DIGNIFYING ARGENTINA

PITT LATIN AMERICAN SERIES

John Charles Chasteen and Catherine M. Conaghan, Editors

DIGNIFYING ARGENTINA

PERONISM, CITIZENSHIP, AND
MASS CONSUMPTION

Eduardo Elena

UNIVERSITY OF PITTSBURGH PRESS

Published by the University of Pittsburgh Press, Pittsburgh, Pa., 15260

Copyright © 2011, University of Pittsburgh Press

Manufactured in the United States of America

Printed on acid-free paper

10 9 8 7 6 5 4 3 2 1

Library of Congress Cataloging-in-Publication Data

Elena, Eduardo, 1972–

 Dignifying Argentina : Peronism, citizenship, and mass consumption / Eduardo Elena.

     p. cm. — (Pitt Latin American series)

 Includes bibliographical references and index.

 ISBN 978-0-8229-6170-3 (pbk. : alk. paper)

1. Peronism—Economic aspects. 2. Argentina—Economic policy. 3. Argentina—Economic
conditions—1945–1983. 4. Argentina—Politics and government—1943–1955. 5. Consumption
(Economics)—Argentina—History—20th century. 6. Households—Economic aspects—Argentina
—History—20th century. 7. Citizenship—Argentina—History—19th century. 8. Populism—
Argentina—History—20th century. I. Title.

 F2849.E54 2011

 982.06—dc23

                    2011020850

Contents

Preface vii

Introduction: Peronism and the Midcentury Moment 1

Chapter 1. An Imperfect Abundance 18

Chapter 2. Standards for a New Argentina 52

Chapter 3. The War on Speculation 84

Chapter 4. Needs, Wants, and Comforts 119

Chapter 5. Parables of Prodigality 154

Chapter 6. The Counterpolitics of Voice 187

Chapter 7. Ironies of Adjustment 221

Conclusion: The Dignified Life and Beyond 251

Notes 261

Bibliography 301

Index 323

Preface

This book is the product of many years spent working on Peronism, one of the most discussed topics in modern Latin American history and among its most controversial. Indeed, it is impossible to study twentieth-century Argentina and not constantly get questions about what one "really thinks" about Peronism. Here one must tread carefully. Scholarship on this era has often borne the marks of Argentina's fractious political struggles. In the past, these intense disputes lent a degree of clarity to interpretations but also discouraged dialogue between pro- and anti-Peronists and narrowed the scope of subjects considered by each camp. The measured tone and pluralism of recent works is, I believe, an improvement worth preserving. In addition, non-Argentines (I among them) must be especially on guard against the temptation to pass judgment. While foreign observers have made important contributions to the field, they have displayed a regrettable willingness to levy totalizing opinions about a country and people not their own. With these caveats in mind, readers may still quite reasonably want to know where an author stands. In the following pages I criticize features of Peronist rule, in particular the tendency of state authorities to pervert laudatory ideals of egalitarianism, inclusion, and participation into tools for command and indoctrination. But I seek neither to demonize Peronism nor to dismiss its supporters as misguided—far from it. The study of history need not be solely about the search for inspirational heroes or the condemnation of villains (each surely a worthy cause). It is crucial as well to consider those cases that irritate and provoke, that are not easily categorized or squared with received wisdom, but that illuminate historical problems still pressing in our contemporary world. Few subjects are better suited to this approach than the politics of social justice in Peronist Argentina.

In short, those looking for a straightforward polemic will be frustrated by this book's arguments, which show an appreciation for Peronism's multiple legacies and contradictions. Instead, I hope that my interpretation of the Peronist case encourages deeper thinking about the collision of two major midcentury trends: the widening of market relations associated with consumer society and the experimentation with nationalist politics. In Peronist Argentina, as in countries across the globe, everyday consumption became a particularly intense field of contention in attempts to conceive, communicate, and realize paradigms of the just society. Many of us living in the aftermath of the midcentury era clearly tend to minimize its political stakes and trivialize populist movements such as Peronism. But we equally clearly resist coming to terms with the problems of inequality illuminated in the midcentury moment, just as we continue to struggle with the question of how to enhance collective welfare that these actors raised but by no means resolved.

WHILE the book's interpretations are my own, as are its remaining flaws, I have been fortunate to receive generous support and counsel from many quarters over the years. A number of institutions made this book possible in the first place. As a graduate student and then lecturer at Princeton University, I was backed by the Department of History, the Graduate School of Arts and Sciences, the Program in Latin American Studies, and the Fellowship of Woodrow Wilson Scholars. A Fulbright fellowship from the U.S. government funded an extended stay in Argentina in 1999–2000, and Princeton's University Committee for Research in the Humanities and Social Sciences facilitated return trips to the archives. At my current academic home, the University of Miami, completion of the manuscript was aided by a series of Provost Summer Awards, a junior leave from the history department, and a sabbatical from the newly created Center for the Humanities. Many thanks to the center's director, Mihoko Suzuki, its staff, and the inaugural class of fellows for their thoughtful assistance down the final stretch.

Archivists and librarians were instrumental in tracking down the scattered remains of the Peronist era. Employees of the following Argentine institutions deserve special recognition for their assistance under sometimes woeful conditions: the Archivo General de la Nación, the Banco Central's Biblioteca Tornquist and Biblioteca Prebisch, the Biblioteca Nacional, the Biblioteca del Ministerio de Economía, and the Centro de Documentación e Investigación de la Cultura de Izquierdas en la Argentina (CEDINCI). Much of the groundwork on this manuscript was done in the halls of Firestone Library (Princeton), the Butler Library (Columbia University), the New York Public Library, and the Library of Congress. As the project came to a close, the resources of the University of Miami's Richter Library proved invaluable.

Throughout my training as a historian, I have benefited from the wisdom of many advisers. During my undergraduate years at the University of Virginia, Herbert "Tico" Braun challenged assumptions; the fact that I, too, have become drawn to the mysteries of populism must owe much to our conversations. Before the book came the dissertation, and I was lucky to be guided by a skillful committee. More than any other professor, Jeremy Adelman has contributed to my intellectual formation as a Latin Americanist: his willingness to ask big questions and engage with audiences across disciplines and geographies are an inspiration. His repeated interventions ensured that I had the resources to stay afloat even when it seemed the ship might sink. With his endless goodwill, Kenneth Mills too has kept me going during tough times, and his creativity as an interpreter of documents sets an impossibly high standard to emulate. Christine Stansell's historical imagination and encouragement to avoid the snares of academic cant have motivated me. As an outside reader, Barbara Weinstein lived up to her reputation as a leading scholar by suggesting where to head during revisions.

This work has benefited from incisive readings by many other eyes. From the earliest days, the members of the Writers' Kollectiv—Meri Clark, Kristin Roth-Ey, Todd Stevens, and Ashli White—have been at once my most argumentative and my most sympathetic critics; I cannot begin to recognize the value of their solidarity enough. I am grateful as well for the advice offered by former and current colleagues at Princeton University; the State University of New York, Stony Brook; and the University of Miami. Fellow Latin Americanists at these institutions and others—including Stanley Stein, Paulina Alberto, Jesse Hoffnung Garskof, Karen Caplan, Paul Gootenberg, Brooke Larson, Steve Stein, Bill Smith, Martin Nesvig, and Kate Ramsey—sharpened my thinking, at times unwittingly, through our discussions. The members of the University of Miami's Department of History have spent more time and care on this manuscript than I had any right to expect. In the latter stages of this book's gestation, the editorial team at the University of Pittsburgh Press saw the project through to completion. Acquisitions editor Joshua Shanholtzer, series editors John Charles Chasteen and Catherine M. Conaghan, copyeditor Bruce Bethell, and the two outside readers have improved the manuscript immeasurably along the way. I thank them for their fastidious care in making a text into a book.

Scholars across the Americas lent a hand by providing welcome opportunities to exchange ideas. Whether they read chapters and shared their own writing, answered my queries and extended invitations to present my work, or simply argued over coffee, I have prized their intellectual camaraderie. Special thanks are due to fellow students of Peronism and twentieth-century Argentina: Anahi Ballent, James Brennan, Lila Caimari, Jim Cane-Carrasco, Oscar Chamosa, Flavia Fiorucci, Katherine Fuller-French, Donna Guy, Mark Healey, Joel Horowitz, Matthew Karush, Sandra McGee Deutsche, Natalia Milanesio, Jorge Nállim, Rebekah Pite, Karina Rammaciotti, Line Schjolden, and César Seveso. Cambridge University Press and Duke University Press kindly allowed the use of earlier versions of my work published in their journals and an edited volume. Two impressive academic couples, Victoria Basualdo–Juan Santarcangelo and Vania Markarian–Leandro Delgado, have come to my rescue on more than one occasion and kept me in the loop. Other names have surely escaped me, but I would like to recognize the contributions of all those who provided feedback at scholarly events. I appreciate in particular the patience shown by Argentina's academic community in my sometimes clumsy attempts to tell their stories to audiences abroad. This book represents an attempt to reach different publics located from North to South America (and across oceans to the west to east) while remaining attuned to the needs of my main constituencies in the United States. At times bridging these worlds has not been easy, but it never ceased to be a worthwhile endeavor.

Over years of researching and writing, I have racked up personal debts throughout the Río de la Plata region and beyond. With the project already well underway, I had the good fortune that my father, Jorge Elena, relocated to Buenos Aires. Not only has he welcomed a graying son under his roof without (much) complaint, but he shared freely his historical acuity and faith in the promise of Latin America. His wife, Elena Milla de Elena, has been a consummately warm host. On the river's eastern shore, my extended family in Uruguay provided distractions from academic travails (including occasional trips to the Centenario). *Mil gracias* to all the Elenas and Cassinonis: it is a shame that Irma, María Esther, Mirta, and Poupée were unable to see this book in print. The return of my mother, Fanny, to Montevideo has given me yet another reason to revisit my birthplace, while her unconditional support and curiosity have sustained me over the project's long haul. From New York City to Virginia, a circle of friends and family have collaborated by offering refuge during research trips: thanks to my brother, Alejandro, and his wife, Julie; my lovely mother-in-law, Annemarie White; P. M. White and family; Dionne and Rod Searcy; Cullen and Kristin Woehrle; Aaron Lemons and Lara Posner; Mike and Shannon Spaeder; and John Farrell. My daughter, Paulina, has displayed a wonderful knack for devising better plans for me than revising the manuscript.

To my closest collaborator, Ashli White, I dedicate this book. Whether at home, late at night on the subway, or from the opposite end of the world, she endured far too much talk about it. But her brilliance and devotion to the cause has made all the difference.

DIGNIFYING ARGENTINA

INTRODUCTION

Peronism and the Midcentury Moment

[handwritten annotation: Perón + Eva reminding people of their accomplishments]

JUAN DOMINGO PERÓN reached a crossroads in November 1951. Facing reelection, Argentina's president desired a strong showing at the polls to remind supporters and critics alike of his enduring popularity. To this end, Perón and his legendary wife, Eva Duarte de Perón, addressed massive audiences at open-air rallies, while speeches broadcast on the national radio network reached a larger public still. The couple offered a panorama of their administration's accomplishments during the preceding six years: public works projects, nationalizations, social programs, and labor reforms—the types of initiatives that now feature prominently in histories of Peronism. Yet they also spoke about smaller but no less significant improvements in everyday life. In one radio speech, Perón contrasted the poverty of previous decades with the bounty of the present: "Today one eats well and four times a day. Those who in the past had one suit of clothes now have a closetful. Those who in the past went to the cinema or theater once a year now can go every week. Those who in the past spent their summers sitting in the doorway of their tenement [*conventillo*] now go to the mountains, or to the sea shore, or if not, to the comfortable resorts around Buenos Aires itself." At the same time, Perón lashed out at his enemies, arguing that only egotistic elites could bemoan the lack of imported goods, such as whisky, perfume, and refrigerators (*frigidaires*). He assured his listeners that, thanks to government action, the popular majority lived with true "liberty and dignity."[1]

This historical juncture inspired appraisals from other commentators, among them individuals far removed from the commanding heights of the state. A few weeks after Perón's reelection triumph, Hilda Benítez de Maldonado, a working-class housewife from a small town in the western province of Mendoza, wrote a letter to the nation's leaders.[2] Like hundreds of thousands of similar petitioners, this woman recounted daily struggles. She lamented that her husband, who belonged to a rural workers' union, earned wages too low to meet the family's needs. Rising prices threatened, and by her estimate the cost of living in town had increased threefold during the previous year alone. Benítez de Maldonado accused local merchants of buying off state inspectors assigned to crack down on profiteering and of plying them with cold drinks and favors. Moreover, her family's attempts to secure relief through other channels had been unsuccessful: "I'll tell you, my general, that my mother stayed for three months in Buenos Aires to see if she could speak with Our *Compañera* Evita, but they did not give her an audience." Nevertheless, she described herself as a "good Argentine and good Peronist" who prayed tearfully for Eva Perón's recovery from illness. Her letter expressed her gratitude for having received consumer goods as holiday gifts from the regime's authorities (a fruitcake, a bottle of cider, and a toy for her son). "Many thanks and forgive the errors and the boldness of having contacted you both," she declared in closing to the president and First Lady.

What should we make of these two contrasting accounts from late 1951? On the surface, Perón and Benítez de Maldonado seem an unlikely pairing. One was the leading figure in twentieth-century Argentine history, a man who held the reins of the state and positioned himself at the apex of one of Latin America's most powerful mass movements. The other was a poor and barely literate woman from a provincial backwater. Despite the gulf between them, however, Perón and Benítez de Maldonado shared certain inclinations that suggest much about the changing political landscape of this historical moment. One may have extolled national plenty and the other recounted personal troubles, but they were joined, however loosely, by a preoccupation with the ordinary stuff of life. Both Perón and Benítez de Maldonado considered getting and spending as matters worthy of public attention and state intervention and thus vital to understandings of citizenship. While neither invoked *consumo* (consumption) explicitly, each viewed popular acquisition and the satisfaction of household-level needs as crucial to living with "liberty and dignity." Perón and Benítez de Maldonado were not alone. They were joined by a host of other actors who grappled, in their respective and sometimes competing ways, with the quandaries posed by this era's commercial offerings, social inequalities, and material aspirations.

Indeed, the Peronist era (1943–1955) was a historical watershed that reconfigured state-citizen relations around new conceptions of entitlement and national development. Peronism has lent itself to countless interpretations, yet scholars have tended to mine certain lines of inquiry repeatedly, and the significance of consumer controversies has not received the scrutiny it deserves.[3] But the deep resonance of Peronist politics rested at least partly in its articulation of quotidian consumption as an essential element of social justice. The movement's protagonists adapted relevant social scientific concepts, such as the *nivel de vida* (level of living) and *standard de vida,* (standard of living), drawing them out of narrow reformist debates and thrusting them into the center of mass politics. It is difficult to overstate the importance of the standard of living to the period's contests. The language of "levels" and "standards" guided an array of initiatives intended to lessen vulnerabilities to market forces and to uplift "submerged" populations to a higher plateau of well-being. Through these actions, political authorities sought to transform a marginalized majority into modern citizens—and, it was hoped, loyal and disciplined partisan subjects. What begs for further explanation, in my view, is the process through which individual yearnings intersected with statist visions of progress and Peronist ideals of "dignified" living standards.

Rather than collapse state-citizen negotiations into a familiar tale of repression versus resistance, we should explore the multiple (and often unexpected) outcomes of struggles over consumption. This history cannot be reduced to top-down manipulation of the "masses"—despite efforts to impose ideological consensus—for such an interpretation dismisses popular aspirations out of hand instead of inquiring into their social origins and political deployment. Most important, as Benítez de Maldonado's letter reminds us, the pursuit of the *vida digna,* the dignified life, was never free of friction. Even among the regime's staunchest sympathizers, state consumer policies were never fully synchronized with individual desires and the intensity of local demands. For the roughly one-third of the Argentine population who rejected Peronism, the era's politics represented a disturbing challenge to norms of property, order, deference, and personal liberties. An awareness of these antagonisms serves, then, as a necessary counterbalance to comprehending how the "Nueva Argentina" modeled by Peronist authorities overlapped, if imperfectly, with the futures imagined by ordinary citizens.[4]

Telling this story, however, is complicated by the current tendency of many historians to compartmentalize culture and economics into separate boxes, at times presenting them as nearly isolated spheres of existence. To better understand Peronism's innovations, we must bridge the divide that often separates studies of political culture from those of political economy, using tools of cultural analysis to examine economic subjects, such market regulation, while contextualizing Peronist discourse and imagery in the specific material conditions of midcentury Argentina.

Placing norms of morality, patterns of exchange, and personal ambitions in the same interpretive framework offers a far richer portrait of the way contemporaries experienced the era's politics. As state authorities made their presence felt in domestic spaces and the marketplace, the prosaic took on new meaning for pro- and anti-Peronists alike. Everyday objects—from an imported frigidaire to a child's Christmas toy, a humble hunk of cheese to a brand-name motor scooter—became freighted with significance as competing symbols of elite selfishness and social justice, populist excess and national progress.

Rethinking Midcentury Politics

Investigating these conflicts will lead to the reconsideration of a central problem in Latin American history, the shifting terms of political membership and participation —in a word, citizenship. The midcentury era was a crucible in which existing citizenship practices were wrested apart and forged anew across much of the region. Nevertheless, some observers choose to emphasize Argentina's exceptionalism, claiming misguidedly that the country's history stands outside some imagined Latin American norm. Studies of Peronism can occasionally display an insular tendency common to all national histories, but they have also provided perceptive ways of thinking beyond borders. The study of consumption can follow along these lines, pushing at the limits of current studies of citizenship to consider how controversies surrounding consumption contributed to reshaping political subjectivity. Foregrounding these issues reveals the larger constellation of economic forces bearing down on citizenship in Argentina and its neighbors during this historical conjuncture, a time in which novel strategies of development expanded the connections between national politics and the microlevel practices of popular households.

To be sure, Latin American societies were not alone in experiencing a recasting of politics, for the midcentury moment was marked by a global crisis of liberalism. The faith in laissez-faire economics, the individual rights of property holders, and constitutional-parliamentary systems, so solid at the beginning of the 1900s, was battered by two world wars and a major economic depression. By one estimate, in 1944 there were only twelve elected constitutional regimes remaining out of the more than thirty-five that had existed worldwide in 1920. The drift was extreme in Europe, the "dark continent" that witnessed the ascendance of inventive, if noxious, authoritarianisms (from fascism to Stalinism), followed by social democratic attempts to retool liberalism.[5] The inhabitants of Latin America—at once part of both the "West" and the "Global South"—confronted the limitations of their own liberal republics, including their exposure to external economic shocks and harsh social inequities. Across the region, the collapse in international trade associated with the Great Depression acted as a catalyst that undermined ruling blocs. Argentina exemplified these trends. The early 1930s saw a military coup over-throw the country's civilian president, ending over fifty continuous years of elec-toral succession and fifteen years of popular republicanism. This turbulent decade was punctuated in 1943 by another military coup, one from which Perón would emerge, rising to prominence and ultimately achieving victory in the 1946 elections.

These were times of enormous political experimentation in Latin America. At the crest of this wave was a remarkable generation of leaders, including Brazil's Getúlio Vargas, Mexico's Lázaro Cárdenas, Colombia's Jorge Eliécer Gaitán, Peru's Victor Haya de la Torre, and Guatemala's Jacobo Arbenz, in addition to the most famous of all, Juan and Eva Perón. For all their differences, these figures shared a drive to reform liberalism while stopping short of a total transformation of repub-lican institutions and capitalist structures. Most stressed popular inclusion within more vibrant national orders freed from the threats of excessive social stratification and the overconcentration of wealth. Although their promises outstripped their abilities (and, ultimately, willingness) to implement change, this generation broke with many political conventions and identified closely with the interests of the common person–or to use the preferred term, *el pueblo* (the people). Scholars grouped these leaders and their followers under the label "populism." A notori-ously elusive term, loaded with derogatory connotations, populism has been sub-ject to endless definitional controversies.[6] For all its slipperiness, the notion of populism remains a valuable means to draw comparisons between different na-tional histories and the region's political practices. That said, the strict categoriza-tion of Peronism as populism can unnecessarily close off other avenues of inquiry, at worst minimizing the issues at stake to matters of raw clientelism and exotic cari-catures of charismatic leaders grandstanding before malleable masses (populism in its "Don't Cry for Me, Argentina" mode).

While the populists were prone to a dramatic style, they went to the core of liberalism's crisis in the concerns they raised—the inadequacies of republican in-stitutions, the desire to assert anticolonial forms of economic sovereignty, and above all, the drive to incorporate the citizenry within a more just, modern nation. Perón and his peers inaugurated an era of contention that, when combined with the onset of the cold war, set into motion accelerating cycles of civil strife and radicali-zation. In this sense, the mid-twentieth century was another "Age of Revolutions" during which the very terms of state authority and political action were thrown open to debate. Like their counterparts, Peronists presented themselves as picking up the flag from their independence-era forebears, as embarking on a revolutionary project to found a "New Argentina." This rhetoric was exaggerated and self-serving: actual revolutions were far less frequent than thwarted nationalist campaigns and fragile state reforms. Unlike those of the early nineteenth century, the upheavals of this mid-twentieth-century generation did not lead to the full collapse of the *ancien régime* (at least outside of Cuba). Yet before the phase of counterrevolution and neoliberal restoration took hold in the 1970s, Argentina and its neighbors went through convulsions that burst the established boundaries of political life.

Despite the importance of this historical moment, we lack the conceptual framework to appreciate its significance fully. This is part of a larger interpretive problem: our analytical tools are borrowed mainly from Anglo-U.S. cases seen as universal norms (based, for instance, on a fundamental distinction between the state and civil society). Latin Americanists have displayed creativity in adapting this terminology to fit the subject at hand. This impulse is only logical: Western examples shaped the region's political systems, and for academics in this field, the task of translation is inescapable (even if one cannot ignore the imperial implications of less-than-voluntary choices).[7] But the labor of tailoring concepts to the specific historicity of Latin American societies results in interpretations that do not fit comfortably, that pinch in certain areas and leave others uncovered. This holds especially true for that vexing political keyword "citizenship." The return of civilian rule after savage dictatorships in many areas of Latin America during the 1980s sparked renewed interest in citizenship as a category of analysis not only within academic circles but also among a wider public energized by the promise of democracy.[8] In Argentina research on citizenship has revolved around locating where democratic traditions are "nested" within society and has opened new vistas on elections, civil associations, and neighborhood-level politics in the late nineteenth and early twentieth century.[9]

But the midcentury moment, the heyday of experimentation with mass politics, remains something of a black box. The consensus is that T. H. Marshall's elegant account of the history of citizenship in England—the progressive accumulation of civil, political, and social rights from the eighteenth to the twentieth century—does not jibe with the more fitful expansion and contraction of rights in Latin America. New research has addressed the region's uneven citizenships, characterized by the distance between rights talk and social practice (what one recent work on Brazil calls the problem of "disjunctive democracy").[10] But the literature on citizenship in Argentina hits a snag with the 1940s. When viewed from an Anglo-

American interpretive tradition, Peronism scrambles our bearings. What is one to make of a government that was democratic in the sense of being popularly elected and boasting majority support but that employed mobilizational and authoritarian methods of rule? Can one talk about "civil society" with respect to a context where associational life was heavily suffused with partisan politics? How do theories of citizenship apply to the Peronist government, which extended entitlements and collective modes of participation in public life but abrogated of civil liberties and minority rights?

One response has been to conceive of Peronism as advancing a form of "social citizenship." In this view, Peronist politics stoked a sense of empowerment among working-class Argentines that mitigated earlier experiences of exclusion. According to Daniel James's pathbreaking interpretation, Peronism supplied a "credible vision" of change that redressed class inequities through labor reforms while mounting a "heretical" challenge to cultural norms of deference.[11] Social citizenship offers a welcome antidote to the traditional emphasis on governing elites and electoral politics, but this approach leaves unanswered crucial questions about the meaning of social citizenship as realized in practice, especially outside the much-studied arena of state-union relations. How were individual perceptions of inclusion in society influenced by the characteristics of Argentina's capitalist order and emerging consumer society? How did political feelings of belonging translate into everyday ways of being, if they did at all? In short, the "social" component of citizenship warrants more thorough consideration.

We might begin probing these thorny questions surrounding citizenship in Peronist Argentina by taking a closer look at the era's political lexicon. Contemporaries spoke about citizenship in terms of rights. The Perón administration extended the franchise to the country's female majority and drafted a constitution in 1949 that proclaimed new social rights for workers, the elderly, and families. Yet rights talk complemented other ways of framing entitlement and membership in the national community. Peronist officials deployed the standard de vida and other developmentalist concepts with perhaps greater frequency in outlining their vision of a New Argentina.[12] They modified descriptions of the improved living standards enjoyed by the citizenry with expressions including *dignidad, bienestar* (well-being), *confort,* and above all, *justicia social.* (It was not mere coincidence that Peronists referred to their movement as *justicialismo.*) Keywords such as "dignity" are admittedly wooly terms, the type that make hardheaded social scientists cringe. Depending on the time, place, and observer, they can reflect various religious and ethical principles, economic circumstances, and political possibilities (to name but a few factors). Given their charged connotations and protean qualities, they are extremely difficult to handle, which provides another reason populist strains of nationalism have been called a "politician's delight and a historian's nightmare."[13]

Sometimes overlooked, however, is the fact that these seemingly eternal concepts have a specific history. Thus, we can attempt to historicize what contemporaries meant by, say, the term "social justice," which served as a focal point of state power and mass politics in the midcentury moment to an extent that it never had before (or ever would again). The content of this flexible concept varied from case to case, but certain issues attracted repeated attention in Argentina and elsewhere, principal among them, how to elevate the material living conditions of "vulnerable" families. References to the vida digna reveal how Peronists reformulated understandings of justice around an ideal of enhanced citizenship and elevated living standards. One need not accept actors' terms at face value to use them as a starting point for critical analysis. To be clear, I do *not* use the phrase "dignified life" in a normative sense or as an accurate description of the actual conditions of Peronist rule. Instead, it provides a useful way of organizing the era's field of debate over national inclusion and progress. A lingering uneasiness with "dignity," "justice," and other capacious terms should not prevent us from recognizing a basic fact: this looser language of entitlement was arguably more central to Peronism—and to the politics of midcentury Latin America more broadly—than the scholarly rhetoric of constitutionalism that prevails today was.

There was no unanimity as to what justice comprised among Peronists. Yet conceptions of social citizenship privileged ideals of class and gender comportment, and discussions of living standards focused on the needs of male-headed households and heterosexual, married unions. The vida digna encompassed more than consumer purchasing power; it required a *comprehensive* elevation in working-class standards that included everything from poor relief programs to public education. Labor featured prominently in these considerations—indeed, officials never tired of pointing out that all collective benefits and individual gains derived from productive sacrifice to the nation. The broader "dignification" of working people depended, in turn, on interventions to reshape everyday life along gender norms. The New Argentina's architects stressed that laboring men should occupy the role of economic breadwinners and women would serve primarily as wives, mothers, and household managers. While both men and women gained shared rights, their public and private responsibilities as citizens derived from distinct understandings of masculinity and femininity deemed natural by authorities. Peronist rule thus both opened new political opportunities for Argentina's female majority and imposed constraining expectations regarding their domestic duties.

The freedoms associated with elevated standards rested on a model of gender relations that mirrored campaigns across the globe committed to the "modernization of patriarchy."[14]

In the struggle to define social citizenship, other factors, such as race and ethnicity, were by no means unimportant. As I will show, these issues structured assumptions about the specific populations that merited reformist attention, and they were brought to light in heated partisan confrontations (as in slurs about "*los negros peronistas*"). But the emphasis on interethnic harmony in the Peronist paradigm of the vida digna is notable. This may seem at first counterintuitive given the frequent comparisons between Peronism and fascism, not to mention the xenophobia of certain right-wing factions allied early on with the movement. Nevertheless, Peronist ideals of mass entitlement and assertions of pride aimed at maligned "creole" groups served much the same strategic political purpose as did talk of "racial democracy" in neighboring Latin American countries: it reinforced nationalist ideals of common purpose within unquestionably heterogeneous societies.

State and party officials occupy a prominent place in this story, for they were responsible for producing and disseminating these visions of worker empowerment, family respectability, and national unity. But a "top-down" study of political power can take us only so far. Peronist initiatives were met with a mixture of enthusiasm and resistance among their intended subjects. Women identified themselves in ways that complemented Peronist authorities' notions of femininity, but they did not confine themselves to meeting domestic burdens. Likewise, ideals of masculinity that equated men with workers did not preclude them from expressing concerns related to purchasing and household provisioning. Individuals of diverse social backgrounds took advantage of opportunities to voice displeasure with living conditions and, on occasion, launch biting critiques of government inaction. Argentine populism must thus be considered from the perspectives of both the "regime" (the state-centered mechanisms of governance) and the "movement" (the web of networks among leaders and followers). This interplay tells us much about the location of Peronism in Argentine society—its configuration within the state, allied organizations, and autonomous associations—in ways that defy conventional definitions of mass mobilization and civil society.[15] At the same time, it is necessary to look beyond these internal dynamics. Anti-Peronist critics, too, deserve attention for influencing political outcomes through frontal resistance and surreptitious noncompliance.

Illuminating these controversies permits a consideration of Peronism in areas overlooked or at best partially considered in previous studies.[16] Over the past two decades, this field has witnessed an explosion of interest. New studies have built on pioneering works of labor history to examine the Perón government's ties with other key players, such as the Catholic Church, intellectuals, business organizations, and provincial parties. We now have, alongside older biographical treatments of Perón and Evita, a more detailed picture of their government, including efforts to forge consensus through cultural rituals and various ministerial-level initiatives. While new histories of Peronism have deepened our knowledge of the "regime," most have devoted far less analysis to the subaltern sectors that constituted the "movement" and, more generally, to the way popular organizations and individuals engaged with the overtures of the central state. The dearth of accessible sources is partially to blame, but so, too, are historical approaches that stress policymaking and cultural production over reception and social practice. We still know relatively little about the lives of laboring Argentines outside the factory floor or the majority of the population that was not unionized. Peronist authorities made appeals on strict class terms, but they also reached out to populations subsumed within the category of "el pueblo." The protagonists of my story here include familiar actors, such as the state authorities who designed propaganda and programs and the union members who clamored against high living costs. It features, however, a far wider spectrum of social types: neighborhood organizations railing against commercial "speculators," partisan critics lambasting consumer wastefulness and tackiness, impoverished families seeking access to Peronist networks, merchants attempting to elude regulations, and housewives balancing tight budgets against yearnings for a greater plenty. Focusing on these actors and the world of everyday consumption reveals an alternative path through the political history of Peronist Argentina and the key nodes of related activity, from the formulation of reformist knowledge about social need to the tactics pursued by sympathizers and detractors at the grassroots level.

Recasting Consumer Society

It is perhaps easy to see that Peronism challenged existing paradigms of citizenship, but the fact that these contests were waged in part around problems of consumption is less obvious. For all the attention lavished on the history of citizenship in the past two decades, the history of consumption in Argentina remains uncharted territory. In fact, this subject's relevance may strike some readers as immediately suspect. Consumption calls to mind other places—above all, the suburban landscape of the postwar United States and its glowing television sets, streamlined appliances, and wide-body cars. Histories of twentieth-century consumption have emphasized the rise of a distinctly modern acquisitive spirit ("consumerism") and innovations in retailing practices. Viewed in this light, societies such as Argentina seemingly have little to offer; at best, they appear to reflect trends first manifested elsewhere. The study of the consumer marketplace may be fine for the United States, Western Europe, or East Asia, so the argument goes, but isn't Latin America's problem fundamentally one of enduring poverty and the inability to achieve consumerist prosperity on a massive scale? These are issues worthy of consideration, but the geographical contrasts rest on false assumptions that reinforce global disparities, not to mention an excessively limited view of consumption's scope. There is no reason the history of consumption cannot tell us something about the relationship between abundance *and* scarcity, about models of economic progress that proved elusive, and about the commercialization of everyday life that stoked new desires while reproducing old material inequalities (and not just in societies south of the Rio Grande).

It is somewhat ironic that domestic consumption has featured so infrequently in studies of Latin America's past, given the region's fame as a global producer of consumables. The land and labor of its inhabitants enabled modern consumption: sugar became a staple of diets in industrializing nations; coffee allowed populations in the developed West to keep pace with frenetic times (while tobacco and cocaine provided a temporary escape); edible commodities, such as wheat, beef, and bananas, fed urban workforces; and copper, tin, nitrates, and other ores facilitated the rise of manufacturing empires. Nevertheless, the study of consumption *within* the region's societies is only now coming into its own. The prevailing wisdom (sometimes well founded) was that the average resident of Latin America was too poor to purchase much in the way of commercial products. The largely peasant populations of the colonial and early national eras devoted themselves primarily to subsistence and homespun goods, simply not earning the wages necessary to fuel mass consumption. Over the past decade, however, scholars have begun to reconsider this portrait and have used consumption to explore colonial encounters, the role of U.S. business in trends of "Americanization," and the impact of commercial mass culture on nation building.[17] As it does in other geographical areas, the twentieth century stands out as a period of seismic shifts that accelerated changes in commercial practices and consumer habits throughout Latin America.

Argentina presents an all-important case in this regard, for many of the transformations that characterized midcentury Latin America were felt there first and with particular intensity. The overlapping trends of "modernization"—explosive urban growth, industrialization, the spread of wage labor, a shrinking peasantry, and the integration of regional markets, among other forces—affected the region's societies, albeit in an uneven manner. Domestic manufacturing and large-scale agriculture unleashed a flow of new goods into the marketplace, where they joined foreign imports in altering everything from popular diets to recreation. Widely perceived as having the region's wealthiest economy, Argentina stood at the forefront of these changes. By 1930 a majority of its population already belonged to working and middle classes that depended on the exchange of wage income for commercial wares. Residents encountered an expanding variety of consumer offerings, especially in urban and suburban areas. Buenos Aires, then the biggest metropolis in Latin America, was an emporium that gathered the fruits of local industry, agriculture, and international trade. For travelers and local observers alike, the city's grand department stores and shopping avenues presented unquestionable signs of consumer society.

Yet the onset of mass consumption brought unease. Individuals may have embraced novel experiences and striven to satisfy desires, but many expressed frustrations with their powerlessness before the economic pressures that governed their lives. With constrained purchasing power, popular households in Argentina confronted an inability to enter the marketplace that lay tantalizingly before them. Social critics lamented the scandal of indigence in this celebrated land of opportunity and the economic gaps that paralleled the divide between urban and rural areas (and marked divisions within the modern metropolis itself). In turn, political leaders pledged to impose greater order on the chaotic swings of commerce. In nation after nation, debates about the standard of living ran up against similar dilemmas. To be clear, popular consumer spending was rarely the main, explicit object of attention. Demands for enhanced rights—especially those concerning labor and social protections—acted as a driving force behind reformist and revolutionary politics alike. Highly divisive matters of rural property and industrial production generated the greatest debate, and land reform was undoubtedly the region's most hotly contested topic, especially in rural societies with large peasantries, profitable export commodities, and powerful landholding elites. But for city residents and wage-earning populations dependent on the cash nexus of the marketplace, pocketbook issues could not be ignored. Latin America's rapid urbanization in these years only elevated the stakes: by 1950 nearly half the region's population lived in urban areas (a figure that has continued to increase, with roughly four out of five inhabitants now urbanized).

Peronist policies that affected consumer purchasing (e.g., price controls, subsidies, public credit, tariffs, and commercial inspections) were adopted simultaneously in neighboring countries. Their ubiquity under both dictatorships and democracies, counterrevolutionary and socialist regimes, must not be taken as signs of timeless patrimonial tendencies or, as neoliberals would have it, a cultural predisposition to meddle in free markets. Rather, these measures represented political attempts to cope with the "maelstrom of modernity" as it swept through the region and created more commercialized and thus more unsettled societies.[18] The Peronist ideal of the vida digna illustrated the inroads made by changing consumer expectations. It represented an effort to remedy the insecurities of commercial exchange and to loosen the knot of needs that constrained households.

A certain "double movement" characterized state responses to issues concerning the standard of living in Peronist Argentina.[19] On the one hand, officials sought to shield predominately working-class sectors from the ever-present risks associated with illness, old age, overwork, and accident. The goal of domestic policy was to defend and regulate, to remove certain areas of life from market exchange. On the other hand, political authorities strove to incorporate ordinary citizens more fully into the nation as economic actors. In the mid-1940s the Peronist leadership supported a redistribution of income to wage earners on a scale unprecedented in Latin American history, a move that contributed to a rapid surge in consumer spending power. But Perón's regime did not tame market forces along purely socialist lines. Rather, its officials saw themselves as charting a "third way" between the extremes of laissez-faire liberalism and Soviet-bloc communism. They aimed to domesticate markets, to bring capitalist forces in line with nationalist priorities, and to erect protections for laboring Argentines as producers while enhancing their capacity as consumers. *Standard of living movement*

The Peronists' hybrid approach demands a flexible use of consumption as a category of analysis, which some readers may find initially disorienting. "Consumption" is itself a deceptively simple term. Although the tendency is to equate it with retail purchasing, there is virtually no limit to the way members of a given society consume—that is, acquire, use, and display goods and services. When contemporaries referenced consumo in Argentina, they did so in varied ways: in references to retail sales, in reformist discussions of worker nutritional deficiencies, in reports on macroeconomic planning, and in statements on social programs. Tracing the winding route of the standard of living requires trespassing across conventional categories to reveal historical connections among different facets of consumption and addressing topics typical to most histories of consumption but also touching on matters that fall under the purview of social policy, such as housing, subsidized leisure, and health care. (For clarity's sake, I will refer to these areas as "collective consumption" or "nonmarket consumption" to distinguish them from retail spending or mass consumption.)[20] Recent scholarly calls to move "beyond consumerism" to issues other than individual acquisitiveness encourage greater appreciation of the full spectrum of consumer acts.[21] While there is something to be said for preserving this tradition, which grants us welcome respite from the din of the commercialized present, consumption lends itself to other ends in exploring the past. Looking backward, historians have created two parallel literatures (one on the rise of mass consumption and the other on the welfare state) that flatten the complexity of debates about living standards in midcentury politics. Latin American populists and their peers had no reason to heed these artificial scholarly barriers.

The Peronist vida digna therefore spanned various spheres of consumption (individual and collective, commercial and nonmarket) but by no means erased the differences among them. Elements of so-called ordinary consumption (food, clothing, simple household products, and the cheap amusements of commercial entertainment) preoccupied reformers and, naturally, the members of popular households themselves. Consumer politics extended up the chain of acquisition, too. By the early 1950s the Peronist regime was experimenting with new forms of retailing (creating its own department stores and shops) and the manufacturing of technologically complex products (most famously, in the mass production of a coche justicialista, a Peronist automobile). Partisan institutions were tasked with using nonmarket channels to deliver goods and services judged too important to leave to supply and demand. In other areas, the designers of welfare programs looked to the marketplace, adapting prevailing aesthetics and distinctions of taste and at times emulating discourses of consumer pleasure associated with the private sector. In this sense, Peronist living standards were about satisfying an elastic range of needs, delivering basic justice *and* a higher order of comfort.

The problem, however, lay in striking a stable balance between these impulses, for the Peronist double movement was rife with contradictions. Although officials celebrated working-class spending, they perceived mass consumption as a potential threat. Perón and Evita attacked oligarchic elites but also reprimanded popular consumers for their supposed wastefulness and indiscipline, essentially offering their own variation on midcentury criticisms of consumerism. Over the 1950s state policymakers retreated from their initial commitment to augmenting purchasing power. This move did not mean an abandonment of commercial regulation; nevertheless, it added to tensions between authorities seeking to manage market relations and consumers faced with incomplete citizenship. In this manner, Peronist-era contests over consumption summoned a range of aspirations and anxieties—dreams of upward mobility, fears of falling, class resentments, myths of plenty—that charged national politics with an intense energy.

Nations and Frameworks

As these examples suggest, the nation-state looms large in this story of midcentury citizenship and consumption. In Peronist Argentina conceptions of social justice were yoked tightly to ideas of national liberation, premised on throwing off the shackles of foreign economic imperialism and pursuing an independent path in the emerging cold war order. Perón and Evita can be grouped alongside a generation of leaders who pursued similar projects, including not only Latin American populists but also a cohort of iconic nationalists in Asia and Africa. The terms of national politics were by no means identical across the Global South. Whereas Perón and his Latin American peers sought to carve out greater autonomy for their flawed republics, their counterparts elsewhere faced the daunting task of creating entirely new nations from the remnants of empire. In political style Perón differed markedly from Third World liberators, certainly from progressive figures, such as Ghana's Kwame Nkrumah and India's Jawaharlal Nehru, and even from uniformed contemporaries, such as Egypt's Gamal Abdel Nasser. Yet sovereignty was their shared preoccupation, a problem that cried out for greater state intervention in society and for better organization of national resources to elevate standards. The fact that this generation became a lightning rod for such controversy, remaining to this day larger-than-life historical figures, should alert us to certain commonalities. Midcentury nationalist movements threw open existing political orders, usually under pressure from a hopeful populace. Excluded majorities assumed a larger presence in the public arena in country after country, both as voters and rights-bearing citizens and as participants in mass movements and agents of national development.

Despite the shadow cast by the legendary figures of this era, the nation has fallen out of favor in certain academic fields. Historians in the United States especially have come under increasing fire for their parochialism and complicity in reinforcing narrow ideas of national exceptionalism.[22] The cosmopolitanism of newer transnational approaches is long overdue, even if it runs the risk of minimizing the nation-state's historical significance in the twentieth century. Yet the study of national politics need not confine itself to nationalist ways of thinking. It can, for example, situate Argentina within trends beyond its borders by tracing transnational flows of knowledge, especially by illustrating how the social policies of the New Argentina emerged out of global debates about the state's responsibility in managing market forces. Perón's advisers borrowed ideas from Argentine reformist circles and Atlantic currents of thought, ranging from techniques of measuring living standards to projects of postwar planning. Similarly, Peronist politics had national ambitions and were, in fact, felt across the country's territory, from remote rural areas to urban slums. But the nation did not experience justicialista rule uniformly; one must therefore look critically at Peronism's variegated impact at the local level. Although issues of consumption extended to the countryside, small towns, and provincial cities of Argentina's vast territory, this study concentrates primarily on the largest population centers. The forces of commercialization were most concentrated in the urban and suburban areas of the littoral region, especially in the metropolis of Buenos Aires; not coincidentally, Peronist consumer politics had the greatest visibility and intensity in these areas.

Adopting this framework on national politics requires drawing on a range of sources. The obstacles faced are familiar to specialists; even by standards of collections elsewhere in Latin America, archival materials for midcentury Argentina are especially fragmented. The country's infamous institutional volatility has caused the destruction of state documents, while waves of anti-Peronist purges over the past sixty-five years have taken a toll on private papers and other sources. Partisan appointees who serve as gatekeepers over surviving collections and the chronic lack of funding for archival preservation—verging on a conscious attempt to eliminate traces of a fractious past—present additional hindrances. The sources for this book were gathered from multiple sites, and they include social scientific tracts, business publications, commercial films, mass-market periodicals, and government materials. My analysis draws on the archives of the Ministry of Technical Affairs just recently opened to researchers. This set of internal reports and other documents provides a wealth of insights into Peronist planning. It includes an unexpected cache of materials: thousands of letters to Perón's government mailed by individuals and local groups across the country. This public correspondence offers glimpses into the political imaginations of "ordinary" Argentine men and women. When augmented by neighborhood newspapers, labor publications, and other rare ephemera, the letters help us move beyond state-centric concerns with policymaking and propaganda.

At the center of this investigation lies a question pondered in Argentina and across midcentury Latin America: what does it mean to live with dignity in a modern society? The answers to this problem varied tremendously, as commentators in each country took stock of the political opportunities open to them, the social conditions that surrounded them, and their places in the world. Some launched projects that addressed the failings of liberal orders and set new thresholds of citizen entitlement. For those living in places that, as did Argentina, included extremes of wealth and indigence but saw a growing majority of their populations marching to the rhythms of a consumer society, the "deficiencies" of popular households carried particular political significance. Perón and his ilk spoke as never before to the economic frustrations and aspirations that characterized life in these societies. The search for a more substantive, inclusive citizenship in the region was not limited to matters of redistribution and purchasing power alone. But without paying closer attention to the realm of popular consumption, one cannot comprehend the potency of nationalist politics in this era, the strategies pursued by leaders such as Perón, or the resonance of appeals to "liberty and dignity" for Hilda Benítez de Maldonado and her contemporaries.

1

AN IMPERFECT ABUNDANCE

Primary sure

IN 1928 the newspaper *El Mundo* hired Roberto Arlt to write a series of observations about life in Buenos Aires. This was a promising arrangement: the newspaper offered a new tabloid layout aimed at popular audiences, and Arlt was an iconoclastic novelist who had worked as a store clerk, machinist, and jack-of-all-trades before earning his living as a journalist. His column, *"Aguafuertes porteñas"* (*aguafuerte* meaning "etching" and a *porteña/o* being a resident of the port city Buenos Aires), provided everything from mock scholarly analyses of slang terms to vignettes of unusual urban scenes. High on Arlt's list of fascinations was the commercial pulse of the metropolis. Foreign visitors often marveled at the modernity and elegance of Argentina's capital (the "Paris of South America," according to the prevailing cliché). Arlt's "etchings," however, revealed a grittier side of life. One newspaper column about Corrientes Avenue, a major city artery, offered a walking tour beginning at the urban fringes and then moving closer downtown. Along the way the reader encountered a commercialized landscape: first, blocks of warehouses, workshops, and factories whose employees assembled everything from electric fans to plumbing fixtures; then down-and-out storerooms where traveling salesmen came to resupply their stock of cheap wares; next, the Jewish quarter, with its dense knot of retail shops ("cloth merchants, perfumists, electricians, boot polishers, cooperatives") and a few "Turkish" businesses on the side streets; and finally, the most famed blocks of Corrientes, dotted with cafés and restaurants and lit up by the marquees of the theaters and cinema palaces beloved by nightowls.[1]

Above all, Arlt's chronicles examined the psychology of the inhabitants of this mercantile environment. They documented the social types who embraced the era's competitive, profit-driven spirit: the neighborhood grocer who schemed to undermine his rival or the café owner who let customers ogle his attractive wife because it was good for business. Greater sympathy was afforded to those city residents compelled to sell their labor to survive, such as the tired washerwomen walking the streets with baskets of laundry on their hips. His writings did not romanticize the virtues of the poor; rather, they probed the commercial appetites that shaped the dreams of these "ordinary" city residents both big (shopping sprees after winning the lottery) and pitifully small (saving up to buy a half-kilo of fruitcake for Christmas). With his world-weary irony, Arlt questioned the dominant faith that these conditions constituted signs of *progreso,* a term he once summed up as the achievement of commuting on a packed subway car, working all day under electric lights, returning home to a stifling apartment, and buying a pair of flimsy shoes every three months, a suit, every six.[2]

Arlt was one of this era's most insightful cultural observers, and his renown as a writer has only increased over the decades. But he was not alone in drawing attention to questions of acquisition. During the 1930s scores of commentators assessed how getting and spending influenced social relations. While most lacked both fame and a novelist's acuity in probing individual motivations, they focused on issues of collective, if not explicitly political, concern. Like Arlt, these critics looked beyond the affluent districts of Argentina's "Paris" to its less celebrated barrios and suburbs (and, more rarely, to the nation's rural expanses), where the cracks in the façade of national progress were hard to ignore. They narrowed their vision on laboring populations exposed to the capriciousness of their country's market economy. In particular, discussion revolved around the social category of the *familia obrera*—that is, the working-class family—and the predicament of households pinched between meager incomes and material needs. The awareness that life could be cruel or that a gaping divide separated rich from poor was nothing new, of course. What troubled observers was the unpredictability of modern times: all it took was a sudden accident, layoff, or other mundane twist of fate to send most families hurtling into indigence. The impressive economic advances and technological innovations on display in Buenos Aires only sharpened the contrast with the misery that existed alongside them.

Whereas Arlt styled himself a chronicler of metropolitan types, other contemporaries adopted the mantle of would-be reformers who would shed light on the causes of dislocation and devise practical strategies for amelioration. In targeting various facets of life, their muckraking reports offer unexpected insights into the characteristics of Argentina's consumer society in the 1930s and early 1940s. These chroniclers and critics may seem an unlikely place to begin, given the country's reputation in the early twentieth century as a land of material prosperity on the verge of joining the exclusive club we now call the "developed world." One could concentrate instead on the fertile countryside of the pampas, the wellspring of Argentina's much-vaunted riches; the ships docked at the nation's ports, loading cargos of wool, meat, wheat, and other commodities for export; or the retail emporiums crowded with every imaginable imported ware and local manufacture. Without question, these are essential places for understanding advances in commerce and consumption, but not all Argentines saw their society as marching on an upward economic slope.

Among the reformers, two groups were especially important: social scientists who inquired into aspects of household consumption through, among other means, surveys of family budgets, and a broader cohort of activists preoccupied with the ethics of exchange and "immoral" commercial practices. Both camps represented a spectrum of competing ideological leanings and political constituencies. Motivations varied as well. Fears of unrest competed with humanitarian sentiments; interests in boosting labor productivity with limiting the predations of capitalism; and a sense of paternalist duty with feelings of popular solidarity. At the core, however, reform-minded observers shared similar causes of dismay. In their eyes, the vulnerability of the working family and the inescapability of acquisitive imperatives required immediate action. Nevertheless, these debates were often overshadowed at the national level. Commonly referred to as Argentina's "Infamous Decade," the years 1930–1943 were bracketed on either end by military coups (the first overthrowing the elected president Hipólito Yrigoyen and the second setting the stage for Colonel Juan Domingo Perón's rise). A loose alliance of conservative politicians assumed state control, resorting to electoral fraud and other methods to ensure their hold on power. Limited in political influence, the era's critics nonetheless expanded ways of thinking about the conundrum of penury amid plenty. By the early 1940s the Peronist movement would take up their conceptual tools to address the acquisitive demands of modern life.

In examining how contemporaries came to terms with commercial transformations that produced unquestioned wealth but also a confusion of unsettling risks, pressing wants, and perilous inequalities, we must depart from two familiar interpretations of this period. One stresses the complete marginalization of working people from the nation's material bounty. Peronists argued along these lines to make a sharp contrast between the inaction of preceding administrations and Perón's efforts to improve living conditions. Another interpretation, associated with Peronism's

Past research

2 faces "

detractors, presents a far less pessimistic view. While acknowledging the impact of the worldwide depression, it sees this period as part of the golden age of economic expansion. These stark positions obscure the fact that by the 1930s Argentina had many features commonly associated with modern consumer societies *and* that contemporary critics saw unsatisfied needs as imperfections in national plenty. Multiple, seemingly unrelated forms of cultural expression, from social commentary to scientific reports to popular protests, were interconnected, however loosely, by shared preoccupations with the working family's exposure to midcentury market forces.

Mass Consumption and "Little Economies"

Whether harvested from the land, manufactured in a nearby factory, or shipped from across the seas, bountiful consumer goods were on display in Argentina. A patriotic booster wishing to show off this side of the country's material plenty might have led another walking tour along the streets of Buenos Aires, one with an itinerary markedly different from Arlt's. This guide would have inevitably taken a visitor to Argentina's most famed commercial thoroughfare, the calle Florida. Running through the capital city's downtown area, this pedestrian street, as well as its surrounding district, was home to a mixture of office buildings, restaurants, clothing shops, fine boutiques, emporiums, and department stores (including an outpost of the world-famous Harrod's of London). Passing through the front doors of the shops, one could find almost any type of domestic or imported good—linens, perfumes, men and women's clothes, household appliances, and other sundry items—displayed artfully in different sections, each with full-service staff to assist shoppers. If feeling more adventurous, the guide might have pointed out another monument to urban commerce: the city's central wholesale food market, the Mercado del Abasto. Surrounded by the types of barrios more familiar to Arlt, this enormous building of honey-colored granite occupied multiple blocks with its warehouse spaces and countless stalls. Through it passed the riches of the Argentine countryside, the grains, produce, and meats destined to find a place in thousands of neighborhood shops across the metropolitan region and eventually on residents' tables.[3]

In fact, these landmarks of mass consumption did attract interest from foreign visitors during the 1930s and early 1940s. Travelers to Buenos Aires were suitably impressed by the commercial hustle-and-bustle of the port city. Echoing the cli-

Primary source (handwritten annotation)

FIGURE 1. Corrientes Avenue in Buenos Aires, typical of the mercantile landscape of the modern metropolis; the famed Gran Rex theater stands in the middle. *Archivo General de la Nación, Departamento Fotográficos, box 6, envelope 11, doc. 153453 (1947); reproduced courtesy of the archive.*

chés prized by porteños, these visitors extolled Buenos Aires by removing the city from its national and regional context; as one Frenchman exclaimed, "This city seems to be a New York set on top of Barcelona, and curiously enough by this method they have created a new type of Paris!"[4] The congested frenzy of the metropolis elicited dystopian judgments as well, and none more famous than the architect Le Corbusier's pronouncements made during his 1933 stay: "Buenos Aires is one of the most inhumane cities I have known; really, one's heart is martyred. For weeks I walked its streets 'without hope' like a madman, oppressed, depressed, furious, desperate."[5] Recapitulating his efforts to reconstruct Paris, Le Corbusier left behind designs (thankfully never implemented) for imposing high modernist order on Argentina's mercantile capital.

Other visiting commentators eschewed Atlantic comparisons in favor of local color. One pair of particularly astute observers, Ruth and Leonard Greenup, a U.S. couple who lived in Argentina for four years during the early 1940s, commented on the habits of residents. As modestly paid journalists who sought to pinch every penny, the Greenups were well aware of the financial obstacles to accessing the city's bounty. Yet they marveled at the profusion of goods for sale, especially when it came time to eat. "Evidence of the abundance of food is everywhere," the Greenups wrote with Rabelaisian glee; "standard window equipment for the city's hundreds of restaurants is a large barbecue spit, on which great sides of meat, a dozen or so chickens and quantities of fat sausages turn round and round to a sizzling golden brown." They were struck by the number of eating establishments and the array of "every kind of food" (a list that, for this couple, was exhausted by "French, Spanish, Argentine, American, Russian, and Italian"), and the cornucopia would not be complete, they wrote, without the mountains of fresh pasta, wheels of cheese stacked to the rafters, and ornately decorated cakes on display in specialty stores. In their view, this truly was the "land of the stretched belt."[6]

For all their differences in opinion, local commentators and foreign travelers were equally captivated by the social consequences of Argentina's remarkable economic transformation. The country was much more than simply a breadbasket and butcher to the world. Its reinsertion into the global economy after decades of postindependence turmoil unleashed a host of modernizing forces at the domestic level from the late nineteenth century onward. The combination of mass immigration and local population growth altered the very the fabric of society: from only 1.8 million inhabitants in 1869, Argentina's population increased to 7.8 million in 1914 and reached over 14 million by 1946.[7] The impact was especially visible in urban areas positioned along advantageous water and rail routes that swelled into sprawling, multiethnic cities. The metropolis of Buenos Aires led the way; by 1910, among the cities along the Atlantic seaboard of the Americas, it was second in population only to New York City. Export-led economic expansion in turn propelled local business activity and foreign investment, sped further along by a steady rise in purchasing. The nation's overall capacity for consumption grew ninefold between the 1890s and 1930s, thanks largely to higher per capita real incomes and demographic increases.[8]

The wheels of commerce were pushed along by the rise of domestic manufacturing. Whereas the commitment to agriculture was once thought to have thwarted the country's industrialization, recent research has illustrated that factories emerged in the shadow of Argentine wool, meat, and grain exports.[9] Buenos Aires and Rosario, for example, served as transportation and commercial hubs not only for the agricultural hinterlands but also for industrial cities—not to the degree that, say, Detroit or Manchester did, but the large plants and thousands of smaller workshops that they contained made them leading manufacturing centers in Latin America. Local factories were devoted to light industry (food processing, beverages, cosmetics, and textiles), although by the 1930s they were also assembling electrical appliances and other durables. Argentine-made manufactures replaced the imported goods already consumed by the population: whereas approximately 50 percent of all consumer goods were fabricated locally in the 1920s, by the 1930s the figure had climbed to around 65 percent and would top 80 percent by the early 1940s.[10] Calling this trend "import substitution" fails to do justice to its innovations. Entrepreneurs helped to create tastes for new products and adapted prevailing foreign fashions to local conditions. Over time, industrialization contributed to the formation of a broader market for everyday staples and higher demand for other commercial goods (such as ready-to-wear clothing) purchased on a mass-market scale.

The nationalizing trends associated with domestic consumption, however, should be kept in perspective. The boundary between the foreign and the domestic in the world of goods was permeable, and Argentine manufacturers were rarely independent from the international economy. They relied, to a greater or lesser degree, on foreign-made machinery to outfit their operations, imports of raw materials (e.g., coal and sheet metal) to supply them, and investment capital to keep their enterprises running. Imports continued to have an appeal. The fact that immigrants made up a large share of the country's residents—around one-third of the national population in 1914 and higher still in major cities—only added to the cosmopolitanism of the marketplace. Over time consumer practices followed the dictates of local tastes, but wares from London, Paris, and elsewhere continued to possess distinction, and Argentines consumed prodigious quantities of them. To provide but one example, over 3 million liters of foreign alcohol were imported in 1937 (including 840,000 bottles of whisky) to satisfy the local thirst, and this in a nation with established wine-producing regions and newer beer and liquor industries.[11] Through the countless lines of trade and communication connecting the nation to its trading partners in the Atlantic world, residents also looked abroad for the latest fruits of machine-age progress (e.g., automobiles) and monitored the changing whims of fashion.

The cornucopia of goods on display in urban areas added to Argentina's reputation as an international success story in the early twentieth century. Yet the expansion of the domestic marketplace was punctuated by the fitful rhythms of growth and contraction. The country's commitment to free-market liberalism ensured that economic crises in Western Europe and the United States were felt at home. During the Great Depression, business activity dropped off across the country as demand for grains and meats slackened abroad. The early 1930s were dark times for many Argentines; unemployment surged into the double digits, and those fortunate to keep their jobs endured sluggish incomes and poverty for years manuf ↑ agri ↓

afterward. Mass consumption slowed accordingly.[12] But the pendulum began to swing in the other direction by the middle of the decade. Argentina came out of the crisis more quickly than other nations, and employment improved as local businesses gathered momentum. Disruptions in the global economy were not entirely negative news, especially for domestic manufacturers who seized on disarray abroad to enlarge their operations. Factory owners faced serious challenges in acquiring raw materials and capital from abroad, but there was a burst of manufacturing activity in textiles and other sectors producing goods destined for local consumption. In fact, manufacturing rose by 35 percent between 1930 and 1939, and the sector gathered additional force during the war years. By contrast, agro-exports fell 60 percent from 1928 to 1938, another sign of the shifting balance toward the domestic market. For the first time industry now matched agricultural activity in terms of overall contribution to the GDP.[13] In the end, Argentina came out of the Great Depression and World War II with a larger industrial sector and a denser web of local commerce than it had before those crises.

Foodstuffs and manufactures may have led the way, but by the 1930s Argentina had also developed a vibrant commercial culture, an array of modern entertainments, services, and media that quickly became a feature of everyday life. The kiosks that dotted the city streets and small towns enticed passersby with publications of every stripe: daily newspapers (including those written in multiple immigrant languages); illustrated magazines on subjects ranging from science to gossip, women's beauty, sports, and family life; and cheap editions of popular fiction. Circulation figures for traditional Buenos Aires newspapers, such as *La Prensa,* placed them among the top ten dailies worldwide.[14] The colorful covers of *Radiolandia* and *Sintonía* and other such magazines, adorned with the faces of celebrities, provided an additional sign of the local fascination with the mass media. Commercial culture was linked to the world of consumer goods most obviously through advertising, and businesses employed the pages of periodicals, radio waves, and movie screens to court potential customers. Print, radio, and film were aimed at audiences with sufficient disposable income, including the country's sizeable middle class. Nevertheless, those in the working-class majority avidly consumed commercial culture as well. Most domestic manufacturers and media magnates sold their wares to as broad a public as possible. Spending power varied greatly, of course, but few ingrained cultural taboos or legal proscriptions blocked popular consumers from the marketplace.

Indeed, one of the appeals of mass consumption was precisely that it resonated, for some members of society at least, with one of the era's prevailing ideals: social opportunity. Argentina's mythic reputation for abundance gave shape to the spectrum of individual ambitions. To put it in familiar terms, there existed something of an "Argentine Dream"—a sense that this was a land where status was not necessarily fixed by family past or birthplace but could improve with hard work and luck. Obviously, the realization of mobility was limited in practice. But historians have suggested that the largely immigrant working- and middle-class residents of cities such as Buenos Aires and Rosario viewed advancement in essentially similar terms. These popular sectors longed to move out of congested downtown areas and into new neighborhoods, to become homeowners, and to ensure an education for their children.[15] In addition, smaller aspirations—to eat and dress a little better, to acquire a radio set, or to enjoy commercial entertainments—also served as markers of familial progress and modernity.

Raw competition and status seeking unquestionably accompanied such impulses. These tensions were mitigated, or at least masked, by a conception of mass consumption gaining force internationally at this time. Commentators argued that expanding commerce produced a social leveling across occupational lines and that strict class identities gave way to the formation of a broader mass of consumers sharing basically the same tastes and desires.[16] The perceptions of "consumer freedom" elicited predictable complaints about the erosion of standards but also favorable judgments regarding the lessening social divisions and the profits to be reaped in meeting popular demand for merchandise. Travelers from Europe came to comparable conclusions from their walks around downtown Buenos Aires. One such foreigner, Eduardo Aunós, who formed part of a Spanish government mission in 1942, offered this portrait of female consumers along the calle Florida: "At the commencement of night, when the street fills with shining signs and the windows of the elegant stores envelop in light all the lavishness of their wares, this becomes the reception room of the city. Along it circulate the elegant ladies who rub elbows with the maid, the servant, or the simple female worker [obrerita], who defeats through her sparkling jovialness the modesty, though not without taste, of her clothing."[17] Aunós did not deny that status distinctions existed, else how could one tell female workers apart from the wealthy? Rather, he suggested that social differences were muted amid the backdrop of the city's commercial plenty; women of humble standing shared the same public spaces as the well-to-do and dressed proudly to show off the "good taste" they had acquired. In this manner, everyday encounters in the urban marketplace were taken as optimistic evidence of a lack of deep-seated conflict, as a sign of the country's democratic social tendencies and capitalist progress.

Yet Argentina comprised more than just Buenos Aires, and the capital city included more than just calle Florida. Indeed, the spaces where most acquisition occurred lay distant from the districts frequented by wealthy businesspeople and travelers. Judgments about the inclusive, open character of mass consumption represented only one set of perspectives on the commercial transformations underway, impressions gathered with little effort to understand the everyday living conditions of the "masses." Consumption may have offered participation in an emerging social mainstream for some, but spending also differentiated social strata. While individual choices cannot be reduced to sociological categories, consumer acts were shaped by collective identities: one's ethnic or immigrant group; one's class and status ranks; and feelings of membership in generational, regional, or national solidarities. In short, the encounter with mass consumption was shaped by cultural variations and social inequalities that have been overlooked in the patriotic myths of easy plenty but that nevertheless determined the specific ways in which Argentines acquired goods.

At the most obvious level, the density of the consumer marketplace was uneven across the national territory. Turn-of-the-century economic transformations came at a cost of accentuating regional imbalances. The effects of growth were concentrated in the fan-shaped area of the Litoral (comprising the provinces of Buenos Aires, southern Santa Fe and Entre Rios, and southeastern Córdoba), responsible for the bulk of the nation's agro-exports and home to dominant manufacturing, transportation, and commercial centers. At the other end of the spectrum were regions with a narrower economic base, especially the provinces in the northwestern and northeastern regions, reliant on a combination of subsistence farming; enclaves of plantation agriculture; and extractive industries, such as forestry. Between these extremes were provincial zones that benefited from internal and foreign demand for their products (wine making in Mendoza or sheep herding in southern Patagonia). Each region was in turn subdivided into a checkerboard of areas with differing degrees of economic vitality; even within the booming Litoral, patterns of consumption in Buenos Aires were a far cry from those in the towns of its rural hinterland. Yet Argentina's regions were tied together, if weakly, by the sinews of a transportation infrastructure. Residents of the interior made use of the national railway and road system to adjust these regional imbalances, and they migrated toward the cities in ever-larger numbers during the 1930s. By this period, nearly one-half of workers in metropolitan Buenos Aires had lived in the region less than five years, and approximately one-third of this region's population had been born in the interior.[18] Attracted in part by the booming factories and commercial enterprises, migrants added to the already large populations of cities.

In addition, the increasingly national reach of mass communication linked the provinces and major cities into a consumer society. Take, for instance, the town

FIGURE 2. Rural workers at a flour mill in Santa Fe display the bounty of Argentina; the lack of room inside the bursting warehouse has forced them outdoors. *Archivo General de la Nación, Departamento Fotográficos, box 3061, envelope 8, doc. 155734 (Mar. 9, 1927); reproduced courtesy of the archive.*

of Venado Tuerto (population 14,000), in the province of Santa Fe, a middle-sized community in a typical Litoral agricultural zone. The town's residents were mainly laborers who worked seasonally in the fields or the local flourmill, sharecroppers and small farmers (*chacareros*), and a small middle class of professionals and merchants. Although the inhabitants were still restricted in their abilities to consume the latest modern manufactures, they were aware of commercial innovations. By the early 1940s, even this modest town boasted three movie theaters that regularly played Argentine, European, and Hollywood films. Radio programs from Buenos Aires and other cities reached the town, too, as did newspapers and magazines; a public address system set up on the main street broadcast music and advertisements at noon and in the evenings to passersby.[19] The social phenomenon of commercial culture became a theme for Argentine films, as in Mario Soffici's *Kilómetro 111*, a portrait of life in a small Litoral town where young people were obsessed with Cary Grant, Greta Garbo, and other celebrities. In the film, one female teenager is so besotted with stardom that she moves to Buenos Aires, where she enrolls in the sham "New Cinematographic Academy of Hollywood in Buenos Aires." A similar itinerary was pursued by some provincial residents (most famously, by a young woman named Eva Duarte, who left her pampas town to make her name as an actress in the big city).[20] For those who chose to remain in their hometowns, mass communication kept them informed about life in the Argentine metropolis and beyond.

In practice, the commercial landscape traversed by city residents only partially resembled cinematic representations of modernity. Even in Buenos Aires and Rosario, most consumer acts had a decidedly pedestrian character. The reign of self-service and the chain store lay in the future, and the supermarket would begin to make small inroads in Argentina only during the early 1950s. Patterns of buying and selling at the neighborhood level remained vibrant, and even the city streets were home to traveling salesmen and itinerant sellers. The term "marketplace" (*mercado*) had a more physical meaning than the current abstract sense. Popular barrios were converted into temporary bazaars during market days and open-air fairs (*ferias*), and shoppers relied on the ubiquitous bulk goods grocery (*almacén*), which sold dry goods, beverages, and sundry foodstuffs. These were typically full-service operations where merchandise was stored in bulk containers and on shelves behind the counter and where the storeowner attended to clients personally and sold household wares on weekly or monthly credit. Amid the clutter of the corner almacén and the pungent smells of its hanging cheeses, cured meats, and sacks of flour, locals gathered for a round of gossip. Consumers in urban areas did venture out of the neighborhood to other shopping and entertainment districts, but most purchasing probably occurred in places and among merchants familiar to consumers rather than in an impersonal mass setting.

For those living within this variegated marketplace, it was impossible to ignore the basic fact that consumption was linked inextricably to the demands of wage labor. Although subsistence farming remained important in some regions, as did artisan production and petty trading in urban areas, a growing majority of Argentines depended on market exchange for their survival—in other words, on the conversion of wages into commercial goods and services. For those who toiled in the nation's fields, docks, and factories, employment fluctuated with the harvest season and the vagaries of the business cycle. Earnings were often unpredictable, resulting in periodic belt-tightening and a tendency toward short-term purchasing. Social observers agreed that the high cost and poor quality of popular housing, especially in urban areas, imposed some of the heaviest burdens on discretionary spending. Surveys showed that in the late 1930s nearly nine out of ten working-class individuals in Buenos Aires lived in one or two rooms; in the average case, a *eco goes instability*

five-person family crammed into a room of roughly eighteen square meters. A typical rented lodging had a simple cooking area and access to a central patio, but it shared the bathroom with other tenants and often lacked any ventilation other than the main apartment door.[21] Crowded living conditions discouraged or obviated the need for elaborate household furnishings and appliances (with exceptions, such as the radio); in any event, paying for food and rent left most workers with limited disposable income.

The constraints on purchasing faced by popular households attracted attention from entrepreneurs, for whom establishing potential customers' spending power was integral to selling their wares. The "science" of marketing lacked the professionalization that it would achieve a generation later, but one major study from this period suggests how business experts viewed local consumers. In the early 1940s the Argentine Corporation for the Promotion of Trade contracted the U.S.-based Armour Research Foundation to write a report on the country's economic prospects. The Armour foundation was a private research agency headquartered in Chicago and specializing in engineering and industrial matters. To prepare its report, which it issued in 1942, the agency employed a team of over two hundred researchers who cooperated with Argentine businesses and government officials. The Armour team encountered initial pessimism regarding the depth of mass consumption; as one unnamed local businessman told them, "You must never forget that the Argentine market consists of three and a half million persons—not thirteen million."[22] Undiscouraged, the researchers noted that this judgment depended on the product under consideration, a high-end import (e.g., an automobile) versus a laborer's standby (e.g., *alpargatas* [cord-soled shoes]). To gain a better sense of proportion, the researchers resorted to comparisons with foreign countries. They focused specifically on the "unskilled laborer"—whom they assumed to be male—in Western European nations and the United States. The use of these areas, and not, say, neighboring Latin American countries, stemmed from the information available to the researchers and from perceptions of the nation's "advanced" status. Yet this comparative approach was fraught with problems. Incomplete statistical data were the least of these shortcomings. The category of "unskilled laborer" had no universally applicable definition, and it was clear that consumer preferences and the supply of goods were not the same across different nations.[23]

Despite these flaws, the Armour report drew broad conclusions about working-class purchasing power at the end of the 1930s. For one thousand hours of work, an unskilled urban laborer in Argentina earned only two-thirds the wages of his peers in Germany, one-half of those in Great Britain, and one-third of those in the

United States. A similar trend held true for unskilled rural workers, who earned less than urban laborers in all countries (although the gap between city and country was smaller in Argentina than elsewhere). But the data also suggested that Argentina's myth of popular plenty was not entirely fictitious. The lower prices charged for basic consumer goods there placed workers at a relative advantage. This was especially true with local staples, such as beef, milk, and bread. Other items, including sugar and potatoes, were more expensive, but on the whole, Argentine laborers could buy as much food as could their counterparts elsewhere, and sometimes more. These findings appeared to confirm the country's reputation as a land where the workingman's belly was full. This picture changed, however, when one looked at other features of mass consumption. The Argentine laborer's wages allowed purchases of only one-third to one-fourth the quantity of textiles that the comparable wages would buy in the United States. A radio receiver was seven times more expensive, an automobile five times more, and a sewing machine three times more than these items were for a U.S. worker.[24] These findings reinforced the primary conclusions of the Armour report, namely, that Argentina faced obstacles in further industrialization because of its workers' low wages and its relatively small internal market. Implicit in this conclusion was the assumption that the type of industrial capitalism pursued by the United States—the production of cheap goods on a large scale, relatively high wages to prop up consumption, and technologically intense manufacturing—was the ideal path for Argentina to follow. Based on this presumed model, Argentina had achieved an incomplete sort of consumer society, one in which the internal production of "ordinary" commercial goods had reached a high level, but the upper tiers of mass consumption fell short of the mark.

Strangely, the report said virtually nothing about the spending power of their "average worker" relative to that of other social groups, including those with higher incomes. By the 1930s middle-class households in Argentina were becoming avid purchasers of radio sets and electrical home appliances. These products were imported from the United States and Western Europe, but an increasing number were supplied domestically by companies such as SIAM Di Tella, which became Latin America's largest manufacturer of such goods.[25] Moreover, the Armour report's conclusions about Argentina's shallow domestic market were culturally relative; by contrast, the Spaniard Eduardo Aunós saw the ready availability of consumer credit as a sign that the country's "*yanqui* neighbors" had "notoriously influenced" patterns of life. Soon after landing a job in the country, he claimed, one would be solicited by the "infinite tentacles of credit," with offers of "furniture, clothes, work implements, if one needs them, and everything else needed to begin a life with the comfort that in other countries is realized only after years of sacrifice and saving."[26] This account of easy financing was an exaggeration, but it suggests that consumers found ways to obtain desired goods. As newspaper and magazine advertisements indicate, larger retailers and department stores offered installment plans of ten to twenty monthly payments on radios, furniture, kitchen stoves, electric irons, and bicycles, all of which expanded their pool of potential customers.

For all its omissions, the Armour report was fundamentally correct in highlighting the gaps that characterized mass consumption in 1930s Argentina. The guiding myth of Argentine national wealth and modern mass consumption emphasized openness and egalitarianism, but even in prosperous urban areas, most consumers faced another reality. Getting and spending necessitated all manner of cunning tactics. In their 1940s memoir, Ruth and Leonard Greenup described some of the methods employed by ordinary wage earners. While they extolled the abundant food on display in Buenos Aires, they also cast an eye at the use of credit and scrimping (they dubbed this the practice of "little economies") by which urban residents acquired consumer goods. For instance, they described the habits of the twenty-year-old "copy boy" who worked at their newspaper office. With his wages of $4.50 a week, this young man would buy one suit a year, paying for it on weekly installments of seventy-five cents and then purchasing a new one the following year when it wore out. Although the Greenups felt that their co-worker was able at least to eat reasonably on his meager salary, as middle-class Americans living abroad, they thought these common routines of thrift to be "a dreary little rut."[27] Arlt may have remarked sardonically in his newspaper column about benchmarks of progress (such as buying a new suit every six months), but many of his fellow citizens did not have it even that good.

In the pursuit of these little economies, gender played a fundamental role by structuring consumer tactics. As the example of the copy boy suggests, the marketplace was not an entirely feminine sphere, and one must not fall into the familiar trap of equating women with consumers, men with producers. Nevertheless, women were tasked with the primary responsibility for housekeeping, and they were expected to possess special knowledge in regard to purchasing, not least of which was knowing how to stretch tight incomes and maximize household well-being through thrifty shopping. Female duties in provisioning extended to household production—such as making and repairing garments, tending to vegetable gardens, and cooking—as well as cleaning and other forms of housework. These norms reinforced the ideal of the domestic sphere as the primary, legitimate domain for women and served to buttress the institution of heterosexual marriage, which rested on an idealized division of labor in which female adults would tend to men and children. As the commercial offerings grew with each passing year in Argentina, so, too, did the demands on women as consumers. Positioned at the point where the household met the marketplace, female consumers possessed authority within the domestic sphere and, at least potentially, within everyday commercial spaces.

Advertisers targeted women as consumers, inspired both by paternalistic notions of the malleability of the female mind and by their supposed command over the purse strings. Popular magazine ads invoked their domestic authority: "In my house, I'm the boss," announced a smiling housewife in a mid-1940s ad for canned ham.[28] Commercial culture contributed as well to an ideal of the female consumer that transcended narrow status categories. Women's magazines, such as *Para Ti* and *Rosalinda,* were pitched at middle-class audiences but also reached out to working-class consumers anxious for respectability. Advice columns teaching female readers how to groom themselves with "*clase*" on a modest budget suggest how these publications sought to channel the social aspirations of women, and not only in their role as household managers. Young women readers were encouraged not to despair when confronted with photographs of high society debutantes, film stars, or other examples of feminine perfection. Under the tutelage of the magazine's experts, they, too, could learn the "harmonization of colors," new hairstyles, skin treatments, and other techniques of beauty required for women to shine in society.[29] While most ads stressed household provisioning or ideals of personal beauty, some, such as Mum deodorant ("for women who work"), featured images of typists and nurses, suggesting that businesses recognized the demands of laboring women.[30]

Indeed, female consumers engaged in wage work both inside and outside the home (in addition to performing unpaid forms of household labor) and made up around one-quarter of the official workforce in the 1930s.[31] Argentine women from the middling strata could lessen these burdens by hiring domestic servants to carry out duties, such as food provisioning. (Apparently some contemporaries considered it bad form for women of a certain class to be seen carrying packages or bags in public; if one had the money, one could get almost anything delivered, and an untold number of people earned meager livings shuttling goods from department stores and local shops to their customers.)[32] Such niceties of conduct were rarely possible for working-class females, who presumably envisioned other ways of distinguishing between proper and disreputable behavior. The majority of women faced a grinding double shift as income earners and household managers, which left little time or disposable income for other purchasing. Perhaps more than any other social sector, working women were exposed to the contradictions between the abundance of the marketplace and the constraints of domestic wants.

There was little doubt, then, that Argentina in the 1930s possessed the basic features of that which observers later came to call "consumer society," even if full access to the nation's commercial bounty remained elusive for most inhabitants. Merchants placed an ever-wider offering of commercial services and wares—both imported and domestically harvested, processed, or manufactured—at the disposal of would-be buyers. The era's vast marketplace comprised spaces ranging from downtown department stores and movie palaces to neighborhood shops and small-town street fairs. Acquisitive practices varied tremendously, as they did in even the most affluent consumer societies, and were modified by regional, ethnic, and class differences, individual economic circumstances, and norms of gender comportment and domesticity. Boosters claimed that a general climate of plenty and democratic well-being prevailed, as even those who lacked income aspired to emulate the purchasing habits of their social "superiors." More careful observers acknowledged that in the famed "land of the stretched belt," working people struggled to get by. While some moved along the acquisitive path of upward mobility, most continued to live at the edge of subsistence only through constant labor and by dint of "little economies."

Sizing Up Spending

Consumption attracted interest from more than just local commentators and curious travelers. Observers working in the social sciences, for example, studied consumer behavior in the 1930s, if often indirectly. Unlike the Armour foundation and other such business outfits, which compiled information to foster sales, these professionals and would-be reformers amassed data on buying power for ameliorative ends, seeking to illuminate "deficiencies" and propose practical solutions to remedy material wants. Their conclusions about the widespread existence of unmet needs among the country's working majority contradicted the prevailing national myths of Argentina's abundance; partly as a result, they were disregarded by those in positions of authority. The results hardly make thrilling reading, especially compared to the vibrant chronicles of Arlt and other street-level observers. But contained within dutiful statistical reports, charts of spending patterns, and surveys of working-class family life were powerful conclusions about unmet material needs. By adapting the standard of living metric and other analytical tools to local circumstances, researchers helped frame consumer spending as an object of public debate and reformist attention. Although most social scientists who probed into areas of household consumption remained obscure figures, their ideas would have tremendous political resonance in the years that followed and would inform Peronist programs to elevate workers from poverty.

Studies of worker spending habits formed part of a much larger field of inquiry. The scope of social politics was enormous, as is reflected in the investigative output of experts: reports on congested housing; journalistic exposés of child labor and workplace safety; studies on public sanitation, hygiene, and health care; legislative proposals for social insurance and retirement systems; sociological investigations into criminal behavior—and these were but a few of the major controversies. This field resembled less a conversation around a common table than the chaos of a noisy cafeteria, with many separate pockets of activity. Left-leaning activists and liberal reformers were well represented; right-wing groups also weighed in, some inspired by the examples of interwar fascism in Europe, and others, by the Catholic Church's efforts to create a more pious nation.[33] Nevertheless, there was a surprising degree of consensus among experts regarding the causes of dislocation. The so-called social question focused on the risks facing urban wage earners, who had employment but nonetheless lived at the brink of complete destitution.[34] Critics were convinced that the free play of economic liberalism in Argentina had created wealth and plenty for some but left too many ordinary workers behind. Markets were not entirely to blame, for life itself carries inevitable risks of disease and accident and the unavoidability of old age. Yet the critics felt that these problems were worsened by the thirst for profits and frenetic swings in supply and demand. Without seeking to eliminate market forces entirely, reformers wanted to remove especially sensitive areas of the household from market transactions, especially "essentials," such as shelter or health care. As a result, consumer spending became relevant only to reformers interested in the way laboring people converted wages into commercial goods and services needed for survival. The term "consumo" was all too often reduced to minimal definitions that encompassed only the most basic food and clothing.

Despite their blinkered view of working-class material life, researchers could on occasion display creativity in thinking about the politics of social need. In surveying spending habits, for example, advocates of the working class explored a new vocabulary for thinking about the collective entitlements of individuals living in a competitive order. These changes were reflected in a conceptual innovation employed to understand consumption broadly defined: namely, the nivel de vida, or "level of living." Like its close cousin the "standard of living," this term included flexibility among its principal attractions. It allowed researchers to draw connections among issues of production (wage income), commerce (the cost of living), and consumer spending (household budgets). As was the case for other concepts used in Argentine social politics, the adoption of the standard de vida metric was inspired by developments elsewhere in the world. These ideas flowed mainly one way, with the latest, cutting-edge methods arriving at South American shores across the Atlantic from Paris, London, and New York. In this regard, local experts were consumers of imported journals and books just as others were consumers of radio sets or bottles of whiskey. Investigators made foreign comparisons not only out of a drive for intellectual cachet or sense of inferiority but also because they considered Argentina itself to be standing on the cusp of a transition to capitalist modernity. Rather than simply mimic their foreign peers, they adapted methods devised abroad to illuminate local conditions. Research on the standard of living gained currency elsewhere in the world roughly at the same time, as in the 1929–1931 Ford Company–International Labour Office inquiry conducted across western and southern Europe.[35] Argentine investigations proceeded independently but in a roughly parallel manner and with little lag time in diffusion compared to studies elsewhere.

The standard de vida became such a feature of the political vocabulary of post–World War II Argentina that we tend to assume it always to have been so. It is surprising, then, to see how little it figured in social politics a generation earlier. Take, for example, Juan Bialet Massé's muckraking classic *El informe sobre el estado de la clase obrera* (1904). A physician and lawyer, Bialet Massé was commissioned by the Argentine government to investigate worker conditions in the provincial interior. For months he traveled across the expanse of the country's northwest and central regions, documenting the deprivation of local populations in a final report of three 400-page volumes. The study contains no references to levels or standards of living: Bialet Massé did insist that working people deserved a "minimum ration" but offered only a few passing references to an adequate diet, shelter, and "simple" and "inexpensive" clothes.[36] The author failed to imagine what a more comprehensive satisfaction of wants would entail—perhaps understandably so, given the desolation he witnessed during his journey.

Compare Bialet Massé's assessments to the approaches adopted a generation later. The economist Alejandro Bunge followed the path set down by his precursor but attempted a more quantitative assessment of regional divergences. One of the best-known social scientists of 1930s Argentina, Bunge devoted his professional life to researching nationalist issues, bringing attention to them in policy journals (including his own *Revista de Economía Argentina*) and, more broadly, through frequent editorials in major newspapers. Bunge saw Argentina as requiring greater state involvement in expanding industrialization and managing natural resources. Inspired by right-wing Catholic doctrine, he further argued for government action to address the "deficiencies" of the population—including measures to strengthen the "white race" through a reduction in child mortality and improving workers' living conditions. This nationalist vision was captured in his most influential book, *Una nueva Argentina* (1940), which offered a mixed message on the question of consumption. Bunge suggested that conditions for the Argentine "working population" and "petit bourgeoisie" were generally adequate; invoking the familiar trope of national plenty, he proclaimed, "They have nothing to envy in their standard of life, in their well-being and possibilities of betterment, from any other country in the world, with the exception of the United States."[37]

But Bunge also argued that in many regions the working population suffered from exceedingly low living standards, the consequence of a phenomenon he called underconsumption (*infraconsumo*).[38] Based on his calculations, regional differences in economic productivity left the residents of the interior with a meager "acquisitive capacity" relative to their peers elsewhere. "In the country of beef," Bunge wrote, "there are regions where its inhabitants rarely consume it." He devised social scientific yardsticks to measure the impact of infraconsumo and other socioeconomic problems across a vast territory. According to Bunge's estimates, the Litoral (defined as the arc within 580 kilometers of the city of Buenos Aires) represented only 20 percent of the total national territory but was home to almost 70 percent of its inhabitants and an overwhelming majority of the country's capital investments, businesses, and modern technology, including 70 percent of the nation's telephones and 80 percent of the automobiles.[39] Bunge argued that uneven development meant that the economic capacity per inhabitant—which included the ability to consume commercial goods—differed sharply from place to place. In metropolitan Buenos Aires it was ten times greater than in Catamarca, a sparsely populated, arid province on the slopes of the Andes. His perceptions of social difference further widened the sense of a regional divide in underconsumption. The Litoral's disproportionally large population stemmed in part from heavy overseas migration to the region; by the mid-1930s nearly 80 percent of the nation's resident foreigners lived there. The northwestern and northeastern areas were comparatively less affected by immigration and tended to have populations with roots that went back generations. In these areas, many native-born inhabitants came from mestizo backgrounds (indigenous, African, and European ancestry), or to use the period's more common term, *criollo* (creole).[40] When seen through the lens of Bunge's racist ideology, which privileged recent European ancestry and whiteness, these ethnic characteristics accentuated a sense that Argentina's prosperous Litoral and other regions were worlds apart.

As Bunge established living standards in regional terms, his circle of followers sought to quantify the microlevel dimensions of consumption. A close associate, Emilio Llorens, explored consumo through statistical analyses of nutrition. Llorens defined this term mainly as caloric intake, which was a new social scientific tool that was being applied in Argentina and elsewhere to study and compare populations. Llorens relied on nutrition data published in other countries (including neighboring Latin American nations) to assess "levels" of consumption in Argentina. Using international nutritional "standards" developed by social scientists in the United States and Europe, he concluded that urban workers in Argentina had a diet based on ample total calories (if short on fresh vegetables). But Llorens was quick to note that residents of poorer provinces faced nutritional deficits, and he proposed policies—including education, food subsidies, and augmented worker incomes—to elevate the levels.[41] For Llorens, the problem of underconsumption began at the most fundamental level of nutrition, draining the nation's workforce of its full potency and health. Accordingly, the members of Bunge's circle favored an inward-oriented economic model, where the intensification of production in poorer areas and urban industrialization would speed a virtuous cycle: higher consumption of domestic goods, an elevated nivel de vida, and ultimately greater sovereignty for the country as a whole.[42] This nationalist faith in the curative effects of domestic consumption would later prove influential, but it is worth noting how consumption-oriented concepts, such as the standard of living, helped link working-class consumption to larger reformist designs. The issues that Bialet Massé had emphasized—basic food, shelter, and clothing—remained a center of scholarly attention, but they were combined with analyses of macroeconomic policy, statistical efforts to assess nutritional thresholds, and other "scientific" assessments of the material requirements for a decent life.

As these examples suggest, quantitative knowledge was crucial in orienting discussions of living standards in the 1930s and early 1940. Perhaps the most comprehensive attempt to measure consumption in this era was conducted not by private social scientists but by the Departamento Nacional de Trabajo (DNT). The DNT, or National Labor Department, was the branch of federal government that mediated workplace conflicts between labor and management, but it lacked the authority to impose arbitration and suffered from underfunding. From the mid-1930s to the early 1940s, the agency's small staff made a more ambitious push to gather knowledge about laboring populations. A series of surveys documented the household budgets of an "average working-class family" (defined in 1937 as a male wage earner, wife, and three children under the age of fourteen living in Buenos Aires or that city's suburbs). The individual responsible for this research was the department's chief of statistics, José Miguel Figuerola y Tressols. Born in Spain and relocated to Argentina in the early 1930s, Figuerola epitomized the internationalism of social politics. In his native land he had supported the right-wing Primo de Rivera regime during the 1920s and had served as an official in the labor ministry that had helped draft Spain's national labor code.[43] After immigrating to Argentina, Figuerola established himself within the social scientific community (joining the board of the *Revista de Ciencias Sociales* and the Social Politics Institute of the University of Buenos Aires) and forged ties with nationalist circles. By 1933 he had been appointed to his post at the DNT and published policy tracts on the side.[44]

The surveys assembled by Figuerola provided unprecedented detail on household consumption. A 1937 survey of the nivel de vida revealed that the "average" family allocated 57 percent of its total income for food (with an additional 4 percent going to fuel for cooking and heating). Food choices reflected the regional variety of Argentine agriculture and the city's immigrant influences: wine and oil from the Andean provinces; milk and butter from Litoral dairies; and from the northeast, *yerba mate* (the local "tea"). "*Pan francés*" (French bread), pasta, beef, and other staples formed the basis of the local diet. Rental housing costs came next (20 percent), and one got very little for the money: one or two poorly ventilated, overcrowded rooms. Household members devoted much smaller shares of the budget to other consumer goods, 10 percent for clothing, for example, and 8 percent for "general spending," a catchall category for personal hygiene, entertainment, medical, and transportation expenses.[45] Looking over these charts and figures, one can trace the minutia of quotidian life: the grams of flour, sugar, or dried beans purchased; the quantities of wine drunk or cigarettes smoked; the pairs of pants and blouses bought yearly. It is surprising, then, that Figuerola provided little analysis of the data. The agency's mandate was to publish information for the use of researchers, not necessarily to offer interpretations of its own, but these missed opportunities betray a lack of curiosity about consumer behavior. In hindsight, the unexamined implications of these surveys beg to be drawn out. For instance, the

DNT figures belie gender stereotypes by suggesting that working-class households spent much more on men's clothing than on women's. In fact, as much as two-thirds of the clothing budget was devoted to men's suits, hats, work overalls, and other garments.[46] We are left wondering why certain articles were selected over others—why, say, did working men apparently purchase ready-made suits, while women bought cloth to make dresses? What is one to make of the fact that, despite devoting only a fraction of income to clothing, an urban working-class family used 106 different pieces of clothes and accessories each year? The lack of answers makes it impossible to fully weigh the significance of consumer choices within material limitations and cultural tastes.

There were a number of questionable assumptions built into the DNT's portrait of the nivel de vida that colored its view of living standards despite pretensions of objectivity. The labor department's conception of the working class was based on unskilled laborers (*peones*) in the metropolitan region's bigger industrial workplaces, ignoring the numerically larger ranks of day laborers, service workers, petty artisans, and others.[47] Regional variations and rural populations lay outside this scope as well. Most problematic, budget calculations rested on the supposition that a sole male breadwinner within a married household was the norm. The DNT reports hammered home a central conclusion time and again: namely, that the average working-class family did not earn enough to satisfy basic consumption needs. While the male "head" earned 127 pesos, household expenditures totaled 164 pesos; the resulting 37-peso deficit in the monthly budget represented nearly 30 percent of the average laborer's income. Statistics on white-collar wage earners (*empleados*) proved a bit more reassuring, for their salaries (calculated at double that of unskilled obreros) allowed most to provide for monthly expenditures.[48] The data on the wages earned by women and children were either not gathered or erased from the calculus of household budgets. This omission was more than an oversight. From Figuerola's viewpoint, the true social scandal was not the deprivation endured by working households on tight budgets but rather the fact that the male breadwinner alone was unable to satisfy family income needs. The fact that women and children constituted part of the official workforce was presented as a calamity that demanded immediate solutions.

Despite the grave concerns expressed about the working-class family, social scientific inquiries into living standards did not spur immediate reforms from state authorities. Experts recommended the same sorts of measures proposed throughout Latin America and elsewhere at this time: nutritional supplements for children (such as milk rations in public schools); minimum wage legislation; and above all,

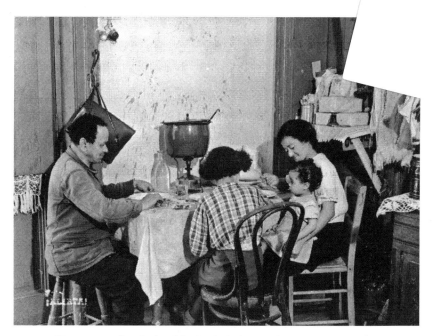

FIGURE 3. Newspapers often depicted the "typical" *familia obrera;* the one-pot meal and small, sparsely furnished room shown here suggest this one's constrained consumption. *Archivo General de la Nación, Departamento Fotográficos, box 1023, envelope 15, doc. 320039 (Oct. 2, 1941); reproduced courtesy of the archive.*

"family wage" subsidies for male workers that would boost income and safeguard the masculine provider of the nuclear family.[49] Conservative rule enabled the ascendance of groups on the more extreme nationalist and Catholic right, and it is not coincidental that right-wing individuals, such as Bunge and Figuerola, were responsible for leading research, for they enjoyed the resources (meager as they were) to explore such matters. Nonetheless, the weight of laissez-faire traditions presented serious barriers to policy experimentation, and policymakers focused their attention elsewhere (e.g., on economic recovery from the Depression). Faced with this inhospitable climate, the majority of social scientists with liberal and leftist leanings either retreated to their research or directed energies toward local activism.

But even as statistical reports on *"capacidad adquisitiva"* gathered dust on library shelves, awaiting an eventual political champion, the discourses associated with living levels and standards helped those terms steadily work their way into the lexicon of public life. By the early 1940s this terminology appeared with increasing frequency in the pages of daily newspapers and politicians' speeches.

With increased application outside circles of expertise, the notions of levels and standards proved their usefulness once again as malleable concepts that allowed bundling multiple aspirations for a better life under one umbrella. They surfaced as well in the publications of organizations representing working-class constituencies— "the Living Level Must Be Elevated," proclaimed a headline of a railway workers' union newspaper in 1939. In this case, the article's author shared the reformists' concern about the nuclear family, suggesting that the problems affecting male laborers—"lack of food, misery, minimal wages, unsanitary housing"—kept the level of living so low that it contributed to reduced birthrates among working families.[50] How readers responded to these ways of discussing wants and needs is unclear, but the social scientific language reached at least a segment of the working class. The social knowledge that experts used to measure consumption may have remained foreign to most popular audiences in the 1930s, but their discursive tools became objects of interest to politicians, employers, and labor organizations seeking to set a new agenda for the post–World War II era. By the mid-1940s, "standard de vida" and similar terms would be freed from the confines of the academic journal to become keywords of Argentine public life.

The Ethics of Exchange

Talk of levels and standards, however, represented only one mode for thinking about the defects of Argentina's market economy. Rather than assess differentials in nutritional intake, other observers worked within older traditions of critiquing commercial pressures. The sobriety of social scientific reports vanished among those favoring a rowdier approach that involved taking to the streets in protest. Here the focus shifted from household consumer behavior to villainous property holders—not least of which were "unscrupulous" merchants and profiteers accused of swindling the needy and gouging customers out of their hard-earned pesos. Critics summoned the frustrations of a laboring public burdened with constrained spending power. Their rhetoric tapped into a deep reservoir of cultural attitudes regarding the ethics of exchange, stretching back to popular responses to the market transformations of nineteenth-century liberalism, if not further back to colonial-era conceptions of usury and greed. Taken together, these attitudes constituted a "moral economy" of sorts, famously defined by E. P. Thompson in the context of eighteenth-century England as "a consistent traditional view of social norms and obligations, of the proper economic functions of several parties within the community."[51] While everyday commerce was not the sole object of attention for Argentina's moralists, the undeniable acquisitive imperatives and commercialization of modern life provoked repeated unease.

Ethical judgments against unfair commerce did not entail a complete rejection of market exchange or mass consumption in 1930s Argentina. Concerns with injustice operated in a milieu far different from that of the moral economy of peasant societies. Argentina may or may not have been born liberal, but by the 1930s the values of economic liberalism had seeped into the worldview of its inhabitants. Accommodations to the logic of a market-driven society bred a familiarity with the quotidian demands of earning, buying, and selling. This did not mean a total acceptance of the existing order, however, for exposure to economic pressures sparked resentments among those kept at the margins of national plenty. Discontent manifested itself in everything from private grumbling to organized forms of protest, while competing revolutionary and religious utopian visions of a better world beyond capitalism still inspired large sectors of the population. But attacks on avarice often had more immediate aims and reformist goals consonant with political projects for tighter state regulation and economic intervention.[52] Moreover, moralizing often fell short of embracing total asceticism before the material world. Frustrations with merchant greed could exist, albeit uneasily at times, alongside aspirations in the realm of mass consumption, and even actors adopting anticapitalist positions at times displayed a surprising openness to the allure of the marketplace.

Various camps voiced concerns with commercial injustices, but Argentina's leftist and labor organizations were by far the most consistent in doing so. Sizable by Latin American standards and prominent in the urban areas of the Litoral, the Argentine Left nevertheless represented only a minority of the national population. The Socialist Party had managed to gain a few seats in Congress and Buenos Aires's municipal government; other players included the remnants of a once vibrant anarchist movement and a small but growing Communist Party. Leftist activists maintained close ties with labor unions, which increased in membership from 15 percent to 20 percent of the industrial workforce in the late 1930s.[53] All Argentine leftists targeted more or less the same social types in their denunciations of capitalist relations: rapacious bosses who exposed laborers to unsafe workplace conditions, employers so obsessed with profit that they paid starvation wages, greedy financiers responsible for market panics, and corrupt government officials who imposed burdensome taxes. Although workplace-related questions featured prominently, the line separating labor from other economic realms was not always sharply drawn. If leftists rejected the dehumanizing premise that labor is just another commodity to be bought or sold, with little regard for the person behind the physical work, this realization propelled many activists to look at working-class life in other dimensions—especially matters of collective consumption. There was, moreover, room in the rogue's gallery of capitalist villains for those involved in commercial buying and selling: the retailer who cheated customers with overpriced goods, the *almacenero* (shopkeeper) who cooked the credit ledger to keep his clients in debt, and the stall owner who sold tainted milk. Condemnations of merchant cupidity peppered declarations in public speeches and the pages of leftist newspapers and smaller labor publications, which together reached audiences numbering in the hundreds of thousands.[54] The measured terminology and statistical forms of knowledge deployed by social scientists found a home among these activists. But leftist critics relied on impassioned language, tarring merchants as speculators, railing against hoarders and profiteering intermediaries, and arguing that high prices constituted a "criminal assault on the dignity of workers," as one labor newspaper proclaimed in 1935.[55]

As they had for other social commentators, urban working-class households attracted the lion's share of leftist attention. Reformist anxieties about the vulnerability of the male-headed nuclear family merged with more pragmatic considerations, for the urban workforce was clearly the Left's target constituency. Nevertheless, these city-based critics did not entirely ignore populations elsewhere. Alfredo Palacios, a socialist member of Congress representing the capital, documented bleak conditions during his travels through the northwestern region in his 1944 book *Pueblos desamparados*, exclaiming, "My pride as an Argentine suffered a rude blow, confronted with the misery of this good people, sad and resigned, whom we shamefully forget." Like his predecessor Bialet Massé, he passed through regions where subsistence farmers lacked water for their crops and laborers working on the estates of large landowners endured long periods of unemployment punctuated by brutal harvest seasons. Palacios recounted the coping tactics of local inhabitants in arid, resource-poor provinces, such as Santiago del Estero, marginalized from the circuits of mass consumption. Faced with a lack of food, some parents served their children a breakfast of only *té de brasas*—"ember tea," an infusion made from a piece of burnt wood coated with a bit of sugar and then dropped in hot water.[56] In these regions of Argentina's interior, the constrained spending power of city dwellers gave way to a constant fight against malnutrition and starvation, but this struggle attracted only occasional concern from activists.

The pressures weighing on urban wage earners also shaped the agenda of the Left's rivals for popular support, including centrist, liberal, and religious organizations and, most notably, Argentina's largest political party, the Unión Cívica Radical (UCR), or Radicals. During the party's heyday in 1916–1930, President Hipólito Yrigoyen and other Radical politicians styled themselves as defenders of the "people" against entrenched economic interests. Politicians affiliated with the UCR forged alliances with organized labor and echoed leftist condemnations of commercial avarice. Patronage networks operated by the Radicals in Buenos Aires and other urban areas provided direct assistance through the distribution of low-cost bread loaves (dubbed "*pan radical*"). Yet UCR leaders faced a classic bind of Argentine politics that ultimately hampered their ability and even willingness to deploy the state to this end. Government measures favoring urban consumers often conflicted with the interests of powerful rural producers. Distinguishing Argentina from many other nations in Latin America, its main agricultural exports were also the core of its domestic consumption—namely, foodstuffs (e.g., grain and meat) and not, say, coffee or tin. In general, the Radicals opted not to antagonize landowners, and their efforts to shield urban consumers through commercial regulation or subsidies were minimal (such as modest rent laws and controls on the price of sugar).[57] Committed to the liberal order, UCR politicians nevertheless continued to present themselves rhetorically as defenders of the people, and throughout the 1930s they emphasized their signature themes of moral government and popular republicanism.

By comparison, Argentina's conservative and religious organizations voiced more selective condemnations of commercial injustice. Nationalist intellectuals warned of the harmful dominance of foreign capital (especially telephone, transportation, and utility companies that fleeced their customers), while religious commentators bemoaned the excessive materialism of modern times. Catholic leaders referenced biblical proscriptions against usury (*agio*) and merchant greed in their commentaries on contemporary economic issues. So-called social Catholic politicians coupled their antimaterialism with a desire to shield families from economic threats through state regulations. From their vantage, the thirst for consumerist acquisition clashed with the barely hidden reality of working-class poverty. As one of the leading figures in these circles, Congressman Juan Cafferata, noted in a report on housing conditions: "How can one talk seriously of progress and civilization when amid the skyscrapers, department stores, and grand avenues of Buenos Aires were families living in deplorable slums incompatible with basic notions of human dignity?"[58]

Irrespective of their ideological leanings, reform-minded contemporaries found it hard to ignore the contrasts of abundance and misery evidenced in the capital city and communities across the nation. Ironically, similar criticisms about unethical exchange and inequality circulated through the very networks of the consumer marketplace assailed by detractors of modern-day materialism. Popular frustrations with commercial pressures were not entirely the domain of activists and politicians, for they were ventilated in public life as well through radio programs, mass-circulation magazines, and other cultural forums. The feature films of the day exemplified this blending of discourses, providing moviegoers with accounts of consumerist pleasure and critiques of social injustice often within the same work. Argentine films from this period, for instance, often told rags-to-riches stories that resonated with the nation's ideal of social fluidity: typically, a worthy but unfortunate heroine was plucked from poverty to live in wedded bliss.[59] (The fear of falling was expressed in a tragic inverse: the girlfriend being cast off by a rich beau or the heartbroken man whose lover leaves him for a wealthier suitor—not coincidentally, the classic theme of the era's popular commercial music, the tango.) Fizzy comedies, including those of the formulaic "white telephone" variety, ruled the day, but these representations were occasionally counterbalanced by forays into social realism.[60]

One such film, *Mujeres que trabajan* (working women), directed by Manuel Romero, offered portraits of female salesclerks in a large department store.[61] In this 1938 melodrama, the daughter of a wealthy financier falls from grace after his suicide and then finds herself toiling alongside the women wage earners whom she had previously mocked. Despite the serious issues the film broaches (the store owner's affair with one worker leads to an out-of-wedlock pregnancy), the story ends happily with the protagonist, Ana María, marrying her handsome, wealthy boyfriend. Its storyline is set against an urban commercial landscape. One scene takes place in a "*bar lacteo*" (literally, "milk bar," a sort of U.S.-inspired diner); many others were shot on location on the floors of a downtown department store, called "Stanley Ltd." in the film. Amid the bustle of this noisy, brightly lit emporium, the women sell perfume and gloves to mainly female customers, pushy bourgeois types decked out in fashionable hats and handbags, all while reflecting on their own attempts to make ends meet. As they wrestle with personal setbacks, Ana María and the other salesclerks suffer jibes from their more affluent customers: "I have no idea what these idiot employees must be thinking," one lady exclaims. The film's potentially controversial contrast between the wastrel rich and burdened workers is defused by its somewhat comic portrayal of the salesclerk Luisa, a worker-intellectual who espouses arguments in favor of class struggle and unionization. Mocked as an embittered, uptight *comunista* by her friends, in the end she, too, longs for the love of a man who will take her away from her books. Hewing to gender conventions, the populist message of Romero's *Mujeres que trabajan* is clear enough: despite their lack of wealth, working people are honest and proud.

Commentary on the pressures of the marketplace, whether proffered by politicians or film directors, served a variety of purposes. In some cases, these complaints operated as a springboard for collective action. Leftist groups in particular sought to translate anger at consumer-related matters into public protest. During the 1930s party and labor activists staged rallies, led boycotts, and engaged in other mobilizations around high living costs and unfair merchant practices, much as they had in preceding decades; small-scale victories did not, however, lead to broader changes in commerce. Consumer cooperatives provided alternatives to private sector provisioning by selling low-cost food and other goods; some of the largest were run by the Socialist Party, while labor unions, including the railway workers' organization La Fraternidad, operated similar facilities for the rank and file.[62] Proponents considered cooperatives not just a means of distributing lower-cost goods but also a first step in moving beyond capitalist modes of exchange, one that would instill habits of righteous consumption in workers subject to the materialistic enticements of sellers.

Yet cooperatives and calls for greater market regulation made little headway during the 1930s. Cafferata and other social Catholics helped push through the adoption of palliative measures such as urban rent control legislation but mirrored the Church hierarchy in conservative opposition to further redistributive measures. Driven by anti-immigrant xenophobia, right-wing nationalists were hardly predisposed to address the consumer needs of an often foreign-born urban workforce. And while those on the political Right lacked the desire, other groups did not possess the means. After the 1930 military coup, prominent Radical Party politicians were forced from office and lost access to patronage resources. While some UCR members, including the former president Marcelo T. de Alvear, restyled themselves in a populist mold, calling for economic measures to favor working people, the party failed to regain the presidency (though it did win back some seats in Congress).[63] Leftist condemnations of capitalist greed may have reached large urban audiences, but the movements behind them were hamstrung by their lack of broad-based national support, limited finances, and repeated waves of hostility from state authorities. Interparty rivalries also discouraged support for state intervention under Concordancia rule; in these circumstances, even some leftists supported low barriers on trade and feared that state commercial regulation would benefit well-connected businesses, not ordinary consumers. From their perspective, the biggest threats were capitalist monopoly and collusion with state authorities, not retail exchange.[64]

The development of a more ambitious consumer politics was further hampered by problematic assumptions about consumers themselves. Gender played a crucial role, for political overtures were directed toward male wage earners and voters, not disenfranchised female purchasers. The fact that working-class women performed the bulk of household provisioning and thus might be predisposed to mobilize around issues of consumption did not lead to organizing campaigns for women—although female involvement was fundamental in boycotts and protests. When viewed in this light, the positions staked in 1930s Argentina conform to a conventional view in the history of consumption. On the one hand, dour social critics, distrustful of commercial appetites, made broad appeals to morality, measured acquisition, and popular solidarity; on the other, an emerging consumer society, driven by business interests, sought to propagate an inclusive, classless view of social well-being gained through individual purchasing acts.[65] There were, of course, extremely good reasons communists and social Catholics, for all their differences, shared a lack of interest in such matters. Why bother with mass consumption when many workers lived at poverty's edge? To their credit, critics focused creative energies on issues of collective consumption, such as health care and housing; after all, these too had become commercialized in modern times, paid for with wages through market forms of exchange. It made sense to frame consumer politics around attacks on capitalist greed, but lost from sight was how the commercial interests of a modern marketplace exerted an appeal on popular constituencies.

In practice, however, the barriers separating commercial detractors and mass-consumption enthusiasts were more permeable than they might first appear to have been. For starters, the pull of the consumer marketplace could not be completely ignored, even by those who quite rightly emphasized its inequities. Even though they faced severe constraints on spending power, Argentine wage earners lived in a competitive social world in which goals of greater inclusion, higher status, and progress were pursued partly through acts of consumption. Not all critics of capitalism, even those on the Left, were entirely consistent in their asceticism. To offer but one example, the publications of Argentina's two largest labor organizations—the railway workers' Unión Ferroviaria and La Fraternidad—offer insights into the porous border between economic moralizing and consumer aspiration. These union papers reported on workplace conflicts, legal decisions, and high living costs, much as did leftist periodicals. Appearing alongside these articles and editorials, however, occasionally on the same page, were advertisements for a variety of consumer goods. These ads hawked not just staples but also items higher up the chain of acquisition: cabinet radios, sewing machines, and dining and living room sets.

Merchants highlighted the availability of installment plans, which suggests that these wares were still a stretch on a railway worker's salary. Nonetheless, potential buyers were courted with descriptions of fine fabrics, the "*confort*" (comfort) of furnishings, and the technological sophistication of imported products. In home décor, ads seemed to favor the angular lines of art deco furniture, though they included items in more ornate styles, including a "Chippendale bedroom" decked out with "fine walnut frames, crystal mirrors, and platinum-colored hinges."[66] Clothing advertisements eschewed the brawny laborer trope of leftist visual culture in favor of more stylish models. The classic image of the male proletarian in overalls and cap was replaced with the trim man in a tailored pinstripe suit complete with handkerchief, striped tie, strawhat, and walking stick. As they played with these images of the natty worker, advertisers still invoked the ideal of workingmen as family providers, now encouraged to buy kerosene-powered kitchen stoves and electric irons for use (one supposes) by women household members. The ideal of the manly provider and the yearning for conventional elegance sometimes converged in unexpected ways: an advertisement from *La Fraternidad* offered union members, on terms of credit, a variety of women's fur coats made of fox, seal, and imported animal skins.[67]

These advertisements offer glimpses into the complexities of class and consumption in 1930s Argentina. It might be tempting to see these representations as evidence of a "labor aristocracy" trapped in longings for middle-class respectability. We do not, however, know enough about the meanings that workers assigned to these products or about their own hierarchies of taste; one cannot infer emulation from ad copy alone. Rail workers (especially conductors and other skilled workers) were among the highest paid blue-collar laborers; for most laborers, however, electrical appliances and the like remained out of reach even with credit. Moreover, advertisements shared space with condemnations of exploitative bosses and capitalist avarice. At least the editors of union papers (and perhaps their working-class readers) saw few contradictions in coupling the ethics of exchange to aspirations for small comforts and consumer wares. As do the treatments of "moral economic" themes in commercial films such as *Mujeres que trabajan* or the lingering liberal influences on Argentine socialists and other critics, these examples suggest that longings for social justice were not necessarily incompatible with desires for greater access to the abundance of the marketplace. Grappling with the uneven distribution of economic plenty, few observers were limited to an either/ or choice between a total embrace of market forces or their wholesale rejection.

※

With regard to ambivalence toward the market, Arlt and other literary chroniclers proved to be more perceptive than activists or social scientists were in understanding how commercialized fantasies merged with other material aspirations and feelings of injustice. Arlt's newspaper column profiled the types of individuals caught in the routines of making do but still dreaming of making it, whether through scrimping and hard work, get-rich-quick schemes, or poorly conceived criminal plots (the subject of his famed novels *Mad Toy* and *The Seven Madmen*). To be fair, reform-minded critics had other priorities in mind: it was their goal to modify economic conditions rather than document individual consciousness in its full, contradictory detail. Their reduced understanding of needs and wants was compensated for, at least in their minds, by clarity of vision about society's ills. They eschewed an ironic, Arltian sensibility in favor of moralistic tones through which they asserted new forms of expertise and spread the terms for a public conversation about ethical exchange.

It is important, however, to keep the period's criticisms of infraconsumo and living standards in perspective. While these concerns reached sizable audiences through various means (press coverage, grassroots organizing, and even commercial entertainments), reformist calls for state action remained diffuse during the 1930–1943 era. Many Argentines (including those in the laboring majority) no doubt considered the challenges of everyday getting and spending to be essentially private struggles, with little relevance to national public life or worth in terms of major government intervention. As a result, the little economies practiced by popular households lacked sustained political visibility, especially within state institutions controlled by conservatives preoccupied with other affairs (above all, rescuing agricultural exporters threatened by the world depression). Faced with this climate, most critics focused on ameliorative, stopgap measures. Family wage subsidies and other palliatives failed to coalesce into a coherent platform of social policy strong enough to bridge the era's ideological divides. Despite a slackening faith in the tenets of laissez-faire liberalism, few observers advanced projects for comprehensive commercial regulation or direct economic redistribution.

Political responses to the acquisitive imperatives of modern times may have lagged, but the social changes that accompanied mass consumption—widening industrialization and retail commerce, population growth and urbanization, wage labor and commercialization, the coupling of new material ambitions and frustrations —continued their advance in 1930s Argentina. From the metropolis of Buenos Aires to Venado Tuerto and other settlements, trade networks linked the various parts of the national territory using the sinews of the mass media and transportation. Argentina was not exceptional in this regard, for its own wheels of commerce were pushed along by global capitalist trends. Other regional centers, including São Paulo, Mexico City, and Havana, served as nodes that concentrated the commercial offerings and social pressures associated with mass consumption in mid-century Latin America. Yet early twentieth-century Argentina witnessed the play of a particular combination of economic, demographic, and cultural factors that acted as a wellspring for public concern regarding the marketplace and the working-class family. The country's status as a leading agricultural producer and exporter of food sharpened the contrast—in the eyes of some contemporaries, at least— with the misery endured by ordinary wage earners. In addition, Argentina's reputation as an economic success story, as well as nationalist guiding myths about its being a land of opportunity, made the unevenness of its material abundance harder to ignore. The country's much-vaunted affluence bred complacency among many contemporaries, but the gap between plenty and penury led others to new thinking about living standards. It encouraged not just well-known figures, such as Bunge, Palacios, and Cafferata, but also countless anonymous observers, among them working men and women exposed to market pressures, to ponder the cracks in national progress. How could it be that in the country of beef, there were regions whose inhabitants rarely ate it? How was it possible that wretched slums existed only blocks from grand department stores and shopping avenues? Why was it that in a country dubbed the "land of the stretched belt," some citizens struggled with belt-tightening little economies or, even worse, subsisted on té de brasas?

2
STANDARDS FOR A NEW ARGENTINA

THE DILEMMAS of constrained consumption figured only marginally on the agenda of state officials in the late 1930s, attracting sporadic attention during cost-of-living protests and justifying modest surveys of family budgets—yet how different the political landscape looked just a few years later. During the mid-1940s, the national government and its allies took bold strides to lift all Argentines above a minimum threshold of well-being. The combination of full employment and rising wages loosened the budgets of popular households and placed new commercial wares within the reach of the working class, enabling many to become not only purchasers of daily staples but also consumers of manufactured products and leisure services. Those kept on the margins of mass consumption quickly became more active participants in the marketplace, while an array of social programs lessened life's risks and moderated inequalities. In highlighting the significance of these changes, the country's leaders proclaimed that the days of laissez-faire liberalism were over and that a new era had begun. Citizens were now living in the Peronist Nueva Argentina.

It was no coincidence that the political transformations Peronism ushered in began during the World War II period. Argentina was removed from the main theaters of battle and areas of civilian devastation in Europe and Asia, and to this day, its government's formal neutrality during the conflict remains a source of re-crimination. Yet the war's presence was undeniable. A host of Argentine observers met the global conflagration with anxious questioning: Could local industries withstand disruptions in trade and shortages of imports? Would economic troubles spill over into unemployment and social unrest, as had occurred with World War I?

The predicaments underlying these questions generated discussion on a range of issues related to national progress. Perhaps more unexpectedly, they refocused attention on the vulnerability of the urban working-class family. Earlier concerns with household deficiencies and infraconsumo were drawn into debates about national economic policy; accordingly, they took on intensified urgency among groups outside the usual social scientific and activist circles, including new business organizations tasked with preparing for the postwar era. Military officials, too, consulted local experts as they groped for answers and drew inspiration from experiments with state intervention proposed across the globe. From 1943 onward, Peronism would emerge from the confluence of these domestic and transnational currents.

In particular, Perón and his early followers adapted existing frameworks for identifying need and satisfying wants. Their brand of social politics applied new strategies for removing critical areas of life from the profit-driven logic of the market. What merits closer scrutiny is why these actors envisioned reform not just in terms of subsistence minima and poor relief but rather as a far-ranging redistribution of income and comprehensive improvement in living conditions—a process best illuminated by tracing the evolution of the notion of the standard of living during this watershed moment. Following the concept's winding path through competing projects of national reform will ultimately help explain how the Peronist vida digna came into being. Such an approach will require us to reconsider Peronism's origins, one of the most trammeled roads in Argentine history. Rather than echo conventional narratives of the "rise of Perón," however, it will be worthwhile to explore how the groundwork for social citizenship was laid during the wartime and immediate postwar eras. It is tempting in retrospect to collapse this historical conjuncture into its outcomes, to assume that economic inequalities were simply waiting for state action. Such an account distorts the political process. It neglects the multiple steps through which needs were identified and acknowledged as meriting immediate attention, paired with potential solutions, and finally remediated by those in positions of power, who were often driven by hardnosed struggles to outmaneuver rivals.[1]

Instead of pointing inevitably in one direction, the war years inspired competing ideas about Argentina's future, only some of which would be taken up by the government after 1946. Perón and his advisers were protagonists in this process, but they were not solely responsible for determining the course of social politics. Organized labor and other allies exerted pressure, and the decision to support a remarkable increase in worker spending power owed much to factors beyond governmental control, including global economic conditions and international relations. By the same token, the men and women attracted to the nascent Peronist movement performed their own translations of social scientific language into still fluid conceptions of justice. While many Argentines remained skeptical or fearful of these changes, an increasing majority of citizens hitched their aspirations for a better life to the Peronist state's designs for national progress.

Postwar Possibilities

The prospects for such a sweeping political reorientation appeared extremely unlikely at the start of the war years. Frustration prevailed among many social critics. One of them, the architect Fermín Bereterbide, attended the First Pan-American Housing Conference in Buenos Aires in October 1939, just as the war began spreading across Europe. Bereterbide, an avowed socialist, presented a proposal for reducing urban overcrowding. His architectural sketches and cost analyses, like those of fellow conferees, represented part of a transnational conversation about living standards that referenced initiatives from red Vienna to fascist Italy. Local sources of social knowledge were also key, and Bereterbide used the National Labor Department's budget surveys to tailor public housing to working-class spending patterns. (The man responsible for the surveys, José Figuerola, attended the conference as well, although the two stood at opposite ideological poles.) Bereterbide's report concluded that public housing alone was not enough; other measures were required—minimum salaries, social insurance, and a restriction of "artificial" rises in the costs of food and essential consumer goods—to guarantee a "decent level of living" for Argentine families.[2] Yet when Bereterbide and his peers compared their country to favored models in Western Europe or the United States, Argentina's laggardness came into sharp relief. Their nation seemed politically mired in another time, outstripped even by policy experiments elsewhere in Latin America. For signs of innovation in social politics, one had to look west to the programs of the center-left popular front governments of Chile, east to the labor legislation of Batllista Uruguay, or north to the corporatism of Brazil's right-leaning Estado Novo and the nationalist land reform of Cardenista Mexico. In his report Bereterbide tartly concluded that there was no housing problem in Argentina, at least in terms of funds or popular demand: "What is lacking, and here lies the problem, is a feeling of humanity, confidence in those knowledgeable in these matters, and a will to act."[3]

Few of those at the 1939 conference could have foreseen the transformations that ensued. In the span of a few years, the locus of discussion about living standards shifted to organizations commanded by business and military authorities. Some social scientists (including Figuerola) accompanied this move, becoming influential assistants to those in positions of power; other experts, Bereterbide among them, fell by the wayside. Interest in social politics became restricted to ensuring a productive, stable workforce in a time of international crisis. Growing interest in limited social services, designed to provide a modicum of security for the nation's workers, was inspired by two major trends in international economic thought: the notion that the state should help prop up aggregate demand so as to spur economic growth and the idea that increasing the industrial workforce's buying power would help expand domestic markets—objectives lumped under the familiar if ill-fitting labels of Keynesianism and Fordism. Yet thinking about consumer-led growth was tempered in Argentina by business concerns of excessive "statism" and higher wage costs, as well as military interest in heavy industrialization rather than mass consumption. In the end, the tentative alliances among business, military, and social scientific camps suffered from internal divisions similar to those in earlier reformist efforts.

The roots of wartime experiments with social politics could be traced to the Depression era. The policymakers of the Infamous Decade moved simultaneously in two directions. On the one hand, the ruling bloc favored an elitist brand of conservative rule, motivated by a rejection of the perceived demagoguery of President Yrigoyen and the Radical Party in the late 1920s. As they tried to roll back the clock on popular republicanism, Argentina's conservatives displayed a forward-looking willingness to build the regulatory capacity of the state. New institutions, including the country's first central bank, enhanced technocratic control over monetary and credit policy.[4] President Agustín Justo's administration (1932–1938) refined a system in which the federal government managed agricultural output, for example, by setting minimum crop prices. Agencies known as Juntas Reguladoras acted as cartels to benefit large agricultural and commercial interests. These juntas were established for grains, beef, and other export commodities, as well as for staples destined primarily for domestic consumption (wine, sugar, milk, yerba mate, and cotton). Not surprisingly, prices for rural producers were stabilized at the expense of higher costs for domestic consumers.[5] Officials could not afford, however, to neglect the "social question" entirely. Responses to Depression-era poverty included school meal programs and the organization of a junta to study the problem of unemployment. This body devoted its scant budget to employer-friendly measures, such as hiring trains to relocate rural workers (its allegiance was hardly surprising, for the junta included members of the Sociedad Rural and other elite economic groups). One report cautioned that more extensive aid, such as income subsidies for unemployed Argentines, would cause "moral disintegration": noting the regrettable example of the English dole, authorities warned against social programs that spawned legions of "parasites" easily swayed by unprincipled politicians.[6]

Given this restrictive climate, most social policy initiatives sank because of their proponents' political weakness or quickly ran aground on the rocks of conservative indifference. These impediments did not preclude, however, some provincial governments from putting modest proposals into practice. In Santa Fe and Córdoba, opposition parties passed legislation in the late 1930s offering social insurance for public employees and "family wage" schemes. Along similar lines, a project to finance public works in Córdoba justified itself as a mechanism to relieve rural unemployment and "strengthen the edifice of popular consumption."[7] Under the leadership of Governor Manuel Fresco (1936–1940), the province of Buenos Aires embarked on similar experiments along a decidedly rightist tack. Fresco had become governor by rising through the ranks of a corrupt political machine, and ideologically he was an anticommunist of the "*Dios, Patria, Hogar*" (God, Fatherland, Home) variety, an admirer of Mussolini and Salazar, and a disparager of representative democracy. Nevertheless, Fresco's minister of government, Roberto Noble, argued that "modern times" demanded an end to laissez-faire liberalism and the creation of "redistributive justice" based on the "delivery of the benefits of civilization and comfort" to the working majority.[8] Backing up this rhetoric, the government of Argentina's largest province augmented public works funding for schools, health clinics, and housing; subsequent decrees extended collective bargaining and installed a minimum wage. The goal of Fresco's measures was ultimately a reactionary one: to impose social peace, thereby protecting traditional values, respect for order, and hierarchy. To this end, police forces censored leftists and hunted down communist labor organizers gaining converts in meatpacking plants and factories.[9]

Federal meddling in provincial affairs often derailed social policies. Even Fresco would find himself at odds with fellow conservatives, and during a short-lived drive to clean up corruption, he was deposed following a fraudulent reelection. Eventually, however, national-level bodies took tentative steps to address the material needs of popular households. World War II served as a catalyst, especially among those who remembered the domestic turmoil of World War I (indeed, in economic terms, the Great War was in many respects more devastating than the

Great Depression in Argentina).[10] Trade disruptions with Europe in the 1910s had led to a cascading crisis; unable to secure needed raw materials and imported goods, Argentina's urban manufacturing, transportation, and commercial sectors had been thrown into disarray, and unemployment levels soon reached nearly 20 percent. Many feared a repeat of episodes such as 1919's "Tragic Week," a spate of urban rioting that left scores dead and hundreds injured on the streets of the Argentine capital. With these memories in mind, the government adopted preventative measures soon after the start of hostilities. The Argentine Congress approved emergency wartime price controls in September 1939 (law 12.591), providing new legal tools to set maximum levels on urban rents, staple foods, and other consumer goods. The legislative reform built on both the 1930s trend of federal regulation and the precedent of consumer price controls enacted briefly during World War I.[11]

The measures, however, lacked adequate enforcement, and consumers soon saw their spending power threatened by shortages and climbing prices. The country's surging industrial economy, operating at near full employment, was to partly blame, for local production could not always satisfy demand, and wartime barriers to imports exacerbated the situation. Yet merchant hoarding and profiteering were allegedly rife in early 1940s Argentina. Unions and leftist groups responded with a wave of protests. The Confederación General de Trabajo (CGT) organized a "campaign against the cost of living" in 1942, hosting allies in major cities and provincial labor halls. Similarly, a group called the Junta Popular Pro-Abaratamiento de la Vida y Contra los Monopolios organized meetings in the city of Buenos Aires, including the so-called Congress against the High Cost of Living in March 1943. The Socialist Party and other leftist political forces issued sympathetic declarations against commercial trusts, and newspapers carried regular reports on the skyrocketing prices of charcoal fuel and potatoes. Editorialists accused public officials of turning a blind eye to rapacious commercial practices. Tapping into the cultural reservoir of norms regarding unethical exchange, critics tarred greedy merchants as "*especuladores*" (speculators) and lambasted commercial conspiracies as the "sharks of capitalism" and the "Mafia of lucre."[12]

While the federal government attempted (unsuccessfully) to assuage urban consumers, its policymakers proposed other mechanisms to augment living standards. In 1940 Federico Pinedo, the architect of the government's Depression-era recovery strategies, drafted a legislative package of measures; soon dubbed the Plan Pinedo, this proposal consisted of economic measures to assist producers, industrialists, and other employers avoid ruin. It also included the largest government proposal to date for financing housing construction. Intended partly as a job creation measure, the housing reform represented an acknowledgment from within official circles that greater action was needed on the social front. Once again, however, political circumstances remained unfavorable. Congress rejected the Plan Pinedo, mainly because of partisan infighting over federal interventions in provincial politics that had little to do with the merits of the proposal itself.[13]

This string of failures by no means ended the debate over living standards in Argentina—if anything, the Plan Pinedo's demise had the unintended consequence of encouraging activity among nongovernmental actors. While Bereterbide and other reformers continued to devise ameliorative strategies, much as they had for decades, new actors weighed in on the question of living standards and consumption in the early 1940s. They included elements of Argentina's business community and military institutions with acute fears of wartime calamity. Lacking the ability to shape policy directly, these groups focused their energies on the near future, or what in this climate of anxious optimism was dubbed "planning for the postwar." These would-be planners adopted the notion of nivel de vida and related concepts, embracing them as modern tools of technical knowledge while stripping them of any inconvenient associations with progressive activism. The language of social politics was thus subsumed within larger preoccupations with ensuring a smooth transition to a peacetime economy. The Unión Industrial Argentina (UIA), the country's largest umbrella group for manufacturers, took the lead in creating an institutional framework for postwar planning. In 1942 the UIA established the Institute for Industrial Studies and Conferences, which brought together professors, engineers, factory owners, and military officers for regular discussions of policy matters. (Individuals in the last group were typically civil engineers and directors of military-run arms factories, part of the country's small military-industrial complex that had built up since the 1920s.) The UIA founded a parallel organization in May 1943 with the unwieldy title of the "Permanent Congress for the Study of Problems of the Postwar and General Economy of the Country." Comprising hundreds of members from the institute's proindustry ranks, the congress included representatives from agriculture and business, such as the Sociedad Rural Argentina and the Bolsa de Comercio.[14] In considering these matters, UIA-sponsored organizations relied on previous debates among social scientists—most notably, nationalist figures such as Alejandro Bunge, whose 1940 book, *Una nueva Argentina,* was read widely in these circles. Although attracted by the promise of government support, participants warned against excessive state involvement in private sector affairs. In their view, "planning" was a process of coordination among business representatives and experts as more or less equal actors, not a rigidly formal system of corporatism or top-down state dirigisme.

While industrial policy and other related matters dominated attention, some participants used these forums to address the living standard question. Within this emerging camp, the industrialist Torcuato Di Tella became a voice for moderate reform aimed at industrial workers and their households. Di Tella was a prominent figure: he helped create the UIA's industrial studies institute and was the founder of SIAM Di Tella, a major manufacturer of electrical appliances. As did a few other factory owners in Argentina, Di Tella operated rudimentary programs in the workplace and offered wage subsidies for laborers with children.[15] Di Tella embraced social scientific methods as well, and in 1940 he commissioned a survey of housing quality among workers in his Avellaneda plant. The SIAM study revealed that nearly half the factory workers lived with their families in just one room. Only 60 percent occupied brick or concrete housing, while the rest lived in structures cobbled together from wood and scraps of metal in Avellaneda's barrios, just outside the Argentine capital city.[16] In thinking about reform, Di Tella also looked internationally for inspiration.[17] His journeys abroad included attendance at a 1939 International Labour Office conference in Geneva (followed by a short tour of Nazi Germany and the Soviet Union to satisfy his curiosity) and a 1943 voyage to the United States, where he gained insights on New Deal planning. In his short book *Problemas de la posguerra* (1943; problems of the postwar), Di Tella reflected on his experiences abroad. Lauding the steps taken by the National Resources Planning Board in the United States, he warned his compatriots, "We run the risk of being unprepared for peace without having drawn up any plan that addresses our economic future." Di Tella sought to convince fellow factory owners to accept the responsibilities of social leadership; he maintained that U.S. industrialists had already realized that attending to employees' well-being eased class tensions and expanded the potential pool of consumers for their goods. "It is not enough that workers merely subsist," explained Di Tella; "rather, it is necessary that one elevate their material level of living, their 'standard,' and provide a minimum of social security that merits their person and economic function."[18] This assessment of U.S.-style Fordism ignored the serious divisions that persisted between U.S. labor and management, but it chided Argentine business owners that they were falling behind modern trends. Nodding to his more skeptical peers, Di Tella concluded that nothing could be more "authentically conservative" than spending resources this way: to do so was to invest in "pacification" and "social stability."[19]

Through Di Tella and other intermediaries, the language of living standards and minimum needs was incorporated into the postwar planning discussions of business and military representatives. The crucial issue of the proper amount to elevate standards along a Fordist ideal remained vague, but state reforms were now seen as a mechanism not only to defuse strife but also to prop up consumer demand among workers. As a sign of this turn, UIA president Luis Colombo peppered his speeches with mottos from the New Deal and the Beveridge Plan, proclaiming at a 1943 conference, "We have wanted and still want to defend the worker: 'From the cradle to the grave.' That's the way it should be." Yet for all this high-minded rhetoric, the UIA's institute and economic congress failed to reach a consensus about reform. After years of indifference, if not outright hostility, to social policy, business owner apprehensions about the cost of welfare programs and infringement on employer autonomy remained high. Under Colombo's leadership, the UIA lobbied against congressional proposals for a minimum wage; conservative organizations within the planning coalition questioned the most restrained family subsidy and insurance systems.[20] Moreover, pleas for social responsibility received less attention than economic controversies. Even on issues more directly related to business, such as industrial policy, opinions differed widely about the terms of state involvement.[21] Competing interests stymied the development of a unified voice, making "postwar planning" an uneasy marriage at best.

The ambiguity that characterized postwar planning extended more generally to the place of popular consumption in wartime politics. For Bereterbide and other experienced social reformers, the emphasis lay on assisting working-class families to satisfy essential needs. Union members and leftist activists framed consumption in terms of high living costs to protest merchant profiteering. In planning for postwar life, industrialists and military officials saw the elevation of living standards in a paternalist, managerial vein—namely, as a way to ease class tensions and ensure an ordered workforce. Inflation would be combated not through popular mobilization in the streets but via closed-door economic coordination between business and government. As suggested by the range of actors involved in these debates, wartime anxieties increased the visibility of working-class consumption. By 1943, however, there was little clear sense of how, or even whether, this tangle of competing views would be accommodated in a coherent agenda.

Dawn of the Peronist Era

Instability in national politics further complicated matters. On the morning of June 4, 1943, a military coup led by General Arturo Rawson overthrew President Ramón Castillo. The government had shown increasing signs of weakness, deriving from a series of disagreements with business over wartime tax policies and a deepening succession crisis. Unwilling to stand by as Castillo passed the presidential sash to an archconservative politician, a disaffected faction within the military led a preemptive coup. A temporary alliance of army colonels and lower-ranking officers, known by its mysterious acronym "GOU," emerged as the dominant leadership after the so-called June Revolution of 1943.[22] Disgusted with civilian politicking and scandals, Argentina's uniformed men saw themselves as the nation's stewards, the only force that could impose an order based on respect for God and the patria. The leaders of the June Revolution were guided by an amalgam of various right-wing nationalist ideologies circulating in society. The nation's enemies, in their view, included progressive political sectors, and soon after the coup, the regime censored the leftist press, imprisoned activists, and interdicted major unions. Officials cultivated ties with extreme nationalist and Catholic organizations, offering the latter group long-coveted concessions, such as religious education in the public schools.[23]

Lasting but three years, this episode of military dictatorship nevertheless recast contemporary reformist preoccupations—living standards, household constraints, family vulnerabilities, regional inequalities—in unexpected ways. The officials of the June Revolution saw themselves as leading a drive to "rationalize" the state. They hoped to create a central government better prepared for the mayhem of a world at war, replacing what they viewed as the outdated, inefficiently bureaucratic cronyism of the Radicals and conservatives with an industrial-age model of technocratic governance. To this end, officials adapted 1930s regulatory institutions to their brand of economic nationalism, either by creating new agencies or by reshuffling ministerial arrangements. Military rulers borrowed notions of postwar planning but placed stronger emphasis on the central government's role in setting priorities. Although the forceful rhetoric of planning did not always match the reality of policymaking (especially as each ministry operated with de facto autonomy), the June Revolution further boosted the state's managerial capacity.

Military rulers sent the clear message that henceforth matters related to all domestic industry and commerce, not just export agriculture, would be a government priority. Lieutenant Colonel Mariano Abarca, a military engineer with manufacturing experience and an occasional contributor to Bunge's policy journal, was placed in charge of the first-ever Secretariat of Industry and Commerce. Under his guidance, a new financial institution, the Banco de Crédito Industrial, was created (with a UIA textile manufacturer at its helm) to expand the flow of investment capital to domestic businesses. State support for industrialization had the secondary effect of raising the profile of mass consumption as a policy issue, and Abarca himself spoke out in favor of industrial growth spurred by higher domestic demand.[24] The secretariat widened its scope to include areas of domestic commerce previously under the purview of the Ministry of Agriculture—most notably, it assumed control over the juntas reguladoras for consumer staples. The revamped juntas provided a means to adjust the flow of goods to urban areas and to fight inflation, which figured within the military's anxieties regarding wartime unrest.[25] Days after seizing power in June 1943, the regime adopted an 18 percent reduction in rents and a subsequent rent freeze in Buenos Aires, hoping to shore up support among the city's consumers (even as union and leftist protesters were harassed).[26] Throughout 1943–1946, officials pledged better enforcement of existing wartime price controls on consumables.

The June Revolution sent ripples throughout those groups debating the living standard problem. For the Left and reformist liberals, the new regime was hardly a cause for celebration: obstinate conservatives had been finally pushed aside, but the antirepublican authoritarianism of the military rulers was alarming. By contrast, rightist nationalists, such as Alejandro Bunge and his circle, greeted the military government as an opportunity to implement their long-deferred projects. Sectors of the UIA gained potent allies within the Secretariat of Industry and Commerce who could help them accomplish their economic policy aims. The type of alliance imagined during postwar planning discussions appeared to be on the verge of realization. The issues of the standard of living merged with still hazy ideas of industrial progress, while the more critical edge of social justice was blunted by the managerial priorities of army colonels and factory owners.

Given this military-industrialist alliance, one might imagine that subsequent developments would have included a modest expansion of state programs targeting the minimal health and housing needs of urban workforce but aimed primarily at building the military's legitimacy and preventing potential disorder. This scenario did not come to pass, however, at least not as expected. Out of the June Revolution emerged another political force that soon eclipsed all rivals. Juan Domingo Perón was a member of the GOU faction. Unknown outside army circles prior to 1943 and without experience in civilian politics, by 1946 he had become famous across the world. The story of his meteoric rise is by now familiar. Perón's life prior to his involvement in the June Revolution, at forty-eight years of age, was surprisingly commonplace. He spent his childhood at his middle-class family's struggling sheep ranch in Patagonia and later with relatives in the city of Buenos Aires. A career military officer, Perón had advanced through the ranks and held a number of posts, including professor of military history and strategy at the army academy. The military provided him the opportunity to travel, and assignments in Chile and Italy during the 1930s afforded Perón firsthand views of popular front and fascist movements in other nations.[27] Postings in impoverished areas of rural Argentina gave Perón direct contact with the realities of exploitation. As with many officers of his generation, Perón embraced ideas of national regeneration. Yearnings for liberation from foreign economic influence and mistrust of civilian politics meshed with views of the military as the nation's savior.

Shortly after the 1943 coup, Lieutenant Colonel Perón was appointed to the National Department of Labor (DNT) and from there forged ties with organized labor that later catapulted his campaign for the presidency in February 1946. Although historians once emphasized Perón's sharp break with the politics of the past—perhaps because he subsequently portrayed himself in these terms—most studies now place his movement within a longer historical trajectory, tracing the roots of Peronism in union struggles and growing state intervention during the 1930s. But in the study of Perón's origins, a fundamental question remains largely unanswered: how did this politically inexperienced army officer become the driving force behind a campaign to elevate living standards? While the DNT ascended with Perón at the helm, its impact on the inexperienced lieutenant colonel is often ignored. Yet the DNT's staff and social knowledge conditioned Perón's political outlook and reformist agenda in crucial ways. The principal intermediary was the department's chief of statistics, José Figuerola, who almost overnight became Perón's closest policy adviser. Figuerola brought vast experience as a social scientific researcher to the table. In a 1966 magazine interview, Figuerola described his first meeting with Perón at the Labor Department: "We began talking at six in the afternoon. He wanted to see my files, to look at socioeconomic statistics and graphs of standard of living curves for the last 12 years. We exchanged ideas and drank many cups of coffee and smoked dozens of cigarettes." The meeting finally ended at two in the morning, with Perón taking home a stack of charts on the nutritional deficiencies of working-class families.[28]

Figuerola's anecdote suggests how social scientific expertise helped shape Perón's perception of the nation's problems, building on the army officer's raw thinking on state intervention. With the additional resources that Perón brought to the Department of Labor, Figuerola conducted additional surveys of working-class conditions; between 1943 and 1946 he further refined his thinking on breadwinner needs and pinched household spending power.[29] The overarching conclusion of Figuerola's household budget surveys—that male workers were unable to satisfy the basic consumption requirements of family dependents—was reflected in Peronist responses to the standard of living question. Even if the chain-smoking Perón never finished reading the statistical reports, the agency's staff lent authority and guidance in creating new policies. Together, they transformed the DNT from a mechanism of social observation into an agent for regulating markets and courting organized labor. Bringing together expertise and political power, Perón turned the National Department of Labor into his base of operations. Under his direction, the department became one of the most energetic arms of the wartime state, and a mere month after his arrival in November 1943, it jumped to a higher bureaucratic rung. The Secretaría de Trabajo y Previsión, as it was now known, rivaled the Secretariat of Industry and Commerce as the central node of policymaking within the military regime.[30]

Unions initially (and understandably) regarded this representative of the right-wing military government with distrust.[31] The army officer moved cautiously as well, but his courting of unions grew only stronger as his overtures to other potential allies (including industrialists and Radical Party politicians) stalled. Here, too, Perón's assistants served as crucial intermediaries: Lieutenant Colonel Domingo Mercante and Atilio Bramuglia, for example, acted as liaisons to major unions and the government.[32] The simple fact that ambitious government officials wanted to meet face to face with labor leaders represented a welcome departure. But Perón did more than entertain demands; he also used the Labor Secretariat's authority to help unions negotiate with employers from a position of greater strength. In 1944 nearly one thousand collective agreements were signed, over five hundred in the province of Buenos Aires alone. Contracts contributed to a 12 percent rise, on average, in unskilled workers' real wages from 1944 to 1945—not a radical change, but one with promises of more to come.[33] Perón's Labor Secretariat assisted workers in asserting their authority vis-à-vis employers—for instance, helping them to gain greater influence over shop-floor rules—and the agency backed unions by stepping up hitherto lax enforcement of existing labor laws governing hours, benefits, and pay. Support from the secretariat helped new unions form in the rural harvesting and food-processing industries, while more established unions expanded the services they offered to members.[34] Eager to gain worker loyalty, Perón distributed loans and gifts of land to the Unión Ferroviaria and promised to help fund additional hospitals and recreational facilities. Such programs (known as *obra social*) remained a dream for the average union, but these gains stirred hope for greater changes.[35]

Perón counted on the support of his superiors in the army, especially the president, General Edelmiro Farrell, who converted his policy proposals into executive decrees. In 1944 Farrell signed into law the Estatuto del Peón, a measure that spelled out the rights of farmworkers as had never been done before: defining wage levels for specific tasks, instituting equal pay for male and female workers, mandating leisure time (rest breaks, Sundays off, and paid vacation), and enhancing employer responsibility for basic medical and housing needs. Nevertheless, it was the urban workforce that received the lion's share of Perón's attention. Industry, transportation, and commerce constituted the path to the future, in his view, and unions were already densest in these sectors. The intimate ties between the Labor Secretariat and organized labor met with strong opposition from some quarters, especially among leftists who remained targets of military persecution. For these skeptics, Perón represented a homegrown version of fascism, and they complained that unions had traded democratic liberties for bread-and-butter concessions. Perón responded by isolating his critics; over time, a majority of union members were drawn into his orbit—in part because, at this juncture, the labor secretary required little in exchange. It is worth noting that expanding household consumption did not weigh heavily among these issues, aside from concerns with wartime inflation and boosting wages. On the whole, labor leaders privileged other issues. They pursued longstanding claims, such as asserting union rights to legal standing and presence in the workplace. From this perspective, the elevation of living standards was defined in terms of obtaining sturdier contracts from employers and, when possible, adding to their decentralized system of social programs.

While unionists focused on securing gains, Peronist perspectives on popular consumption were being shaped by debates about state economic intervention. As a sign of Perón's growing prominence, Farrell promoted him to the additional posts of vice-president and minister of war in June 1944 and soon thereafter head of the new federal planning board, the Consejo Nacional de Posguerra (National Council of the Postwar). This council was staffed by a mix of officers, social scientists, and business representatives, including familiar faces from the UIA's institute (e.g., Di Tella and other prominent industrialists) and from Bunge's group. Between 1944 and 1946, this council evolved from an advisory board to one exerting greater policymaking powers, including oversight over cost of living concerns.[36] Once again, Perón relied on his more experienced associates and appointed Figuerola to serve as the council's secretary general. With his fondness for corporatist modes of state coordination, Figuerola sought to put his stamp on national planning. The Spaniard's emphasis on technical rationalization dovetailed well with Perón's militaristic outlook on public affairs. While lacking expertise in postwar discussions, the former army instructor often invoked the planning metaphors of military strategists, such as Clausewitz, to analyze political matters.[37]

In 1945 the council published a report that publicly outlined its general recommendations under the imposingly vague title *Ordenamiento económico-social* (economic-social ordering). Among the main priorities for the postwar period, the council argued, was preventing the erosion of wartime industrialization, and its experts called for government intervention to create new industries, train the workforce in technical skills, and diversify production in rural areas devoted to monoculture.[38] In comparison to precursors such as the Plan Pinedo and the UIA's conferences, this postwar model did not emphasize export agriculture prominently. The report differed most significantly from earlier planning efforts, however, in the stronger tone it gave to social themes. The "primordial" goal of the state's "economic-social ordering," according to Perón and Figuerola, was to "secure the satisfaction of all the needs of the country's inhabitants, without tolerance for the unjust concentration of resources in the hands of a few." This meant not only full employment but also state guarantees of "social welfare." Short on specifics in this regard, the report called for a comprehensive social insurance system (rather than union-administered programs) in addition to other measures to protect Argentines, "from the cradle to the grave," against suffering caused by "illness, injury, unemployment, old age, death of spouse or parents, etc." While warning against excessive "statism," the council maintained that central government was duty bound to arbitrate "Labor-Capital" conflicts and establish a system more "humane" than the "hard rules of supply and demand."[39]

As in other postwar planning conversations, interest was piqued by concerns about infraconsumo, defined in Keynesian terms as the combination of overproduction and the lack of aggregate demand in the economy. Similarly, participants thought along Fordist lines with respect to intensifying the virtuous cycle between industrialization and domestic consumption, partly by fostering greater working-class purchasing power. The viability of this direction, however, provoked much disagreement. The nationalist economists and factory owners assembled by the council remained preoccupied with postwar inflation and material shortages, problems that income redistribution to laboring families would most likely aggravate. The 1945 report offered a mixed message on the subject of the state's role in managing consumption: on the one hand, it stressed the need to defend consumers against rising living costs and to improve their material well-being; on the other, it called for a reduction in the "excess spending power of the public" to generate investment funds following the war.[40] In the light of the unanswered questions raised by the conundrum of infraconsumo, planners preferred to pass general pronouncements about maintaining full employment and instituting moderate social programs for vulnerable populations.

The question of how the central government should set economic policy regarding living standards and consumption remained far from resolved. Nevertheless, "postwar planning" served as a useful conceptual umbrella under which Perón and his assistants merged social politics and nationalist longings for sovereignty. In presiding over the Consejo Nacional de Posguerra, Perón achieved greater success than had earlier "planners" in establishing ties between the military and other interest groups—including building a bridge with labor unions via the Labor Department, something his predecessors had never attempted. Of course, Perón benefited greatly from his place within the military regime, but his personal authority derived as well from the alliances he forged with emerging political players in the government, unions, and postwar planning circles. It was from these origins that a new political movement was born, still unsure of its ultimate purpose or direction for most of the 1943–1946 period but rapidly gathering national prominence.

The "Dignified Life"

Perón's politics cannot be reduced to the number of new labor contracts the army official brokered or agencies under his command. His agenda incorporated the reformist language of the past but reframed the technical vocabulary of state planning and living standards. Perón's brand of politics depended in no small measure on conveying his vision of a more moral and socially just Nueva Argentina to the broader public of potential supporters. The labor secretary made hundreds of public appearances across the country—over ninety formal speeches in 1944 alone (with an unknown number of private talks and impromptu gatherings)—and the Labor Secretariat published a book of these presentations, giving it the title *The Pueblo Wants to Know What It's All About.*[41] More than any other Argentine leader before him had done, Perón appreciated the importance of the radio as a tool to reach a mass audience, and he made clever use of the state broadcasting chain in his rise to prominence. In this area, the career military officer no doubt learned a great deal from another "intermediary" within his inner circle: his future wife, Eva Duarte, an up-and-coming radio and film actress whose place in the Peronist movement blossomed after the 1946 elections.

It is difficult in retrospect to evoke Perón's appeal as a speaker. Memoirs and oral histories provide recollections of events, and photographs capture the crowds that gathered to hear him speak, but our view of audience reception remains impressionistic for the 1943–1946 period. Even in their truncated written form, however, his speeches can tell us much about the production of a new politics. His synthesis of reformist ideas was paralleled by the heterodox nature of his rhetoric. In a single speech, Perón might reference popular slang and the urban argot of tango lyrics and then, in the next minute, employ the formal *vosotros* verb form and social scientific terminology. This linguistic diversity served Perón well in courting audiences of disparate political sensibilities, and he appeared before an astounding variety of groups: not only union workers but also middle-class professionals, military officers, civic societies, merchant associations, mutual aid groups, trade lobbies, and at least on one occasion, the Argentine Boy Scouts. His nationalist themes of advancement were sufficiently capacious that they could be tailored into more radical or reactionary versions, depending on the crowd at hand.

"Progress" was defined principally in terms of improving the condition of workers. When addressing other than working-class audiences, however, Perón dealt with this subject by invoking the threat of communist revolution and postwar collapse. His famous Bolsa de Comercio speech of August 1944 outlined the danger posed by laboring people who were "unorganized," "abandoned," or "inorganic." Having ignored the needs of the "working masses," he said, previous governments had opened the doors for "professional foreign agitators" to sow the seeds of communism in Argentina. Before union and working-class groups, Perón adopted a far different tone. He still presented communism as a threatening foreign illness, but he emphasized worker entitlement to a better quality of life. Perón defended labor-friendly reforms as central to creating a more unified nation and to the project of state-led modernization. "In modern times," Perón asserted during a speech to railroad workers in June 1944, "one cannot accept the disgrace of misery in the middle of opulence." The Labor Secretariat, under his command, would therefore "bring the Argentine masses the social justice that they have thirsted for during forty years."[42]

In particular, the notion of a "dignified" living standard was key to Perón's discourse of national progress. At a September 1944 union gathering in Mendoza, Perón enumerated the policy goals of his "*política social*": a minimum wage, social insurance, unionization, work regulations, and assistance programs. He situated these policy objectives within a powerful language of individual and collective aspiration: "We want each person to be remunerated in accordance with his efforts, in such a way that he can live a dignified life [vida digna]; but, above all, we defend the supreme dignity of work. We want men to earn enough to eat, dress, and live in a dignified fashion." Backed by promises of comprehensive state programs, the vida digna rested on an ideal of increasing workers' participation in society as both producers and consumers. The labor secretary frequently borrowed the progressive language of contemporary social scientists and planners. At an assembly of commercial retail workers celebrating their union's new retirement program, Perón described the standard de vida, calling the phrase an "English term." The government's main responsibility, he contended, was to prevent the working population from being "*submergidos*" (submerged) below a minimum standard or line ("*línea de vida*"): "It is an elemental obligation of the modern state to uphold through all means an adequate 'standard of living' for all inhabitants."[43] That the terminology was identified as English suggests its novelty to a primarily working-class audience. Partly through these references, Perón and followers did much to popularize this social scientific vocabulary and the simple yet powerful notion of a basic line above which Argentines deserved to live. By incorporating the notion of the standard de vida into his speeches, Perón defined social justice in the seemingly neutral, authoritative language of mid-twentieth-century policymaking.

Time and again Perón emphasized that all productive Argentines merited a greater share of the nation's material wealth and the security of an equitable society. During a July 1944 speech on the "popular economy," the labor secretary lamented that previous governments had turned a blind eye to the imbalanced distribution of the nation's material abundance, including the commercial wares so central to life in modern times. "We are a dignified and proud country," he asserted, "and none of its children should have to tolerate ever again that Argentine workers be converted into shabby people [*gente astrosa*] so that a group of privileged individuals can continue maintaining their luxuries, their automobiles, and their excesses." Perón stressed that the "people" deserved inclusion within an economic order that satisfied basic wants and, if possible, allowed them to enjoy simple comforts: "We are convinced that the economic end of a country should not be only profit [*lucro*], but rather the satisfaction of all the necessities of its inhabitants."[44]

In outlining this understanding of living standards, promises of dignity rested squarely on assumptions about respectability and family life. Like his reformist predecessors (and collaborators, such as Figuerola), Perón highlighted the inability of male household heads to provide for their dependents, or as he put it, to "maintain their families with decorum." The Peronist model of self-worth tapped into popular audiences' expectations about masculine responsibility and the household division of labor. Perón upheld the ideal of separate spheres that few working-class families attained but to which they might nevertheless aspire.[45] The activist state described in Perón's speeches would fortify the authority of the paternal figure through higher salaries and benefits. In practice, social insurance and other social welfare programs were channeled through the predominately male workforce and not extended as universal schemes of protection to all Argentines. At the same time, Perón and his inner circle did not ignore the needs of female workers. Perón established the Division of Women's Work and Assistance within the Labor Secretariat and placed two female professionals at its head; at its inauguration, he opined, "If the modern organization of society imposes on women the double burden of work inside and outside the home, adequate payment for their work becomes an elemental imperative of justice." Unlike most industrialists and Catholic activists, the Labor Secretariat's team favored equal pay for equal work regarding women. This strategy, however, was motivated partly by a desire to prevent employers from substituting lower-paid female laborers for men. In designing policies for wage-earning women, officials had the concerns of male workers and "ordering" the family constantly in mind. Perón told a group of female telephone operators that he hoped to limit their work schedules to protect their delicate "physiological constitution" and give them more time to deal with "household necessities"—a gender traditionalism that members of his audience did not necessarily reject.[46]

The gendered notion of a dignified standard of living further relied on a reworking of conventional status and class distinctions. Perón's speeches exalted the value of manual labor. At an August 1944 gathering, Perón told rural farmhands of their rights to protection in old age, to housing, to rest from work, and above all, to salaries that would allow them to "live with at least a minimum amount of dignity." While references to the "*clase obrera*" abounded, Perón took pains to employ a more loosely popular vocabulary, at times using hybrid forms such as the "*pueblo trabajador*" and "*clases populares.*" Nationalistic calls to "*Argentinos*" were by their very nature multiclass and multiethnic. Perón's definition of a worker as one who sacrificed for the country's advancement was flexible enough to encompass the middle classes (especially empleados and other modestly paid white-collar clerks). On occasion, it reached further to include certain propertied sectors, as when he called shopkeepers the "proletariat of commerce."[47] From this vantage, workers could represent any ethnicity and racial category. Perón shied away from addressing these issues directly, perhaps because World War II had made race a live wire, and anti-Semitism had support among the nationalist right and within the military high command. But his vision of inclusion implied that those in often disparaged groups—including criollos and darker-skinned laborers from the provinces—were just as important to national progress as other groups were.

In promising a better life for *all* working people, Perón presented himself as a man of action and realism, a contrast to the false politicians of the past who made vague pledges of justice. Speeches frequently began with his signature catchphrases: "Mejor que decir, es hacer" and "Mejor que prometer, es realizar" (essentially, it is better to do and accomplish than to promise). His ability to deliver improvements in workplace conditions, benefits, and wages to union workers no doubt lent credence to his claims. The labor secretary walked a fine line between praising the June Revolution and taking personal credit for new policies. Over time Perón became more forceful in his efforts to portray a common movement in which united workers, unions, and the pueblo found common cause with the government. He distinguished the Labor Secretariat from typical bureaucracies, with their impersonal "technical-administrative mechanism." His agency was the "true home of workers," a protective space where dedicated officials served the common man and woman. "Our justice is and will be more feeling than lettered; more patriarchal than legalistic; less formulaic and more expeditious," Perón told workers at a May 1944 rally in Córdoba.[48] Seen in this light, the technocratic efficiency of a reorganized national government would be tempered by the personal, empathetic touch of a leader serving as the people's representative.

This distinction between us and them, between the government-supported pueblo and its foes, lay at the core of Peronist politics even in this early phase.[49] The metaphors used to depict the Labor Secretariat's reforms—new labor contracts and programs were dubbed "social conquests"—reinforced this sense of a joint campaign for justice. The enemies standing in the way included a by now familiar gallery of economic interests: foreign monopolists, oligarchs, and speculators. Perón grew bolder in talking to working-class audiences about the "egoistical" employer resistance he encountered when trying to improve contracts and raise wages, contrasting his "*política obrerista*" to their narrow defense of exploitative capitalism.[50] Until late 1945, Perón's vision of dignified living standards did not constitute part of a formal political campaign. It was undeniable, however, that he was becoming a figure of national renown. His visibility only grew after the January 15, 1944, earthquake in the province of San Juan. The largest disaster of its kind in Argentina, the San Juan earthquake left over 10,000 persons dead and hundreds of thousands homeless. Perón made a name for himself by organizing federal relief efforts (and it was at a San Juan benefit that the colonel first met Eva Duarte). This calamitous event shook up the political status quo, bringing to the surface complaints about the previous government's indifference to popular suffering and thus placing Perón in a favorable light.[51]

Not all quarters welcomed Perón's growing prominence. In particular, his approach to the living standard problem raised red flags among Argentina's business community. Predictably, agricultural lobbies, such as the Sociedad Rural, were none too pleased by Perón's involvement in rural unionization drives and the Estatuto del Peón. Having benefited from Depression-era state recovery measures, landowners now returned to their defense of laissez-faire liberalism. Perón's relationship with industrialists was more complex: factory owners typically adopted a pragmatic approach in the hopes of securing protectionist benefits and public credit from the military government while resisting the Labor Secretariat's encroachments in the workplace. Smaller, less established industrialists (often from the interior) were more willing to endorse national planning than were the owners of booming factories in greater Buenos Aires. Nationalist discourses played better to smaller entrepreneurs than to larger commercial concerns with less need of state protection.[52]

The leadership of the Unión Industrial Argentina at first cooperated with the June Revolution, and the organization's members took part in at least twenty-four government commissions and agencies.[53] Soon after his appointment to the Labor Secretariat, Perón met with the UIA president, Luis Colombo, to coordinate their agendas, but the possibility for cooperation soon broke down. In a January 1945 letter to Perón, Colombo bemoaned the dire impact of government policies on what he considered previously cordial relations between labor and employers. Factory owners, in his view, faced the "lack of discipline that is necessarily engendered by the ever more generalized use of a certain terminology, which presents employers in a position of material superiority and every agreement, not as an act of justice, but as a 'conquest,' that if necessary, workers would defend even with force."[54] The government policies that union workers received with gratitude were considered by many industrialists to be an intrusion into their "private" realm of the shop floor. In their view, Perón's bellicose brand of social justice was making it more difficult to maintain a disciplined workforce.

Argentina's political parties had another set of axes to grind with Perón and the military regime. The leaders of the June Revolution backed their pledges to "cleanse" the political establishment by dissolving all civilian parties, and the leftist press was intermittently shut down between 1943 and 1945. Outrage at the restriction of civil liberties combined with extreme mistrust of Perón. Conservatives derided the activist military officer as a rabble-rouser, but the most intense enmity emanated from those on the left. The Socialist Party and other left-wing organizations seethed with frustration as Perón gained the trust of the union rank and file, copied their reform proposals, and emulated their moral critiques of capitalist excess. Political opponents saw the military regime and Perón's talk of a vida digna largely through the lens of fascism—and not without reason.[55] The leaders of the June Revolution were indeed inspired by right-wing nacionalista currents, even if state reorganization fell short of full-blown corporatism. Key differences separated the governments of Nazi Germany or Fascist Italy from the Argentine military regime, but it made strategic sense to attack Perón as a carbon copy of Mussolini, for doing so built on years of vigorous antifascist campaigning in Argentina.[56] With signs of an Allied victory in Europe, these comparisons attracted international attention to Argentina's domestic politics.

A confrontation between the military regime and its enemies was clearly brewing by mid-1945. On September 19 a massive antimilitary government demonstration—the "March for the Constitution and Liberty"—was held in Buenos Aires. Estimates of the crowd size ranged from 65,000 to 500,000 persons, drawn from all the social classes (but mostly from the middle sectors) and ideological spectra (communist to conservative).[57] In the meantime, Perón continued his polemical efforts to court organized labor, overtures that elements within the military opposed. Two weeks after the march in Buenos Aires, Perón convinced Farrell to sign a decree establishing guidelines for creating industrywide unions and collective bargaining tribunals.[58] The ensuing storm of controversy provided Perón's enemies with a justification for his removal. On October 9, 1945, Perón was forced to step down from public office, and two days later the military imprisoned him.

The following week was a crucial turning point in Argentine history, the subject of countless memoirs, journalistic accounts, and scholarly interpretations.[59] In an effort to free Perón and vindicate his policies, Argentine unions orchestrated a popular march in Buenos Aires on October 17, followed by a general strike the next day. Columns of male and female workers streamed into the city on the morning of the seventeenth; some walked twenty miles or more to reach the city's main square overlooking the presidential palace at the Plaza de Mayo. They congregated peacefully all day in unusually hot weather, occasionally breaking into chants supporting Perón. After much of the crowd had gone home, Perón appeared at midnight on the presidential balcony. Having been freed by officials who feared unrest, he thanked his ecstatic advocates and informed them of his resignation from the military; Perón pledged, however, to continue fighting on the pueblo's behalf, so that, as he put it, "all workers may be a little more content."[60] The show of working-class support encouraged Perón to run for the presidency in elections announced shortly thereafter, and October 17 came to be remembered as the foundational moment of the Peronist movement. His critics described it as the urban invasion of the lumpen proletariat, but for the workers who marched that day, it became a moment of rupture in the status quo when they asserted their authority and class pride before city dwellers. In the words of the writer Raúl Scalabrini Ortíz, this pivotal juncture brought the hidden demands of workers into full view: "Era el subsuelo de la patria sublevada" (roughly, it was the nation's lower strata rising up).[61]

In the aftermath of October 17, political events moved quickly. The military regime announced presidential elections for February 1946, accompanied by a further lifting of restrictions on opposition parties and the press. In November union leaders formed the Partido Laborista (later subsumed into the Peronist Party) and nominated Perón as their candidate. The elections pitted the so-called Democratic Union (an alliance of the Radical Party, Socialists, Communists, and Progressive Democrats) against a pro-Perón coalition of *laboristas,* dissident Radicals, and a motley collection of provincial parties. Echoing the themes of his 1944 speeches, Perón ran on his record as a leader who delivered on his promises of a better standard de vida and his nationalist ideal of an economically independent, well-ordered, and just society. The Democratic Union's candidate, José Tamborini, made references to worker-friendly reforms but emphasized the need to restore constitutionally protected liberties. Perón used tactics that undermined confidence in the opposition's social platform. In December 1945 he secured Farrell's signature on a decree that mandated employers to pay a year-end bonus (called an *aguindaldo*) of one month's wages to all industrial and commercial workers—a sweeping measure that boosted spending power considerably. In protest, the UIA and other employer organizations declared a three-day lockout, effectively shutting down many industries and businesses. The Democratic Union was left in the tricky position of criticizing the decree as electoral demagoguery, despite its obvious popularity.[62]

In the end, a majority of Argentine voters cast their lots for Perón. The Perón ticket obtained roughly 1.5 million votes to the Democratic Union's 1.2 million.[63] The electoral rules gave the Partido Laborista and its allies two-thirds control of both houses in the Congress and control of every provincial government but one. The victory gave Perón a mandate to realize his highest aims but by no means indicated unanimous public support. Perón and his inner circle of advisers were now free to pursue promises of comprehensive state planning, and they could extend the reforms carried out through the Labor Secretariat to the economy as a whole. While fears of postwar collapse lingered, a climate of optimism and expectation hung in the air for those who helped catapult him to the presidency.

From Planning to Redistribution

In the months following the elections, government authorities set about the task of meeting the high expectations raised during the campaign. The president's image was, after all, that of a leader who not only promised but delivered. But where to start in the quest to create a vida digna when so many problems vied for attention? Until this point, Perón and his assistants had focused on the workplace-centered demands of unions. Now, with far greater resources at their disposal, Peronist authorities turned to other facets of living standards. At the inaugural session of Congress in June 1946, Perón outlined the priorities of his government. In the section on social policy, he referenced the Labor Secretariat's statistical surveys on working-class household budgets and pledged to adopt policies that would allow laboring families to reach a "*standard decoroso.*"[64] The specific policy issues identified to reach this "decent standard"—social insurance, labor regulations, public health measures, housing construction—were hardly new. In this setting, the dignified life was conceived as a modicum of safety and security, a threshold of "freedom from want" in keeping with the international catchphrase of the era.

Yet Peronist authorities did not stop at welfare, as unquestionably significant as social programs were to the elevation of living standards. To the surprise of many, the pursuit of the dignified life became a matter not only of meeting subsistence minima but also of expanding the horizons of mass consumption for working-class Argentines. The move to bridge welfarist notions of collective consumption to individual spending power derived from multiple factors: the designs of Peronist policymakers, to be sure, but also the postwar economic environment and grassroots pressures exerted by unions and popular actors. As a result, the early years of Perón's presidency were marked by a rapid increase in working-class incomes that produced one of the twentieth century's most dramatic experiments in income redistribution. Statistical estimates suggest that in the four years following Perón's election, the "average" industrial worker experienced a 62 percent increase in real wages. The share of total national income constituted by worker salaries leapt from 44 percent in 1943 to a peak of 58 percent in 1954, the highest level ever reached until that point—and still to this day—in Argentina.[65] Workers channeled income to various ends, including personal savings and investments, but the largest portion was spent on areas of everyday consumption. As a share of Argentina's gross domestic product, consumption leapt from 81 percent in 1945 to 93 percent in 1948. Consumer spending grew faster than either savings or investments, which still rose during this early postwar period, offering more signs of the country's overall economic prosperity.[66]

The pace and scale of income distribution were unprecedented. Perhaps the closest comparison was the French Popular Front government in the late 1930s; under the guidance of Léon Blum's leftist coalition, France embarked on a short-lived attempt to elevate worker incomes. Yet Blum's government secured agreements for wage hikes of only 7 to 15 percent, which in any event were soon eroded by inflation and financial crisis. Popular Front measures were part of Depression-era strategies for recovery, whereas Peronist redistribution sought to accelerate ongoing trends of industrial growth and economic nationalism.[67] In other Latin American countries, such large-scale economic distribution has centered on land reform rather than a comprehensive transfer of income to urban wage earners—for example, the early 1950s experiments of the Arbenz government in Guatemala and the Bolivian Revolution.[68] Although Peronist authorities raised the issue of land reform in the mid-1940s, its visibility faded over time. Many other political movements called for income redistribution, but far fewer possessed the resources and political will to sustain such promises. Remarkably, the preceding years had revealed few signs that a major attempt at reshuffling incomes was in the cards after Perón's election. The experts at the Consejo Nacional de Posguerra had focused more on the dangers of inflation and supply shortages than on expanding consumer demand. Peronist notions of social justice referenced the entitlement of workers to a greater share of the nation's economic pie. But Perón stressed gender-inflected themes of security and satisfaction—of male providers earning good wages so that their households could "eat, dress, and live in a dignified fashion."

How, then, did boosting spending power come to occupy a prominent place in the early Perón years? Given the lack of sources indicating how the Peronist inner circle devised its strategies, this issue remains somewhat of a mystery, but a few major factors stand out. First, Perón's economic policymakers placed unexpected importance on domestic consumption in the postwar transition. After the election, Perón entrusted Figuerola with formulating a "five-year plan" (the Plan Quinquenal) to establish policy priorities. Completed in September 1946, this sprawling document touched on every major issue: agricultural and industrial policy, public health, social insurance, housing and public works construction, international relations, state finances, and much more. It emphasized the power of the central state, guided by proper technical planning and expertise, to channel the nation's resources more equitably, without seeking an elimination of private enterprise. In his public presentation of the plan, the president went on the offensive against those who might attack his program as socialism: "They talk about a directed economy. And I ask where is there an economy that is free? When the

FIGURE 4. Juan Perón and Eva Duarte de Perón. *Archivo General de la Nación, Departamento Fotográficos, Subsecretaría de Informaciones, AB-2, doc. 244944 (n.d.); reproduced courtesy of the archive.*

State does not direct it, monopolies do instead, with the only difference that the State can ensure a distribution of the benefits of wealth among 14 million Argentines, while monopolies do so to fatten the immense capital in their headquarters, far away, in foreign countries."[69] Redistribution via state planning, in this case, dovetailed with Perón's anti-imperialism and visions of a streamlined economy. The president identified consumption as the reward for a productive populace and an incentive for further growth. He railed against the "egoistical and antihuman economy" of the past, which had been based on the accumulation of agricultural goods for export while the pueblo starved at home. Perón argued that his administration was busy trying to remedy these ills by creating policies to "elevate national consumption in quantity, quality, and variety of products."[70] Yet references to consumption were counterbalanced with other priorities in the still-evolving Peronist model of economic nationalism. The Five-Year Plan and other policy statements provided little in terms of an extended defense of income redistribution or a justification for suddenly spurring consumer demand. Figuerola and other officials apparently placed greater stock in social programs as a means to elevate living standards, in a top-down manner and at a state-controlled rate, than in the potentially messier process of redistribution.

Mass consumption, however, did feature explicitly in the designs of the official entrusted with *implementing* economic policy, the so-called financial czar of the Perón government, Miguel Miranda. Perón handed Miranda the reins of the Central Bank and other financial agencies, making him one of the few industrialists formerly associated with the UIA to hold high-ranking cabinet posts. Despite the importance given to planning and technical expertise in official pronouncements, Perón selected an individual with no formal training in economics or background in public administration to set his government's financial policies. Whatever Miranda may have lacked in these areas, he compensated for it with his reputation as a successful entrepreneur and his immovable faith in his own abilities. The son of Spanish immigrants, Miranda epitomized the trajectory of the mythic Argentine "self-made man," having risen from modest origins to build a personal fortune in sheet-metal manufacturing and commercial ventures.[71] By all accounts, Miranda exuded a bravado that appealed to the president. His fundamental goal was to preserve and, when possible, expand the country's industrial base. Propping up aggregate demand was a crucial piece of his strategy. In Miranda's view, giving greater spending power to Argentine workers would enlarge the pool of domestic buyers for agricultural and industrial goods. To offset higher wages, manufacturers received credit from the Central Bank and other public lenders at generous rates.

Miranda's version of economic nationalism stressed the interlocking nature of industrialization and improvements in the standard of living—a concept defined increasingly in terms of spending power. In his public statements, the financial czar justified a "certain degree of state regulation" by highlighting the social costs of laissez-faire liberalism (he invoked, for instance, the camps of unemployed workers at the Buenos Aires port during the Great Depression). He argued that the nation should not waste its trade surplus by throwing open trade after the war, as he claims was mistakenly done following World War I, when the country "burned up its reserves by importing all manner of goods and consumer articles." Rather, he maintained, resources spent supporting domestic industry would elevate the standard de vida not only by creating better-paying jobs but also, and equally important, by enhancing the offerings available in the marketplace.[72] Similar arguments echoed in editorial pages of policy journals loyal to the new government, such as the influential *Hechos e Ideas.* A September 1947 piece on worker gains noted the importance of social security and redistribution of wealth as elements of the nivel de vida, but it stressed the primacy of material plenty in "reconstructing" the nation: "There exists no other better way to abolish misery than by creating a regime of abundance, given that social justice is inconceivable amidst scarcity." The editorial further argued that the Perón's government's "singular aim" in economic policy was to "increase the volume of consumer goods and place them within reach of the social sectors that make them." In exchange for access to this "regime of abundance," workers were called on to perform their self-disciplined role as productive members of the nation and moderate "excessive" demands.[73]

These examples illustrate Peronist variations on Fordist ideas and national planning circulating among the administration's policy experts during the mid-1940s. Nevertheless, the decision to tailor economic policy to domestic consumption and existing light industries owed a great deal to the weight of existing trends rather than the inspiration of Miranda and his peers. Argentina's economy had been turning more inward since the 1930s, and the disruptions in international trade due to the war only accelerated the expansion of local industry, principally in an attempt to provide substitutes for imports. Production nearly doubled between 1935 and 1946, with established factories leading the way over newer industries. Nearly three-fourths of the factories established between 1939 and 1946 manufactured consumer products, such as textiles and processed foods.[74] In tandem with this expansion, industrial employment continued its steady rise. By 1946 there were 1.2 million industrial workers and employees—an increase from 800,000 in 1940—concentrated mainly in the city and suburbs of Buenos Aires, Rosario, and to a lesser extent, other cities of the interior.[75] Despite the talk of deepening industrialization, many officials focused on defending the recent gains of consumer-goods industries. In practice, full employment and the redistribution of income were prioritized over increasing technological investment, and nationalist dreams of steel mills and other heavy industry were put on hold until after the immediate transition to peace.

The international economic climate further conditioned the Peronist inward-oriented approach to boosting consumer demand. On the surface, it appeared that export agriculture was in a privileged position, for the world war and postwar European reconstruction fueled demand for Argentine grains and meats abroad. But Great Britain and other war-devastated nations lacked the capital to pay for these goods in the short term and with convertible currencies. The U.S. decision to bar Argentina as an agricultural supplier for the Marshall Plan—the product of lobbying from U.S. farmers and an effort to intensify political pressure on Perón—offered another push toward greater autarchy. Relations between the United States and Argentine governments remained strained in the aftermath of the Blue Book affair; between 1942 and 1949, the United States imposed a series of boycotts against trade with Argentina, affecting mainly industrial machinery, fuel, and other necessary inputs. Although domestic factory owners continued to look to the United States and other nations for industrial material, Perón's government sought to lessen the reliance on foreign trade.[76]

Mass consumption, then, was the Peronist policymakers' response to multiple problems at once, addressing the needs to consolidate popular support, shore up wartime industrialization, pursue a vision of national independence, and deliver on higher living standards. Just a year prior to Perón's election, the postwar council had warned of the dangers of "excessive" consumption to investment and industrial diversification. Although concerns persisted among critics, they were dispelled by Peronist officials celebrating increased consumer spending as a sign of social justice. There was an improvised, unplanned character to the redistribution of income and support of consumption in the late 1940s, as reflected by their low profile in the Five-Year Plan. Miranda and other officials realized the full consequences of their actions only in retrospect, and their decisions were subject to political and economic forces beyond their immediate control.

Indeed, pressures exerted from outside the government were instrumental in raising the purchasing power of ordinary Argentines. While the expansion of the *aguinaldo* and other social legislation played an important role, the redistribution of income toward the working class occurred most frequently through the mechanism of new labor contracts. Unions seized the favorable political moment following Perón's election to press for better pay and social benefits. Conditioned by the expectation that Perón's government would back it, organized labor pressed forward in its struggles with management. Yet it was individual unions that mobilized members, negotiated aggressively with employers, and took action when collective bargaining broke down, as witnessed in the spike in strike activity during the first three years of Perón's term. The rapid increase in the numbers of Argentines belonging to unions only emboldened leaders further. By the early 1950s the CGT estimated that over two million Argentines—nearly half the economically active population—belonged to unions, up from just 20 percent a decade before and representing a wider spectrum of the working-class and white-collar sectors.[77] The increasingly close relations between Peronist officials and labor leaders did not preclude tensions between the two camps or divisions among factions within unions, but during the boom times immediately following the war, the government and CGT-affiliated unions shared similar objectives. Their commitment to preserving full employment and increasing the economic participation of wage earners offered a platform on which rested the alliance between labor and the state.

In the end, a combination of factors—union pressure, worldwide economic conditions, and the nationalist inclinations of state policymakers—contributed to the combination of income redistribution and widening mass consumption. Perón's enticing if vague promises of a vida digna began to materialize more clearly during the period of economic prosperity in 1946–1949. The immediate postwar boom helped fuse two models of the standard of living: one based on extending social services; the other, on elevating household spending power. At this moment, political authorities saw these as compatible aims. In exchange for their productive contributions, citizens would become protagonists in the New Argentina as political subjects *and* modern economic actors. The planning state would take a leading role by delivering benefits directly through social programs, favoring working-class consumers through economic policies, and supporting allies to get a greater share of national abundance.

❋

Argentina's political scene was remarkably fluid in 1939–1946, one of those rare periods in which the very terms of national progress are open to redefinition. Perón's eventual victory was the product not only of his own designs but also of a series of unforeseen incidents and positions adopted by his opponents—contingencies to which he responded with dexterity. In the field of social politics, there were many roads not taken. For every expert who rose within the ranks of the government, countless more advocates, such as Bereterbide and Di Tella, were forced aside. The UIA's model of planning, based on probusiness coordination, gave way to a brasher economic nationalism that complemented Perón's own populist strategies. Policymaking authority resided in a UIA member, as the organization's leaders had hoped, but Miranda's approach to planning, with its emphasis on shoring up domestic consumer demand, deviated from the path favored by his more elitist peers. The very coalition assembled around the president—an assemblage of interests that included labor unions, dissident industrialists, right-leaning social scientists, provincial parties, and the military, as well as still "unorganized" sectors of popular support—made it difficult to predict the government's direction in the postwar era. The partisan antagonisms witnessed in the run-up to the elections, combined with the fact that a sizable minority of the public contested the legitimacy of Peronist rule, contributed further to the uncertainty of this histori-cal conjuncture.

In debating their country's future, Argentine political actors understandably focused on domestic conditions, but concern with the nation did not preclude certain types of openness to the world. Although most accounts of Peronism's ori-gins stress its domestic insularity, the movement's nationalist character should not blind us to this context. Perón's references to the "English" concept of the stan-dard de vida offer but one clue; behind the scenes, Figuerola and other collaborators borrowed extensively from international sources in formulating a novel paradigm of national planning. At a deeper level, the issues at stake in debates over living standards in Argentina sparked controversy across the globe. World War II had called into question the very terms of membership in the nation, especially in bel-ligerent countries struggling to rally public support and reward military sacrifice. These pressures crystallized proposals for expanding the state's role in managing social needs, proposals that would be taken up by Western Europe's postwar wel-fare systems. But a spirit of reformism also swept through Latin America during the war and its immediate aftermath, inspired by experiments abroad but also, and more important, by longstanding frustrations with closed political systems and the clash between republican ideals and obvious inequities. Existing regimes faced pressure from new mass movements, labor mobilizations, and calls for democrati-zation. At least until this window closed in the late 1940s, with the onset of cold war counterrevolution, nationalist dreams of integrating social majorities within more inclusive political systems seemed close at hand in Latin America.[78]

As these regional trends unfolded in Argentina, the Peronist redefinition of state-citizen relations combined influences from liberal traditions, wartime think-ing about state socioeconomic management, and midcentury forms of mass poli-tics. There is no denying that the Peronist movement embodied hopes for greater civic participation and social inclusion among a broad swath of the population or that Perón's government sought to establish its legitimacy through formal atten-tion to constitutional procedures. Yet Perón began his political career within a military dictatorship harboring corporatist pretensions, and his own administra-tion continued its predecessor's emphasis on ideological order. While Perón forged ties with unions, he also followed in the footsteps of civilian figures, such as Manuel Fresco, who had coupled social reform to antileftist sentiments. The for-mulation of citizenship in terms of living standards reflected this potent combina-tion of wartime influences. On the one hand, Peronist actors envisioned citizenship in terms of social rights, entitlements, and protections, much as did other incipient "welfare states" in the postwar world. On the other, officials favored a hierarchical conception of modernist development, in which state benefactors would care for the needs of the nation's workers in exchange for unwavering loyalty behind the regime and its supreme "*Conductor.*" Whereas Perón's opponents continued to view politics in republican terms—hence the 1946 march for "the Constitution and liberty"—his movement sounded a new tone. While not rejecting liberal republicanism entirely, Peronist leaders spoke about citizenship in ways that validated the everyday aspirations of working Argentines but that also justified the planning state's tutelary power over its subjects.

The Perón regime's attempts to ensure a decent standard of living stand out because the government managed to effect redistribution on a massive scale. The contrast with other Latin American contexts is revealing. Unlike populist counterparts elsewhere, Peronist leaders were in the rare position of having both economic resources to distribute and the mechanisms to do so. They created favorable opportunities for working-class organizations to press claims on employers while stopping short of defining a radical alternative to capitalism (as would later be the case in 1960s Cuba, 1970s Chile, or Venezuela under Hugo Chávez). Nevertheless, maintaining these "social conquests"—better salaries and benefits, collective relief and social services, the easing of household constraints—would prove no easy feat after the 1946 elections. This was particularly true of the consumer marketplace, the social setting in which rising wages translated into improvements in living conditions and satisfaction of material ambitions. For redistribution was just the beginning. Over the late 1940s, the arena of mass consumption became a site of friction not only between state regulators and defenders of merchant property but also among popular households struggling to realize the vida digna.

3

THE WAR ON SPECULATION

IN ARGENTINA the end of World War II was soon overshadowed by the start of
Perón's presidency. Whether this momentous transition represented the dawn of
a new era or the further decline of the Republic depended on the side of the growing partisan divide on which one stood. While political tensions showed few signs
of easing, the fears of postwar economic collapse that had long preoccupied observers soon vanished. For the remainder of the 1940s, Argentina entered a phase
of impressive expansion, the benefits of which were felt widely. Naturally, officials
in the Perón administration took credit for this prosperity, presenting it as concrete evidence of a socially just nation in the making. When contrasted with the
war's devastation and the sacrifices of reconstruction abroad, the county's good
fortune in the immediate postwar years only added to its renown as a land of plenty.
Yet no sooner had the world war ended than a different war began in Argentina,
not a conflict between nations but rather, as defined by the country's authorities,
an internal struggle. It was a contest to safeguard the living standards of the Nueva
Argentina but framed in far more vivid terms by Peronists as a crusade against the
nation's economic enemies. "It is not tolerable after having raised salaries to just
and reasonable levels," proclaimed Perón in a June 1947 speech, "that by the indifference of state agencies and the lack of scruples on the part of certain dishonest
merchants, the working population suffers wrongs that I am inclined to impede at
all costs."[1]

In response the government assembled a veritable arsenal of weapons to stamp
out "unjust" forms of exchange. These included price controls on all manner of
consumable wares and police inspections of retail shops and manufacturers (with

accompanying fines, jail terms, and other punishments). State-led campaigns sought to mobilize consumers in support of these measures. Recalling his career as an army officer, Perón referred on occasion to these initiatives as the "Guerra al agio" or "Guerra contra la especulación"—the war against usury or speculation. Given the recent global conflagration that had left hundreds of millions dead, injured, and displaced, the metaphor of warfare may seem to have been an odd choice for the Argentine president. But the commitment to "antispeculation" was not merely rhetorical posturing. Creeping inflation threatened income redistribution among working Argentines, while profiteering limited their access to local products and unsettled the regime's inward-oriented strategy of economic growth. Given the high stakes, the defense of purchasing power became an object of widespread concern and controversy.

Amid postwar abundance, Peronists waged campaigns to discipline the quotidian spaces of the marketplace and household. Antispeculation measures thus expanded the terrain of national politics outside the old liberal boundaries, highlighting the new economic dimensions of citizenship while creating opportunities for popular collaboration that drew on traditions of protesting unethical exchange. Naturally, other issues competed for attention on the Peronist agenda, and the regime lavished considerably more publicity on its achievements in labor reform, national planning, and social welfare. The question of spending power, however, was impossible to ignore, largely because it was inseparable from these high-profile issues. As a result, consumer contests provide a window onto struggles to realize promises of dignified living standards in everyday life, and they reveal the competing cultural understandings of the moral economy that Peronism brought to the surface of public life.

It may be tempting to view the "war on speculation" as an idiosyncratic exception, and Perón's overheated rhetoric facilitates this conclusion. Yet the impulses underlying the domestication of markets in Argentina were part of a moment of global challenges to the hegemony of free-market principles. In the wake of the Great Depression, Latin American states experimented with exerting greater regulatory power over daily commerce.[2] Consumer subsidies, price controls, and other regulatory mechanisms were ubiquitous the world over, even in capitalist bastions; the U.S. federal government created the Office of Price Administration, which at its peak boasted 250,000 paid staff and volunteers entrusted with monitoring the marketplace.[3] These policies were accompanied by political efforts to modify liberal citizenship, principally by asserting an active role for "citizen consumers" in line with new modes of nationalism. The rights and duties of citizen consumers varied considerably from country to country, but they reflected the growing national prominence of something Meg Jacobs has dubbed "pocketbook politics" (that is, disputes over wages, purchasing power, and related dimensions of economic citizenship). The Depression and World War II acted as catalysts for these changes in the United States and elsewhere, but it was the emergence of Peronism that redefined the terms of consumer contests in Argentina—and in the process, ensured that pocketbook politics took on an especially fractious, partisan charge.

The war on speculation established norms for the correct behavior of actors in the marketplace (if not always with the results officials intended). In particular, Peronist authorities envisioned female consumers as particularly valuable and loyal allies to the regulatory state. Antispeculation measures advanced an ideal of gender relations that stressed female authority over household consumption and management of the domestic sphere while simultaneously reinforcing the patriarchal position of men as breadwinners. Citizenship was further defined by a collective, moralistic distinction drawn between the virtuous pueblo and a cabal of greedy adversaries, a rhetoric shared with other populist movements. Merchant "speculators" joined selfish elites, oligarchic landowners, and foreign imperialists in the rogues' gallery of national enemies. This distinction succeeded in stirring popular enthusiasm and channeling anxieties associated with competitive consumer societies, but it created a twofold problem. First, antispeculation policies elicited counterreactions within the ranks of property holders, who advanced their own understandings of ethical exchange. Second, promises of "just" commerce often fell short in practice—not surprisingly, given the complexity of regulating something as vast as Argentina's consumer marketplace. Rising prices nagged popular households at middecade but became a more urgent crisis as the postwar boom stalled after 1949. The uneven impact of the antispeculation campaigns thus gave rise to another theater of battle—one less noted publicly and less overtly hostile in its confrontations—within the Peronist movement, as popular sympathizers pressed claims for greater action on the state.

The Paradoxes of Plenty

The fact that Perón's first presidency was remembered by many Argentines as an age of abundance cannot be attributed solely to the prosperity of the mid-1940s. Yet the postwar boom had an undeniable impact on the lives of the populace, contributing to the upbeat mood of the times, acknowledged even by Perón's detractors: "Argentina was a fiesta," to put things in the famous words of Félix Luna, the historian and skeptic of Peronist rule.[4] For a majority of the country's working-class inhabitants, material gains were inseparable from feelings of political empowerment and identification with the Peronist movement. Collective access to an unprecedented share of the national income translated into improvements large and small in the quality of life. In terms of mass consumption, the effects of redistribution were concentrated in urban and suburban areas, where purchasing power was most clearly displayed in the crowded streets of urban shopping districts, the packed houses of theaters and cinema palaces, and the throngs of shoppers in department stores and neighborhood shops. Prosperity, however, brought with it a new set of problems. Memories of a joyous, carefree era obscure the reality that, even at the peak of the boom, certain obstacles continued to block popular aspirations. Rather than simply bask in the bounty of the New Argentina, working households could not escape the competitive strains of the marketplace, which contemporaries called the "*carrera*" (race) between salaries and prices. Postwar conditions lessened the need for rigorous penny-pinching, but keeping up in the carrera created new frustrations.

The politics of this consumer's race took place within a social context marked by working people's broadened access to Argentina's commercial offerings. Sorting out exact purchasing patterns after Perón's election is complicated by an ironic twist. Although surveys of working-class budgets shaped early Peronist social policies, the government stopped publishing statistics on household spending and the nivel de vida soon after the 1946 elections. The lack of social knowledge suggests much about the era's new political priorities: in a time when national authorities extolled the nation's limitless bounty, when the pueblo supposedly had all its needs met, why should one employ tools once used to measure worker poverty (or, more to the point, gather information that might supply ammunition for criticism)? Other sources, however, provide indirect insights into the ways Argentines spent rising incomes in this period. Retail sales figures for metropolitan Buenos Aires indicate an upward trend across the board between 1946 and 1949, both for everyday goods (e.g., food, clothing, pharmacy products, household items, books, and toys) and services (e.g., restaurants and entertainment). The types of consumables remained familiar, and there was an overall continuity in the retailing practices and structure of commercial networks from the 1930s. The real innovation came in the expanding pool of purchasers for the cornucopia of wares available in the Argentine marketplace.[5]

Perhaps the clearest evidence appeared on kitchen tables, for rising incomes meant that the laboring majority could eat more freely. In Argentina this meant one thing: meat. Beef was the most prized food, an important cultural indicator of plenty and an engrained part of culinary habits to a degree that shocked foreign visitors. In middle- and upper-class homes, meat was consumed daily, and it was almost unheard of for lunch or dinner not to include some cut of beef, preferably a juicy steak, as the main dish.[6] Other social strata ate beef more rarely, if at all, but newfound spending power allowed working people to add more meat to their plates in the early Peronist era. Argentina already led the planet in per capita beef consumption, but whereas the average Argentine annually ate around 175 pounds of beef and other meat during World War II, this amount jumped to an astounding 250 pounds in 1950. To put this in perspective, consider that Australia and New Zealand came next at a distant 147 pounds per capita per year, with the United States trailing in fourth position. For residents of war-ravaged Europe and much of Latin America, beef was an occasional indulgence at best.[7] While beef still remained out of reach for indigent populations in Perón's Argentina, the coveted beef-centered meal became a little luxury available to more working families. In addition, shoppers made qualitative changes in their everyday food purchasing that reflected the prosperous times. A pro-Peronist newspaper quoted one neighborhood butcher who reported that demand was so strong that shoppers turned up their noses at the more economical, tougher cuts; he could barely keep better quality meat in his store.[8] Nevertheless, Argentines did not live on steak alone (as much as some might have tried), and greater disposable income allowed for upgrades of other popular dishes, including pastas and stews. Higher salaries meant as well that some working-class families could afford to treat themselves to meals outside the home, in the nation's countless restaurants, pastry shops (*confiterías*), and neighborhood cafés. The era's social scientists still complained about the lack of balanced eating habits and continued problems of malnutrition among the indigent, yet Peronist rule stimulated quantitative improvements in diets. According to one study, the daily per capita dietary intake in Argentina grew from 2,730 to 3,190 calories between 1936 and 1950, reaching levels roughly equal to those of the United States.[9]

Individuals also spent their paychecks on the array of manufactured wares and services available in the 1940s marketplace, with purchases of clothing leading the way. In fact, retail sales of garments and accessories grew faster than expenditures in grocery stores or restaurants. Shoppers headed not only to department stores and emporiums in downtown districts but also to an untold number of barrio-level dressmakers, tailors, and shoemakers scattered across Argentine communities. Thanks to greater disposable incomes, the volume of clothing sales per inhabitant increased by over 30 percent between 1946 and 1949.[10] Sales figures translated into larger, better wardrobes for women and men used to scrimping and mending. Decked out in new outfits, some consumers hit the town in search of commercial forms of entertainments when the workday was through. Attendance at theaters, sporting events, musical shows, and dance halls all rose in the immediate postwar years. The cinema attracted by far the largest crowds at the glitzy downtown film palaces and rough-and-tumble barrio halls of Litoral cities; even provincial towns often had at least one movie house. The city of Buenos Aires alone witnessed a two-thirds rise in cinema attendance between 1943 and 1951, facilitated by government price controls that kept ticket prices low. Dance halls sprouted up, catering to tastes for tango, jazz, and other popular music and offering alternatives to already established ethnic and social clubs. For those benefiting from postwar prosperity, these improvements offered tangible, daily evidence of higher living standards. *other indicators offered prosperity*

It is worth stressing that working people directed disposable income to numerous other ends besides eating more beef, buying new suits and dresses, or enjoying commercial leisure-time entertainment. Further indicating the strong economic climate, personal savings and investments also increased over previous levels. Bank deposits more than doubled between 1943 and 1948, and the holdings of the federal savings and loan institution (the Caja de Ahorro Postal), which served those with modest incomes, grew fourfold.[11] Rising incomes allowed individuals to pursue projects they had put on hold during the war years, including all sorts of activities requiring small-scale investments, such as setting up a business or supporting a child's education. The optimistic mood was reflected in marriage and birth rates, both of which spiked during Perón's first term, as many young people took the opportunity to form their own families or expand the size of their households.[12] These factors contributed to one of the most significant social trends of this period: the expansion of home ownership. Peronist policies helped previously excluded segments of the working and middle classes to join the ranks of home owners, mainly through low-interest mortgages administered by the state's Banco Hipotecario Nacional and public housing construction.[13] Even more important, economic conditions allowed those in lower-income sectors to purchase their own plots of land. Would-be property holders favored by the postwar confluence of full employment, rising salaries, and lower living expenses flocked to the suburban belts that surrounded major cities. Buying a plot was just the beginning, for many suburban residents built their own homes over time with the assistance of friends and neighbors. In the suburbs of greater Buenos Aires, the rates of home ownership soared from 43 percent in 1947 to 67 percent by 1960, as hundreds of thousands of people moved from the city and provinces to newly established neighborhoods.

As Peronist leaders keenly understood, the home was more than an investment: it constituted a powerful cultural indicator of personal progress, both for those able finally to reach this goal and for the millions still aspiring.

In turn, home ownership motivated complementary forms of consumer spending. The postwar boom allowed Argentines to spruce up their current homes or decorate recently purchased or constructed houses. Mass-market magazines educated audiences about fashions in aesthetically pleasing and modern domestic spaces. Advertisements praised electric appliances that promised to lessen the burdens of household labor, providing an alternative (or at least a supplement) to the work carried out by housewives and maids. Campaigns targeted female consumers touting home appliances as necessities for maintaining "proper" homes while alluding to the dominant rhetoric of national independence. "Liberation!" exclaimed the ecstatic housewife in ELNA sewing machine advertisements, for whom the purchase of a consumer good brought, at least in theory, freedom from drudgery and the more complete realization of modern womanhood.[14] The 1946 census revealed that only 17 percent of the population owned a refrigerator (33 percent in the city of Buenos Aires), yet during the first three years of Peronist rule, refrigerator sales more than doubled.[15] Vacuum cleaners and range-style stoves became commonplace in middle-class homes, though they remained priced outside the reach of many lower-income consumers. For laboring families, time-saving manufactured goods, such as electric irons and sewing machines, proved invaluable for in-home upkeep; perhaps more important, they were tools that could be used for sideline sewing and laundering work. Nearly half of all households owned a sewing machine in 1946, and the number climbed throughout the decade.

Of all the manufactures available on the market, the radio was one of the most coveted. Radio sales increased sixfold between 1946 and 1949, and by the end of Perón's first term only the more impoverished (or old-fashioned) households lacked their own receivers. The radio was quickly becoming the dominant means of mass communication, one put to good use by Peronist authorities, who relied on state broadcasting and allied stations to spread propaganda. But radio was also source of popular entertainment, serving as a starting point for daily conversation and a constant background companion during family gatherings. Receivers became less obtrusive in the home as their appeal increased: wooden cabinets gave way to more streamlined sets and, by the end of the 1950s, hand-held transistor radios. Programming ranged from melodramas and children's shows to sports coverage and news reports, and Argentine radio catered to multiple audiences, with stations that targeted the middle class through a more reserved broadcasting style and those that aimed for mass appeal (including Radio Porteña, Radio Mitre, and Radio del Pueblo—"the most popular wavelength," as its motto claimed).[16] Although television came to Argentina in 1951, radio was king during the Peronist era.

The changes in the consumer marketplace were helped by state policies. The Perón government supported a particular type of postwar consumption, one conscious of nationalism and class. The goal was to have more people buy those goods already produced domestically (and thus protect existing industries and agriculture) rather than supply the market with the latest global innovations in mass consumption. Policymakers favored local producers with the expectation that they would deliver the fruits of a modern economy to the nation's inhabitants. In March 1946 Perón entrusted the Central Bank director Miguel Miranda with a new agency, the Instituto Argentino de Promoción del Intercambio (IAPI; the Argentine Institute for Promoting Exchange), which provided a mechanism to address the classic Argentine bind between exporting agricultural goods or consuming them domestically. The end of World War II brought a huge European demand for beef, wheat, and other products, and naturally, the landowners of the pampas looked to sell their crops abroad at international prices. Boosting exports, however, would reduce the supply and raise the prices of staple goods for Perón's pueblo. The IAPI represented the government's solution: through this agency, the federal government arranged the entire sale of agricultural commodities to buyers abroad. Rather than give them full price for their harvests, the IAPI paid farmers and ranchers at approximately half the going international rate. The remaining profits were channeled into government coffers to fund social programs and other federal spending. At the same time, Miranda favored fellow industrialists by providing them with public credit on highly favorable terms.[17] In short, the IAPI redistributed wealth from Argentina's rural producers to the government and then to urban workers and factory-owners—a transfer that, as one might expect, did little to endear Perón to large landowners. As partial recompense, the IAPI offered agricultural producers generous loans and subsidies designed to reduce prices on oil, sugar, and flour destined for Argentine markets.[18]

The administration took additional steps to ensure the supply of affordable consumer goods and services through state intervention. Perón heralded a 1948 agreement to nationalize the British-owned railroads as evidence of Argentina's economic independence; moreover, state control of the rails enabled officials to pursue redistributionist aims by keeping commuting costs down for millions of riders. Federal agencies intervened in behalf of consumers by compelling meat producers to lower beef prices for national consumption, extending credit to meat-packing houses, and covering deficits incurred in supplying beef for the city of Buenos Aires.[19] Municipal officials in the capital and other communities established *ferias francas,* street markets that sold foodstuffs at reduced prices directly to consumers. Most important, the Perón government followed in the path of the June Revolution by consolidating the rent controls in Buenos Aires through a 1946 law that ensured fixed monthly rents and eviction protections for nearly two-thirds of city dwellers. Rent freezes had a huge impact, for the share of income workers spent on housing plummeted from an estimated 18 to 2.6 percent between 1943 and 1957. Renters of agricultural land (*arrendatarios*), who constituted the rural middle-class, benefited, if less so, from comparable controls and antieviction measures. When coupled with moderate inflation, rent controls meant that tenants paid substantially less for housing over time; this money could be used for savings, investment, and other ends, including enriching the quality and quantity of daily consumption.[20]

Inspired by the government's optimistic vision of national plenty, many Argentines put aside fears of postwar collapse and enjoyed the nation's commercial bounty. Millions of citizens rode the rising tide of the nation's economic growth. Individuals pursued previously deferred aspirations in the realm of consumption with purchasing acts both small (more food and better clothes) and large (outfitting a new home). Yet not all were equal participants in this expanding chain of acquisition. Among wage earners, union laborers and government employees witnessed the most sustained increases in income. In general terms, a male factory laborer in Buenos Aires was typically in a better position than his sister who worked as a maid, a neighbor who was a street vendor, or a cousin who made a living as a rural farmhand. The rise in real wages favored working-class residents of urban and suburban areas of the Litoral provinces, which became even more prominent as centers of industrial, commercial, and government activity. The suburbs of Buenos Aires experienced the greatest expansion in retail terms, in part because merchants opened shops to meet the needs of new residents. Between 1946 and 1951 retail sales per inhabitant doubled in the suburban region, with figures in the capital city following close behind. Sales in leading provincial cities, such as Córdoba, grew more slowly, increasing 68 percent in the same period.[21] Retail statistics are unavailable for smaller towns and rural settlements, but one can safely assume that fewer commercial establishments and sources of good employment there limited prospects for mass consumption—additional factors explaining why residents of the countryside continued to migrate to the urban Litoral. To be not always eco prosperous

sure, slight material improvements could have great significance for members of the working poor, but the conditions of indigence facing farmhands and city slum dwellers failed to change overnight, if at all, under Peronist rule.

Even for favored populations at the height of the boom, Peronist-era promises of easy abundance fell short on occasion. Although retail sales of consumer goods increased, shoppers encountered periodic shortages of foodstuffs and fuel, long lines at stores, and high prices for manufactures that dampened the celebratory mood. The popular press voiced shoppers' frustrations (no doubt with some exaggeration), and journalists warned that prices were on the verge of overwhelming salary improvements. The average working family "earns more than yesterday," claimed a 1947 editorial on the cost of living, "but its income does not meet its living needs."[22] Newspapers, such as the liberal *La Nación* and Catholic *El Pueblo*, took up the cause of small property owners. Editorials complained about the Perón government's neglect of the middle class—the "Cinderella of Argentine society"—whose members were being left behind as workers prospered.[23] In fact, inflation did hurt retirees and others on fixed incomes, while rent controls threatened middle-class families who depended on income from small rental properties. Press coverage of these travails reminded the public that not all households were keeping pace in the consumer's race.

Estimates suggest that inflation surged in the 1945–51 period from annual rates of around 8 percent to near 40 percent—levels so far from the hyperinflation of 1980s Argentina but a disquieting novelty for a generation unaccustomed to such conditions. In a May 1947 presentation before the Bolsa de Comercio, Miranda explained the causes of rising costs. In his view, the country was passing through a "transitional phase" during which consumer demand was outstripping the supply of goods. The war was partly to blame, for it had left industrialists without the raw materials and capital to fully meet the expanding desires of a population undergoing a dramatic elevation in the standard de vida. Citizens should be thankful that inflation was lower in Argentina than in other postwar nations. Miranda was partially on the mark. In the aftermath of the world war, economies across the globe experienced inflationary trends, and Argentina's inward-oriented economy was not immune to these larger forces. He omitted mentioning, however, other potential sources of inflation, such as the surge in government spending and the Central Bank's loose credit policies. Furthermore, Miranda suggested that additional support to factory owners would reduce inflation: "As soon as our new industries begin to produce, the flow of new consumer goods will fill the market, and the main cause of the current rise in prices will vanish." The role of the working population was to throw themselves into labor—and here he invoked Perón's motto "producir, producir, producir"—and to set more savings aside.[24]

Miranda's economic analysis highlighted a virtuous cycle of national development in which rising production led to higher wages and spending power. But it was one thing to lay out these arguments before well-heeled business representatives and quite another to resolve the preoccupations of laboring families. The political stakes of inflation were clear, especially because consumer affairs were bound closely together with labor relations in Peronist Argentina. With each price increase during the 1940s, emboldened unions clamored for better contracts from employers and government support for wage increases. Officials were thrust into the tricky position of having to referee this wage-price carrera. Social policies were not enough; they required complementary efforts to satisfy union allies and popular demands without aggravating the problem of inflation. Would salaries keep pace with the growing cost of living? Would the population continue to achieve new "social conquests"? How long would the prosperity last, and who in the end would reap the benefits? The inability to answer these questions created uncertainty even during the boom times.

In response, Peronist officials reframed the wage-price race in terms of a new competitive metaphor: namely, as a war between popular consumers and internal economic enemies. They broadened the scope of state planning to encompass all forms of domestic commercial activity, from the manufacture of consumer goods to their distribution and sale in stores. To justify state regulation, the regime's leaders put a face on abstract economic concepts, such as inflation. In a manner similar to other populists, they identified villains—immoral shopkeepers, unpatriotic traders, and fat-cat industrialists—who conspired against a decent quality of life. Drawing on cultural traditions for criticizing the excesses of commerce, Perón heaped scorn on the mysterious persona of the "speculator," a foil to the patriotic producer exalted by the government. During a 1947 national radio broadcast, he noted that inflation was a common postwar problem, but he condemned in particular the "egoism, greediness, lack of human solidarity, and absence of patriotism" of certain Argentine business owners. "They are the ones," the president exclaimed, "who stir up the river to reap gains as fishermen, who lay the foundations for black markets, who speculate and profit from the labor and blood of the immense majority of inhabitants."[25]

Peronist leaders drew on familiar moralizing discourses and earlier state experiments with regulation but raised the political stakes. Like 1930s activists on the secular left, they leveled attacks on the "unscrupulous" elite that profited parasitically from the working majority. The frequent use of the term "agio" (usury), an archaic, biblical-sounding word replete with connotations of reprobation, echoed the language of Catholics and other critics. In the past these appraisals circulated largely outside the government; after the 1946 elections, however, attacks on speculation and usury became ambitious expressions of state power. Yet Peronist commercial controls were not exclusively anticapitalist. Instead, they aimed to safeguard working-class income redistribution, not to eliminate private property or provide a collectivist alternative to profit-driven commerce. This approach to consumer politics offered a "double movement" in response to the forces of commercialization, seeking to tame the excessive chaos of capitalist forces while extending the comforts of the marketplace more broadly. In the quest to mitigate the paradoxes of plenty, state authorities extended their reach over routines of buying and selling, in the process altering distinctions between private and public affairs that structured everyday life.

Waging the War

The government's initial effort to discipline domestic commerce came a week after the president's inauguration in June 1946. With great fanfare Perón announced the "Sixty-Day Campaign," a package of price controls to limit the cost of consumer necessities. Advertisements filled the pages of popular daily newspapers and enlisted the cooperation of shoppers and merchants alike.[26] The government backed the measures with police inspections of stores, limited for the moment to the city of Buenos Aires. In one of her first high-profile public addresses, broadcast nationwide on state radio, Eva Perón prevailed on women to follow the state's lead in stamping out high prices: "Our home, our sacred space, the altar of our emotions, is in danger. . . . Over it hovers threateningly the unspeakable machination of speculation and usury."[27] Evita exhorted women—in their roles as mothers, wives, and girlfriends—to respect official prices, report offenders, and convince their family members to do likewise. Shortly after Evita's speech, the Secretariat of Industry and Commerce took out full-page ads in women's magazines and other mass publications urging readers, "Don't Pay a Cent More."[28] The drive ended two months later with the regime's leaders claiming victory. Prices of consumer goods had fallen, but as it turned out, only temporarily: in the aftermath of this inconclusive campaign, the real war against commercial injustice would begin.

This first package of measures set the pattern for the regime's consumer politics during 1946–1951. Not merely a technocratic matter, antispeculation initiatives provided repeated opportunities for Juan and Eva Perón to affirm the populist terms of their political project as the struggle between a pueblo of deserving workers and profiteering merchants bent on undermining hard-won gains. Making the presence of the state felt in everyday spaces mattered, especially for authorities who staked their reputations on delivering material improvements and who encouraged supporters to demand justicia social. The steady climb in prices over the 1940s motivated officials to conduct inspections and jail merchants in a struggle to match antispeculation discourses, a process pushed along by energized constituents as well as the counteractions of reluctant property owners. In practice, however, balancing the economic planning and mass-political elements proved difficult.

The orchestration of consumer campaigns fell to several executive branch bureaucracies: the Ministry of Technical Affairs, the Secretariat of Industry and Commerce, the Federal Police, and the Subsecretariat of Information—all newly created agencies that were torn in countless directions by the administration's agenda.[29] Building on the limited price control legislation passed in 1939, the Peronist-controlled Congress approved two new laws, one in August 1946 (12.830) and one in April 1947 (12.983), to entrust federal agencies with stronger regulatory weapons.[30] The first gave the executive branch authority to fix maximum prices on key products (e.g., food, clothing, manufactures, medicines, construction materials) and, if necessary, restrict exports and ration import permits to maintain a well-supplied consumer marketplace. Maximum punishments included imprisonment for up to six years and the closure of businesses. The second law went further, allowing officials to freeze prices, levy fines up to 100,000 pesos, seize merchandise, and deport suspected speculators or detain them for jail terms of up to ninety days. In the years that followed, federal officials added piecemeal to this legal arsenal.[31] Planners occasionally supplanted adjustable controls with more stringent tactics, such as fixing profit levels and all-out price freezes.[32]

Initially the inspections were restricted to the capital and its metropolitan region, not coincidentally those areas with the densest concentration of consumers. This restriction facilitated surveillance, because the location fell within the jurisdiction of the Federal Police, but it excluded the two-thirds of the Argentine population who lived in the "interior." Enforcement in the provinces picked up over time, as local officials created their own institutions to manage prices and as federal authorities increased their presence nationwide. In 1947 Perón's cabinet organized a conference of Argentina's governors to encourage cooperation with antispeculation efforts. Governors from Entre Rios and Salta proposed additional measures, including more extensive controls over profit margins and the creation of state-run stores to sell goods directly to consumers. The provincial government of Santa Fe followed through by forming its own "Junta against Usury and Speculation" to coordinate with national agencies and established local committees (each staffed by the chief of police or mayor, a representative from local unions, and a community representative) in their efforts to monitor markets in cities and towns across the province.[33] In general, however, the impact of the guerra al agio varied enormously from province to province and even from one community to the next, contingent on the diligence of local officials and the means at their disposal.

Leaders invoked ideals of economic efficiency in their presentations of consumer protection measures. Laws streamlined commerce by reducing "middlemen" (e.g., wholesalers and transporters) suspected of hoarding and adding unnecessary costs to the traffic of consumables. Perón made it clear that his government did not intend to eliminate private property altogether, and he argued that speculators were a minority of the otherwise respectable business community.[34] In political terms, it made sense not to alienate potential supporters among the countless traveling salesmen, kiosk and pushcart operators, and shopkeepers of Argentine society. Perhaps for this reason, officials did not resort to overt racial or ethnic stereotyping of the merchant community, a group in which immigrants were very visible. Law 12.830 did allow for the deportation of foreign lawbreakers, and there was a fine line between calls for economic nationalism and xenophobia. If ethnically motivated confrontations did occur, however, the media were careful to avoid reporting them in this manner; regulators apparently considered deporting convicted *agiotistas* (usurers) in a handful of cases but backed down.[35] Perón himself resisted engaging in anti-Semitic or anti-immigrant baiting in his proclamations against greedy merchants.

Yet the bellicose tone of the era's consumer politics tended to drown out measured justifications for regulation. Playing on the popular culture of their audiences, Peronist leaders focused on the insatiable avarice that propelled businesses to prey on laboring people and described the problem of containing inflation as a battle between good and evil. The religious overtones of Perón and Evita's statements (as in her references to the "sacred altar" of the home) highlighted the moralistic terms of the antispeculation campaigns. This rhetoric had a strong "gothic" quality, too, painting commercial exploitation as ghostlike, with the specter of speculation hiding in every corner of the marketplace and haunting the livelihoods of hardworking families.[36] This spectral quality explained why controls were needed in all areas of commerce: somewhere behind a closed door, a merchant or manufacturer was scheming up an "unspeakable machination" to squeeze another peso from the pueblo. Hundreds of laws and decrees spun a growing web that touched the most ordinary transactions. By the end of Perón's first term, regulations determined the prices of a haircut, a movie ticket, and a cup of coffee. Manufactured merchandise, such as ready-to-wear clothing, was required to carry price tags to assist shoppers in compliance. Federal price controls mandated that all food vendors, whether a neighborhood dive or a five-star restaurant, offer a special "economical menu" for their customers. This shift from satisfying basic material needs to indulging other commercial desires reflected the social reality of postwar Argentina. If state regulations struggled to keep pace with rising consumer aspirations, it was, Perón and Evita implied, partly because speculators lurked everywhere from the boardrooms of big business and downtown department stores to the modest barrio grocery.

The mechanisms for imposing order on the consumer marketplace shifted with each spike in prices. By around 1947, however, a basic procedure had been established. The Secretariat of Industry and Commerce published weekly lists of maximum prices along with the percentage markup businesses and manufacturers could charge at each stage of commercialization (e.g., a kilo of salt sold at eleven centavos wholesale and thirteen centavos retail).[37] The Federal Police and its provincial counterparts conducted inspections of businesses, either in response to tips from local residents or as part of regular patrols. If suspicions were raised, the inspectors would seize any evidence of illegal commerce and interview the manager or store owner, sometimes immediately hauling off the person to jail. New laws allowed the detention of a suspected speculator for up to ninety days without a trial. The case file (*sumario*) was eventually turned over to the Secretaría Técnica de la Presidencia for review; suspects had three days to inspect the file before the executive power issued a final judgment. The majority of arrests, deportations, and fines could not be appealed. Graver offences would be reconsidered only by the same executive power; in these situations, the matter came before a police magistrate, and the accused was allowed to bring in counsel.[38] In 1948 the president authorized the creation of the National Office of Price Surveillance (Dirección Nacional de Vigilancia de Precios), which handled citizen complaints and denunciations of merchants while coordinating action with other federal branches and provincial counterparts. The Office of Price Surveillance and the Federal Police conducted approximately 158,000 inspections between 1948 and 1949 (in a region boasting 90,000 commercial establishments). They imprisoned 12,900 suspects in metropolitan Buenos Aires, and provincial authorities held an additional 1,830 persons in custody. While not exactly the constant scrutiny promised in Peronist propaganda, the combination of intermittent inspections and detentions did not go unnoticed by either merchants or consumers.[39]

Certain fields of business activity attracted greater attention in the antispeculation campaigns. Authorities singled out wholesalers (*mayoristas*) as particularly dangerous. In accordance with the ideal of streamlining business through national planning, officials viewed the activity of these commercial intermediaries with distrust and targeted them as potential hoarders. In a 1951 petition presented to the government, a group of pasta wholesalers requested a raise in their profit level. The merchants expressed their loyalty to the regime, noting specifically that they had donated money to the Fundación Eva Perón in the past. Their request, however, was flatly rejected. In an internal note to their petition, government officials concluded that this type of intermediary merchant did "not constitute a fundamental stage in commercialization."[40] The rationalizing impulses of state planners, combined with the political necessity to moderate the cost of living, placed the intermediaries of Argentine commerce in a particularly untenable position. The Office of Price Surveillance also initiated legal proceedings against Argentine factory owners charged with similar crimes of hoarding and profiteering (as well as smaller infractions, including not labeling goods). In special cases, the penalties for those found guilty were steep: in 1947 Sudamtex, a prominent Argentine textile firm, was slapped with a 100,000-peso fine for engaging in monopolistic practices with several smaller firms and a U.S. corporation, while the owners of a rival business received ninety days in jail and penalties equivalent to a third of their total capital.[41] Most manufacturers eluded punishment, but the government extended both carrots (import-export permits, access to raw materials, and state loans) and sticks (fines and jail sentences) to keep them in line.

Notwithstanding promises to go after the kingpins of profiteering, the war on speculation fell on the shoulders of ordinary retailers (*minoristas*). The surviving records offer snapshots of enforcement suggesting that small shopkeepers made up the majority of accused profiteers. In February 1948, for example, authorities processed seventy cases involving a range of speculators, among them butchers, restaurant owners, fruit and vegetable vendors, and ice sellers.[42] The average example of speculation was mundane, as in the case of a butcher from Buenos Aires who received twenty days in jail for selling rump steak at two pesos a kilo when he should have charged ninety centavos.[43] In these cases, typical punishments included a couple hundred pesos in fines, business closures of five to ten days, and jail sentences of fifteen to thirty days (reserved for male merchants alone).

Roundups of alleged speculators occurred not only in working-class neighborhoods, however, but also in businesses located in wealthy districts of Buenos Aires. Fines for restaurants in upscale Barrio Norte that failed to offer an "economical menu" did little to improve the situation of the average consumer, who

FIGURE 5. Closure of the "Mercado Paris" store in a posh Buenos Aires district. *Archivo General de la Nación, Departamento de Fotografía, legajo 1307, envelope 6, doc. 188496 (n.d.); reproduced courtesy of the archive.*

lived and shopped in other parts of town. But such actions communicated the regime's commitment to standing up to commercial interests, even on the home turf of the affluent.

In surveying the consequences of enforcement campaigns, it is worth stressing that usury and speculation were not figments of the Peronist imagination. An untold number of businesses did indeed take advantage of strong demand to gouge consumers. Difficult as it is to separate fact from the layers of propagandizing in the Peronist-era press, newspaper reporters uncovered numerous schemes that reveal the trying conditions facing the average shopper. Inspections discovered rampant cases of hoarding, from everyday staple foods to gasoline and raw materials needed for manufacturing. Some wholesalers forced retail merchants to buy non–price-controlled products if they wanted to receive sugar, soap, and other goods in short supply. One of the more common forms of speculation involved rental housing. The combination of migration to the cities and urban rent freezes inspired some property owners to charge illegal "key fees" and engage in more elaborate subterfuge to avoid housing laws.[44] Likewise, smuggling rings secured access to imported luxuries and exported commodities abroad; in one case, police officers caught a group of Argentine businessmen sneaking shipments of flour intended for internal consumption into Brazil to evade price controls and reap higher profits.[45] In addition, wily merchants designed ways to turn regulations to their advantage. Among the most common schemes was the practice of so-called chain usury. In this deception, factory owners and distributors conspired to forge paperwork showing that an already finished good was sent to multiple businesses for "further elaboration" and thus could be marked up at each stage.

While never ignoring how these practices hurt consumers, these journalistic exposés expressed a grudging respect for the creative guile (*viveza*) behind these schemes. (It helped that antiestablishment cleverness was celebrated in Argentine popular culture, though not with uniform admiration, with viveza criolla extolled in tango lyrics, theater, and commercial film.) One magazine article distinguished between two types of speculators. There were the "clumsy," garden-variety ones— the butcher who pounded tough hunks of meat to disguise them as prime cuts or restaurant managers who added 15 percent to client bills to evade the new ban on tipping. Then there were those truly skilled in subterfuge, or as one journalist put it: "Those who know how to mock the law, who work it so that somebody else is always to blame, or who deflect responsibility for everything on that pan-pretext 'inflation.'" These clever merchants knew how to hide their tracks and showed no shortage of perverse ingenuity in devising schemes to swindle the gullible or needy. This latter category comprised cynical social types, such as one macabre "middle-man" who charged grieving families for "deluxe" funeral services but behind their backs paid the funeral home owner to perform meager "third-rate" burials and pocketed a tidy sum.[46]

Enticed by illicit trade, some business owners circumvented enforcement by securing the complicity of state officials. Although wary of painting the government in a bad light, the popular press occasionally reported on unsuccessful efforts to bribe inspectors, as in the case of one businessman who slipped a policeman a carton of cigarettes loaded with 10,000 pesos and told him with a smile, "Fume y que Dios lo ayude" (Smoke and may God help you). Probity won out in this episode, but the thicket of state regulation provided cover for hiding corruption. Some government officials used import permits and other regulatory controls to line their own pockets. Influence peddlers acted as third parties between these agents and customers, facilitating access to coveted or scarce goods in the nationalist economy of the New Argentina, whether a few thousand typewriters or a new Chevrolet.[47] By the early 1950s, there were rumors that officials in high places, including Evita's brother Juan Duarte, profited from the federal government's extensive management of business. (Duarte was found dead under somewhat mysterious circumstances in April 1953, a probable suicide, at a time of mounting rumors about his shady dealings involving the commercialization of meat.) Partisan investigations after the Peronist regime's 1955 overthrow levied numerous (if difficult to prove) accusations of corruption ranging from top ministers who stashed jewels in bank safety deposit boxes to elaborate schemes to avoid the regime's own economic regulations.[48] Less expectedly, these reports also suggest that Peronist authorities applied their own countermeasures to contain corruption. The head of the Office of Price Surveillance, Miguel Gamboa, was lauded by investigators for having rooted out officials suspected of taking bribes and shaking down storekeepers.[49]

Naturally, the risk of punishment made the business of speculation an ever-more lucrative enterprise for crooked merchants and bureaucrats alike. As state regulations grew, a wider swath of daily commercial activity became dominated by the black market (the *mercado negro,* or to use the period's more common term, *bolsa negra*). Various forms of illegal trading took place everywhere from street fairs to warehouses. For all the talk of commercial conspiracies (confirmed by actual cases of hoarding and smuggling rings), the black market encompassed mostly mundane transactions. One suspects that Peronist officials, those conducting inspections and economic policymakers alike, realized this fact: it was all too tempting for petty merchants to sell scarce goods at higher prices and all too easy for consumers to sidestep the law. What authorities could not ignore, however, was the political threat that the bolsa negra posed, for illegal trade implicitly questioned the regime's ultimate power. Like the agents behind other experiments in state planning, the Peronist government was determined to keep the bolsa negra contained for economic reasons as much as for political imperatives related to their vision of social organization.[50]

The actions of profit-hungry businesses and their collaborators contributed to the high prices and shortages that threatened popular households, and those accused of speculation, whether guilty or innocent, encountered a legal system that was stacked against them. Many detainees ended up in the new wings of Villa Devoto Prison, in the city of Buenos Aires. Fearing incarceration, some merchants and their families pleaded for mercy. Consider the case of Vicente Santos, a man who wrote to the government requesting clemency for a family member, the owner of "El Sol Argentino," an almacén in Buenos Aires. Although the specifics of the case are unclear, the shopkeeper was convicted of speculation. Santos argued that his relative came from an "honest family unwilling to disregard the decrees to obtain a higher profit" but that it was only "natural" for a business to charge a little more for the home delivery of purchases. Claiming that the family depended on the male shopkeeper for survival, this letter writer asked that his relative's sentence be lowered to a fine.[51] On rare occasions, such entreaties paid off. In 1948 one group of merchants imprisoned in Villa Devoto telegrammed a plea of clemency to Perón. Extolling his grandeur, the merchants solicited their release in order to celebrate the holiday on February 24, the anniversary of Perón's election. In the end, these twenty merchants succeeded in obtaining a pardon through this clever tactic, but most convicted speculators no doubt served out their sentences.[52]

Opponents of commercial regulation saw their material interests threatened, but also at stake were basic understandings of the boundaries between private and public authority. Regulation affronted the rights and social status of some property owners. For others, the problem was not state management per se but what they perceived as the chicanery of the war on speculation. In general, state-business relations under Peronist rule defy easy categorization, for property owners responded in multiple ways: allying with the regime, backing opposition parties, or perhaps most commonly, making the most of new opportunities but resisting the state's encroachment on day-to-day practices.[53] With the rules of commerce in flux, however, the differences between the usual truck and barter of business and the crime of speculation were far from clear. A September 1947 letter sent by the Argentine director of International Telephone and Telegraph to its U.S. headquarters described a "typical" encounter with a price inspector. The multinational's representative wrote that inspections were "carried on in the atmosphere of a raid on criminals" by shouting policemen, who threatened to detain merchants if they did not cooperate: "Virtually every large retail store and textile or clothing manufacturer is operating under a sword of Damocles, as it is almost impossible to do business without violating one or another of the many laws and regulations, and the police and inspectors have been raiding one place after another, apparently hoping to unearth some violation by big business that will really be worth publicizing."[54] The representative considered the inspections an invasion of a private commercial space, and troubled by the sudden unpredictability of doing business in Perón's Argentina, he felt that the partisan politics of price controls and nationalism had trumped the rule of law. The letter presented the inversion of older patterns of deference in a negative light: whereas political authorities usually afforded respect to entrepreneurial elites, in Argentina they treated businesspeople like criminal suspects inhabiting an underworld of outlaws.

Trade organizations voiced similar complaints. Argentine retailers advanced policy-oriented critiques of Peronist regulations, publishing their grievances either in the mainstream press or in specialized journals. They supported an alternative model of consumer society based on encouragement of the profit motive. The Cámara Argentina de Comerciantes (CAC), an advocate of laissez-faire liberalism, proposed the abolition of price controls in an open letter to Industry and Commerce Minister Ramón Cereijo. Lauding the social contributions of businesspersons, the "true 'pioneers' of civilization," the CAC contended that a reduction of controls on private industry would benefit consumers. The Cámara de Grandes Tiendas y Anexos, a Buenos Aires store owners' organization, made similar arguments in a letter to the Ministry of Technical Affairs. Only by liberating the "legitimate desire for reasonable profits" from restrictions, the group asserted, would the "tastes and desires of the consuming public" be satisfied fully. Other shopkeeper representatives maintained that greater freedoms of economic enterprise were necessary for achieving stable and sustainable levels of consumption.[55]

Rather than defend liberalism, some trade groups tried to persuade the government to moderate its methods toward building a just consumer society. In a 1950 treatise examining the impact of Peronist policies, the Confederación Económica Argentina (CEA, an organization representing small- and medium-sized businesses) illustrated the counterproductive effects of price controls and other regulations. To contest the government's claims that Argentine sellers were profit hungry and inefficient, their report argued that the local costs of commercialization were similar to those for businesses in the United States and Western European nations; it thus offered a return to the international, comparative definitions of modernity that preceded the inward nationalism of the Peronist era. The CEA asserted that loosening regulations and reducing business costs would lead to the greater production of goods. But this organization stressed that Perón's government should lend a hand and increase loans, tariffs, and tax breaks to nurture Argentine business. Free enterprise (*libre initiativa*), at least as understood by some trade groups, could coexist perfectly well with state probusiness interventions.[56] Trade organizations, as one might expect, painted a bleak picture of business conditions when discussing commercial controls. While acknowledging that total sales had risen, the CEA and other business lobbies noted that merchant profits had plummeted nearly 30 percent between 1946 and 1949.[57] Squeezed between rising labor and production costs and an inability to adjust prices, the CEA contended, businesses teetered at the edge of solvency.

Yet other sources tell a different story. The government's census findings indicate that between 1946 and 1954 the number of commercial establishments in Argentina grew by nearly 60 percent and that the proportion of small retail businesses increased from eleven to fifteen per thousand inhabitants. Statistics suggest a probable shift in the structure of commerce, with a proliferation of mom-and-pop stores in the suburbs of Buenos Aires and other areas of population and industrial growth. Major manufacturers of consumer goods weathered the economic ups and downs and saw their sales climb overall. The postwar years offered opportunities for entrepreneurs—at least those sufficiently skillful, lucky, or well connected—to profit from social transformations unleashed by the *revolución justicialista*.[58] Consumer demand was so great for radios and other electrical goods that it strained the resources of manufacturers. Most appliances consumed locally were domestically produced, a result of the ongoing process of industrialization. Manufacturers found themselves caught between mounting orders and the difficulties of expanding production with antiquated equipment, exhausted stocks, and higher labor costs. Some businesses capitalized on protectionist measures that reduced international competition and on the expansion in spending power, adopting measures that included designing publicity campaigns that delivered messages reflective of the era's politics. During the Sixty-Day Campaign, sly businesses reworked antispeculation slogans as part of their advertising endeavors. One group of retail merchants took out newspaper ads proclaiming, "We Cooperate with the Campaign for Lower Living Costs," and a clothing store announced, "And now . . . we are against inflation / Down with High Prices."[59] Even Argentina's leading manufacturer, SIAM Di Tella, launched an advertising campaign that asked customers for patience as they dealt with the spike in demand and bottlenecks in production. Mimicking the tones of Peronist planning, the company placed advertisements regarding its "Plan SIAM," declaring proudly that production had skyrocketed 600 percent from 1940 to 1950 and would continue to grow to meet the great demand for appliances: "More production, less cost. That is the Plan SIAM, the plan of the pueblo."[60]

In sorting out the fate of business under Peronist rule, it is important to distinguish between broad economic changes, often discernible only in hindsight, and the perspectives of contemporaries. While many entrepreneurs catering to popular sector consumers prospered in the postwar era, reactions to Peronist commercial policies varied by the field, region, and size of business, among other factors.[61] Taking the perspective of these critics for a moment, it is easy to see why the Peronist years were an unsettling time. Many businesspeople shared the ITT representative's opposition to the "intrusion" of the regulatory state into their factories and shops, and they bristled at Peronist attempts to paint business as the mortal enemy of consumers. Other entrepreneurs saw themselves under assault from ill-conceived campaigns to protect working-class interests at their expense.

At the very least, the war on speculation added to the vagaries of doing business: merchants were never certain how regulations might evolve, and the rules of the commercial game had seemingly changed, with established conventions giving way to new state controls that mandated what property holders could and could not do.

Business organizations were not alone in their criticisms of Peronist policies. At least before media censorship reached a crisis point in the late 1940s, the press echoed the chorus of complaints about intervention in private enterprise. Traditional bastions of liberalism, such as *La Nación* and *La Prensa,* maintained that commercial controls hampered business and would ultimately result in higher prices for consumers.[62] Journalists rejected the belligerent terms of Perón's war on speculation, which they felt provoked class antagonisms, and pointed to government spending as another main cause of climbing prices. Media outlets initially sympathetic to the antispeculation campaigns, such as the Catholic daily *El Pueblo,* also took issue with the continued encroachment of commercial regulations.[63] Opposition parties went a step further, lambasting Peronist antispeculation measures as a farce designed to whip up partisan support. In the aftermath of the 1946 elections, the Democratic Union broke apart into its respective partisan branches. The Radical Party remained the single largest force, with a foothold in Congress, but it was divided over the best way to oppose Peronism; in fact, more than a few of its members had defected to the other side, and so too had their supporters. Harassment and limitations on free speech plagued opposition groups. As a consequence, they referenced consumer matters within their broader criticisms of Peronist rule. Socialist activists, for instance, agreed that profiteering was a grave problem but stressed that state overspending was the driving factor behind escalating prices. By their calculations, living standards had remained largely unmoved and the "consumer masses" would pay dearly for Peronist "demagoguery and wastefulness" in the long term.[64]

Nonetheless, disgruntled business owners and political parties found little common ground for unified opposition, and fear of state reprisals thwarted other collective modes of resistance. As a result, antagonism toward Peronist commercial regulation never erupted into cohesive action, and resentment was typically confined to discussions in the back rooms of retail stores, company boardrooms, and party headquarters. By the same token, the guerra al agio itself remained within certain limits. Perón's government was neither willing nor able to regulate all business activity. It depended, as much by practical necessity as by ideological design, on Argentina's producers and businesses to provide the jobs, to manufacture the products, and to distribute the goods essential to creating a society of well-paid workers. Thus the enforcement of antispeculation policy was intermittent from the very start—and given the ubiquity of consumer transactions in midcentury Argentina, it could hardly have been otherwise. The ideal of a justly ordered marketplace remained more an aspiration than a lived reality for consumers, especially as shortages worsened and prices raced upward in the early 1950s.

The Cheese and the Rags

For all their incompleteness, the antispeculation campaigns did produce several political effects. State power now encompassed the minutia of everyday life and quotidian consumption. As that happened, the liberal emphasis on individual rights and property protections gave way to still amorphous Peronist notions of collective justice, national ordering, and mass mobilization. The patchiness of enforcement illustrates that planning remained at best an ideal. Behind the Peronist regime's self-image of centralized coordination was a great deal of improvisation. Keeping pace with Perón, Evita, and their propagandists became a burden for agencies entrusted with commercial regulation, among other duties. The story of mass consumption under Peronist rule is, above all, one of loosening constraints over popular spending and democratized access to the nation's commercial bounty. Yet it is also a history of swindles and scams, arrests and inspections, frustrations with untamed exchange and anxieties regarding the unpredictable application of legal punishments. Most inhabitants were caught in the middle of these countervailing trends, attempting to make sense of regulatory innovations while coming to terms with the realities of economic citizenship in postwar Argentina.

Just as the emphasis on planning belied the messy realities of regulation, the ideal of antispeculation as a state-led crusade oversimplified the era's consumer politics. In particular, the regime's cult of leadership obscured Peronism's decentralized features. Consumer campaigns were not simply top-down mobilizations, a rallying of the masses behind their supreme protector, for beyond state institutions lay a larger movement of supporters and sympathizers. There were undeniable constraints to the era's mass politics (not the least being the concentration of policymaking in the hands of a few). But within these limits, popular sector men and women made creative use of any openings to advance aims. Regulatory campaigns provided subaltern sectors with claims for assessing their standing as citizens and consumers, at times producing skirmishes within the Peronist ranks over the best way to impose justice on the marketplace. Working-class and neighborhood associations were spaces where individuals voiced demands, organized collectively, and exerted pressure to extend redistribution. Formal party institutions served a similar role in channeling discontent up the chain of command, if with less tolerance of overt dissent. Given their close identification with the Peronist cause and, in some cases, outright patronage relations with the state, these various groups do not always fit comfortably in the category of "civil society," which presumes a detachment from mass politics. Associations and mediating organizations nonetheless provided an outlet for seeking improvements in household living conditions—and for many loyalists, a sense of participation in the larger collective project of the Nueva Argentina.

Of all the organizations drawn into contact with the Peronist state, labor unions were the most visibly involved in the politics of purchasing. For government authorities, unions represented a valuable conduit for publicizing the antispeculation campaigns to working-class audiences. As a consequence of their long history of cost-of-living activism and increased clout during the mid-1940s, unions affiliated with the proregime Confederación General del Trabajo (CGT) facilitated a degree of worker coordination with state directives. The CGT requested that workers form local delegations to aid officials by staging rallies and spreading the word about regulations among their peers in factories and on farms. Union newspapers, including the railroad workers' *Obrero Ferroviario,* followed suit, asking the rank and file to lend a hand by denouncing greedy merchants—those "for whom there exists no homeland other than their money in the bank."[65] At the same time, unions enabled the rank and file to draw awareness to flaws in government regulation. Union lobbying identified numerous problems with antispeculation measures, among them the lack of enforcement of commercial controls outside the Buenos Aires region. As early as November 1946, a group representing several unions from Mendoza petitioned the federal government to assume responsibility for the provincial price inspection agency. Their letter claimed that local officials shirked their duties and thus jeopardized the population's well-being; as a remedy, the petitioners suggested, workers should be allowed to advise the provincial government on ways to lower the cost of living.[66]

In addition to navigating the internal channels of state bureaucracy, labor union members expressed demands for broader enforcement in open forums. Workers from Tucumán raised the issue of commercial controls at a provincial CGT congress in June 1948. Labor representatives approved a resolution calling for the appointment of new inspectors and deputizing workers to form a "union police" to inspect stores. The resolution singled out certain types—merchants, the provincial "oligarchy," and corrupt officials—who, rather than adhere to the "patriotic spirit of the laws and the efforts to humanize capital," imposed "their unlimited avarice and unequivocally exploit[ed] working people." While not all such demands were met, in this case union complaints for an expansion of antispeculation enforcement across the national territory produced immediate action: following the conference, the provincial government responded with a wave of well-publicized inspections and arrests.[67]

Other popular organizations sought to guide the war on speculation as well, and here, too, consumers walked the line between supporting government campaigns and complaining about inaction. During the peak of the postwar economic boom, delegations representing middle- and working-class neighborhood groups in Buenos Aires demanded that the government step up regulatory efforts. In 1946 residents of the industrializing suburb of Quilmes established a body they called the "Committee for Social Improvement" to denounce merchants and attract media attention to violations of price laws. This organizing occasionally succeeded in obliging officials to include community members on state commissions. Local chapters of the CGT received an endorsement from Domingo Mercante, the new governor of Buenos Aires, to mount a "campaign against the rising cost of living" staffed by a combination of worker representatives and municipal officials.[68] In other circumstances, entreaties aimed at bolstering antispeculation policy came from within local government. In November 1948 the head of the Peronist bloc in the Avellaneda town council petitioned the Ministry of Technical Affairs for help with enforcement. Officials lamented their lack of updated information on price control levels and the difficulties of dealing with consumer problems. Despite their inexperience, they were as committed as ever to waging the war but needed federal assistance: "We make this request in light of the excessive abuse of certain unscrupulous merchants, who day after day increase the cost of articles of prime necessity, with the resulting harm to the consumer." The lobbying appears to have paid off in this case as well, for the Federal Police launched a series of store inspections in the city.[69]

Civil actors were not always content with lobbying for stricter price controls. Unions in particular frequently called for wage increases to match the rising cost of living. The Perón administration typically backed labor allies once strikes had begun, but it opposed claims for better contracts on occasion (in part to address economic planners' concerns with inflation). In a few especially intense confrontations, state authorities replaced or imprisoned recalcitrant labor leaders, as in the

1948 longshoremen and 1949 sugar worker strikes. Miranda and other top officials turned to the press to warn the public of the dangers posed by militant strikers. During a showdown with sugar workers in Tucumán, Miranda argued that work was a patriotic duty, insisting that "workers must comprehend that to consume it is necessary to produce without egoism and with a fundamental sense of national solidarity, which will bring benefits to them as well." At a 1947 conference of labor leaders, Perón instructed unions not to ask for levels of "remuneration outside the realm of the possible." The pro-Peronist press and union newspapers carried articles linking productivity and living standards, including transcripts of speeches by the popular Eva Perón with such blunt titles as "Social Justice Is Consolidated with Greater Production."[70]

Despite frustrations with lax enforcement, consumer politics brought Peronist sympathizers together around their mutual dismay with unethical exchange. Even as unionists pushed for a greater share, the overwhelming majority did so within the political idiom of Peronist reformism instead of calling for a radical overthrow of property rights. The overall decline in strikes during the late 1940s undoubtedly indicates the state's influence over the CGT and individual unions, but it also reflects the basic fact that many of labor's longstanding demands had been met. Worker organizations succeeded, more often than not, in winning the government to their side. Nevertheless, worries over spiraling inflation renewed preoccupations among Peronist authorities seeking to manage a productive national workforce. During the 1940s economic advisers were content to urge caution and stopped short of imposing austerity on working families or mandating greater productivity. As the regime's leadership saw it, the war on speculation could help direct organized labor away from the bargaining table and toward the marketplace, where they were supposedly allies in combating the evils of usurious merchants.

While Peronist consumer politics revolved around the negotiations between state and civil associations, another major area of activity concerned defining the duties of citizen consumers. As officials faced demands for enforcement, they sought to incorporate individuals within new partisan organizations outside the traditional centers of cost-of-living activism. Women were considered crucial in the fight against unjust commerce, a connection that Peronism shared with other twentieth-century political drives to mobilize consumers.[71] To be sure, state authorities avoided presenting consumption as an entirely female sphere of influence; all Argentines, whatever their gender, age, or occupation, could serve as soldiers in the battle against profiteering. Nevertheless, officials saw female consumers as particularly well suited to the task of ensuring compliance with regulations. In general, Perón and his advisers conceived of women as an underused resource. They sought to win female Argentines over to their side through social and political reforms that highlighted their importance—most notably, the extension of voting rights in 1947.[72] By speaking concretely about the travails of everyday life, the regime's leaders encouraged female collaboration with state initiatives outside the established domain of electoral politics. In accordance with prevailing cultural norms, the government assumed that women commanded the family purse strings and shouldered the main responsibility for provisioning. Implicit in this view was an acknowledgment of the creative element involved in burdensome routines of household upkeep—the art of stretching pennies, haggling with merchants, and canvassing the marketplace for the right product at the right price. Women buyers had experience in judging the value and quality of goods, practical skills that economic planners and propagandists hoped to steer toward political ends.

Eva Perón took the lead in accentuating the special spiritual and moral authority of women. Her approach at once contested and reinforced conventional patriarchal relations: women were presented as politically equal to men but still relegated to a place as supporters and nurturers. Regarding household consumption, they could assert a combative yet dutiful role by working within their sphere of influence, coping with shortages, respecting official prices, taking note of changing policies, and denouncing lawbreakers.[73] It was hoped that they would also exert influence over male breadwinners at home. During the Sixty-Day Campaign, the First Lady instructed her audience: "We must realize that our physical strength extends to where a man's extends; for that reason, we are their mothers, their wives, their girlfriends. There, in the place of struggle, beside the man, that is our place." Although Peronistas did not ignore the fact that women worked for wages outside the home, they deemphasized it in favor of an idealized division of labor between the male provider and female housewife. According to Evita, Peronist rule would allow women to dedicate themselves with greater rigor and commitment to managing the household economy and the needs of the nuclear family. The modernization of patriarchy in this case had an explicitly mass-political dimension.[74] Women would become more complete citizens by participating in public life under the tutelage of the Perón regime and by complementing their primary domestic role.

As Eva Perón gained prominence within the administration, so too did efforts to organize women as political actors. In 1949 Evita founded the Partido Peronista Femenino (PPF) to spearhead the integration of women into the movement. She selected a group of female assistants, known as *censistas* (census takers), who went door to door in communities across the country to enroll women in the PPF and encourage them to vote for Perón's reelection. (The call for censistas appealed to "Argentine-born women, foreigners, and sympathizers of the Peronist Movement" to create as broad a base as possible, including resident immigrants.)[75] Neighborhood-level organizations known as *unidades básicas* (literally, basic or base units), a name inspired by that for "military units," acted as mechanisms to attract new followers, shape a common partisan identity, and mobilize loyalists within the vertical structure of the party. The Peronist regime saw women as particularly valuable allies but also ones in need of special attention given their status as new voters; this attitude explains why the unidades were strictly divided into male and female branches (the latter under the command of Evita and the PPF) and why male organizations retained a greater degree of autonomy in selecting their leadership and policy. Both branches shared an overall purpose, one that authorities defined in opposition to the infamous local "committees" of earlier political parties: "What were once breading grounds of vice, we will convert into schools of virtue. For this reason, we speak of Peronist cultural centers that will educate citizens, inculcate virtue, and teach useful things."[76] If the official estimates are reliable, by 1951 alone there were 3,600 female unidades distributed across the entire country, with the highest concentration in the Litoral.[77]

According to Celina Martínez de Paiva, a censista in Mendoza and Buenos Aires, Evita envisioned the female unidades básicas as more than just a way to register voters. They were designed as "second family homes" for women, combining female domestic responsibilities with the duties of loyal partisans; mothers, for instance, were welcome to bring their children, a policy designed to facilitate greater participation.[78] These spheres of female activism were tasked with the responsibility of "*capacitación*" (preparation or qualification), which Evita and other leaders defined as educating women in the practical skills necessary for fulfilling their "natural" role as citizens in the New Argentina. Unidades offered local women classes in subjects ranging from literacy and civics to cooking, first aid, and housekeeping (as well as lighter fare, such as music and folk dancing). Organizations were required to teach skills, such as sewing, deemed necessary for proper domesticity and family respectability (the classes' apparent popularity among members was due in part to their applicability to wage-earning piecework). Unidades básicas not only provided women with the skills to produce clothing and other consumables but also spread word about antispeculation efforts and promoted cooperation with surveillance of the marketplace.

As Peronist authorities rallied allies inside and outside formal party structures, consumers displayed enthusiasm for the promise of just commerce in more spon-

FIGURE 6. The aftermath of a raid on the store La Defensa, a few blocks south of the presidential palace; the merchant had been detained for hoarding bars of soap, which were immediately sold to the consumers crowding the shop. *Archivo General de la Nación, Departamento Fotográficos, box 1307, envelope 4, doc. 172881 (May 9, 1947); reproduced courtesy of the archive.*

taneous ways. Consider a series of stories, published in the newspaper *Noticias Gráficas*, about the barrio of San Cristobal in Buenos Aires. In May 1947 government inspectors had punished a local merchant, Alí Kichquie, for attempting to bribe a police officer and for stockpiling a scarce though presumably mundane household good—*trapos de piso* (floor-cleaning rags). Fearing similar consequences, stores in this popular district lowered prices on their products, causing neighbors to form long lines outside stores in search of coveted items. By challenging the authority of local merchants, the government inspections fostered a triumphant mood. Women residents congregated outside stores and, with smiling faces, held aloft the rags like victory flags. The newspaper evoked the Peronist leadership's militaristic rhetoric in explaining the joyfulness of female shoppers, proclaiming that the "battlefield has been left seeded with adversaries." The caption to one photograph read, "the struggle is hard, but the prize, a floor rag, justifies it."[79] Press coverage was instrumental to broadcasting scenes of antispeculation policies in action to national audiences and imbuing the microlevel struggles of consumers with political meaning; progovernment newspapers published frequent lists of merchants arrested and fined for violating price controls. Official efforts to fix the significance of these events ought not be discounted, but the incident in San Cristobal points to the groundswell of approval for the antispeculation campaigns. Little victories scored against local merchants, while seemingly trivial, reinforced ethical worldviews. On occasion they fostered fleeting celebrations among *amas de casa* (housewives) entrusted with household upkeep in a time of mounting shortages.

Such scenes were repeated thousands of times, converting ordinary citizens walking down the street into actors and audiences of a Peronist morality play. Indeed, the enforcement of antispeculation measures in the 1940s and early 1950s was an explicitly public activity. Police inspections of stores were rituals that allowed officials to translate the rhetoric of commercial justice into sidewalk spectacles. During raids of commercial establishments, agents searched through stores, and if evidence of malfeasance was found, they tacked up signs proclaiming "*Clausurado*" (closed) over the doorways. As they carted speculators off to headquarters, crowds of local residents assembled. Newspaper photographs capture these tense moments: curious passersby and neighbors gathered on streets to watch the commotion, the people in the back craning their necks to get a look at the "usurer."[80] Some images bear the marks of journalists or state propagandists, who posed audiences to maximize the political message of state-consumer cooperation. Wearing expressions that ranged from uneasiness to elation, residents witnessed the power of the Peronist state in action.

References to antispeculation campaigns and consumer expectations appeared in other mass-cultural settings, too, including the commercial cinema and other perhaps unexpected places. The feature film *Arrabalera* (1950) tells the melodramatic story of Felisa (played by Tita Merelo, one of Argentina's most famous actresses), who overcomes an abusive boyfriend to find happiness with her son and new husband. In one scene Felisa goes to a street market to buy ingredients for a *carbonada* (a traditional stew) that her husband requested for dinner. Walking through the market, she wrangles with stall owners over prices and makes comical remarks about the quality of their goods. Eventually she comes across a vegetable stall and sighs with relief because the price of potatoes has fallen. But the merchant quickly flips over the sign, almost doubling the cost, and in a heavy Italian accent explains, "No signora, it's only that the inspector just passed by." Felisa remarks, "Nice example of a usurer" and berates him about his "gold-plated" produce. At this point, the film returns to its main storyline, but the scene draws attention to essential features of consumption in this period. Confrontations between female shoppers and male merchants were daily routines in an age before standardized prices and supermarkets. The episode was meant to entertain movie audiences by turning the tables on the usual gender and class norms, showing how a feisty heroine let an immigrant businessman have a piece of her mind and in the process representing audience members' own frustrations with high prices and "unscrupulous" practices.

Intentionally or not, *Arrabalera* reinforced tropes common to Peronist propaganda through its choice of language, social stereotypes, and gendered depiction of the marketplace. While the film implies that speculation controls were ineffective, and thus differs from state propaganda, it nevertheless underscores the fundamental moral assumptions of just consumption.[81] As these representations reveal, there was more at stake in consumer campaigns than price levels. The public rituals of the war on speculation challenged expectations of social deference, above all, the conventional balance of power between shopkeeper and customer. They allowed subalterns to vent their dissatisfaction, celebrate their standing in the New Argentina, and in cooperation with the government, score victories against the forces of immorality and greed. Overblown as some reports were, the mass media supplied discourses and images for thinking about state power in everyday life. These representations, combined with the ceremony of inspections, sought to convince popular audiences that daily purchasing was indeed a political act. Newspaper reports illustrated how even a cleaning rag could take on significance as an example of Peronist social justice in action.

Perón's regime wanted popular Argentines to perceive market relations within this ideological framework and deployed the notable resources at their disposal to mold opinion. But the question remains: how successful were officials in shaping the outlook of their audience? Gauging public reactions to state initiatives is a fraught task, but the available evidence clearly shows that the quest to domesticate markets provoked positive reactions among popular consumers, although not uniformly so. Letters sent to government agencies offer rare glimpses into the ways individuals grappled with consumption and citizenship in Perón's Argentina. Salvador Rodríguez García, a man from the city of Rosario, wrote to the Ministry of Technical Affairs in 1947 suggesting that the government create an organization to look into the causes of the rising cost of living, which he felt were clear examples of "extortionist piracy." For Rodríguez García, commercial practices had an undeniable partisan dimension. Those responsible for high prices were "inspired not only by unspeakable yearnings for lucre but also by the deliberate objective of disparaging the 'real and evident Social Justice in progress,' supporting themselves with unspecific theories about 'inflation,' 'devaluation of the currency,' etc."[82] Rodríguez García's letter illustrates how a Peronist vision of extortionists' machinations made greater sense to his experiences as a consumer than classical economic theory did. He expressed a political narrative similar to that advanced by the leadership, depicting in typically populist terms a struggle between a greedy elite and an honest people. Whether this echoing was an example of propaganda's direct influence, a tactic to curry favor with policymakers, or an overlapping of moral worldviews is uncertain, but the commonality suggests the resonance of Peronist antispeculation policies with cultural understandings of ethical exchange.

Other letter writers concentrated on denouncing specific violations of the law, a move that dramatized the lack of effective enforcement. Supporters may have smiled in official photographs of price inspections, but in the more intimate setting of their letters to political authorities, they vented their anger at merchant practices. During the Sixty-Day Campaign, one letter writer grumbled that merchants stocked only limited supplies of price-controlled goods; when these were gone, they offered more expensive, unregulated items. If one asked the local cheese seller for price-controlled goods, the petitioner wrote, he offered a chunk of dried-out cheese ("*un trozo reseco*") and, what's worse, sneered while taunting, "Here, you want some of this Perón cheese."[83] The average consumer was thus forced to choose between expensive and second-rate goods, not to mention endure the jibes of insolent retailers. In this case, a prosaic object epitomized merchant resistance to commercial regulations. If floor rags could become victory flags under certain conditions, a hunk of cheese offered a reminder that the war on speculation had not yet made its presence felt in the lives of many citizens.

By linking Argentina's powerful president to a humble staple, the phrase "Perón cheese" indicated the growing presence of mass politics in quotidian life. The cheese and the rags are emblematic of the range of popular attitudes toward consumption, highlighting the extremes of frustration and enthusiasm that accompanied interventions in the marketplace. Ordinary consumer goods became a reflection both of economic threats to spending power and of the inroads made by authorities in molding the perceptions of consumers. The Peronist leadership's vision of moral commerce provided a goal to strive after, and even when conditions in the street did not match the official rhetoric, men and women looked to political authorities for protection against entrenched commercial interests. Nonetheless, expressions of sympathy and excitement—for example, those displayed by crowds gathered outside stores under inspection—do not mean that consumers played the roles of dutiful loyalists as scripted by party operatives. Through varied institutional means (labor unions, local organizations, and unidades básicas) and modes of communication (from the press to letter writing), sympathizers called attention

to the incompleteness of the New Argentina. Without reje[...]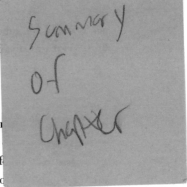
commerce, they made clear that living standards remained f[...]
geared to the imperatives of getting and spending.

❦

According to a familiar historical narrative, the advance of [...]
the postwar world led to political quiescence, the decline [...]
ments, and a retreat from collective engagement to a narrow f[...]
ests. Clearly, this story falls short as an accurate description [...]
if not much of the midcentury world. As with the celebrated examples of the
United States and Western Europe, Peronist Argentina illustrates how historical
actors defined a new political role for the citizen consumer. Yet the Peronist case
stands out by virtue of its particularly acute polarization of public life—and in particular, an escalation of partisan tensions that mapped onto class identities and
populist distinctions. The marketplace became an arena of bitter contention under Peronist rule, as state-led campaigns staked out a presence in everyday routines of acquisition. Commercial practices that undercut purchasing power took
on significance as a threat to the Peronist vida digna and thus to the authority of
the leaders as benefactors and national planners. Antispeculation measures were
designed not only to safeguard redistribution but also, and more important, to
strengthen bonds of solidarity among leaders and supporters. That the guerra al
agio elicited such intense social reactions among irate property holders as well as
working people clamoring for better enforcement indicates the depth of feeling
stirred by Peronism's ethics of exchange.

   This polarization cannot be attributed solely to the forcefulness of the state's
regulatory interventions. Other governments flexed their power over private property more comprehensively. Peronist authorities stopped well short of socialist experiments meant to eradicate profit-driven enterprise in the pursuit of a workers'
utopia, even if they displayed a comparable obsession with hidden commercial
enemies (and with the similar consequence of turning markets into a space of resistance against state strictures). Even the regulatory initiatives of the United States
and other advanced capitalist countries were more far-ranging in their application:
for instance, the Dirección Nacional de Vigilancia de Precios never attained the
managerial capacity of the U.S. Office of Price Administration. By comparison, the
war on speculation was always characterized by its incompleteness, by the gap
between its promise and its practical impact. Antispeculation was therefore many
things at once: a set of policies to restrain the cost of living, a mechanism for

organizing supporters and shaping public opinion, a weapon to intimidate property holders, an assertion of cultural norms about economic fairness, and a political spectacle complete with populist displays of power in the streets. These competing elements made Peronist consumer politics inherently unstable. At times, it seemed that Perón, Evita, and others in the government were flirting with disaster, raising expectations that their agents could not fulfill. By emphasizing the state's ability to deliver real improvements, the administration opened itself to persistent grassroots demands for action. Attempts to match redistribution with regulation created laws that were virtually impossible for merchants to meet fully, let alone for officials to implement consistently (when this was truly their intention). Notwithstanding the emphasis on national order, the Peronist variant of consumer citizenship proved remarkably contentious.

And yet Peronist consumer politics must not be viewed as purely repressive, for its protagonists also articulated desires for inclusion within a market-driven society. Antispeculation policy stressed the punishment of merchant villains but also the preservation a certain type of consumer society, one characterized by a growing demand for domestically produced wares, the satisfaction of essential needs, and inclusion in a commercialized mainstream. Despite the obstacles, working-class sectors did gain access to greater consumer abundance. If the contradictions of antispeculation generated instability, the dual nature of its commercial critique also reveals the key to its allure. In exchange for labor, citizens would, in theory, attain a "dignified" level of material comfort under the planning state's protection— although from the vantage of officials, higher spending power also necessitated increases in workforce productivity. Antispeculation ideals interconnected the spheres of work, home, and the marketplace in ways that went beyond liberalism. The household became an area where one could contribute to the Peronist cause, and the regime's top leaders outlined a political role for women as voters, party members, and housewives. To be sure, the gendered assumptions in this division between male breadwinner and female household manager were constricting, and popular participation ran up against the regime's emphasis on mobilization. But the war on speculation shifted the focus of politics in new directions, above all, by linking ideas of national progress to everyday material struggles and consumer aspirations. The matters addressed were undoubtedly mundane: the price a butcher could charge for a cut of beef, the profit margin on a square of cloth, the cost of a movie ticket or a meal in a restaurant. The ordinariness of these concerns represented an easily overlooked virtue, for it lent concreteness, a prosaic familiarity, to the more abstract ideals of Peronist social justice.

4
NEEDS, WANTS, AND COMFORTS

BY ASSIGNING new political meanings to ordinary purchasing acts, Peronist campaigns illuminated the material aspirations of working households. There was much more, however, to the pursuit of the vida digna than buying plentiful wares in a regulated marketplace. State intervention was necessary in other areas where the play of capitalist forces failed to provide for the citizenry's well-being. Beginning in the early 1940s, authorities responded by extending social services on a scale never before seen in Argentina. Perón's administration presented itself much like other "welfare states" of the era: as an agent defending the common weal against overextended market forces and lessening catastrophic risks. It was no secret that such programs aimed to enhance the regime's standing, for propagandists blanketed Argentina with images of benefactors hard at work. Among these depictions was a 1949 newsreel titled *Señalando rumbos* (pointing the way), which offered a tour of housing projects being built by the Ministry of Public Works.[1] The film's narrator extolled the agency's accomplishments as the camera provided aerial views of the planned barrios being built outside the capital city. Public housing projects were spaces, it seemed, far removed from the pressures of buying and selling.

Yet these projects, like Peronist welfare initiatives more generally, were not completely beyond the orbit of the marketplace. *Señalando rumbos* lingered over one Buenos Aires neighborhood in particular, Barrio Presidente Perón, which consisted mainly of detached, single-family houses built in the "California style" (a trendy adaptation of Spanish neocolonial architecture complete with barrel-tiled roofs and whitewashed exteriors). Cared for by the state in their fashionable homes, smiling residents were dressed "respectably" according to the dominant conventions of the day—adult men in coats and ties, women in elegant patterned dresses, children in new outfits—and shown pleasurably eating meals and entertaining visitors. In contrast to most Argentines, who confronted messy familial relations and tight domestic spaces, the barrio's inhabitants enjoyed a "spacious and comfortable" life. Each family member fulfilled a crisply demarcated role, from the male breadwinner returning from work to the female homemaker attending to her children. The homes had clearly defined areas as well, a conjunction of gendered spaces each of which showcased dimensions of household consumption: separate bedrooms for adults and children, complete with new furniture; a living room perfectly appointed for listening to the radio and socializing; and a modern kitchen with the latest appliances for the housewife. One family profiled in the film even had a gas stove and electric refrigerator, items that remained beyond the means of most working-class consumers.[2] As a finale to this pageant, the film closed in on a framed portrait of Perón that hung above their living-room mantle, making it all too clear to whom the bounty was owed.

This vignette of the well-attired family in the *chalet californiano* was so frequently repeated by propagandists that it remains a familiar symbol of the era. Among historians it has, in fact, become something of a visual shorthand for the Peronist model of social justice.[3] But the idealized family can serve another purpose in the history of consumption, for it offers a starting point to probe the unexpected points of contact between the marketplace and justicialista experiments in social welfare. As revealed in *Señalando rumbos,* the Perón regime's interventions were freighted with multiple meanings. On the one hand, officials intended state assistance to remove "at-risk" populations from cramped, unhealthy housing and provide an alternative to an urban real estate market driven recklessly by the profit motive. On the other hand, as suggested by the newsreel, officials also defined uplift in terms of access to consumables supplied typically through market channels and, more broadly, as a "lifestyle" based on mainstream consumer practices, conventional judgments of taste, and patterns of sociability associated with the middle class. As part of social services, Peronist agencies distributed millions of consumer goods—clothing, toys, foodstuffs, and most famously, sewing machines—directly to the populace through channels that bypassed markets. The regime thus positioned itself as a nonmarket means for pursuing a range of aspirations related to household consumption, from the relief of pressing needs to the satisfaction of a higher order of material wants and commercialized comforts.

Social assistance constituted another example of the Peronist double movement in redefining modern citizenship, one that complemented the similar thrust of consumer politics. Programs identified and critiqued the failings of Argentine capitalism while at the same time widening the citizenry's access to the commercial bounty of the economy. In particular, officials emphasized the virtues of collective consumption—public works, housing, tourism and leisure programs, and other services—as a means of bettering the daily living conditions of laboring Argentines and pulling the poor back from the abyss of indigence. We need not survey the social programs erected during the first Peronist presidency, many of which have received detailed historical treatment in their own right.[4] It will be worthwhile, however, to trace one feature throughout this constellation of experiments: the intermingling of commercial and nonmarket forms of consumption in Peronist assistance networks.

In this sense, one must leave behind the commercial marketplace to fully understand the place of household consumption in Peronist conceptions of citizenship. For skeptics, a film such as *Señalando rumbos* can be dismissed as something cooked up by propagandists. Yet fantasy—or what could less pejoratively be called the political imaginary—was absolutely essential for authorities who sought to mediate popular aspirations for a better life and mobilize the citizenry. Moreover, visual propaganda was but one practice that bridged the worlds of commercial and nonmarket consumption. The Peronist double movement was further manifested in architectural choices, the institutional mechanisms for distributing relief, and the political relationships of patronage. In addition, beyond questions of design and technique, the manner in which aid recipients engaged with providers is revealing. By looking at previously unexamined sources (including a cache of letters to Eva Perón), we can gain insights into the popular tactics employed to obtain dignified living standards. These interactions get us closer to understanding not only how officials hoped their subjects would "consume" social assistance but also how individual citizens assigned meaning to Peronist interventions intended to satisfy collective needs, wants, and comforts.

Freedom and Order

Peronist programs were part of a global trend toward expanded welfare services in the midcentury era. As in other countries, social spending in Argentina was accompanied by new collective rights and entitlements as well as greater state command over the national territory and populace (that is, an increase in the capacity of "governmentality").[5] Like their reformist predecessors, Peronist agents were attuned to the transnational flows of social politics and sought inspiration from experiments abroad. Yet justicialista welfare had its distinctive features as well. Most notably, this was a "welfare state" in which the central government was not the sole or often main provider of relief. Labor unions and ostensibly private organizations, such as the Eva Perón Foundation (the Fundación Eva Perón, or FEP), assumed tasks performed by public agencies elsewhere in the world. At the same time, however, these nonstate institutions were so financially and politically interwoven with Perón's administration as to defy their categorization as part of civil society. For these reasons, we might be best served by using the terminology employed by Perón and his followers: namely, "*asistencia social.*" Without ignoring the power relations implicit in delivering assistance, this phrase showcases the redemptive ambitions of Peronist campaigns to elevate standards. In the words of one Peronist pamphlet, these interventions were not intended as "charity," "alms-giving," or "temporary aid to the needy" but rather imagined more grandly as "all that serves to help man recuperate his place in society."[6]

Contrary to these assertions, however, social assistance was built on an existing patchwork of government institutions and philanthropic organizations, many of which targeted women and children, not men.[7] The philanthropic organizations typically operated as religious charities and ethnic aid societies that relied on a mix of private contributions and periodic federal subsidies to run orphanages and other facilities. Unlike programs attached to state bureaucracies, their day-to-day activities were managed largely by middle- and upper-class women, creating an important female sphere of activism. Nevertheless, these disparate programs faced chronic limitations; by the 1930s charities were under fire from those seeking a more coherent state-based system of provision. The June Revolution military government and Perón's administration expanded command over social policy while phasing out subsidies for philanthropic groups (the largest such group, the Sociedad de Beneficiencia, was directly incorporated into federal agencies). In carrying out this reorganization, Peronist leaders contrasted their approach with the miserliness of state spending in the past and the haughtiness of charitable giving. Under the surface, however, old patterns remained. The federal government continued to subsidize private organizations, especially among its new allies in organized labor. Meanwhile, the Eva Perón Foundation stepped into areas of social relief occupied by philanthropies, much to the consternation of certain state officials.

Perón's administration went much further than its predecessors in terms of the sheer quantity and quality of services offered. As part of the Five-Year Plan, the

Ministries of Public Health and Public Works unleashed a wave of social infrastructure construction. Statistics marshaled in official reports give a sense of the scope of these accomplishments: between 1946 and 1952 the number of hospital beds nearly doubled, growing from 66,000 to 115,000; agencies built or funded an estimated 100,000 new units, exceeding the total public housing from the preceding fifty years.[8] Federal officials also funded scores of new hotels, vacation complexes, and recreational facilities (swimming pools, parks, and reclaimed beaches) as part of popular tourism and leisure programs.[9] Provincial and municipal agencies followed suit, and in Buenos Aires, both city and province, local governments rivaled federal accomplishments.[10] As the reach of bureaucratic institutions radiated outward, new facilities dotted the landscape, and an untold number of Argentines were brought into assistance networks.

State officials had to contend with other players within the Peronist movement. Union programs (obra social) supplemented government initiatives, and swelling membership rolls enabled CGT-affiliated unions to vastly increase the range of services they provided for their members. Thanks as well to government patronage (via loans and land grants), labor organizations built their own health clinics and hospitals, founded small-scale housing projects, and offered home loans to members. Larger unions with preexisting programs, such as the Unión Ferroviaria, amassed a wide array of obra social, including hotels that catered to the leisure needs of working-class members. Most organizations emulated these social services on a more modest scale.[11] Despite the close ties, unions and the state did not always see eye to eye. Labor helped defeat the plans by the Ministry of Public Health and others to create a "universal" system of social insurance. Unions favored instead an expansion of the existing retirement accounts (the *cajas de jubilación*), which gave their managers greater control over resources. Significant modifications to the existing caja system ultimately trumped universalist proposals, and membership in the invigorated cajas soared from 500,000 persons in 1943 to 4.7 million by 1954.[12] What remained was effectively a version of workers' insurance, and benefits flowed through the predominantly male wage earner to his "dependents," further realizing ideals of modernized patriarchy.

Despite these ambitious programs, the Fundación Eva Perón attracted the most acclaim on the social front. By the early 1950s, this "private" foundation rivaled federal agencies as the main force in administrating new health-care, tourism, and public housing facilities. The foundation rose swiftly from modest roots. After Perón's election in 1946, Evita branched out from her advisory role at the Labor Secretariat to pursue her own brand of charitable giving. She distributed a variety of wares—food, clothing, toys, and Christmas gifts of cider and cakes—in person and through the mail. With Atilio Renzi, the presidential residence's steward, initially participating, these informal efforts culminated in the creation of the "Social Aid Foundation María Eva Duarte de Perón" in June 1948 (later abbreviated to the Eva Perón Foundation). The FEP intensified its activities each year, growing from an original staff of two to an organization that by 1954 had around 25,000 employees and a budget exceeding those of some federal institutions.[13]

The FEP pursued assistance in broad terms. Between 1948 and 1955, it operated approximately thirty-five hospitals and specialized medical centers across Argentina, and it also managed housing and vacation complexes.[14] In 1949 the federal government granted the FEP authority to process requests for old-age pensions from individuals who did not belong to the existing retirement system. The foundation inaugurated a half-dozen or so Hogares de Ancianos (homes for the elderly) and constructed fifteen "hogares-escuelas" for indigent children that offered access to public education as well as a battery of health and recreation services.[15] But the FEP is best remembered for its so-called direct social action (acción social directa). As her foundation grew in size and financial capacity, Evita expanded her early campaigns to distribute household goods, food, and other material aid to the poor. During most afternoons Evita would spend hours at the foundation's headquarters presiding over such efforts. With lines stretching outside her office, Evita heard personal stories and dispensed immediate relief, giving one supplicant money, securing scarce medicines for another, or placing individuals in public housing apartments. The quantities involved were staggering: according to its own estimates, the foundation distributed over 2.7 million items of aid (clothing, food, medicine, etc.), 4 to 5 million toys, and a half-million sewing machines *each year* for a population of some 16 million persons.[16] The FEP's scant records prevent knowing how many passed through its tourism complexes and hospitals, but these facilities likely welcomed tens of thousands every year. The consolidation of the FEP as the regime's central provider ensured that millions of Argentines came into contact, in one way or another, with social services, material aid, and new consumer wares.

Through each of these modes of assistance, Peronist officials extended an impressive web of protections and benefits. Still, this "system" operated with a considerable degree of disorganization, perhaps an inevitable consequence of the number of agencies involved, the frenetic pace at which they advanced, and the bureaucratic competitions among them.[17] Union workers were among the principal beneficiaries; other sectors of the population (professionals, farmers, merchants,

FIGURE 7. The stacks of dolls at this Fundación Eva Perón warehouse carried a potent message: like better-off children, the daughters of the poor and needy, too, deserved new, factory-made toys. *Archivo General de la Nación, Departamento Fotográficos, Subsecretara de Informaciones, C-11, doc. 243975 (n.d.); reproduced courtesy of the archive.*

and the self-employed) were only partially covered. Funding reflected this patch-work character, for it came from competing sources. Government revenues from taxes and employer contributions to the cajas de jubilación were fundamental. Congressional allocations of expropriated property, revenue from state lotteries and casinos, and contributions from business owners supplemented the budget of Evita's ostensibly private foundation. Argentine wage earners themselves paid a large share. Evita's organization depended on union donations, and workers were required to offer the FEP a percentage of new wage contracts and full pay on the Peronist holidays of May 1 and October 17.[18] New labor regulations allowed unions to deduct dues from paychecks automatically, the proceeds filling coffers for obra social.[19] These transfers had mixed consequences for popular consumption. Programs loosened spending restrictions for some working families, because income previously devoted to buying housing, health care, and leisure services could be used to increase consumer purchasing (or savings and investments). Social assistance contributed to greater security, but paycheck deductions also cut into the spending power of wage earners, which added to the pressure of rising living costs.

From the perspective of state leaders, however, collective consumption presented a number of advantages over individual commercial spending. Welfare programs fit within the conception of the planning state as a tool of socioeconomic ordering. When compared to the unpredictable race between wage increases and the inflationary marketplace, social spending posed less of a threat to the balance of payments and could be more readily controlled by policymakers (at least in theory). One might argue about erosions in consumer spending power, but it was hard to deny a new hospital or tourism facility. Still, Peronist authorities carefully avoided presenting consumer spending and collective consumption as an either/ or choice. Instead, they allowed the provision of services to enhance their standing as gatekeepers of coveted resources. Social assistance allowed their power to increase by generating a thick web of relationships between providers and recipients.

The humanitarian impulses behind social assistance dovetailed with the Peronist regime's broader drive to organize Argentines politically. "Organization" meant reforming the perceived deficiencies of the national population and creating healthy, productive subjects—goals shared with other welfare initiatives in the midcentury world.[20] But Peronist variants of governmentality stressed the imposition of ideological cohesion, too. The expansion of welfare networks accompanied stricter controls over public expression. To a degree, these two historical trends operated along separate institutional tracks and advanced at different speeds during Perón's presidency. The experts responsible for providing medical aid to the sick or shelter to the poor were motivated by concerns quite distinct from those of state censors or party ideologues. Yet collective consumption and political regulation shared a similar emphasis on managerial power. Ultimately, both impulses were rooted in the leadership's vision of Argentina as a unified, prosperous, and regimented society—what Perón and his allies dubbed the "Organized Community."[21]

Peronist authorities employed increasingly extensive techniques to enforce consensus. They cobbled together a virtual media monopoly by 1950 and commanded the principal national radio networks either through state ownership or through puppet intermediaries. Here, too, distinctions between the state and civil society were blurred. Newspapers were incorporated within a Peronist-controlled media conglomerate known as Alea, nominally a private company but staffed by propagandists for the government and Peronist Party alike. Alea grew into a publishing empire that included dozens of magazines and other publications.[22] At the same time, the state's closure of opposition papers, such as the Socialist Party's *La Vanguardia* (closed in 1947) and the liberal *La Prensa* (closed in 1951), had a chilling effect; the remaining independent newspapers trod carefully to avoid a similar fate. By managing the distribution of newsprint and commercial affairs of the press, Peronist officials made life difficult for independent-minded journalists. Some newspapers did run toned down or veiled critiques; all print and radio media, however, remained under threat of state sanctions.[23]

The Peronist regime coupled these controls with efforts to define an official partisan identity in positive terms, something one leading historian has dubbed a Peronist "subculture." The organizing impulse extended to the production of political symbols, images, and discourses on a massive scale in Argentina.[24] Contrary to persistent stereotypes, Peronist politics were by no means commanded entirely from the heights of the state or party. Even scripted partisan rallies allowed opportunities for more spontaneous displays of support, while mediating institutions, such as the unidades básicas, opened certain avenues for participation to women and others usually marginalized from public life. But the regime's leaders committed themselves to the ideal of partisan consensus, and over time they set down a party line, a "*doctrina Peronista*," to be inculcated among the population as a whole. In this context, *Señalando rumbos* was not simply a piece of self-congratulatory propaganda. It was a newsreel, part of the Sucesos Argentinos series created by an ostensibly private media organization. In offering one view of the vida digna in practice, the film illustrates not only what passed for news in Peronist Argentina but also how social assistance was deployed to shape a partisan worldview.

As one might expect, Perón avoided presenting the constriction of civil liberties as a tradeoff for collective consumption. In fact, he dismissed criticisms of authoritarianism as grousing from the opposition and highlighted instead the newfound *social* liberties enjoyed by worker-citizens. Peronist authorities used their command of the media and other resources to portray the joyous lifestyles associated with elevated standards. Officials discussed consumer purchasing and collective services as complementary aims, as two key elements (among others) of the "dignification" of workers into productive and patriotic subjects. Although they invoked individual sacrifice to national interests, calls for duty were balanced with celebrations of freedoms, including new legal entitlements. In September 1947 the president approved legislation that granted women the right to vote in national elections. Legal reforms also broke new ground in the spheres of labor and family life. In the mid-1940s the administration staged a series of ceremonies proclaiming the "rights of workers" and "rights of the elderly." These efforts culminated in the 1949 constitutional reform initiated by the Peronist bloc in Congress. The Radical Party participated in the convention to revise Argentina's 1853 constitution but later stormed out in protest; the end result was a document very much in keeping with Peronist priorities. For critics, the convention was overshadowed by the Peronist bloc's elimination of the prohibition on presidential reelection, so that Perón could stand for another six-year term. Its ratification sent a forceful message to the Radicals and other political dissidents, who had invoked the old constitution at every turn to critique government procedures; now all public employees (including the congressional opposition) were forced to swear allegiance to "Perón's constitution."[25]

The new constitution also reflected Peronist priorities in social assistance. In particular, the document enumerated a vast series of "special rights" afforded to citizens under article 37. Workers were singled out for particular attention as citizens, and they gained entitlements to adequate pay, social security, and "dignified work conditions." While there was no right to consumption as such, the Constitution alluded to various aspects of household spending. For instance, the "Right to Well-Being" (*Derecho al Bienestar*) guaranteed workers an elevation in the "nivel de vida," defined as the ability to access "housing, adequate clothing and nutrition, to satisfy without worry their needs and those of their family in a manner that [would] allow them to work with satisfaction, rest free of preoccupations and enjoy in a measured fashion spiritual and material gains."[26] Rights were closely tied to productive contributions to the nation and, above all, to one role, that of wage-earning worker outside the home. Seen from this vantage, Peronism constituted a form of "populist constitutionalism" that aimed at correcting inequities through new entitlements and extending older rights to women and other marginalized sectors.[27] These rights built on traditions of popular claims making, including organized labor's efforts to seek redress through the legal system. Even prior to redrafting the Constitution, Perón had from his earliest days at the Secretaría de Trabajo supported a stronger institutional framework for collective bargaining and labor courts.

Yet Peronist rights talk also had a high degree of abstraction that increased as officials turned entitlements into a topic for propaganda. The rights of workers

FIGURE 8. A legal entitlement from the Peronist 1949 constitution enshrined as a parade float bearing the image of a working family standing outside a *chalet californiano*. *Archivo General de la Nación, Departamento Fotográficos, box 2931, envelope 8, doc. 174846 (May 1948); reproduced courtesy of the archive.*

and families in the 1949 constitution were nebulous at best, with scant details on the ways they would be enforced by the courts or used by individuals as legal tools. Nevertheless, officials poured resources into educating the public on its entitlements as citizens of the New Argentina. Early attempts to adapt liberal constitutionalism to an age of mass politics were somewhat stilted. During a rally celebrating the May 1 Peronist Worker's Day, motorized floats representing social entitlements paraded down city streets, each complete with a visual metaphor of the vida digna— including a worker climbing up a statistical chart of rising living standards for the "Right to Economic Improvement."[28] In other settings, however, state authorities displayed more creativity in media representations of entitlements. Indeed, Peronist propagandists were critical in advancing a conception of citizenship rooted at least as much in depictions of lifestyle as in statements of rights, if not more so.

Although various institutions played their parts, responsibility for publicizing the vida digna fell largely on the Subsecretaría de Informaciones y Prensa (the Subsecretariat of Information and the Press, later changed to the Secretaría de Prensa y Difusión [the Secretariat of the Press and Broadcasting]). Its duties included monitoring the private media and producing its own print, radio, and visual propaganda. Created shortly after the 1943 military coup, the subsecretariat became a major player with the appointment of Raúl Apold as its director in 1949. Much of the federal agency's personnel came from backgrounds in the mass media, graphic design, and film industries (Apold himself had directed the Sucesos Argentinos newsreel series before joining the agency), people who now turned their talents to publicizing Peronist triumphs.[29] The military regime that took power after Perón's overthrow in 1955 conducted an investigation of the subsecretariat's activities that suggests the incredible scale of its operation. Between 1949 and early 1951, the organization published approximately 2.1 million posters, 14.4 million pamphlets, and 9.5 million postcards and wall hangings with pictures of Juan and Evita Perón; these quantities doubled or tripled by 1954–1955.[30] These figures appear inflated (especially given the size of Argentina's population), and the rabidly anti-Peronist officers who published the report were predisposed to exaggeration. But even if the numbers are only partially accurate, propaganda invaded virtually every sphere of life in Perón's Argentina, from the busts of Juan and Evita at the summit of Mount Aconcagua, the highest mountain in the Americas, to the posters along the streets of Buenos Aires. This propaganda machine even churned out consumer goods as partisan memorabilia, thereby allowing supporters to display and use the stuff of Peronism. Surviving examples of these consumables include handkerchiefs decorated with Perón's visage in needlework, calendars with smiling photographs of Evita, and similarly adorned matchboxes, ashtrays, and other household objects.[31]

The subsecretariat and other agencies combined exaltations of the leadership with accounts of the lives of ordinary Argentines that showed working people accessing the benefits of social welfare: taking vacations, socializing in new homes, and being cared for in health-care facilities. This propaganda typically contrasted the grandeur of the present with the penuries of the past, thus offering a form of antinostalgia that reminded audiences of collective gains under Peronist rule.[32] "This is how the pueblo trabajador lived in the incredibly rich Argentine Republic," proclaimed one 1948 newsreel. While the rural poor in the northwestern region dwelled in "dark caves, almost ashamed to be alive," and "without water and without bread, a life of perpetual punishment," the film lamented, the nation also endured the "social embarrassment" of filthy tenements just blocks away from the Presidential Palace in Buenos Aires. To correct past injustices and usher in a new age, Perón's government was "raising for the pueblo a house of equality, fraternity, and harmony."[33]

To reinforce this message, propagandists shifted attention from policymaking onto the joy of beneficiaries. In particular, they created fictional scenes in which characters of popular backgrounds acted out thankfulness. A pamphlet on the

FEP's social work noted the improved quality of life for the most downtrodden. Photographs of children with shaved heads and dour uniforms illustrated the lack of care on the part of traditional charity organizations; these "ragged and sad creatures" were victims of irresponsible governments and an "indifferent and cruel society." Thanks to the "extraordinary will and love of Eva Perón," however, boys and girls were now frolicking in vacation facilities, where they were dressed in neat suits and dresses. Before-and-after photographs of the children drove home the message. While the children of the past glanced forlornly at the camera, the smiling youth of the New Argentina, decked out in their brand-new clothes, "looked toward the future without fear."[34] Proceeding along similar lines, a 1949 government-produced radio advertisement proclaimed, "Everyone knows why they are satisfied," thus setting up a series of dialogues between average Argentines. In one of them, a young male worker excitedly tells his female partner, "Look, I received my annual bonus and tomorrow my paid vacation begins," to which she responds, "Oh, that's magnificent!" In another, a boy named Cachito and girl have a conversation in which he explains that he is going to pick up a toy at the local post office. When she asks who is sending him this toy, he exclaims, "Don't you know . . . ? Evita!"[35]

Through these dramatizations of everyday encounters, Peronist officials publicized social policies as a nonmarket means to satisfy desires for services (vacations, housing, and health care) and consumer goods (clothing and toys). Propaganda supplied templates of gratitude for making sense of transformations in material life, connecting individual improvements with membership in a national collectivity and mass political movement. Claims of this nature were not a hard sell, for extreme deprivation eased during Perón's first term—in no small measure because of social assistance provided by the state and its allies. Those with rival political views found this national community anything but inclusive, for they faced constrictions of civil liberties and of the means to contest state authority. Yet Peronist welfare programs were designed to remove key spheres of household consumption from market forces—not "decommodifying" these areas entirely but providing alternatives through nonmarket mechanisms. In reducing the struggle for sustenance and survival, Peronist welfare providers also promised respectability through the satisfaction of higher needs and wants. These efforts were guided by an impulse toward social leveling (that is, creating a new, more equitable order), yet they also reflected a vision of national inclusion within existing class relations and cultural norms of status. As Peronist officials sought to limit market pressures, they looked, paradoxically, to the commercial world for inspiration in defining the terms of collective freedom.

Naturally, what constituted "respectability" was subject to great contention among both the suppliers and the beneficiaries of asistencia social. To a degree, all twentieth-century welfare regimes struggled to decide how much to pattern interventions on the offerings of the private sector. Discussions raged over the significance of aesthetic choices and established cannons of taste, perhaps best witnessed in controversies over the design of public housing.[36] Similar housing debates occurred in Argentina, with the consequence that no uniform Peronist aesthetic or approach ever emerged. Instead, the staff of agencies entrusted with public works experimented with a surprisingly eclectic range of architectural styles: from formal neoclassical to the fashionable vernacular of the californiano, not to mention numerous variations on midcentury high modernism. But the problem of welfare's relationship to the marketplace was more than just a preoccupation for bureaucrats. The regime's vision of dignified living standards made the quality of social services a particularly sensitive political issue, one that attracted the attention of top leaders. These were hardly the first political actors to stress the delivery of quality social aid. Notwithstanding the bleak monotony of many facilities, experts the world over thought carefully about ways to provide a richer quality of life through collective consumption. Moreover, it was commonplace for states to employ propaganda in extolling such gains even when public services left much to be desired. Yet the Peronist stress on justice *and* comfort in regard to collective consumption made Argentina's programs differ in key respects from other contemporary experiments, especially from Soviet attempts to create a new socialist civilization and the intentional miserliness of U.S.-style poor relief. Officials defined respectability in terms of working-class empowerment but often in ways that stressed the incorporation of laboring people into a cultural mainstream created through dominant norms of taste and fashion. Moreover, Evita and others took discourses of consumer comfort to ostentatious extremes rarely seen in other midcentury welfare regimes and delivered supposedly "excessive" luxuries to further underscore the popular abundance of the New Argentina.

The intermeshing of commercial and nonmarket consumption under Peronist rule is most readily apparent in the case of tourism programs. Few other areas of social assistance so clearly drove home the message that the submerged majority could now access comforts limited previously to the affluent. The planners' managerial preoccupations with a ensuring a well-rested and healthy workforce dovetailed with the propagandists' emphasis on consumer pleasure. During the late

1940s, national and provincial governments opened beach and mountain resorts and expanded the parks system across the country, along with creating a cluster of smaller recreational centers around Buenos Aires. The Eva Perón Foundation's vacation complexes ministered largely to the needs of poor and working-class children. Additional state reforms contributed to expanding leisure. Labor legislation shortened the workweek and for the first time extended higher-order benefits, such as vacations, to much of the industrial working class and state employees. New national holidays added to the free time of popular sector Argentines, many of whom now enjoyed for the first time uninterrupted weekends and ten to fifteen days of paid vacation a year. The private tourism industry, too, sought to capitalize on these changes: hotel developers, railroad companies, and the Automobile Club of Argentina and other travel-related organizations took steps to attract and cater to the tourist market. One measure of the surge in mass tourism can be found in the number of vacationers in the premier resort of Mar del Plata, which jumped from 380,000 in 1940 to 1.4 million by 1955.[37]

There were differences between private sector and "social" tourism, to be sure. Peronist facilities were sometimes located in remote areas not usually frequented by tourists, reflecting efforts to promote state-affiliated destinations such as the national parks system and encourage the population to "discover" their nation. Government and FEP hotels offered special services (e.g., healthy meals, medical care, and counseling) not typical to most hotels. Some boasted large communal cafeterias and rooms for accommodating entire families; indoor bowling alleys in some hotels were apparently a populist touch to provide wholesome recreation. The costs of transportation and hotel stays were often subsidized or waived; in exchange, these leisure centers operated as additional spheres for promoting partisan politics and creating loyal citizens among workers, impoverished children, and other populations.[38] But social tourism was guided by the norms of the marketplace as well. Peronist hotels looked much like their commercial rivals, with comparable amenities and aesthetic choices. Many government- and FEP-operated facilities employed the californiano architectural style associated with private sector vacation and country club projects from the 1930s and early 1940s. In other cases, they were simply private hotels purchased and converted to a "social" purpose. Moreover, the geographic location of these spaces underscored developmentalist models of national inclusion. Most facilities were situated in the hill towns of Córdoba and Mendoza or along the beaches of the Atlantic Coast, areas that previously were the stomping grounds of affluent tourists. A union-operated hotel in a former elite playground such as Mar del Plata attested to organized labor's growing power and offered a clear symbol of a phenomenon scholars have dubbed the "democratization of well-being" in the Peronist era.[39]

Like their counterparts in commercial advertising, propagandists stressed themes of attentive service, cleanliness, and pampering in publicizing social tourism. They also drew attention to the political significance of commercial pleasures previously denied to popular Argentines. A 1948 CGT publication boasted about the "sumptuous" hotels built by unions, which stood as "a demonstration that workers have rights and abilities to enjoy the advantages of comfort and ease from which until a short time ago only a minority of those with means could take pleasure."[40] Likewise, government tourism pamphlets touted wider consumer horizons. Laboring folk used to "watch, from the window of their home or workplace, rich tourists pass by, loaded with suitcases, radiant with joy"; now they, too, had access to such pleasures.[41] Whether the comforts were truly "sumptuous" depends ultimately on subjective criteria, but they undoubtedly represented a welcome improvement to beneficiaries previously unable to afford vacations of any sort. Downplayed in these accounts, however, was any sense that workers had contributed to these achievements not only by enduring paycheck deductions but also by pressuring officials and engaging in union activism.

Films offered arguably the most powerful representations of collective consumption as part of the vida digna. Newsreels and documentaries shown before Hollywood features and domestic commercial films reached Argentina's massive filmgoing public. From 1950 onward, a series of state-sponsored short films celebrating FEP social assistance and other Peronist triumphs hit the theaters.[42] For these films, the Subsecretaría de Informaciones secured the cooperation of well-known directors and actors, thus deploying figures within the world of commercial culture to new partisan ends. Some artists were simply drawn to the ideals of Peronism; the fact that the federal government controlled celluloid stock and sponsored the domestic film industry offered additional motivations. These collaborators included Mario Soffici, famed for his melodramas of social injustice. *Nuestro hogar* (our home), a 1952 short directed by Soffici, acclaimed the achievements of housing policy through documentary-style footage and fictional vignettes. In one scene, a male worker in the pre-Peronist years comes home to a crowded tenement room filled with his fighting children and tired-looking wife. Fed up with the noise, his teenage daughter proclaims threateningly that she would rather go hang out on the street. Another scene shows a fatherly figure facing the repossession of his home by the "Company" for having fallen behind on mortgage payments.[43] In both cases, the private sector not only has failed to meet material needs but also has undermined paternal authority within the family.

Later in the film, however, Soffici offers contrasting images of the comfortable lives enjoyed by residents of Peronist housing in the present. An elderly rural couple praises the state housing loan they received, while a male worker returns from his job to be greeted by his smiling wife and children outside a new home. The film's narrator (a teacher instructing his elementary school class) reinvents rights talk in line with simple pleasures, arguing that public housing guarantees families "the unalienable right to the benefits of sun and happiness." Unlike the generation raised in tenements, the laboring Argentines profiled by Soffici lived in tidy new houses with home furnishings that bespoke a quality of life similar to that of an urban middle class. In its portrayal of domestic life, Soffici's film mirrors earlier propagandistic newsreels, such as *Señalando rumbos* (not coincidentally, some of the film's housing projects resembled the capital's Barrio Perón). The camera shows children playing on the lawn and adults relaxing on a front porch, all protected by "un techo digno, un hogar felíz" (a dignified shelter, a happy home). In presenting the home as a means of social uplift, the narrator offers a final reminder at the film's conclusion that this family, like thousands of others, "must not ever forget that they acquired it thanks to the sound foresight and justicialista spirit of an exemplary government."[44]

Nuestro hogar mixed the Peronist language of living standards and allusions to social rights with other discourses of justice, including moralizing scenes of popular anguish and joy that resembled those of Soffici's 1930s commercial films. This heterogeneity was characteristic of Peronist propaganda. In other cases, images of the ordered, "respectable" family coexisted with more forcefully heroic "proletarian" depictions. Officials employed working-class icons (such as the burly, shirtless male worker) borrowed from leftist traditions and other influences.[45] Nevertheless, the depictions of working-class comfort and family life favored by Soffici and his peers merit special attention. For some observers, these "bourgeois" workers reveal the inclination of Peronist authorities to lull laboring folk into a stultifying state of contentment (and thus forestall more radical demands). Others see this as an example of Peronist leaders' appeals to popular aspirations and desires for upward mobility rooted in the national myth of Argentina as a land of opportunity.[46] But these debates often overlook how images of domesticated comfort offered an alternative vision of midcentury consumer society. These depictions of the working family emphasized measured pleasures rather than consumerist hedonism or individual spending. Although film propaganda about Barrio Perón revealed that the neighborhood had a gas station (ostensibly for residents' cars, thus suggesting a higher tier of mass consumption), filmmakers situated the trappings of the good life within a moral community. The overt presence of Catholicism in the housing project acted apparently as moderating force: *Señalando rumbos* focused attention on the state-built church, located at the central hub of the housing project, and the female residents dutifully at prayer within it. Barrio Perón and other housing projects were presented as socially harmonious, with different sized units and residents of working- and middle-class backgrounds interacting with one another. In fact, the apparent message was that distinctions mattered less than they ever had before; thanks to the intervention of Peronist benefactors, here one could not distinguish blue- from white-collar wage earners by their appearances, homes, or practices of sociability. In these model neighborhoods, clothing and other consumer goods were not weapons used to struggle up the competitive social ladder and set individuals apart. Rather, they were part of the material standards that all productive, moral members of society deserved and, in theory, would soon acquire in the Nueva Argentina.

As this example suggests, Peronist image makers attached competing values to their programs but presented the vida digna as superior to mere consumerism. The pleasures of quotidian consumption that came with elevation to a more secure, comfortable lifestyle were ultimately contained; references to social justice as a spiritual concept counterbalanced more sensual descriptions of living standards. Quantity was as important as quality. Peronist agencies inundated the population with facts and enumerations—the hundreds of hospital beds built, the thousands of new housing units erected, and the millions of persons helped by the social insurance system. Similarly, the imagery of technological modernization sometimes overshadowed consumption. Newsreels regaled audiences with white-frocked doctors and nurses caring for the sick in impoverished rural areas, and press reports on union-operated clinics emphasized their "*modernidad*," complete with photographs of X-ray machines and other new medical equipment.[47] Peronist leaders raised similar themes in public appearances. At a 1949 rally, Labor Minister José María Freire described the gains of his own union and played to the audience's sense of working-class pride and masculine responsibility: "We have doctors in every district and other benefits; our female companions [*compañeras*] no longer give birth in our own homes, a place without proper facilities, nor do they go to the public hospital; they now go to the maternity ward of our own health-care centers, where they, the mother and child, are taken care of with the best facilities and modern means."[48] As it did in film depictions of living standards, the Peronist ideal of the ordered family operated as the connective thread between various representations of asistencia social as technical advancement, social hygiene, and working-class conquests.

In some circumstances, however, Peronist providers downplayed the importance of balanced, collective forms of consumption in favor of more exuberant celebrations of comfort. This impulse informed many of the programs operated by the FEP, which often supplied overtly excessive forms of generosity to populations seeking relief. In attempting to define a new modality of social assistance that would break with the meagerness of charity efforts in the past, Eva Perón devoted particular attention to the issue of high-quality services. The FEP reworked larger Peronist ideals of social inclusion and leveling in new directions. Not only did the organization use design to convey the message that the poor and needy merited a level of treatment comparable to that given to affluent Argentines, but FEP facilities adapted cannons of bourgeois luxury and commercial fashion to "social" ends. The result was often an exaggerated, kitsch reflection of the original sources of inspiration, but these choices were not the outcome of a lack of attention.[49] Their political significance lay precisely in the fact that they sent a clear message— to recipients and a wider public alike—that the "democratization of well-being" extended well beyond the satisfaction of basic needs and wants. By bringing the trappings of high-class taste to the pueblo, Evita's foundation positioned itself as a powerful agent of social redistribution while defending a paradigm of justice that rejected the elites' monopolization of commercial comfort.

The FEP applied these principles most overtly in a series of welfare facilities erected in Buenos Aires. Located in affluent zones of the city's urban landscape, these spaces became known to national audiences through pamphlets and other propaganda. Three "Hogares de Tránsito" in the capital offered temporary lodging and counseling to single women and mothers with children. Situated in former homes of the urban elite, the buildings were turn-of-the-century manses with marble floors and staircases, each facility appointed in opulence: tapestries and paintings adorned the walls, Persian rugs covered the floors, and Louis XVI–style furniture filled the rooms. The obvious luxury of these settings contrasted with the backgrounds of the hogares' residents. Whether they were migrants to the city, recent widows, or victims of abusive husbands, thousands of women passed through the hogares every year. The FEP's team of social workers helped residents find better employment and secure public housing; in the meantime, they made temporary child care available and offered classes on clothes making, nutrition, and religious worship.[50] Women and children were given new clothes that they could take home at the end of their stays, all carefully selected to meet the day's standards of respectability and fashion. In rescuing individuals from need, these interventions thus also aimed to transform subjects according to Evita's own ideals of femininity, among other things, by encouraging habits of "respectable" behavior, acceptance of the status markers of the good life, and compliance with conventions of beauty and sexuality.[51]

This combination of luxurious accommodations and attentive assistance carried over into the Hogar de la Empleada General San Martín. Occupying an imposing eleven-floor building in the heart of downtown Buenos Aires, the "Maids' Home" opened in December 1949 and provided services for domestic laborers and other female workers. This facility followed in the steps of a similar program for low-income women begun in 1923 by a Catholic organization, but the FEP raised it to another level of comfort. The hogar offered low-cost housing to approximately 500 individuals who had to meet basic criteria of eligibility, including the lack of family in Buenos Aires and certification of "good conduct." The residents had access to on-site medical and dental clinics as well as counseling and recreational and educational activities organized by the FEP's staff. The hogar operated a cafeteria that cooked subsidized three-course meals for some 1,500 persons a day, among them workers and state employees who entered free of charge by displaying their union membership cards.[52] Like those of the other FEP homes, the hogar's lobby and common spaces were lavish. Each floor was decorated in a different high-class style—"Norman," "Viennese," "French"—complete with antique chairs, pianos, crystal chandeliers, fine vases, and sundry objets d'art, many of which Evita had collected on her 1947 European tour. The bedrooms were less ostentatious but aesthetically well-ordered spaces (what a propaganda pamphlet called "the picture of comfort and good taste"). Under the watchful eye of the foundation, which imposed a 10 p.m. curfew and other measures to inculcate ideals of "proper" behavior, this facility turned established material hierarchies on their head: maids lived in a style close to (and perhaps even beyond) the manner of their wealthy employers.

The FEP took the emulation of commercial pleasures to something of a peak in the Hogar de la Empleada. Despite the building's conservative style of décor, the institution provided its residents with the latest in entertainment technology, including televisions and record players, and every room had a radio. The second floor of this facility contained an almost unbelievable replica of a downtown shopping avenue complete with mock sidewalks, storefronts, and shops stocked with goods—even a miniature version of Harrods department store. (And all this only a few blocks away from the real Harrods on the calle Florida.) In describing this commercial simulacrum, an FEP publication presented consumer desire in gendered terms, much as did the era's advertisers, arguing that "nothing is more logical

FIGURE 9. Residents of the "Maid's Home" enjoying a moment of leisure in luxurious material comfort. *Archivo General de la Nación, Departamento Fotográficos, box 820, envelope 12, doc. 258973 (n.d.); reproduced courtesy of the archive.*

of course than providing women the possibility of window shopping, a custom so agreeable and rooted in the feminine sex." Under the caring protection of a Peronist institution, women workers could enjoy the pleasures of urban shopping spaces without ever stepping foot outside.[53]

Clearly not all FEP programs were so elaborate, and propaganda coverage favored the more opulent centers over simpler facilities. The FEP extended more modest material aid as well, including food and consumer wares. Most famously, the agency allocated millions of sewing machines to popular households. Like other appliances manufactured in local factories, sewing machines constituted a marker of Argentina's industrial modernity and, more broadly, an international emblem of technological progress.[54] But the FEP's distribution of sewing machines also reflected prevailing gender expectations. Viewed from the vantage of the foundation's staff, this device offered women a means to meet household upkeep duties and, by necessity, earn additional income through seamstress work (much as Evita's mother had done in the backcountry towns of the province of Buenos Aires). A propaganda pamphlet from the era entitled *La Carta* illustrated this point through the story of a traveler who takes refuge in a rural shack and is received by a mother and children: "Soon there appeared three barefoot children, the eldest wearing a shirt with mends and patches; the other, a tattered and torn blue shirt, and the smallest, a shirt almost without sleeves. Seeing this portrait of true poverty, I felt ashamed." On the narrator's return a few months later, this grim scene has changed: a sewing machine had arrived following a letter written to the Fundación Eva Perón. The family is no longer in debt, their *rancho* has been spruced up, and the smaller children march around yelling "Perón-Evita, Perón-Evita."[55] As did other such depictions of relief, this one placed a premium on outward appearance and proper clothes, which seen from the FEP's vantage reflected deeper transformations in self-worth. This direct material assistance may seem a world away from the simulated shopping avenue of the Hogar de la Empleada, where consumer provisioning was a pleasure rather than a burden. In both cases, however, FEP interventions focused on the "feminine" characteristics of consumption, whether by immersing women in a fantasy setting or by providing them a lifeline to the domestic economy.

Even when the material aid distributed was not luxurious, Evita made certain that those who solicited the FEP came away with an impression of limitless generosity. Staff and foreign visitors who observed Evita during her afternoons at the organization's headquarters noted that she often gave supplicants more than they requested; she assumed that they were too intimidated to ask for all the things they really needed. Anecdotal evidence suggests that displays of abundance continued outside Evita's office. Residents of Peronist public housing projects typically moved into bare-bones units; they were expected to outfit their own kitchens and purchase the most basic bathroom fixtures. However, some of those fortunate enough to secure a place in one of the FEP-run housing projects discovered spaces of plenty. The closets of their new homes and apartments were filled with clothing, the rooms were furnished and decorated, and kitchens were stocked with supplies.[56] Impoverished beneficiaries suddenly found themselves elevated beyond their station and freed from immediate material worries, as if transported by some miraculous power to a previously unattainable rung on the social ladder. In these cases, the level of care and attention to detail was purposefully antibureaucratic.

Evita reflected on the motivations behind this approach to social assistance in her autobiography, *La razón de mi vida*. Published in 1952 just months prior to her death, this lyrical description of Evita's life and personal philosophy became a bestseller, and it reached a larger audience still as part of the curriculum for school-age children. Compiled mainly by a ghostwriter and Evita's handlers, *La razón de mi vida* was presented to the public as Evita's own reflections. The book draws a sharp contrast between the "sordid" charity of the past and the grandeur of justicialismo. Prior to Perón, the wealthy offered the poor mere "crumbs of alms" and "miserable and cold coins"; it was the oligarchy, Evita asserted, who created the specter of communism through their greed. They fomented class resentment by dressing needy children in "gray uniforms" and keeping them poorly fed.[57] In *La razón de mi vida* Evita presents her brand of social assistance as an effort to counteract the spiritual and psychological damage caused by traditional charity. "It is because of this," she argued, "that my 'homes' are generously rich . . . [;] what's more, I want to exceed myself in this task. I want them to be luxurious. It is precisely because a century of miserable asylums can be erased only by another century of hogares that are 'excessively luxurious.'" Evita anticipated the potential objections of her critics, who did not understand the purpose of such assistance or feared what would happen if the poor grew used to Peronist-style luxury. "No, I am not afraid," she claimed. "On the contrary, I want them to grow accustomed to living like the rich . . . , [to] feel dignified living with greater wealth. . . . In the final analysis everyone has a right to be rich who lives on Argentine soil and anywhere in the rest of the world."[58] These statements evoke claims applied in other times and places in Latin America: namely, that the poor secretly desire lavishness and that only bureaucratic experts think in terms of minimal needs. Whatever the merits of this logic, Evita's biographers have suggested that these concerns were rooted in her own childhood, which provided her intimate knowledge of the poor's needs and desires (or at least the confidence to make these judgments). Through Evita's personalized brand of social assistance, the FEP sought to relieve suffering while also acknowledging the significance of mundane consumer goods and the political value of "excessively luxurious" collective services.[59]

Although the FEP took the pursuit of comfort to occasional extremes, its programs reflected broader impulses of social leveling and national inclusion. With few exceptions, the goal was not to dispute what was tasteful, beautiful, or pleasurable but rather to break down the monopolization of comfort by a privileged few. There was a transgressive edge to these interventions; in the hands of a figure as polarizing as Evita, the distribution of luxury to the downtrodden and ordinary directed a sharp rebuke at the affluent for their unpatriotic selfishness. Likewise, the stress on generous, high-quality services posed a challenge to existing class distinctions and status stratifications. Peronist authorities, however, stopped short of rejecting cultural hierarchies of taste altogether or replacing them consistently with radical aesthetic innovations. While their propagandists celebrated the virtues of hardworking male proletarians and devoted housewives, they envisioned a future for the working class patterned largely on norms of security, improvement, and prosperity in line with a commercial mainstream.

Accessing Assistance

Portrayals of a satisfied population elevated to a comfortable nivel de vida by their caring benefactors mask the complexity of subaltern responses to social assistance. Peronist welfare networks staked their presence in communities across the country, whether in the form of a construction project in an urban neighborhood or an FEP social worker visiting a family in a provincial town. It is clear, however, that many Argentines did not wait idly for help to arrive. Individuals sought to engage with resource holders through the means at their disposal, and social programs were swamped with solicitations (e.g., the federal housing authority saw the number of requests for home loans increase sevenfold during 1946–1955).[60] Until recently, the literature on social assistance has focused on policy outcomes and the professionals who designed services rather than the popular constituents they targeted. We still know far more about Evita as she sat behind her desk at the foundation that bore her name than we know about the motivations and actions of the individuals who congregated outside her office. Oral histories suggest that individuals who received aid at the FEP's hogares now look back on these interventions with deep gratitude, but varied forms of assistance must have surely provoked a range of reactions.[61] When moviegoing audiences sat in theaters awaiting the start of a Hollywood comedy, what did they think about the newsreels depicting the vida digna in housing projects? How did Argentines struggling to make ends meet envision their relationship to providers? Inevitably, one is left with few answers to these questions.

Political authorities controlled access to resources and set the institutional terms of engagement, but within the constraints of these uneven power relations, those soliciting aid pursued numerous tactics. Supplicants communicated in discourses intended to attract officials' attention, framed personal needs in ways to maximize sympathy, called on personal connections, displayed partisan loyalties and affiliations, and if successful, pressured for additional improvements. The public correspondence of the era provides a particularly fruitful means of gaining entry to these popular responses. Written requests sent to Peronist officials allow insights not only on the "agency" of ordinary women and men—that is, the choices available to them in this historical moment—but also on the ways individuals imagined themselves as working in concert with leaders.[62]

Public correspondence was itself a centuries-old practice in Argentina that became more widespread with growing literacy in the twentieth century. By the 1940s literacy rates for adults had climbed to nearly 90 percent, allowing most citizens direct recourse to letter writing as a means of communication.[63] This practice reached a massive scale thanks to the populist characteristics of Peronist politics, above all, Juan and Eva Perón's ideal of unmediated communication with the pueblo. Propagandists encouraged individuals to address letters personally to well-known figures, including Evita (an approach that many employed spontaneously), and to contact public servants at all levels of government. The volume of public correspondence in Peronist Argentina was staggering: according to the recollections of her assistants, Evita alone received some ten to twelve thousand letters each day at the Presidential Residence.[64] Even a conservative approximation suggests that hundreds of thousands, if not millions, of Argentines put pens to paper to request relief.

What do these documents reveal about the tactics of popular citizens and their efforts to satisfy needs, wants, and comforts? To begin, we must acknowledge our limitations: almost all the correspondence sent to social agencies (including the Fundación Eva Perón) has been destroyed or lost. One can, however, approach the subject through a more indirect route by examining records from the Ministry of Technical Affairs (MAT). In addition to serving as the coordinator for federal planning initiatives, the MAT received letters commenting on every imaginable subject: proposals for inventions, complaints about rude neighbors, elaborate policy suggestions, and denunciations of merchant speculators, to name but a few topics. But the agency's directors also entertained requests from individuals seeking personal recommendations and favors, including employment. For many petitioners, it was a coveted position in government—not a specific good, social program, or form of collective consumption—that represented the ultimate prize in pursuing the vida digna. Compared to their private sector counterparts, civil servants enjoyed good wages and a greater range of new social benefits, and thus government employment offered an attractive route toward upward mobility for lower level white- and blue-collar workers.[65] Although distribution of jobs as patronage antedated the Peronist era, the expansion in the size of government created new opportunities and energized would-be job seekers.[66] This does not mean that securing public employment was a simple feat. For instance, in 1946 a woman addressed a letter directly to the ministry's director, José Figuerola, asking him to find her son a position as a clerk in a post office or bank. She claimed that without a recommendation from someone with influence, it was impossible to obtain a good job or civil service post. Nevertheless, the ministry rebuffed her request and offered a stock response stating that it was not the planning agency's role to act as a placement service.[67]

Other petitioners, however, had more success in swaying MAT officials to intervene in their behalf, some even obtaining the desired forms of social assistance. Personal connections were particularly useful during the ministry directorship of Raúl Mendé, who served as the agency's head from Figuerola's dismissal in 1949 until 1955. Figuerola had been best known for his technocratic planning expertise, but Mendé was a different political beast altogether. Prior to his appointment, he had served as a delegate to the constitutional convention and a provincial minister of welfare and social security in Santa Fe. Mendé eventually made a name for himself nationally as a Peronist ideologue, heading the Escuela Superior Peronista (a sort of ideological training camp for party officials), authoring the *Doctrina peronista del estado* and other dogmatic works, and ghostwriting Eva Perón's autobiography, *La razón de mi vida*.[68] Given his high rank, Mendé not surprisingly received entreaties for favors from across Argentina but especially from his former constituents. Mendé was the former mayor of Esperanza, Santa Fe (an agricultural community of around 10,000 inhabitants). Thanks to the MAT director's intervention on their behalf, residents of this region acquired posts at various government agencies.[69]

Equally important, Mendé helped open the doors of social assistance to these individuals. Within the MAT correspondence, I have located a cache of approximately thirty letters sent by supplicants to Mendé in the early 1950s and then forwarded to Evita's office in the Presidential Residence (also included are letters mailed originally to the First Lady and then passed on to the MAT). This handful of letters provides a rare window into the internal dynamics of delivering social assistance. First, the winding route the letters took underscores the interconnections among state planning and Peronist civil organizations—in this case, facilitated by the friendly ties between Mendé and Evita. These requests crisscrossed networks spanning federal, provincial, and municipal governments, as well as private foundations and party institutions. Although it is impossible to determine how the authors compare to the universe of those soliciting social assistance, their identities match the general characteristics of populations targeted by the FEP: women outnumber men, and most came from apparently working- and lower-middle-class origins. The petitioners were all individuals, not organizations, predominately from Mendé's home province of Santa Fe (with one-third from Esperanza alone). A majority solicited access to new public housing programs, a fact that signals the continued problem of shelter in Argentina and, perhaps, the favorable grassroots response to propagandistic depictions of housing residents enjoying a secure, comfortable standard of living. Individuals also asked for other types of social assistance, including medical care and household consumer goods ranging from clothing to sewing machines.

In presenting requests before Evita and Mendé, letter writers crafted what can be called "narratives of despair," accounts of personal misfortune that situated experiences of deprivation within the conventions of epistolary practices. Popular Argentines did not express longings for a higher order of consumerist wants or comforts in this forum, nor did they demand that authorities respect social entitlements guaranteed by constitutional rights. Instead, individuals presented themselves as supplicants before powerful resource holders. For instance, one woman described the tragedy of her house burning down. Her father died in the conflagration, and she had lost all her clothing, furniture, and humble possessions and would likely have to postpone her marriage. Like many similar petitioners, this woman did not make a specific request of Evita but simply shared her poignant story in the hopes of obtaining whatever relief was deemed necessary. Other letter writers were more direct, as was Dolores García, who asked Evita to grant her father the pension that he had been trying to secure for ten years. Expressing confidence that her wishes would be granted, García wrote, "I feel protected by your generosity and know that your noble feelings are directed toward doing good for humble, heartfelt Peronists."[70]

As these examples suggest, this genre of public correspondence offered an opportunity for petitioners to act out a Peronist identity, inspired by a combination of their own political sentiments and a tactical sense of the sort of thing their readers wished to hear. The case of Tulia Gaute, a twenty-one-year-old factory worker from a Buenos Aires suburb, further exemplifies the type of life stories petitioners told. In her letter Gaute described how the fourteen members of her family lived crowded together, forced to share a bathroom with four other families. Despite the fact that her father was a construction laborer and all her siblings worked, they could not afford better housing; their situation had worsened after the recent birth of a new baby girl (whom her parents named Evita). Gaute laced her letter with expressions of humility that lent credence to her needy status: "I beg that you will know how to pardon me for the boldness I take in directing myself to

FIGURE 10. Evita reviewing a letter and interviewing a supplicant as part of her direct assistance efforts. *Archivo General de la Nación, Departamento Fotográficos, box 3185, envelope 60, doc. 194700 (n.d.); reproduced courtesy of the archive.*

you without previous introduction, but I find myself in such a grievous situation and knowing that many persons have directed themselves to you not in vain. I plead with you to do me the favor of listening to me." After relating her family problems, she closed her letter with a declaration of loyalty: "An Argentine and Peronist worker salutes you respectfully."[71] Rather than direct herself at a bureaucracy, Gaute corresponded in personal, even intimate terms to the First Lady, reaching out to her not as an equal but as a special authority with the power to elevate Gaute's family from the abyss. She allowed Evita to decide the assistance that her situation merited. And like fellow female petitioners, Gaute discussed suffering in terms not of individual wants but of pressing familial needs; she identified herself not as a rights-bearing citizen but as a worker, Peronist, and dutiful daughter.

In accordance with the expectations of this style of personal solicitation, letter writers regularly contrasted their meekness with acclaim for the Peronist movement and its leading couple. In particular, petitioners described Evita in highly empathetic terms, underscoring her "heart," "generosity," and compassion for the downtrodden. Correspondents asked Mendé to act as an "intercessor" between them and the larger-than-life First Lady. María Teresa Martí, a woman from Buenos

Aires, pleaded with the MAT director to "take [her] humble petition to the magnanimous heart of the most Excellent Señora Eva Perón." Paeans to Evita's goodness often had religious overtones that blended metaphors of devotion with mass-political slogans. A Catholic worldview was evidenced in descriptions of Evita that evoked the cult of the Virgin Mary. One devotee even included a poem titled "Angel of Generosity" that recounted a dream in which Evita was surrounded by angels who gave her bread for the poor. Religious symbolism was joined with partisan politics, as this amateur poet proclaimed in rhyming couplets that all good Argentines should not only "idolize" Evita but vote "now and always" for Perón. The saintly view of Evita was, in fact, encouraged by propagandists. Texts for adults and school-age children, such as the foundation's own 1948 publication *Por la ruta de los cuentos mágicos* (on the path of magical tales), stressed the angelic generosity of the First Lady in ministering to the needs of the poor.[72] The exact impact of these influences is unclear, but supplicants drew from a cultural milieu infused with both Catholic religiosity and Peronist depictions of Evita's righteousness.

Male petitioners, too, employed religious sentiments in seeking social assistance, but their letters to Evita and Mendé also asserted their sacrifice to the Peronist cause in militaristic terms. Eduardo Chesaux, a resident of Rafaela, Santa Fe, asked Mendé to endorse his request for a "little house or apartment in one of the neighborhoods built by the government and the Fundación de Ayuda Social" to improve the lot of his family. In addition to offering the requisite gestures of meekness, he described himself as a "soldier of the justicialista cause of General Perón, the cause of the Patria and Pueblo." Those soliciting aid echoed the bellicose spirit employed in antispeculation campaigns and other forms of mass politics.[73] Whether petitioners chose to highlight Evita's generosity or their own fidelity to the cause, they situated partisan and patriotic duties within a framework that acknowledged the power of welfare authorities and presented social need in terms of familial responsibilities.

That letter writers identified themselves in this manner is not unexpected, given that these discourses resonated with the Peronist leadership's stress on family order, political consensus, and uplifting submerged populations. But narratives of despair were often not enough. Most of the petitioners in this subset used their relationship with Mendé (however tenuous) to ensure their letter would reach Evita's hands. It is safe to assume that the vast majority of those who solicited assistance from the FEP and other providers lacked these high-level contacts and therefore simply presented their claims either in person or in letters. Some requests were undoubtedly met immediately, and the case was closed. In this sense, the circuitous route of the surviving cache of letters is somewhat exceptional. Yet displays of partisan loyalties and personal connections were characteristic features of Peronist social assistance more broadly—indeed, an unavoidable part of negotiating the era's politics of welfare. Even supplicants with ties to Mendé provided additional evidence of their good standing. Some letters included recommendations from local unidades básicas, labor unions, or elected officials to bolster the writers' requests. In an appeal for a "special subsidy" to overcome a serious illness, Federico Cano, a resident of Esperanza, assembled a dossier with statements from the town's CGT officer and mayor, who described him as a "disinterested Peronist of the first hour" (i.e., a longtime supporter). Likewise, a letter from another resident of Esperanza, soliciting placement in a Buenos Aires public housing project, carried the following valuable handwritten note in the margin: "Renzi, he is a Peronist of the first hour/R. Mendé," a message from the MAT director to Atilio Renzi, Evita's right-hand man in administering programs.[74] Whether this identification paid off is unknown, but these recommendations suggest that supplicants and their patrons considered them necessary in navigating pleas through the webs of social assistance.

The fates of job seekers depended on similar displays of credentials. A 1952 decree mandated that all federal employees become members of the Peronist Party, but MAT letters make clear that a de facto "Peronization" of the bureaucracy was underway earlier. Susana González, a woman who sought a teaching assistant job in 1950 and offered a letter of recommendation from her town's mayor, saw her request denied by an MAT official. "Not a Peronist," the official concluded after a brief investigation, and the case was closed. Eventually, the procedure for job requests to the MAT began to follow a pattern. An individual mailed in his or her request, sometimes with additional letters of support from some local authority, whether a mayor, CGT officer, or priest. After receiving these documents, a ministry bureaucrat replied, asking the petitioner to prove his or her "*antecedentes peronistas*" (Peronist credentials) and in some cases, those of family members. The petitioner sent in a party identification number or a note from a local unidad básica, and the case was then forwarded to the appropriate official or to the Presidential Residence for consideration.[75] Without evidence of partisan loyalty, job requests apparently failed to advance very far at the Ministry of Technical Affairs during Mendé's tenure.

Yet this evidence of shared partisan loyalties did not mean that petitioners blindly followed the commands of welfare authorities. Viewed from the vantage of those soliciting assistance, identification with the Peronist cause went hand in hand with an acknowledgment of the New Argentina's limitations. Self-effacing supplicants also demonstrated clever thinking about how to direct their claims through justicialista networks. The Presidential Residence, Fundación Eva Perón headquarters, and federal agencies were awash in popular demands, so that many petitioners encountered delays or failed to have their wishes met. Tulia Gaute noted in her sad letter to Mendé that she had written to Evita a year earlier and received a brief reply. Months had passed, however, and she had heard nothing more about her case. Other petitioners complained about pension claims and other paperwork that languished without action. More than simply a sign of the way popular Argentines conflated religious sentiments and patronage traditions, the practices of intercession illustrate the skill with which supplicants reacted to the opportunities provided by Peronist relief and patronage. Those individuals who communicated with the MAT director had often first contacted Evita's foundation without success and so pursued backdoor ways to make their voices heard.

For some the challenge lay not just in getting a plea endorsed but also in making sure that it was fulfilled to their liking. Welfare authorities and letter writers had divergent definitions of legitimate requests for succor and divergent views about the threshold at which needs were adequately satisfied. For an illustration of these tensions, consider the case of Elena D'Alessandri de Létora, a forty-four-year-old unemployed widow from Villa Urquiza, in the province of Buenos Aires, who had a disabled daughter. She first contacted the FEP by mail and succeeded in acquiring a wheelchair for her daughter and a "Category B subsidy" (a form of disability payment). But in April 1951 she wrote to Mendé complaining that when she tried to get her promised subsidy, officials informed her that there were no funds available. The widow was not satisfied with the assistance she had received. Proclaiming, "I think my case is one of true social justice," she enumerated a detailed list of additional goods that were required: an orthopedic bed, food, skeins of jersey wool, two lengths of cloths to make overcoats, and two pairs of shoes.[76] D'Alessandri de Létora and many other letter writers defined justicia social in these everyday terms, mentioning specific household wares (in D'Alessandri de Létora's case, both factory-made consumables and materials with which to fashion clothing for her family). Her skills in domestic provisioning and degree of self-sufficiency from the commercial marketplace, however, did not preclude voicing further demands to providers of nonmarket consumables. This petitioner's confidence translated into a sense of entitlement based on her needy status and conviction that Peronist resource holders would fulfill promises of generosity.

To be sure, responding to the piles of correspondence concerning housing, material aid, and personal favors must have proved a daunting task for the FEP staff. Social agencies faced the dilemma of deciding which cases warranted action and which ones should be ignored. In theory, supplicants after 1950 were required to submit a "certificate of poverty" signed by the local justice of the peace or police chief, but most no doubt failed to comply with such efforts to regulate communication with Evita.[77] In addition, letter writers sometimes presented entreaties that pushed the limits of the regime's model of assistance. One correspondent bypassed the nationalist framework of Peronist welfare entirely and asked for medicines to send sick relatives in Italy.[78] In a more problematic instance, a justice of the peace from Santa Fe requested a sewing machine from the FEP for his wife. Although he supplied a letter of support from the local unidad básica, MAT officials were unconvinced that he was truly needy. Evita's distribution of sewing machines was associated, after all, with working-class women who faced the double burden of housekeeping and providing for their families. The FEP wrote back asking this local government official and Peronist loyalist to provide a detailed account of his monthly income—presumably to determine whether he and his wife were poor enough to merit their desired household appliance.[79]

In the light of these frictions between providers and solicitants, the regime's representatives sought to smooth things over by asserting their virtues as benefactors. Propagandists suggested that officials were laboring diligently to meet legitimate demands. Consider an article titled "A Letter for *Compañera* Evita," published in *Mundo Peronista* in January 1952.[80] This piece described the experiences of a fictional man who was troubled by an unspecified personal problem and decided to contact the "little mother of the poor." The *Mundo Peronista* article presented letter writing as a way for individuals to establish contact with Evita herself and portrayed the First Lady as saintly figure who, like a candle, "burned" her life away working day and night for the downtrodden. (Hardly subtle, this propaganda piece also referred to Perón and Evita as a "miracle from God" and the "personification of Hope.") Tracing the path of this individual's letter, the article painted a picture of an open, empathetic government that would respond to any sort of entreaty. Ignoring the holdups that were part of public correspondence, propagandists even claimed that Evita would eventually read each letter after it had been processed by her trained staff. When one's letter—described as "a prolongation of yourself"—arrived in Evita's hands, they said, "you too have reached her." These descriptions reinforced the regime's antibureaucratic image and heightened the sense that Evita wielded almost superhuman command over the resources of social assistance.

Regardless of the prodding they may have received through articles in *Mundo Peronista,* petitioners sought out the openings offered by Peronist bureaucracies. To be sure, staunch anti-Peronists would have been loath to participate in networks so colored by partisan identities (or at the very least, it would have required subterfuge). For differing factors—sheer persistence, talents with a honeyed pen, friends in high places, or truly desperate conditions of life—some individuals were better able than others to attract the attention of providers. Petitioners no doubt told Evita and Mendé what they believed these figures would want to hear, but in performing the role of the loyal supplicant, many seemed as interested in forming communicative bonds with authorities as in obtaining immediate relief. In turn, officials controlling coveted resources applied various criteria to determine needs, and they sought to shape loyalties as they ministered to social suffering. Supplicants did not always get what they wanted or get aid as soon as they would have liked, but for the moment, these tensions were mitigated by the enhanced opportunities for political participation and communication with resource holders.

These maneuvers between authorities and citizens are also revealing for what is *not* there. If letter writers saw themselves as entitled to collective consumption and material aid, they rarely invoked the rights talk of populist constitutionalism. By the same token, one finds few subaltern appropriations of Peronist discourses about popular comfort, although the longings for a miraculous salvation some writers express are compatible with Evita's modes of "excessively" generous uplift. It was not, of course, the place of the supplicant to demand rights or luxury, for such a stance would have clashed with dominant portrayals of joyous gratitude. Although the elevation of living standards assumed productive contributions from the citizenry, social assistance was most often presented as a form of grace received from above, a sentiment captured in the classic slogan of this era: "Peron cumple, Evita dignifica" (Perón delivers, Evita dignifies).

❧

Peronist "welfare" had a complex relationship to the world of buying and selling. Whether directed by the central state or allied institutions, new programs supplied palliatives for the damages Argentine capitalism wrought on workers and their families. Yet the standards of the vida digna as defined by top leaders, the designers of social programs, and propagandists rested on the notion of incorporation into a social mainstream, an incorporation marked in part by the ubiquity of commercial consumption. This is not to say that officials simply mimicked the private sector (or, for that matter, shared identical views on dignification). Rather, they made cultural judgments about "respectable" household consumption by appropriating elements from contemporary discourses of comfort, fashion, and sexuality, as well as hierarchies of taste and beauty. At times social providers presented their brand of ordered, collective consumption as superior to the excessive consumerism of individual purchasing. In other cases, however, Peronist authorities sought to deliver forms of assistance patterned on the idealized consumption habits of middle-class sectors and even the splendor of the urban bourgeoisie.

Peronist representations of collective freedom may seem strangely familiar to us, for in certain respects they resemble depictions of the good life in other postwar consumer societies. There is more than a passing resemblance between portraits of mass abundance in postwar U.S. suburbia and Peronist-era propaganda, especially in their idealizations of domestic space and gender relations, which at times look like scenes taken from classic U.S. television programs of the era.[81] While U.S. television had minimal impact in the Peronist era, Hollywood movies and other mass-media imports were enormously popular; these products may have influenced the style, if not also the content, of print and film propaganda in the New Argentina. The "Ozzie and Harriet" vision of postwar Argentina may remind us of the permeability of social politics in this era and the transnational circulation of consumer culture. Yet there were also significant differences between these cases. Argentine mass consumption bore influences not only from the United States but also from other parts of the globe, especially Western Europe and the Spanish-speaking world. The "stuff" of the good life was not the same in each case (notably, there was less emphasis on the automobile as a marker of popular plenty in Argentina than in the United States). Most important, with regard to delivering a plentiful life, Peronist portrayals stressed the role of the state and other institutions rather than that of the supposedly free play of market forces. Officials envisioned nonmarket consumption as creating not a carnival of consumerist pleasure marching to a capitalist beat but an ordered social parade in which laboring majorities were no longer mere spectators but joined other classes in enjoying a share of the economic bounty of modern times.

Through this approach to welfare, Perón and his followers turned key assumptions of Argentine social politics on their head. They replaced the pinched rhetoric of minimum thresholds and necesidades básicas employed by earlier reformers (who, in their defense, were concerned with making proposals palatable to stingy governments). Flush with postwar prosperity, Peronist officials adapted earlier schemes to fit their ambitious paradigm of social justice. The Allies' wartime slogan "Freedom from Want" was reworked with an emphasis on achieving a higher order of enjoyment and comfort. At the same time, the importance some reformers placed on relief as liberation from restraining conventions was stripped away, replaced by an emphasis on national duty, partisan loyalty, and gratitude.

One mark of the Peronists' success in reframing social politics is that, whether willingly or not, individuals seeking to access to assistance were obliged to consider their assigned roles. As reflected in Evita's letters, those pursuing the vida digna presented themselves as meek if enthusiastic supplicants before resource holders. Services may have sometimes fallen short of mounting expectations, but frustrations had little visibility in an increasingly restricted public sphere managed by advocates of an "organized community." Instead, the populace encountered representations of benefactors elevating working Argentines to the plateau of well-being —taking vacations, receiving modern health care, and enjoying family life in tidy domestic settings—that defined social justice globally in the midcentury moment.

5

PARABLES OF PRODIGALITY

As WORKING Argentines saw their consumer horizons widen, both through enhanced purchasing power and access to social assistance, their everyday behavior elicited commentary from fellow members of society. In sizing up the significance of these changes, contemporaries told stories that drew moralizing conclusions about the relationship between consumer choices and Peronist politics. Take, for instance, a 1948 cartoon from a union newspaper, the meatpacker's *Trabajador de la Carne*. The illustration presents a conversation between two persons standing in a doorway. A workingman in factory overalls criticizes an inebriated peer, dressed in a disheveled suit, who boasts that he spent the night partying ("me pase la noche de farra corrida"). The drunkard claims that salaries exist "for having fun, for working when [you] feel like it." The upstanding worker counters with a rebuke: "You are wrong, *compañero*. . . . The economic and social conquests that we have obtained are not for that . . . [;] they are so our families can live better and be happier. Don't waste your money and your health. Consider that you are a soldier of the revolution who has a duty to exert himself producing more to consolidate the economic independence of our patria, so that all Argentines may be happy."[1]

This visual parable formed part of a broad cultural trend of thinking about the dangers of mass consumption in the late 1940s and early 1950s. These two contrasting social types, the diligent provider and the selfish wastrel, circulated throughout Argentine society in this period and helped further set the parameters of citizenship under Peronist rule. Individuals in all societies regularly sift through the stuff of life and assign meaning to acts of consumption. Given the right political conditions, however, even seemingly ordinary consumer practices can become topics of sustained public controversy.[2] The polarizing impact of Peronism created circumstances ripe for such cultural conflict, and antispeculation regulations and other marketplace interventions only added to a fractious environment. Contemporaries focused on populations thrust into the spotlight of mass consumption in the postwar era, above all members of the urban working class. These interpretations were highly subjective, of course, and what one observer considered a frivolous luxury another viewed as a much-deserved material reward. Yet judgments clustered into patterns, with certain types of daily consumption garnering persistent attention from diverse onlookers. Working men and women had their own views on consumption, and it is difficult to know how they responded to such representations of revolutionary duty as the meatpacker's cartoon: did entreaties to the "soldiers of the revolution" provoke a sense of paternal guilt among male laborers, stir feelings of solidarity, or elicit amused smirks?

Despite these individual silences, the wider cultural commentary about everyday acquisition offers crucial insights on the politics of citizenship and consumption under Peronist rule. Most famously, disapproval of popular spending habits reflected the deepening partisan divisions of this era. Anti-Peronist critics from predominately middle- and upper-class backgrounds leveled well-known accusations of wastefulness against the laboring majority. Yet as the meatpacker's cartoon indicates, consumer commentary was not confined to the opposition. In fact, state officials had their own concerns regarding excessive spending that bore unacknowledged commonalities with anti-Peronist views of a populace governed by unruly appetites. In conjunction with efforts to mold loyal, productive workers for the Nueva Argentina, Perón's administration launched campaigns to shape citizens into thrifty consumers. Peronist leaders deployed state institutions and rallied their allies in civil society to inculcate "ordered" purchasing habits. Although officials had previously preached the virtues of measured spending, the intensity of these calls increased as inflation became more acute in the early 1950s. However, rather than open a rift between Peronist leaders and their sympathizers, this direction in consumer politics had a more ambiguous impact: on the one hand, it strengthened ideas of partisan solidarity and mass participation, while on the other, it confirmed the central state's desire to set limits to the vida digna.

As the regime expanded its institutional presence in daily life, Peronist authorities articulated new connections among the home, marketplace, and nation. Their goals resembled those of other midcentury attempts to forge "citizen consumers" that sought to encourage feelings of national membership through consumer acts deemed patriotic.[3] Argentine officials stepped up efforts to enhance female command over the household economy and family members. Nominally civil institutions (e.g., the Fundación Eva Perón, unions, and local party associations) were once again entrusted with carrying out the designs of the planning state. The application of tutelary power over citizen consumers reflected Peronism's particular tension between top-down mobilization and the less orchestrated, grassroots expressions of partisan enthusiasm. Within this historical context, the most useful question is not whether consumer spending was "excessive"—a normative judgment that implicitly places one on the side of working-class critics—but rather how consumer purchasing became a source of cultural discord and a justification for state-led projects to forge citizens into economically disciplined subjects. In short, how and why were working people perceived by others as Argentina's prodigal sons and potentially thrifty daughters?

Waste, Plenty, or Justice?

From the mid-1940s onward, observers in Argentina's rival camps pointed to patterns of popular spending to advance competing agendas. The boom in postwar spending power and state-supported redistribution led many commentators to equate working-class consumers with Peronist supporters. There was widespread agreement that working people were eagerly acquiring commercial wares and services, notwithstanding contrary evidence of continued struggles against high prices, shortages, and other constraints revealed in antispeculation campaigns. Debates about prodigality, however, largely ignored these issues. While critics contended that the government was allowing laboring folk to fritter away the country's wealth on fleeting pleasures—in essence, creating a bubble of prosperity that would eventually burst—sympathizers argued that greater buying power allowed deserving working populations to reach a higher plateau of living standards. This war of opinion over the "consuming masses" contributed to a demarcation of political antagonisms that supplanted a loose populist distinction (the people versus the elite) with a far stronger conflation of class and partisan identities (Peronist workers versus an anti-Peronist middle class). Within this climate of worsening acrimony, ordinary acts of consumption became a subject for contentious evaluations of the nation's present condition and future course.

The fact that some observers looked down on the perceived crudeness and base appetites of ordinary folk was hardly new, for the leveling aspects of mass consumption had provoked hand-wringing in earlier decades. Yet for Peronism's most vehement critics, anger at populist politics exacerbated anxieties about social displacement. Peronism was perceived, rightly or wrongly, as seeking to erode markers of class distinction, deference, and cultural hierarchy. Affluent sectors too may have seen their incomes rise during the postwar boom, but some felt their gains were matched, if not outstripped, by those of blue-collar workers and grew uneasy about being overtaken by their "inferiors." The fading of economic prosperity only added to concerns about social standing and feelings of invasion from below. Consequently, working-class consumers became the grist for rumors and jokes that appeared sporadically in the mass media but circulated more widely through word of mouth as censorship tightened in the late 1940s.[4] Onlookers weighed consumer habits in the light of cultural expectations of proper comportment, and the rules of respectability were perhaps less strict in urban areas, but the visibility of the working class in public spaces, particularly those devoted to modern retailing and commercial leisure, caught the eye. Regarding the crowds of shoppers in downtown areas of Buenos Aires and other large cities, commentators noticed more working-class individuals milling about the district's avenues and department stores or lingering in the cafés, restaurants, and movie houses in areas frequented by "respectable" sectors.

Several commonly accepted social types serve as guideposts through the cultural criticism of Peronist mass consumption. In his recollections of the 1950s, the writer Ernesto Goldar remarked on a fashion contemporaries labeled the "Divito" style of dress, favored by workers in Buenos Aires. The very name "Divito" was part of commercial culture, originating in the name of a buffoonish character from a cartoon strip in the humor magazine *Rico Tipo*. The male Divito could be identified by telltale features: he wore high-waisted, peg-legged pants and long, double-breasted coats (in blue or brown) that reached almost to the knee; a white shirt and florid tie completed the ensemble. Interestingly, Goldar saw this as a holdover from the tango-inspired styles of earlier decades but also claimed a U.S. influence via Hollywood: "it is the clothes of the jazzman in a technicolor picture." The female variant wore stiletto heels, narrow pencil skirts, and tight blouses set off by wide belts and tailored jackets; for accessories, she donned hoop earnings, necklaces, and heavy red lipstick. Goldar suggested that these styles were borrowed from middle-class fashions, but by the 1950s they had become so associated with the denizens of popular barrios and suburbs that the urban middle class sought new means to distinguish themselves (for men, by wearing shorter, single-breasted suits).[5] It is unclear how working people responded to this stereotype and whether they found a feeling of group identity in this style of clothing, perhaps even in self-conscious defiance of dominant norms of taste. Viewed from the perspective of the middle class, the Divito was the essence of tackiness, recognized as a marker of the pueblo, which mistook flashiness for elegance.

Other stereotypes spoke to the broader sociological transformations of the period. Gazing on urban crowds, observers discerned a new social character: "*los veinte y veinte*" (the twenty-twenties). Los veinte y viente were recent rural migrants who hung out in the modest urban barrio cafés. On their days off, these workers spent their wages by paying twenty cents for a slice of pizza or a glass of wine and twenty cents on the jukebox to hear a song by Antonio Tormo, the celebrated singer and popular idol.[6] The implication was that these individuals had the narrowest tastes: even with bigger paychecks, they could think of spending their money only on the simplest foods and "vulgar" commercial music. As a reflection on rural migration, this image of the "twenty-twenties" suggested that migrants remained country bumpkins out of place in the cosmopolitan metropolis.

Class-based stereotypes such as the "twenty-twenties" had a comical tone, but they took on a racist edge in another moniker of the time: the *cabecita negra*. Translated literally as "little black heads," the cabecita was also a recent migrant, one to whom city dwellers ascribed backwardness and a slavish identification with the Peronist cause. The prejudice inherent in the term "cabecita negra" (or simply "*los negros*") was rooted in Argentina's longstanding racist thinking about the relationship between the civilized city and barbarous countryside. As a result, some residents of the capital greeted the appearance of more individuals with dark complexions and so-called Indian features on their streets as a social invasion, a perception captured by one legislator's famous description of the Peronist revolution as unleashing an "*aluvión zoologico*" (a "zoological flood"). The sense that the big city was overrun with cabecitas negras or "*negros peronistas*" was shaped by the massive turnout of Peronist supporters for regular partisan rallies such as October 17, during which sympathizers proudly occupied the capital's central square. But these views also reflected the presence of the working class in other public spaces, including downtown commercial thoroughfares, where they challenged older patterns of stratification by rubbing shoulders with members of other classes. In turn, the racially charged persona of the cabecita became a way for critics to project their definition of a Peronist supporter onto certain social sectors. This stereotyping asserted an anti-Peronist identity in Argentina, one rooted in ingrained perceptions of whiteness and feelings of membership in the "civilized" classes defined in opposition to atavistic rural hordes.[7]

In conjunction with collective stereotypes, one individual served above all others as a lightning rod for accusations of waste: Eva Perón. She embodied the negative values detractors associated with Peronist consumption. In their view, Evita was unable to shake her humble origins and upbringing: without putting a fine point on the matter, they claimed that she was a social climber, an arriviste of illegitimate birth from a provincial town who clawed her way up to become the president's wife through her crude sexuality. Her fondness for excessive luxury was seen as a sign not only of her low birth but also of the Peronist regime's hypocrisy. As one critic asked, how could one take seriously the so-called Lady of Hope, the spiritual mother of the poor, if she presented herself as "richly bejeweled, more splendid and shining than Cleopatra"?[8] Evita's enemies focused particular attention on her body, deriding her rough manner of speaking and "common" physical appearance (in particular, her supposedly fat ankles). They complained that she looked like a cast member from a bad commercial film who was enamored of enormous hats and gowns in garish, ill-matching colors; as these observers saw it, Evita's faux pas of wearing evening garments to daytime receptions illustrated that she was not cut out to be the nation's First Lady. Like the Peronist masses, so the argument went, Evita lacked the refinement to know what to do with wealth that had fallen in her lap.[9]

What some opponents found particularly galling was the high cost Evita's tastelessness imposed on the rest of society, for it encouraged gluttonous excesses among the masses. Among anti-Peronists, the classic liberal view of the populace as a pool of potential citizens who could be improved gradually gave way to a pessimistic outlook. The pueblo was seen instead as governed by coarse passions rather than reason, as obeying the impulses of the stomach over the intellect. This reaction explains in part why many anti-Peronists invoked the defense of culture—defined broadly as spiritual and aesthetic refinement, education, and civilized comportment—as a strategy of opposition. Aside from a cohort of mainly right-wing nationalist and Catholic writers, the overwhelming majority of Argentina's intellectuals attacked Peronism as an expression of irrational, antienlightenment values. They pointed to the regime's purges of the public universities and cultural institutions as a sign of Perón's tyrannical bent.[10] Literature served as a forum to take out their frustrations, often in thinly veiled allegories or overtly hostile accounts published abroad and after Perón's fall. The most extreme representation can be found in "La fiesta del monstruo" (the fiesta of the monster), a 1947 short story by Bioy Casares and Jorge Luis Borges that tells the tale of a band of grotesque workingmen: they are virtual animals who speak a nearly impenetrable patois and terrorize a bookish citizen on their way to a political rally.[11] The socialist Américo Ghioldi and other political opponents adopted a similar defense of Enlightenment reason while holding out hope of revealing the true face of Peronism to working-class supporters. Ghioldi's 1946 volume *Libros y alpargatas en la historia argentina* (books and cord-soled shoes in Argentine history) referenced the famed slogan reputedly chanted by working-class Peronists in their confrontations with student groups and others: Alpargatas sí, libros no. The socialist leader sought to rework the symbolic opposition between these material goods: in his view, working people were entitled to both enlightenment and the satisfaction of basic material needs, to both books and plain footwear, and not the false affluence proffered by justicialismo.[12]

Foreign visitors tended to echo these negative assessments about the lack of culture; in addition, they described Perón as another "Latin strongman" and even as a fascist behind the times. While they expressed sympathy for the opposition and decried the constraints on political liberties, most could not help commenting on the spending they saw around them, all the more noteworthy when contrasted with postwar reconstruction elsewhere in the world. These social portraits of Argentine plenty repeated familiar tropes. Following in the steps of turn-of-the-century travelers, one visiting Frenchman claimed that it was impossible to find a man wearing work coveralls, for even lowly workers dressed like department store mannequins: it seemed as if "the entire city of Buenos Aires [were] inhabited by only ministers or bankers or businessmen," he joked.[13] On occasion, travelers offered more probing insights into economic prosperity. The U.S. journalists Ruth and Leonard Greenup noted the difficulties ordinary wage earners faced in making ends meet during the mid-1940s. Nevertheless, they suggested that Argentine workers did not fully appreciate what they enjoyed compared to their counterparts in the United States. They illustrated their point by way of an ironic anecdote about their "criolla" maid, who was a devotee of Perón. Although the maid supposedly ate a "T-bone steak" every day for lunch, she continued to complain to her U.S. employers about the unjust poverty of workers who could afford only large meals of pasta with meat sauce, cheese, and wine. The Greenups implied that their maid and other Argentine workers had been inspired by Peronism to expect more, perhaps even too much.[14]

Indeed, stories about the way maids responded to Peronism as consumers abounded during this period, no doubt because domestic servants were the working people with whom most elite commentators, whether Argentine or foreign, had greatest contact. The gendered associations between women and consumption played an obvious role as well. A former U.S. ambassador to Argentina, James Bruce, recounted one such story in his memoirs. Bruce claims that when he asked his housemaid why she supported Perón, she answered that now she had money to spend on small pleasures such as having her hair done at the beauty salon every week: "Before Perón, we servants never enjoyed such luxuries. Now we do. Other things may be costlier. But to us life has always been expensive and we have had nothing to show for it. Now at last we can feel like ladies."[15] In this case, consumer satisfaction was not about meeting basic needs or providing for one's family. Rather, it was primarily a perception of feminine respectability that came with experiencing commercial services, described as luxuries, that were previously out of reach. For this anonymous maid at least, Peronist rule appears to have meant, in part, "feeling like a lady." Bruce's anecdote should be taken with a large grain of salt, for the ambassador was distanced from the routines of working-class life.[16] Nevertheless, his tale of consumer spending power departed from the ironic tone of most anti-Peronist stereotypes. It suggests that what Bruce's maid and her female peers really wanted was the possibility of emulating the habits of social superiors and participating, if for a few hours at least, in a society with fluid class distinctions.

Yet alternative conclusions could be drawn from these accounts. Some Peronist observers told the stories of well-dressed maids differently, highlighting the affluent classes' resentment at worker gains. In this telling, employers were put off by the better wardrobes and comforts their domestic servants enjoyed, for they supposedly feared a loosening of social distinctions with manual laborers, who would no longer know their proper place.[17] In general, many of the practices and stereotypes that provoked ire from critics were cast by these more sympathetic observers in a favorable light. Derided as a tacky social climber by some, Eva Perón was embraced as a paradigm of rags-to-riches aspiration by countless others. Even as she emerged as a political figure in her own right, one who exerted power behind the scenes and took on an increasingly public persona as the defender of the humble born, Evita retained a self-consciously "feminine" image of glamour through her appearance.

This issue was at times an uneasy one, and Peronist propagandists tried to brush aside the lowlife connotations of her past as an entertainer while still playing on the mystique of her celebrity. But it is clear that the First Lady was something of the nation's First Shopper as well. Accompanied by her closest aides and her mother, she regularly made shopping expeditions to Buenos Aires's top department stores, boutiques, and jewelers. Professional hairstylists attended to her requests, while renowned Argentine fashion designers including Paco Jamandreu made sure her closets were stocked with the latest garments. In 1947 Eva Perón received an invitation from Spain's dictator, General Francisco Franco, and embarked on a European voyage. When not meeting with foreign dignitaries, she added to her collection of gowns and arranged with Christian Dior to have the latest Parisian couture sent to her back home.[18] To some Peronist supporters, Evita represented a model of beauty to admire; her fashion and hairstyles style were rumored to be a source of inspiration for barrio seamstresses and their customers.

For individuals who lacked the funds or desire to emulate the First Lady, however, her public persona conveyed an acceptance of prevailing norms of tastefulness and fashion supplied by the consumer marketplace. As a political figure, she rejected the inequities of capitalism and the greed of "oligarchic elites," but as a consumer, she accepted bourgeois ideals of material luxury and feminine beauty. Without making her any less controversial, Evita's own style captured the sense that one could be a proud Peronist and still "feel like a lady."

But Evita was certainly not the only Peronist consumer. In fact, political authorities extolled their administration for having made life better for the pueblo. Perón and his assistants focused their propagandizing energies on elements that fit within their productivist ethic: public works projects under construction, diligent state employees hard at work, crops being harvested, and factories in full swing. Not surprisingly, then, the regime's propaganda makers favored the iconography of smokestacks and burly male workers over that of the shopper in the department store. Nonetheless, high-ranking officials contrasted the bonanza of the present with the deprivations of previous decades. Perón maintained that justicialista planning had boosted production and freed the pueblo from the hold of "trusti-fied capitalism." Instead of ending up in the hands of "four or five capitalist consortiums," Argentina's great natural wealth now flowed to those who deserved it most. He boasted in August 1946, "Every one of us can thank God that we live in this veritable paradise, recognized by all the foreigners who visit us, who spend the majority of their time in restaurants or milling about in shops or buying goods at prices that in today's world are almost inconceivable."[19]

The second tier of state, union, and party officials elaborated on these glowing opinions. At a union rally in September 1949, Labor Minister Freire enumerated the workplace protections, social benefits, and "*jornales dignos*" (worthy wages) obtained by workers. But he also told his audience, "Today one consumes much more beef, much more bread, etc. And despite the fact that chicken is more expensive than before, one eats twenty times more of it than when it cost $1.50." Although this statement acknowledged inflation's threat to popular spending power, it implied that incomes were winning the race against prices—an argument that did not fully jibe with the antispeculation rhetoric of other officials. A former glass worker, Freire reminded his peers of conditions in the past and maintained that Peronist prosperity extended to other realms of consumption besides food: "Now one cannot find a worker without a tie, without a good shirt, without good shoes."[20] In this case, the image of the well-dressed worker was deployed not in a mocking tone (as in the Divito stereotype) but as visual evidence of the little improvements accompanying Peronist rule.

FIGURE 11. A multigenerational family from the barrio of La Boca enjoying a Christmas celebration, including traditional year-end gifts distributed by Peronist organizations. *Archivo
General de la Nación, Departamento Fotográficos, Subsecretaría de Informaciones, V-3, doc. 247711
(n.d.); reproduced courtesy of the archive.*

Authorities took pains to stress that consumer gains occurred on a national
scale and not just for a select labor aristocracy in the capital. In speeches to working-
class audiences in Buenos Aires, Freire described his recent visit to the interior
provinces (unknowingly repeating the itinerary of reform-minded individuals, such
as José Bialet Massé and the socialist Alfredo Palacios, who documented the privations of rural families in earlier decades). In Santiago del Estero the nivel de vida
had grown by leaps and bounds, according to Freire. Now one no longer saw mal-
nourished, barefoot children, he claimed, and thanks to higher purchasing power,
the inhabitants had "begun to live like people, not like slaves." Playing on patriotic
pride and class solidarity, Freire recounted his conversation with a female telephone
operator in El Chaco who described the changes brought by Peronism in everyday terms: "Now, we not only dress well and drink coffee with milk, but we also
eat steak."[21]

Celebrations of material abundance, however, also tended to highlight the
class struggle required to achieve these gains, a tendency best illustrated in the

most famed Peronist stereotype, the *descamisado* (the shirtless one). The term became central to Peronist political discourse, bundling together a potent, complex set of associations regarding labor and social status. The descamisado referenced the modest resources of the average worker, but it turned a source of shame—having no dress shirt and, by extension, no coat or tie—into a badge of honor. (A similar inversion was performed with other negative stereotypes, including the anti-Peronist racial epithet "cabecita negra," which Evita employed as term of endearment for her supporters and a rallying point for an oppositional partisan identity.) As one of the era's central propagandistic tropes, the descamisado was adopted by various organizations allied with the Peronist movement (including a pro-regime mass-circulation newspaper of the same name). While acknowledging the proletarian virtues of the (male) laborer, the descamisado illuminated the changes in material living standards experienced by working people. Pronouncements made by Freire and his counterparts drove home the point that laborers were now secure and contented, well-fed and better dressed than they had been in the past. At union gatherings labor leaders adopted the ritual of removing their suit coats before the meeting started as a gesture to the desamisado past. But they were not left literally shirtless (in fact, critics wagged their tongues at the expensive shirts and silk ties worn underneath union bosses' coats). The descamisado thus balanced between extolling the humble sacrifice of working people and bucking the social insults of the past by displaying their new standing.

Focusing on the war of opinion over the meanings of popular consumption—a war waged by Peronists and anti-Peronists, local commentators and foreigners alike—one can easily to lose sight of social practices that fell outside questions of prodigality. Despite the political significance attributed to consumer acts and actual improvements in spending power, many consumer routines were not radically altered. In popular neighborhoods and small communities, shoppers faced a familiar marketplace. Working Argentines likely spent the bulk of their wages in local stores rather than in downtown commercial districts, if only because the lack of home refrigeration encouraged frequent purchases of food from stallholders and corner almacenes, many of which offered short-term credit between paychecks to retain customers. Webs of mutual dependence and sociability similarly linked working-class consumers to local clothes makers, peddlers, and other merchants. The business institutions that girded mass consumption in Peronist Argentina resembled, in most fundamental respects, those forming the commercial landscape of the 1930s and early 1940s. In short, the debates surrounding consumption during Perón's first term had more to do with controversies over spending power than with "retailing revolutions" and other innovations in commercial practices.

Moreover, purchasing was not exclusively a topic for cultural criticism and partisan mobilization, for it also could provide an escape from the era's acrimonious politics. Flipping through the pages of women's magazines or other mass-market publications from this time period, one entered a fantasy realm with few references to clashes between Peronists and anti-Peronists. In these commercial cultural settings, advertisers presented avenues to individual satisfaction rather than evidence of divisive "social conquests." These representations underscored the sensual delights of consumer products, complete with mock testimonials from women who owed their glowing skin to Manuelita soap or the man who regained his lost love after shaving with Palmolive razors.[22] Despite the Peronist regime's nationalist rhetoric, businesses continued to appeal to their customers' fascination for foreign goods and international fashions. Commercial regulations may have limited the influx of imported wares, but local manufacturers found ways to satisfy desires for foreign items, in some cases passing off domestic products as imports, as in advertisements for Heather lipstick and Helen Harper sweaters, each a "North American creation" made in Argentina.[23]

Yet the Peronist presence in the marketplace was impossible to avoid entirely, be it the "Clausurado" sign plastered across a local store, the newsreels that preceded feature films, or the descriptions of popular plenty offered by state officials. Even the regime's supreme leaders used the allure of commercial culture to boost their own popularity. Unlike their staid predecessors, the president and First Lady mingled regularly with theater and film stars, recording artists, and athletic champions (most famously, the boxer and folk hero José María "El Mono" Gatica). They were photographed attending public events of all types, including soccer matches at the Racing Club's newly constructed President Perón Stadium in Avellaneda. In these contexts, Peronist authorities presented widened access to commercial culture and mass entertainments as evidence of collective triumph. The emphasis was on spending power as a means of achieving greater egalitarianism—a social order where all workers could satisfy basic needs and enjoy comforts—rather than on consumption as the constant striving to satisfy personal appetites. The consumer pleasure experienced by workers came partly from the fact that others were sharing in the bounty.

That is not, however, how all Argentines saw the matter. For some, these perceptions of expanded working-class consumption stoked fears of a loss both of social hierarchy and of the patterns of decorum and cultural distinctions that structured their lives. In a charged partisan environment where class was becoming increasingly mapped onto political divisions, some critics perceived claims of egalitarianism advanced by those in power as a destabilizing threat. Contemporary observers became more aware of popular types along certain links in the chain of acquisition (downtown shopping districts, department stores, cafés and restaurants). Other anti-Peronist critics cared less for such matters and targeted what they considered the crimes of an authoritarian regime. But aspects of consumption surfaced repeatedly in the dismissive rumors and stories told by detractors. These accounts shared a preoccupation with the wastefulness of consumer behavior attributed to the Peronist movement. Whether critics addressed the vulgar appetites of the "masses" or the needless luxury of national leaders, they focused on the uncontrolled nature of consumption, which was cited as a lamentable consequence of the era's political transgressions.

Creating the Consumer

In publicizing the Nueva Argentina, Peronist officials adapted old myths of national plenty, insisting that their country was now a land where even humble workers could eat steak and dress in fine clothing. Behind the scenes, however, government authorities were preoccupied with certain dangers of "excessive" consumption. Naturally, the regime's leaders did not turn up their noses at Divitos, los viente y viente, and cabecitas negras; their concerns ran more toward inflation and other economic problems. Praise of consumer gains did not fall away, but from the late 1940s onward the political emphasis shifted to the responsibility of dutiful citizens as consumers. Through appeals to patriotic sacrifice and partisan solidarity, Perón and Evita encouraged consumers to practice more efficient household management. As part of state-supervised campaigns, Peronist organizations invoked ingrained cultural assumptions about the unrestrained appetites of ordinary folk. Working-class men, in particular, were singled out as lacking the control of their female counterparts. By calling on women as consumers, officials outlined opportunities for mass-political participation for housewives and other popular actors while further justifying interventions at the household level to create more disciplined national subjects. At this juncture, Peronist forms of tutelary power emphasized moral suasion through propaganda outreach and deployed partisan networks to convince audiences of their duty to the nation and movement. Whereas the war on speculation extended regulatory capacity over market forces, the new direction in consumer politics aimed to manage the microlevel practices of ordinary households.

From the earliest days of Perón's presidency, policy experts inside and outside government ranks warned about the "dangers" of mass consumption. Although theories of infraconsumo inspired Miguel Miranda's audacious inward-oriented economic model, government advisers identified purchasing power as a potential source of instability. Short-term spending could detract from long-term investment, and if domestic production did not keep pace with the demand for goods, then inflationary pressures could build. The social scientists associated with the prestigious *Revista de Economía Argentina* approved of the general outlines of the Five-Year Plan and claimed that its nationalist priorities followed in the path of their founder, Alejandro Bunge. But soon after Perón's election, figures associated with the Instituto Bunge argued that labor policies might augment consumer spending power without deepening national investment or industrial development, asserting paternalistically that "a pueblo is not happier because it has more cars, refrigerators, mechanical devices, or simply liquor and cigarettes." In the view of the social scientific establishment, redistribution was a matter of satisfying minimalist definitions of need through social programs rather than through programs that channeled income to working households.[24]

While actors weighed the macroeconomic implications of consumer acquisition, the regime's antispeculation campaigns began to define the duties of consumers as collaborators with state designs. As early as 1946, Eva Perón encouraged housewives to adopt careful spending habits and keep in mind their contributions to the greater good of the Peronist cause.[25] Even at the height of postwar economic prosperity, top officials stuck a similar tone of restraint. Labor Secretary Freire warned that the family subsidy given to workers with dependents should not be wasted on buying "superfluous things" but rather spent on maintaining a healthy, restful home. The president, too, called on his supporters to combine collaboration with commercial regulations by avoiding waste at home and increasing production at work: "Your collaboration should consist not only in your responsibilities as citizens, but also in maintaining the rhythm of production, ignoring bad counselors, or to be more exact those enemies that suggest to you some other way of achieving social gains."[26] Although concerns with economic destabilization were key, Peronist authorities fixed consumer thrift within midcentury notions of governmentality, including the idea that measured habits would contribute to collective health and proper functioning of each laboring citizen's "human motor."[27]

Officials stepped up institutional efforts to shape the behavior of supporters as thrifty consumers during the twilight of the postwar boom. Miranda argued it was possible to expand both consumption and investment, and the results bore him out for around three years; by 1949, however, evidence to the contrary was mounting. Try as they might, state officials had not escaped Argentina's classic bind between exporting agricultural goods and consuming them at home. With rising domestic demand, there was less beef and grain to export and thus a dwindling source of foreign exchange. Ranchers and farmers responded to Peronist management of agriculture by reducing their investments and output, which added to trade imbalances; scarcity of imported raw materials and capital goods contributed to slumping domestic manufacturing. As in other Latin American cases, inward-oriented development in Argentina succeeded at first but soon ran into obstacles: declining agro-exports set off a cycle of yawning trade deficits, foreign-exchange scarcities, and barriers to further industrialization.[28] It was clear that Peronist antispeculation controls could not contain market forces. Shortages of food, clothing, and other staples became more frequent as a result of weak agricultural harvests and bottlenecks in production. At the same time, the official consumer inflation rate in Argentina reached 31 percent by 1949, the highest annual level since 1890.[29]

These trends posed two serious problems for Perón's government. First, policymakers' inability to stamp out rising prices presented a political challenge, for the flouting of commercial regulations in the black market lent credence to opponents' accusations that the Peronist vida digna was a sham. Second, these pressures led labor unions to press for higher wage contracts from employers and the government. The tensions between these Peronist allies—one fighting to stop the slide in spending power and the other hoping to restrain inflation—flared during contract negotiations and strikes.[30] Perón responded to these conditions by reshuffling his inner circle of advisers. He forced out Miranda and his collaborators in January 1949 and replaced them with a new body, the National Economic Council, a team of ministers who, unlike Miranda, had formal training and greater experience in public administration. The council looked for ways to tighten government spending, impose order on credit policies, and address the slowdown in agricultural exports. Alfredo Gómez Morales, the minister of finance, and his counterparts moved slowly so as to attract a minimum of public attention, primarily, it seems, because Perón wished to delay any major actions until after the 1951 elections.[31] Rather than institute a complete change in direction, the economic team devised a patchwork of solutions. Like Miranda, they were not averse to moderate inflation, which would operate as a hidden tax on property-holding sectors while benefiting others (including industrialists and recipients of state bank loans, who enjoyed negative real interest rates). When combined with continued rent freezes and other measures, inflation could serve the interests of workers as well, at least as long as wages continued to increase more quickly than prices. Policymakers were concerned, however, that the days of favorable inflation were over and that it now threatened to erode income redistribution and the popularity of the regime itself.[32]

In line with the shifting economic priorities, Peronist organizations shaped an ideal of the rational consumer. Propagandists broadcast speeches about spending habits on state radio and reprinted them in the press, incorporated lessons on frugality into commercial mass magazines and films, and published materials on practicing thrift in everyday life. One such initiative, a pamphlet titled *Guerra a muerte a los especuladores dijo Perón* (fight to the death against speculators, says Perón), compiled speeches given during a well-publicized September 1950 conference about the problem of high prices.[33] As the title suggests, Perón continued to lash out at the "vulgar thieves" and "economic delinquents" behind speculative conspiracies. Nevertheless, he focused on the shortcomings of Argentine shoppers, who he felt had become complacent with the material benefits of Peronist rule. He criticized in particular the "*rastacuero*" (literally, "upstart") behavior of fellow Argentines, the custom of living beyond one's means and publicly displaying the illusion of wealth and high status, or as Perón put it, the need to "give the appearance that we are more than we are." He contended that people threw money around at restaurants and stores without checking to see whether they were being ripped off. The president grumbled that there were too many "loafers" (*harraganes*) and "fools" (*zonzos*) who complained about inflation but spent money recklessly on needless vices (such as gambling at the horse track). Using an example that he would repeat frequently, Perón bemoaned all the perfectly good meat and bread he saw dumped in the trash on his way to work in the morning; while postwar Europe languished in penury, the president noted, fellow citizens failed to appreciate their land of plenty.[34]

Other figures within the Peronist movement echoed these judgments about excessive comfort while also minimizing anxieties over the postwar boom's end. Ángel Gabriel Borlenghi, who held the posts of interior secretary and secretary-general of the commercial employee's union, put a positive spin on long lines and lingering shortages, treating these consumer travails as evidence of social justice in the making. Addressing an audience of commercial workers, he claimed that crowds waiting for cinema and theater tickets were actually "blessed lines" and signs of "our prosperity and our joy," since they meant that the working majority could afford such entertainments. For those who complained about these conditions, Borlenghi illustrated how material life had improved: "Today we stand in line [for taxis] because nobody wants to walk even five blocks; everyone has money to pay for a car, we fight over taxis. Before there were entire generations that never had taken a taxi because they could not afford it."[35]

These statements illustrate the ambivalence with which Peronist leaders viewed mass consumption. It was an integral facet of social justice but also a potentially corrupting force that threatened their conception of the ordered nation. Enticed by sudden spending power, popular households could become obsessed with satisfying consumerist desires. At a basic level, officials were correct in their assessment: price controls failed because shoppers accepted the higher than official prices offered by merchants. But motivations were complicated. Some consumers paid no heed to controls out of a lack of concern or even spite, yet many Argentines simply lacked the time to track down goods at official prices or had no alternative to buying black-market products. Rather than acknowledge these realities, Perón created a new persona—the negligent consumer—to stand alongside the speculator in the rogues' gallery of the people's enemies. Criticisms of unpatriotic consumer behavior played on supporters' guilt, while Peronist leaders presented themselves as tutors who would instruct Argentine citizens in measured comportment. Perón asserted that "every Argentine should be his own price inspector" and gave the public practical advice on shopping: he recommended carrying a list of price controls when going to buy socks; offer the store owner the official price, he said, and if he does not accept, call the police and have him carted off to Villa Devoto. If every citizen did this, the president concluded, speculation would be eliminated in a mere forty-eight hours.[36] This type of populist discourse pushed the boundaries between public and private. Earlier governments had rebuked profiteering and praised savings, but no previous president had taken household economics to the extreme of offering citizens advice on shopping for socks.

"Home economics" (*economía doméstica*) thus became a political buzzword. At the 1950 conference, Eva Perón named María Rosa Calviño de Gómez to head a new mediating institution simply called the Organización de Consumidores. In January of that year she had entrusted Calviño de Gómez with opening the first unidad básica, which illustrates the intimate ties between the new consumer group and the partisan networks of the Partido Peronista Femenino.[37] The most ambitious consumer education campaigns were directed through the PPF's female unidades básicas as a complement to practical classes on domestic management and other areas defined as "naturally" female skills. While women were seen as instrumental in the crusade against speculators, they were even more important "weapons" in reducing wastefulness. It fell on housewives to act as "tutelary angels of home economics" by ridiculing the wild spending of the men in their households and honing their skills at managing family budgets.[38] By focusing on the significance of housewives, state officials highlighted the political importance of women, and not only as maternal agents of reproduction and childrearing. They insisted on the importance of the household economy—shopping, food preparation, and forms of self-sufficient production (tending gardens, fashioning clothes, and so on)—to the vitality of the national economy as a whole. In rhetorical terms at least, housewives were depicted as analogous to state planners, employing rational techniques to ensure maximum efficiency in the use of national resources. Propagandists replaced the emphasis on sensual pleasure found in advertisements pitched at female consumers with a more somber tone, one that presented consumption as a serious business of civic duty.

This political strategy was reinforced by Peronist-era social trends. Reforms boosting wage-earner incomes allowed a greater number of families to withdraw women (and children) from the official workforce. The mid-1940s witnessed growing rates of marriage and family formation as well, which reflected optimism about economic opportunities. By 1947 only one in five women over the age of fourteen reported having a paid job, an all-time low in Argentina: it is probable, therefore, that more women than ever were devoted exclusively to the duties of being a housewife. To be sure, state officials courted female laborers outside the home and did more than previous administrations to support principles of equal pay for equal work; women's wages in industry crept closer to matching those of male workers, and female laborers swelled the ranks of unions.[39] By equating women with housewives and mothers, then, Peronist authorities backed a restrictive paradigm of gender relations in which the home was their most legitimate sphere.[40] Within these patriarchal boundaries, women were presented as loyal agents who would follow the instructions of the state and who, unlike feckless male wage earners, were assumed to be more responsible and malleable to partisan instruction. Officials did not ignore male consumers or union members entirely in their reeducation efforts; antispeculation speeches were reprinted in union newspapers, and handbooks on home economics were written in gender-neutral terms with illustrations of both husbands and wives.[41] But they depicted legions of thrifty and loyal female consumers as an alternative ally to the predominately male unions demanding higher wages. These initiatives were part of a larger drive to offset the influence of organized labor by reaching out to women, children, the poor, and other unorganized sectors.[42] This distinction may explain why Peronist authorities focused mainly on consumer education propaganda and instruction through mediating institutions instead of, say, supporting consumer rights advocates.

The reeducation of female consumers fell under the control of Eva Perón and her agencies, including the Partido Peronista Femenino and the Fundación Eva Perón. As was mentioned previously, neighborhood-level unidades básicas offered their members classes on home economics, nutrition, clothes making, and other skills designed to shape their behavior as shoppers, producers, and consumers. From 1950 onward, they also distributed lists of official prices to women in each district, an effort aimed at securing popular compliance with antispeculation campaigns. The lists were also published in newspapers, but materials for the unidades came with explicit instructions on how to act: "If the merchant does not keep to the established price, this requires the intervention of the closest police agent to confirm the infraction and make an official report, avoiding in all cases discussions or altercations given that the authorities have precise instructions on how to proceed."[43] The warning reveals how Calviño de Gómez and other party operatives envisioned consumer politics in hierarchical terms: they would issue orders, and female consumers at the grassroots would comply in an efficient manner. Likewise, the subdelegate in charge of each unidad básica was instructed to inspect markets and stores but similarly told to leave punishment to the police. Perhaps because officials feared that popular anger at profiteering could get out of hand, women were prohibited from forming larger "neighborhood commissions" to patrol businesses.

To provide information about duties complementing those regarding the marketplace, the PPF also gave women propaganda on household thrift published by the Caja Nacional de Ahorro Postal and other state agencies.[44] One such pamphlet, titled *Economía familiar* (1950), offered instruction on prioritizing daily expenditures, designing written budgets, and controlling every peso. By applying the methods of economic planning at the microlevel of the home, families would act much as the state did at the national level and contribute to defending living standards. Recalling the household surveys conducted by Figuerola in the early 1940s, these sample budgets allotted the male "head" of the family with the largest share of disposable income, to be used for basics such as food and clothing but also for little pleasures, such as cigarettes and socializing with co-workers. Although women were assumed to control the purse strings, men were once again granted a larger share of consumption in the era's "scientific" guidelines for domestic management. Both sexes, however, were expected to control their impulses and thereby contribute to the defense of their own spending power and the quest for national economic independence.[45]

These manuals on planning household consumption dovetailed with broader campaigns to encourage saving among the populace. The Caja Nacional de Ahorro Postal's main function was to act as a savings institution for low- and moderate-income groups; founded in 1915, the agency stepped up its outreach efforts to educate children on the values of thrift. Lesson plans for elementary school children concentrated on practical skills such as distinguishing between necessary and superfluous spending, often by references to the aphorisms of Bernandino Rivadavia, José de San Martín, and other national founders. Older students read treatises on the importance of present-day savings for future consumption. The caja's directors believed that ultimately savings could best be inculcated through practice, and to this end, the agency had offices located in public schools where students could make deposits; additional outposts were set up in factories and workplaces. There were some 790 total savings branches in existence by 1949 (almost half in the city of Buenos Aires), up almost 40 percent from 571 the previous year.[46] These various efforts appear to have paid off (or at least complemented savings trends). Even accounting for inflation, the value of deposits in the caja and other savings accounts increased in the Peronist era (with a dip in the early 1950s). Savings occurred despite the existence of negative real interest rates, which discouraged placing money in the bank.[47] It appears that in addition to spending on consumer goods, setting up a new home, and investing in property or land, many popular Argentines saved at least a share of their rising incomes for a rainy day, notwithstanding the cost posed by inflation.

In establishing their model of the thrifty consumer and saver, officials combined positive appeals to duty with the suggestion that wasteful habits were unpatriotic and thus anti-Peronist. This was a central message of the official speeches and pamphlets on budgets, but it was raised by allies of the Peronist movement outside the government as well. For instance, in the lead up to Perón's 1951 reelection campaign, the famed tango lyricist Enrique Santos Discepolo took to the airwaves to lend his support for the cause—a particularly high-profile example of commercial celebrity deployed to mass-political ends. Santos Discepolo performed a series of comical radio pieces in which he addressed the criticisms of an imaginary anti-Peronist *contrera* called "Mordisquito." Among the scores of accusations and rumors that Santos Discepolo sought to refute were the complaints of consumer shortages and high prices. In particular, he mocked those who lamented the absence of foreign goods from store shelves, labeling them pretentious elitists who placed the right to purchase imported tea above a national economy that benefited the pueblo.[48]

The Peronist drive to shape behavior in the economic sphere of everyday life raises difficult questions about popular engagement with thriftiness campaigns. I will return to audience responses to these overtures, but for now it is worth noting that as discouragements of wasteful spending trickled down into society, the messages resonated with some individuals. This type of reaction can be seen in a 1951 letter sent to the Ministry of Technical Affairs by Selva Zulema Durán de González, an outspoken *empleada* (employee, possibly a domestic servant). Hailing from the provincial city of Santiago del Estero, this woman expressed her admiration for Peronist public works and other accomplishments, but she also disparaged the consumption habits of fellow residents in her community. Despite her proud identification as an average person ("one who mixes every day in the crowd," as she put it), this woman argued that salary improvements caused more harm than good: "The majority of the beneficiaries are not ready for the benefits, and are guilty of the economic disequilibrium that almost all we housewives know about the hard way. The money that they earn is now spent with full hands; they spend it away without any control, and that's why from everywhere emerge speculators, usurers for whom no fine or arrest is enough." Male workers should have devoted their "splendid salaries to better their conditions of life, their homes, their clothing, the future of their children." Instead, the letter writer claimed, these wastrels blew their wages at local stores and sent their children out to buy wine for a "continual drunken spree." Durán de González felt that these individuals should be made to invest their money, thereby punishing speculators and allowing their children to live in a more "decorous," socially responsible manner.[49]

There are multiple issues that merit commentary in this remarkable document. Clearly this woman saw the issue of consumer waste largely through the lens of gender relations, in particular a supposed lack of responsibility among male workers and the negative consequences their consumer habits had for wives and children. These were certainly not the self-sacrificing descamisados of official propaganda. She expressed familiar concerns about the pleasure-seeking appetites of working people, although she seemed to lay the blame on a lack of "preparation," that is, on ignorance, more than on an innate crudeness. Likewise, her letter drew a connection between spendthrift behavior and the predations of speculators, who like parasites suck the lifeblood from undisciplined men. While she praised ordered spending habits, she focused on denouncing the excesses of others instead of recounting her own measured routines. At no point did her letter describe compliance with official mandates on thrift or participation in the types of activities organized by unidades básicas (although she comes across like an ideal candidate for such campaigns). Rather than reject all forms of purchasing, the petitioner distinguished consumer squandering from beneficial outlays on housing, clothing, savings, and so on. The letter's conclusion is clear: if many working people could not rationalize their spending willingly, then the government should take command in their best interests.

These opinions would have been music to the ears of state authorities, but one cannot assume that all Argentines viewed contemporary debates about waste and plenty in these terms. Campaigns to order household spending did not stop unions from demanding higher contracts or consumers from voicing their displeasure at merchants. Continued demands for better antispeculation enforcement suggest that many ordinary consumers were struggling against the burdens of high prices and shortages and not living the high life some claimed them to enjoy. By calling attention to the supposed prodigality of their supporters, state authorities risked alienating their base. This concern was strong enough that policymakers waited until after the elections to enact measures that would not just encourage but actually impose economic discipline. Nonetheless, although consumer education carried an implicit critique of working-class behavior, it also opened additional avenues of political participation that could draw sympathizers further into state and allied partisan networks.[50] When discussing the duties of thrifty subjects, Peronist leaders downplayed the notion of formal rights, and they ultimately did little to encourage consumer organization along these lines. Instead, their pronouncements emphasized a notion of citizenship resting on patriotic collaboration with a collective cause. In rallying supporters behind voluntary austerity, the Peronist regime called attention to the political significance of seemingly mundane transactions of the marketplace, and in the process, they advanced the boundaries of politics by validating prosaic routines as worthy of attention by the powerful Juan and Eva Perón.

Peronizing Commerce

By the early 1950s, mass consumption in the New Argentina was equated with restrained abundance, with moderate purchasing that ensured the value of every peso. This paradigm of economic citizenship, however, left numerous other facets of everyday getting and spending open to intervention. Actors within the Peronist camp worked to move citizen consumers in other directions, doing so through, among other things, direct interventions in the marketplace. State resources supported the formation of consumer cooperatives and union-run department stores to compete with merchant businesses, and a chain of shops operated by the Eva Perón Foundation targeted a working-class clientele. Other loyalists took influencing consumer habits a step further. Building on state involvement in the mass media, a group of Peronist intellectuals published a general interest magazine, complete with instructions on measured consumption and "cultured" comportment. "Peronist" forms of commerce were designed not to supplant the private sector but rather to provide alternative models. These initiatives operated in more circuitous ways than did campaigns for household economics, working to create national subjects who were not only loyal and thrifty but also amenable to norms of consumption authorities deemed efficient, modern, and "tasteful." Despite their high visibility, most such experiments failed to live up to their creators' expectations; as a result, they shed light on the limits of Peronist consumer politics as a tutelary force.

From mandating neighborhood-level inspections of stores to undertaking consumer education, the Peronist regime exerted an undeniable influence over the domestic marketplace. Nevertheless, officials displayed little interest in the direct sale of consumables to the populace—unlike their counterparts in Mexico, Peru, and elsewhere in Latin America who offered state-run stores for the urban poor.[51] Had they wished to embark on a similar path, officials would have faced an uphill climb, given the high demands Perón's wide-ranging agenda placed on them. Yet government authorities did support institutions that represented working-class consumer interests and sought to create alternatives to merchant retailing. In particular, they channeled aid to consumer cooperatives run by labor unions and other entities. The Five-Year Plan and other policymaking statements stressed the virtues of consumer collectives, and Perón appointed figures such as Jorge del Rio, a leader in attacks against gouging by foreign-owned utility companies during the 1930s, to federal posts.[52] As in the delivery of social assistance programs, allied organizations rather than federal bureaucracies took responsibility for day-to-day operations, attracting and building constituencies and addressing the demands of their members.

These "private" cooperatives complemented state antispeculation and thrift campaigns. Peronist advocates highlighted their importance not only in supplying low-cost, high-quality goods and warding off greedy merchants but also in keeping individualistic consumerism at bay through responsible spending. Although cooperatives were envisioned as a nationwide response to market pressures, those social sectors with prior exposure to the leftist-inspired cooperative movements of the past provided the most fertile ground for expansion. In the Buenos Aires suburb of Quilmes, for example, a committee of twenty-five unions came together with municipal officials and other community representatives in 1947 to form a "workers consumer cooperative." An announcement in the local paper repeated familiar attacks against commercial profiteers and "shameful speculation," and it reached across gender and occupational lines to attract potential members from suburban residents: "*Compañeros* workers, *compañeras* housewives, in this great cooperative you will be well served, you will pay for each article what it is truly worth." Thanks to these appeals to good service and ethical exchange—and, more important, state support and the growth in union ranks—cooperatives reached new heights. According to official estimates, the number of cooperatives nationwide jumped from 844 to 1,249 between 1945 and 1949 alone, with a total membership of approximately 650,000 persons.[53]

These organizations varied enormously in the scope and quality of consumer services they provided. The average cooperative, or *proveeduria*, operated out of a union headquarters and stocked foodstuffs, dry goods, and other household essentials. Notwithstanding the emphasis on women as household managers, membership in union cooperatives hinged on the role of male workers as providers. Given the limited offerings, most working families undoubtedly supplemented cooperative purchases with those obtained from private retailers. But unions with strong government ties strove to create a higher order of shopping experience. The members of the Buenos Aires municipal workers union (an estimated 45,000 strong) could shop at their imposing multilevel store, located on prime real estate near the national Congress building.[54] This and a few other high-profile cooperatives emulated commercial rivals, even as they sought to supply wage earners a refuge from capitalist pressures. This tendency can be best seen in an exceptional cooperative operated by the commercial employees union. In 1951 the union acquired one of the largest department stores on the famed calle Florida of downtown Buenos Aires. The building was an eight-floor belle-époque structure purchased with union funds and a loan from the Fundación Eva Perón. It opened its doors under the name "Grandes Almacenes Justicialistas" (Grand Justicialist Stores, also known simply as "Gran Just").[55]

The union that represented shop attendants and clerks now boasted an impressive commercial facility of its own that functioned as a hybrid cooperative and department store. This experiment with retail sales had many parallels with union-owned hotels: the general public was welcome to shop for goods, with prices kept scrupulously at official levels, while the union rank and file obtained additional discounts. At the store's opening, the union's secretary-general, Ángel Borlenghi, struck a tone of militancy: "It is a revolutionary act which offers proof that we are not in agreement with the manner in which the capitalistic system of the world was developed and that we are helping to resolve these problems by a practical and juridical modification of its structure." Yet Gran Just fused the spirit of worker solidarity with a sense of entitlement to a level of commercial service defined by business practices of the private sector. The overarching goal was to provide a shopping environment for workers comparable to that of other retail emporiums along the commercial thoroughfare. Local businesspeople groused privately that the former owner of the department store had been seeking to unload this property because it had been losing money and had never attracted as "discriminating" a clientele as those its neighbors drew in. Nevertheless, the union hired the former branch manager of Gath y Chavez, one of the city's leading department stores, to direct Gran Just.[56] In the end, working-class consumers and other shoppers strolled down the same aisles that private customers had occupied before, eyeing the racks of clothing, milling about the housewares and linen displays, and circulating among the scores of other products—but now a self-avowed Peronist labor organization was protecting the shoppers from merchant exploitation.

This cooperative was an exceptional case, but a similar impulse to combine shopping pleasure and material abundance with an emphasis on class solidarity and ordered consumption informed other Peronist forays into retailing. Most famously, the Fundación Eva Perón opened its own chain of proveedurias in the early 1950s to sell food and other consumer goods at reduced cost. Like their cooperative counterparts, the FEP stores were presented to the public as streamlining the winding route from producer to consumer and eliminating the commercial intermediaries responsible for profiteering. By selling goods at official rates, the proveedurias would drive down prices in the marketplace. At the inauguration of the first proveedurias in 1951, Eva Perón argued that she intended the stores "to address the needs of housewives, to bring them basic staples at an official price," not because the foundation wanted "to compete unfairly with anyone," but because it did not want "anyone [to] be exploited either."[57] By 1954 the foundation operated approximately 208 stores, 182 of them in Buenos Aires. While consumers in the metropolitan area were the main beneficiaries of this offshoot of the FEP's social assistance programs, propaganda coverage of Evita's proveedurias reached audiences across Argentina.[58]

The FEP's shops exemplified the multiple dimensions of Peronist attitudes toward popular consumption as an element of social justice—above all, the double move of both criticizing and emulating the marketplace. Typically painted a signature shade of light blue, the proveedurias were a visible presence within the urban commercial landscape. Their layout was in some respects similar to that of the classic almacén, with a variety of everyday products on offer, but remade with the clean lines of modernist aesthetics. In contrast to dim, musty shops of the barrios, the FEP's stores gleamed with windows and electric lights, their shelves stocked with carefully arranged dry goods and canned products. Unlike the average corner store, where wares were rarely labeled, the proveedurias posted lists of prices at their entrances. According to propaganda, modern efficiency did not trump old-fashioned service: an attentive full-service staff offered greetings to the amas de casa and children who frequented their establishments ("Be careful with that, Tito. . . . Don't lose your change, Luisito").[59] In the words of one pamphlet, the employees' "plain but attractive uniforms and amiable disposition offer[ed] a pleasing contrast to the appearance of assistants in certain suburban stores, who often attend[ed] clients with marked displeasure while wearing inappropriate attire." Descriptions of the proveedurias made pronouncements about commercial desire that one might find elsewhere in the postwar world: "The client feels at ease in the salesroom. Everywhere about him are appetizing food products symmetrically arranged in their stands." But unlike other representations of abundance, those attending to consumer satisfaction were Peronist authorities, not private store owners.[60] From the signs outside the shops and the ads in the newspapers to the images of the president and First Lady plastered on the walls inside, these were clearly Peronist spaces.

The stores represented a social political attempt at uplift and offered a pathway to inclusion within consumer society. According to Evita's pronouncements, her proveedurias provided staples to housewives and other shoppers struggling to make ends meet. In addition, the staff was trained to educate consumers about buying cheaply and offered lessons on nutrition, thereby serving a tutelary purpose in keeping with the state's domestic management and public health campaigns. But newspaper advertisements reveal that the FEP proveedurias stocked consumer items of another sort, too, including pâté and brandy (domestically produced, one assumes). These markers of luxury perhaps enticed a more skeptical urban clientele into the shops, at least those who could tolerate making the partisan gesture such an act would entail. Thus, the FEP stores were driven by ideas of uplift and inclusion in a social mainstream for deserving producers, or as the tagline to a proveeduria advertisement read, "General Perón offers justice, not charity."[61] Hence the interest devoted to creating modernist spaces that would surpass the humble neighborhood almacén and rival retail emporiums. This approach to ordering mass consumption sought to strike a balance between two seemingly incompatible goals: providing access to low-cost staples through mechanisms outside the commercial marketplace and swaying consumer aspirations of acquisition.

It is not coincidental that those institutions most involved in asistencia social —namely, unions and the FEP—were most actively involved in Peronist retailing. The underlying impulse was similar: to compensate for the failings of market forces

FIGURE 12. Interior of a Fundación Eva Perón proveeduria. *Archivo General de la Nación, Departamento Fotográficos, Subsecretaría de Informaciones, C-13, doc. 242793 (May 1951); reproduced courtesy of the archive.*

and ensure an elevation in living standards for constituencies identified as particularly vulnerable (and politically valuable). Unlike most social programs, these cooperatives and Evita's proveedurias were not exactly "nonmarket" mechanisms, for their members and clients still engaged in the exchange of wages for consumables. Instead, these were protected spaces at once inside and outside the marketplace, both standing apart from and enmeshed within the consumer webs of urban Argentina. Through retailing alternatives, the Peronist regime's allies staked a presence within a society characterized by higher expectations of working-class consumption; they reached out to popular constituencies not only as rights-bearing citizens and workers but also as thrifty consumers, female managers of the purse strings, and pleasure-seeking shoppers.

For others within this political camp, the quest to reshape consumer behavior went beyond retail sales into the realm of commercial culture. By the late 1940s, the regime had already staked a major media presence through its loyalist newspapers, newsreels, radio stations, and publications. One cohort of Peronist collaborators broadened tutelary campaigns to encompass cultural matters of taste and distinction, breaking new ground in efforts to forge partisan subjects. The mechanism for achieving these ambitions was an unusual magazine called *Argentina*.[62]

In content and format, this magazine, which was published from January 1949 to July 1950, closely resembled mass-market commercial publications, such as *Mundo Argentino* and *Qué Sucedio en 7 Dias* (or their closest U.S. counterpart, *Life* magazine). It began with a series of editorials, followed by news and nonfiction articles, light entertainment, how-to guides, and fictional pieces. Many features dealt explicitly with subjects assumed to be of special interest to women, such as cooking, fashion, and romance. Rather than celebrate proletarian virtues and the rejection of social hierarchies, the creators of *Argentina* upheld an understanding of nationalism based on transforming the behavior of popular majorities in line with urban, middle-class norms.

While *Argentina* was sold alongside mass-market magazines on newsstands across the country, it was published under the auspices of the Peronist government. Its director was no less than a top minister, Oscar Ivanissevich, who was an accomplished physician and early Perón supporter, rewarded for his service by an appointment as minister of education. Ivanissevich saw the role of public education as a means of inspiring loyalty to the Peronist cause among the nation's youth. The magazine's editorial board and contributing writers shared this outlook, as well as their director's conservative Catholic and nationalist take on Peronism.[63] In a 1949 speech, Ivanissevich proclaimed that the magazine's goal was to widen this pedagogical scope in order to "improve and perfect the education of adults," specifically by "replacing that toxic venom of foreign literature." In his view, the combination of public schooling and wholesome, didactic mass media would help rid the nation of "cabecitas negras." Rather than convert this slur into a badge of honor, the minister argued that education would eliminate the cabecita by uplifting the downtrodden and developing a "social conscience, an awareness of social responsibility" among all the nation's residents.[64]

To accomplish these goals, the magazine editors courted the enormous audiences for commercial culture that already existed in midcentury Argentina.[65] Although issues related to consumption were not the exclusive focus of *Argentina,* they did occupy a place of prominence in this "commercialized" genre of propaganda. For the contributors to *Argentina,* the question of taste revolved around what it meant to be "*culto.*" In this context, the term encapsulated a set of understandings regarding how "educated" individuals should behave in society, in an implicit contrast to those seen as backward, uncouth, and barbaric. The definition of "culto" was subject to contestation, but it centered on the idealized practices of the urban bourgeoisie and held up the high arts, literature, and classical music as markers of taste. Articles instructed readers on correct "*costumbres*" and "*modales*" (loosely, customs and comportment) at home as well. A feature entitled "La mesa bien puesta" (the well-set table), written by "Tatiana," informed readers on proper place settings, decorative centerpieces, and recipes for "*Tomates a la hortelana*" and other delicacies.[66] These discussions assumed a degree of affluence: the accompanying photos showed elegant dining rooms with white table cloths, china, crystal, and the accoutrements for multiple courses. In this regard, the magazine's paradigm of good taste was not drastically different from that found in general interest and women's magazines.

Yet the editors of *Argentina* tailored their didactic messages to the political context of Peronism. The workers portrayed in the pages of *Argentina* showed how even the humble-born could aspire to be culto. Take, for example, the magazine's profile of Mr. Fortini, a thirty-six-year-old former tire factory laborer who had become the mayor of the Buenos Aires suburb Lomas de Zamora. The article and accompanying photographs took pains to show Fortini hard at work in his new job as a public servant. Whether eating breakfast in his office at 7 a.m., personally supervising the construction of new roads in the suburb, or visiting sick children at the local hospital on the weekend, Fortini was emblematic of the "new Argentine worker" created by Perón. The author of this profile, Margot Guezúraga, called him a "complete man," and she praised his agreeable appearance: "I am in admiration of how he dresses well and I ask myself where he discovered the secret of true elegance and how he did not fall into the *snobismo* of those recently ascended from their habitual sphere." This passing dig at social climbers aside, the article extols Fortini not only for his much deserved upward mobility and accomplishments as mayor but also for his manners. Naturally, the fact that Fortini was married and had children resonated with the Catholic tone of this publication, as did his measured tastes and "nationalist" preferences: "Fortini smokes little. At the table he drinks a good glass of Argentine wine. His favorite dish is steak. . . . [A]lthough he gets up at the official Argentine hour, sometimes due to his work at city hall he returns home at 3 a.m." Moreover, the fact that he was concerned with the landscaping of his suburb shows his "soul as a poet." Guezúraga concludes that Fortini was certainly not one of those "workers who runs around with a bomb hidden under a hirsute beard"; he was instead an exceptional representative of the Peronist worker.[67]

The female working class received more oblique treatment by *Argentina*'s editors, probably because their conservative vision of the family rested on a gendered division of labor with a stay-at-home mother and breadwinning father. Working-class women appeared in the guise of housewives, and the magazine carried articles encouraging females to be disciplined consumers. "Dress Well without Waste," proclaimed a how-to guide on fashion that offered practical tips on avoiding fleeting trends, choosing quality fabrics, and so on. Far more frequent, however, were advertisements enticing women to spend money on beauty products and other consumer goods. In an apparent contradiction, articles on thrifty clothing were followed by pages of illustrations for lavish garments of taffeta, lace, and silk, suggesting the challenges faced by the magazine's contributors in coupling their notions of taste to the political demands of moderation. Designs for floor-length evening gowns, complete with jeweled accessories, seemed of scant practical use for transforming working-class women into disciplined consumers. Class biases and ideals of female sexuality crept into these columns, as in the case of an article on this pressing issue: which women should wear fur coats? According to the magazine's resident fashion expert, Eugenia de Chikoff, the fur coat was the "dream of all women." But not all individuals had the appropriate body type to wear them. Some women simply lacked the right silhouette—tall and slender, like the elegant, fair-skinned models depicted in the illustrations—and instead were too small and stocky (*redonditas*), body traits that in this era had negative connotations.[68]

Despite voicing such opinions, the contributors to *Argentina* did not see themselves as cultural elitists. The magazine invoked its popular appeal in every issue. According to its own survey, readership was split almost evenly between men and women; a quarter lived in the capital, Buenos Aires, with the remainder in the interior (a distribution matched roughly by the population as a whole); the majority (68 percent) of households where *Argentina* was read earned less than 1,000 pesos a month, which placed them within the ranks of blue-collar and modest white-collar sectors.[69] Monthly circulation averaged 55,000 copies during the first year, and multiplying this factor against circulation figures, the editors concluded that *Argentina* had a massive readership of 715,000. Naturally, this numerical sleight of hand placed the magazine in the best light.[70] One article argued somewhat clumsily that there was a frenzied buzz about *Argentina* on the street, with people desperately seeking to borrow a copy from their friends and struggling to get their hands on the latest issue: "We will not comment on the fights, on the readers who go to the police station to complain about the seller who sold the magazine's issue that should have been reserved for them. We will not comment on merchant profiteering [*agio*]."[71] It was ironic that a magazine published by the government would point to usurious merchants as evidence of popular success. Such inconsistencies were less important, it appears, than was creating an image of this state-funded magazine as commercially viable and "nonoligarchic."

In the end, however, this commercial cultural experiment ended abruptly, though apparently not from a lack of audience. Ivanissevich was forced to step down from his position as minister of education in May 1950, and the magazine vanished shortly thereafter.[72] In the wake of *Argentina*'s demise, cultural policymakers pursued other attempts to reach mass audiences via magazines, including publications, such as *Mundo Peronista,* with a more heavily partisan tone. Reflecting the deteriorating economic climate, *Mundo Peronista* tackled other consumption matters, above all, coordination between household economy and planning authorities. The failure of *Argentina* magazine reflects the larger pattern of Peronist interventions in commercial culture, how officials did (and did not) seek to mold consumers into political subjects. Despite their occasional embrace of cultured taste, the regime's leaders were reticent to condemn commercial media and popular entertainments as inherently depraved, corrupting, or immoral. Eva Perón's background as a radio star made this a particularly untenable position, and officials favored an approach to propagandizing that drew elements from the appeal of commercial culture.

Argentina formed part of the "culture wars" of the Peronist era. It suggests how officials were concerned about their own legitimacy in the eyes of the largely anti-Peronist middle and upper classes—their social peers, after all—and thus had a personal stake in crafting a paradigm of Peronism as culto.[73] Although the magazine's perspective on elegant fashions, luxury goods, and polished behavior was somewhat unusual, the adaptation of orthodox styles and aesthetics was not limited to matters of consumption; it could also be found in the architecture favored by Peronist builders, the décor of social welfare facilities, and state policies toward the arts. In this regard Perón's government resembled other midcentury regimes that retooled mass politics while largely accepting established notions of tastefulness.[74] For all their attacks on foreign trusts and imperialism, Peronistas exhibited a more muted nationalism when it came to the origin of consumer goods and commercial culture. State regulatory policies clearly favored domestic producers, but authorities devoted only sporadic attention to encouraging the population to "buy Argentine"; their bigger concern was that popular consumers become measured purchasers and loyal subjects. What is noteworthy is not the magazine's moralizing about irreligious, foreign influences but the editors' inability to make these themes more central to Peronist politics. In short, certain aspects of mass consumption mattered more than others: lessons on cultured consumption occupied a decidedly subordinate place to antispeculation campaigns, calls for rational spending, and alternative retailing through cooperatives and FEP-run stores.

＊

Argentina magazine represented the outer limit of Peronist efforts to assert tutelary power over consumer purchasing. Prodigality, not taste, garnered the greatest attention in shaping popular sectors into consumer citizens. By contrast, anti-

Peronist critics drew extended associations between wasteful spending and taste. By mocking the consuming masses and the false luxury of their leaders, detractors took stock of perceived challenges to the cultural order from a working class defined as uniformly Peronist. Anxieties about economic decline played a role in piquing interest in "excessive" consumption, but the debate about prodigality cannot be fully attributed to the inflationary crisis of the early 1950s. In the heyday of postwar prosperity, the presence of working people in the commercial spaces of the modern metropolis elicited commentary both critical and laudatory, stoking fears of social invasion and inspiring exaltations of social justice alike. For the regime's representatives at least, the steak dinners and other improvements in diet among working families became symbolic of the "dignified" standards associated with national inclusion in the New Argentina—and increasingly, a reminder why the population owed loyalty to authorities in their calls for measured spending. But Peronist discussions of spendthrift tendencies rested on assumptions similar to those of their partisan opponents, for they, too, looked askance at the insatiable appetites of the laboring majority. The regime's officials hoped that women, in their position as household managers, could influence wage-earning men (and clamoring union members), subjecting these troublesome actors to greater discipline and controlling purchasing to aid state economic planners.

The emphasis on ordered spending in 1950s Argentina ran against postwar trends across much of the world, which favored an unfettering of mass consumption and the advent of innovations in mass merchandising. Perón's Argentina stood as a symbol of affluence in the war's immediate aftermath, but by the early 1950s times had changed. In Brazil and other neighboring nations, foreign investment contributed to ongoing domestic industrialization and growing markets, complete with new consumer offerings geared primarily to urban middling and affluent sectors. Sears and other U.S. retail chains set up shop in Mexico City, Havana, and other large Latin American cities and influenced local residents' expectations of consumer modernity in the postwar period.[75] Recovery was still a long way off in war-ravaged Western Europe, and austerity measures remained the reality across the region, but business boosters invoked the promise of greater consumer spending just over the horizon to yearning populations. By comparison, the Perón regime's drive to organize consumers collectively and contain individualistic desires was reminiscent of an earlier era. These aspects of Argentina's consumer politics appeared to be a throwback to the "command consumption" practiced by interwar governments in Fascist Italy and elsewhere, which struggled to assert national sovereignty over the capricious marketplace and warned of the dangers posed by excessive consumerism.[76]

One crucial difference, however, was that disciplining citizen consumers in Argentina went hand in hand with attempts to extend the pleasures of mass consumption more widely. Replacing the dourness typical of most skeptics of consumerism, Perón's regime staked its political legitimacy partly on depictions of a contented populace enjoying the fruits of modern industry and agriculture. As the leadership criticized capitalist injustices and sought to impress measured habits on households, their politics spoke to the acquisitive desires of popular consumers— even by adapting commercial techniques for propagandizing and catering to clients. This populism for an era of postwar "consumer society" was not simply a top-down process of economic planning and mass mobilization. It was pursued by actors within the Peronist movement but outside the central state: in union cooperatives styled after department stores, in FEP stores that created a pleasurable shopping environment in a manner not unlike private chain stores, and in political experiments with commercial media and magazine publishing. Rather than ignore the marketplace entirely, Peronist institutions responded to the inroads made by mass consumption among the Argentine populace, particularly those sectors that had been excluded from full economic participation. However, the new "freedoms" of consumption touted by Peronist representatives clashed at times with orders from authorities to contain consumer appetites. By the early 1950s, housewives and other members of the pueblo would no longer be expected to voluntarily control spending as loyal citizens; rather, changing commercial conditions and the policies of national leaders would foist thriftiness upon them.

impact of women shopped

6

THE COUNTERPOLITICS OF VOICE

THE AVERAGE worker awakens refreshed just before 5 a.m., eager to begin a new day. After washing up and breakfasting with his family, he leaves a house in the suburbs of greater Buenos Aires and commutes to the city, where he earns his wages through skilled manual labor. Once the day is through, he journeys home again, pausing now and then to admire the displays at bookstores and newsstands. Unlike the downtrodden laborer of the past, this worker is happy to return to a restful domestic life, and he is greeted at the front door by a "smartly dressed and likeable" wife and a "loving, healthy, and tidy" son. Although the cost of living has increased, the male breadwinner's income still allows the entire household to enjoy a robust meal with all the trimmings. After dinner, the family goes out for a stroll around town, popping into a shop to buy women's shoes and a café for some refreshment. Seeing this man dressed in a pinstriped suit and a tie and surrounded by his confident family, a passing tourist might mistake him for a business magnate. And when the weekend arrives, this proud man spends his leisure time in pleasant but industrious pursuits: helping his son with homework, going to church, tending to a home garden, and fixing up the house to make room for a growing family.[1]

Part of a magazine piece titled the "Un día en la vida de un obrero argentino" (a day in the life of the argentine worker), the foregoing account was one of countless representations of the Peronist vida digna that circulated in the 1940s and early 1950s. These portrayals of the satisfied working-class family reveal much about the outlook and designs of state authorities. But the ubiquity of such propagandizing presents a serious interpretive barrier to historians, for it obscures how working Argentines and other subaltern sectors engaged with ideals of just living standards and social citizenship. Understanding the influence of state power from the perspective of its subjects is notoriously difficult, and it is a particularly acute challenge in cases of mobilizational mass politics, oriented around myths of seamless coordination between leaders and followers. Scholars have employed multiple means to get behind the façade of unanimity. Oral history has offered a crucial method for exploring popular mentalities; studies in this vein, however, are necessarily restricted to a given individual, community, or occupational group and thus typically afford a detailed but closely cropped portrait showing how the past is remembered.[2]

A careful reading of the era's public correspondence offers an alternative approach—in the present case, one facilitated by an unusually rich collection of letters that shed light on the cultural dimensions of state planning. On December 3, 1951, Perón informed the public that his government would entertain suggestions for the upcoming Second Five-Year Plan. Under the slogan "Perón Wants to Know What the Pueblo Wants," the president called on the populace to mail in their policy recommendations and commentaries to the Ministry of Technical Affairs (MAT). Tens and perhaps hundreds of thousands of Argentines responded to this letter-writing campaign. The petitioners represented a virtual cross-section of society: women and men of all ages; residents of urban centers and rural hamlets; manual laborers and professionals, farmhands and housewives; and members of neighborhood, civil, and political organizations. Their letters offer invaluable perspectives on everyday life at the beginning of Perón's second presidential term (1951–1955). The Perón Wants to Know documents resemble other public correspondence from this era (such as the entreaties sent to Eva Perón), and individuals used this forum to voice pleas for succor. But petitioners did not limit themselves to requesting small-scale relief. Rather, most had other ambitions in mind. They took stock of the accomplishments and failures of Perón's regime, comparing official ideals of the vida digna to personal aspirations and understandings of justice rooted in local conditions.

The documents generated by this unusual epistolary campaign do not, of course, allow us to peer into the hearts of their authors. The letter writers' demands were shaped by the structures of communication with state authorities, and petitioners fell into roles common to the genre of public letter writing: the dutiful worker, the meek supplicant, and the suffering mother, among others.[3] The opinions expressed in these documents are largely sympathetic to the leadership; those with overtly anti-Peronist views apparently chose not to take part. (The absence of such letters from this collection suggests that hate mail, if it existed, was separated or discarded.) In most cases, petitioners responded to the president's call by proclaiming their devotion to Peronism, a move not entirely surprising given the nature of the campaign. But a closer look at these documents reveals how letter writers pursued forms of "counterpolitics"—that is, tactics that reflected back the strategies of state power onto authorities (in this case, national planning).[4] Although counterpolitics is often associated with frontal forms of resistance to power, it was no less important in other types of engagements, including subaltern efforts to voice demands to state officials and define personal membership in a mass movement. The significance of these reactions is evidenced in the subset of correspondence on matters of household consumption. While numerous concerns garnered commentary, petitioners targeted a cluster of consumer problems: the gap between stagnant wages and the rising cost of living, the uneven distribution of the nation's commercial abundance, the threats posed by merchant profiteers and unpatriotic speculators, the failure of state economic regulations to control the marketplace, and other obstacles that blocked what participants themselves referred to as a "decent" and "dignified" life. Their planning requests balanced enthusiasm for Perón with scathing criticisms of government inaction at the local level and complaints of continued injustice in the marketplace. Understandings of partisan duty blended with assertions of a more activist citizenship that pushed against the limits of Peronism as a mass movement, leading some letter writers to demand greater collaboration in ensuring the effective implementation of state measures to improve their lives.

The Perón Wants to Know event was an experiment, one overlooked until recently in historical studies of this period.[5] It pales in fame compared to the era's open-air rallies and other partisan rituals, but the overriding purpose of the call for planning suggestions—to generate popular enthusiasm for the state, mobilize loyalist institutions, and renew bonds of solidarity—was of a piece with other expressions of mass politics. The correspondence supplies insights into the making of political subjectivities of this era and, above all, the meanings assigned to nonelectoral modes of (at least putative) participation by Peronist authorities and their supporters alike. In the epistolary campaign, letter writers enjoyed a degree of relative autonomy in presenting their requests for the Second Five-Year Plan. Petitioners were able to choose those policy matters and daily frustrations that most concerned them, not necessarily those that dominated the attention of Perón and his planners. Expressions of loyalty did not preclude criticism, and even diehard Peronists combined effusive gestures of supplication with assertions of their entitlements. The question is not whether involvement in the letter-writing event was truly heartfelt or cynical—resolving that issue, though tempting, is impossible given the nature of the sources. Instead, the more intriguing problem is how writers adopted tactics of self-representation that were intended to meet the expectations of authorities but that also may have resonated with their own lived experiences.

Planning and the People

Like state planners elsewhere in the midcentury world, Peronist officials sought to concentrate authority in the hands of executive branch ministries and their expert staffs rather than allow policymaking to be subject to wider political contention. The letters that poured into the Ministry of Technical Affairs had, as far as one can tell, a minimal impact on the formulation of the Second Five-Year Plan. In this respect, Perón's regime can be accused of "seeing like a state" when it came to devising and implementing a modernist project of national planning.[6] There were, however, limits to this technocratic impulse. Federal agents had to contend with jostling among other institutional actors (including provincial governments, non-state organizations, and branches of the Peronist movement). Equally important, officials did not simply impose master plans on society; they also took steps to enhance the legitimacy of their grand designs and generate public goodwill, a too often ignored dimension of the history of state planning. Although central planners had little desire to cede real decision-making power to the grassroots, the letter-writing event reinforced the populist message that average citizens had a stake in the national government and that its representatives were on the people's side. Even as real policymaking authority remained with state officials, citizens encountered indirect modes of participation characteristic of midcentury mass politics.

Political participation is itself an exceedingly slippery concept, one that cannot be separated easily into purely symbolic and substantive forms—or, for that matter, reduced to electoral contests alone. Without losing sight of the central state, it is useful to examine the Perón Wants to Know event to discover how contributors saw openings for participation within national planning. Letter writers themselves did not necessarily experience the new opportunities for communication as illusory or manipulative. Instead, the campaign resonated with popular audiences because of both its innovativeness and its underlying similarities to existing political practices. For one thing, many petitioners were captivated by the prospect of conveying their thoughts to Perón himself (or at least to other top officials). Rather than cast their votes anonymously or cheer from the crowd at a rally, they had a chance to express their opinions at length and in a seemingly more private, interpersonal manner. Argentines had long employed face-to-face lobbying and epistolary communication with government resource holders to address individual and communal problems. In fact, the 1951–1952 letters often described involvement in neighborhood organizing and other forms of associational life that antedated the eruption of Peronism. Grassroots civil society survived beneath the surface of Peronist mass politics, and in certain respects, the two complemented each other, for some petitioners saw local self-help practices reflected in the actions of planners. These factors can help explain why, in a time of mounting restrictions on free speech and centralizing state power, tens of thousands came to view the Perón Wants to Know campaign as an unprecedented expression of authentic democracy.

The keen grassroots response to Perón's call for planning suggestions was conditioned, in turn, by the political climate of the early 1950s. The letter-writing event immediately followed months of campaigning for Perón's reelection that had summoned partisan sentiments with particular intensity. In 1951 the CGT instructed its members and all "patriotic Argentines" to attend a mass gathering in Buenos Aires on August 22. Dubbed the "Cabildo Abierto" (an allusion to the 1810 town council meeting considered the first step toward Argentine national independence), this rally was not a party convention but rather an overwhelming show of enthusiasm for the as-yet unofficial Juan Perón–Eva Perón presidential ticket. A steel-girder stage erected at one end of Buenos Aires's mammoth central avenue bore insignias and sixty-foot-high images of Perón and Evita's faces. A massive audience estimated at one to two million persons arrived from across the country to line the streets.[7] Time and again the crowd cheered for Evita to accept the vice-presidential nomination; she stalled but finally concluded with the declaration: "I will do what the pueblo wants." Two weeks later, however, she removed herself from consideration, an act commemorated soon after in Peronist circles as the "*Renunciamiento*" (renunciation).

While the display of enthusiasm at the Cabildo Abierto renewed solidarity within Peronist ranks, it encouraged some opponents to wreck what seemed like an inevitable electoral victory. On September 28 General Benjamín Menéndez led a small detachment of troops against the government; after a momentary commotion, loyalist units quashed the revolt. Although the Menéndez coup revealed the mounting displeasure within the military, in the short term it backfired. The uprising offered authorities an opportunity to rail against antidemocratic conspiracies, and shortly thereafter Perón won reelection to a new six-year term. Despite the darkening economic clouds, the incumbent obtained 63 percent of the total votes, a more than 10 percent increase over his margin of victory in 1946. His closest opponent, the Radical Party's Ricardo Balbín, received only 35 percent of the ballots. Taking part in a national election for the first time, Argentine women voted for Perón slightly more than men did and were an integral part of his triumph. The

FIGURE 13. Buenos Aires during the Cabildo Abierto. *Archivo General de la Nación, Departamento Fotográficos, Subsecretaría de Informaciones, G-4, doc. 240057 (Aug. 22, 1951); reproduced courtesy of the archive.*

president made new headway among nonunionized sectors of the working class but slipped further among middle-income groups and better educated voters; he won barely half the votes in the capital city yet secured ample margins in heavily populated Buenos Aires province and much of the interior.[8] Some dissidents took courage in the fact that despite the regime's resources, Peronism had not won over all Argentines. Many, however, saw their latest defeat as confirmation of the president's seemingly unshakable appeal.

It was in this context that Perón issued his call for suggestions to the Second Five-Year Plan a mere month after the elections. The event balanced the scientific trappings of modern statecraft with the personalism of populist rule. The president promised to appoint "technical commissions" to collect suggestions from laypersons and civil organizations alike, thereby fine-tuning the designs of planners.[9] He noted that the federal planning agency would directly contact provincial and municipal governments, partisan institutions, and labor groups for their input. Although listeners were instructed to mail their requests to the Dirección Nacional de Planificación, Perón implied at the same time that he would be the final arbiter of planning decisions. (How letters would shape policy outcomes or who would read these documents were matters left conveniently vague.) This entreaty drew on previous efforts to inspire collaboration with the central state. Officials emphasized the primacy of planning throughout Perón's first term: newsreels and other mass media coverage of the Plan Quinquenal profiled the New Argentina in the making. One poster for the plan showed a cauldron of molten metal being poured into an Argentina-shaped mold: industrial-age technology was forging a new nation.[10] By the same token, signs proclaiming "Perón cumple" (Perón delivers) placed beside the hundreds of public works projects made clear who was responsible for planning improvements. The objective of the new plan was to build on this success—or as Perón put it in December 1951, to "consolidate [the nation's] greatness and secure the happiness that the pueblo now possesses"—by further synchronizing state bureaucratic power, personal authority, and popular support. To this end, the government erected an elaborate display of propaganda for the Second Five-Year Plan along the calle Florida, marking the presence of Peronism in this prominent commercial space and allowing passing shoppers and other urban audiences to gaze on the power of planning.[11]

While the specific origins of the 1951 letter-writing campaign are uncertain, the world of commercial entertainment suggests another intriguing precedent. Argentines in the 1930s and 1940s participated in frequent write-in contests organized by radio stations and magazines. There is more than a passing resemblance between these contests and the Perón Wants to Know event, and the propagandists at the Subsecretaría de Informaciones had experience working in these media professions.[12] In turn, the scientific mystique associated with the Plan Quinquenal inspired, whether intentionally or not, the "technical imagination" of petitioners in a society fascinated with science fiction, how-to publications, and popular science magazines. Devotees of the technical (some reputable, others from the lunatic fringe) adopted the mantle of amateur planners. They used the letter-writing campaign as a chance to mail homespun policy proposals, blueprints, and schematics for mechanical inventions to the Ministry of Technical Affairs.[13]

The opportunity to participate in planning was too tempting to pass up for many Argentines, and the response was immediate and vigorous. The Ministry of Technical Affairs received some 21,000 pieces of correspondence within seven weeks of the announcement and an equivalent number over the next few months. Given that multiple authors and organizations often signed one letter, the number of those who participated in the campaign is hard to estimate but surely reached the tens of thousands. The range of the writers' social backgrounds comes across in the physical qualities of the letters themselves. Some are neatly typed treatises from professionals, while the shaky hand, cheap paper, and obvious spelling mistakes of other letters reveal the limited means and formal educations of their authors. In some group petitions, illiterate laborers offered crudely scrawled signatures or thumbprints in making their claims. Letters poured in from urban centers and remote towns with quizzical names, such as Flor de Oro. Estimates of the surviving documents now housed in the National Archives suggest that the volume of letters roughly matched the geographical distribution of the country's population by province (with variations depending on the type of issue addressed).[14] The Peronist leadership achieved at least one its central goals for this event, for it was able to elicit participation on a truly national scale.

What did the public have in mind for the Second Five-Year Plan? Mirroring the scope of Peronist planning, the correspondence dealt with virtually every major social and economic issue of the day: health care, housing, transportation, education, trade, industrial and agricultural policy, and technical training, to name but a few main areas of concern. Public works of one sort or another attracted the most widespread attention. The largest subset of letters concerned infrastructure and collective consumption at the community level, particularly paved roads, sewers, running water, electricity, and other public works projects.[15] These requests reflected the concerns of Peronist planning, for propagandists devoted attention to improvements in the built environment. Yet the fact that petitioners sought basic public services provides a reminder of the continued struggles facing ordinary Argentines, obscured partly by idealized images of abundance and comfort. For a majority of the petitioners, progress was defined in terms of improvements to the built environment. Letter writers repeatedly invoked the keyword "*urbanización*," encapsulating a spectrum of household and community-level aspirations. María del Carmen Albuerne, a resident of a working-class suburb in greater Buenos Aires, captured these sentiments in a letter describing the "sad and desolate" condition of her neighborhood, with its muddy streets, unfinished homes, and lack of transportation. While in her view many did not think that laborers deserved any better, she reworked the political discourses of this era to assert, "somos dignos de calles asfaltadas" (roughly, we are deserving of paved roads).[16] These problems were typical in the recently settled neighborhoods of greater Buenos Aires, where rapid population growth fed the parceling of land into individual lots and left new suburbanites of modest incomes to build their own housing. Residents of rural towns and poorer urban districts elsewhere faced similarly insufficient services.

In contrast to media depictions of a population generously cared for by the state, accounts from letter writers often mentioned the authors' own efforts for community improvement. Correspondence arrived from individuals and grassroots organizations with activist experience in sports and social clubs, mutual aid societies, religious groups, and *sociedades de fomento,* the last being associations, common in working- and middle-class neighborhoods, that served as focal points for improving the built environment. Staffed by local residents, they both lobbied government officials for aid and collected funds to complete infrastructure projects on their own. These advocates saw the Peronist planning state as an ally in furthering their goals. Take, for example, a letter sent by the Sociedad de Fomento "Villa Spinola" of Valentin Alsina, in the northern suburbs of greater Buenos Aires.[17] According to the group's director, one-third of the neighborhood lacked running water, while unpaved streets flooded frequently (the resulting mud forced residents to use horse carts to transport corpses out of the barrio, a situation that, he said, was "profoundly hurtful and incredible in the twentieth century"). The sociedad had taken some steps itself, for instance, building a makeshift library with member dues; in addition, it had contacted government agencies repeatedly since the 1920s for additional assistance, but to no avail. With the new five-year plan, however, the situation had seemingly changed: "Today your excellency offers us this magnificent opportunity, we cannot but become happy and proud of this magnificent example of pure democracy that you have offered us."[18] Viewed in this light, Peronist planning appeared as a continuation, on a national scale, of the self-help efforts undertaken by the residents of popular barrios.

The Perón Wants to Know event sparked interest among an impressive variety of local organizations. These actors included associations closely allied with the Peronist regime, most notably, male and female branches of the unidades básicas and chapters of CGT-affiliated labor unions. Distinctions were not always clear between older forms of civil society and newer organizations with a more partisan, overtly Peronist character (what one historian has labeled the era's "political society").[19] In fact, the letters offer numerous examples of temporary alliances forged across civil and political society. Residents of popular barrios and provincial communities came together to present lists of requests. For example, a list from the small town of La Puerta, Córdoba (soliciting, among other things, a day-care facility, a vocational school for women, and running water), included multicolored seals from a range of local boosters and authorities (unidades básicas, the Partido Peronista Femenino, public school officials, the police department, and a justice of the peace). In other cases, unlikely pairings were established between local government agencies and fomento societies or between business owners and labor unions.[20]

These examples call into question common assumptions about citizenship and associational life. Here we have forms of civil society such as sociedades de fomento, which many Argentine historians consider to have been incubators of grassroots, democratic sociability, dovetailing with the state-centric model of planning commanded by Peronist officials.[21] A few conclusions can be drawn from this apparent contradiction. The 1951–1952 correspondence confirms that citizenship practices linked with civil associations were flexible enough to adapt to changing political climates. The durability of fomentismo is one of its most noteworthy (if often overlooked) characteristics: community organizing continued under military and civilian regimes alike, surviving despite the nation's political turmoil over the twentieth century. For many petitioners, Peronist planning presented an opportunity to meet local goals that complemented their own views on associational life. It evidently outweighed opponents' criticisms about the regime's authoritarianism. As the declarations of some letter writers demonstrate, the epistolary mode of communication was itself perceived as democratic, both in allowing the possibility of contacting authorities and in providing a mechanism by which to improve local conditions.

The Perón Wants to Know letters illustrate that the image of total state power over society must be qualified in this particular context. Peronist authorities did seek to place limits on associational life and clamped down on opposition groups and other dissenters, in keeping with their understanding of the "organized community." Yet this orchestrated event relied on a sphere of relative autonomy in which local organizations operated. Community-level groups enjoyed a space for activism that lay partially outside the state's effective reach. The representatives of Peronist political society (such as unidades básicas) were probably more circumscribed than other civil actors, but their members, too, were able to develop planning proposals and local alliances with an apparent degree of independence. While this mode of political participation fell short of ideals of pluralist democracy, it was greeted by some community organizations as an opening for making claims. The epistolary campaign was an innovation, but its success in generating a public response owed a great deal to its intersection with older traditions of citizen engagement with the state. Lobbying government resource holders for improvements in collective consumption is a central mode of political participation, arguably more deeply rooted in the region than voting—particularly in countries, such as Argentina, that have experienced frequent disruptions in electoral politics and swings between civilian and military rule.[22] In this case, the modernizing aura of the planning state complemented the routine business of "grassroots planning" and community building. Perón's sympathizers scrambled to present their proposals to top officials, but so, too, did all manner of individuals and groups located outside the formal movement. Mobilization behind the Second Five-Year Plan was a messier, less orchestrated process than the regime's managerial self-image suggests.

Obstacles to the Vida Digna

Participants in the Perón Wants to Know event often had specific goals in mind; their policy suggestions addressed the circumstances of their own families, neighborhoods, or towns, in some cases supplying detailed instructions on the placement of a new paved street. But not all petitioners focused on the built environment. Other letter writers dealt with less physically tangible but no less important aspects of living standards. In particular, popular sector Argentines used this opportunity to express concerns about modern life's acquisitive imperatives. Letters addressing consumer purchasing were fewer in number than those on public works, although once again, estimates are complicated by the fact that petitioners tackled multiple issues, and some combined appeals for sewer lines with a commentary on the marketplace. It is noteworthy that spending aspects of consumption appeared at all in this correspondence, given that this was not a central theme in Five-Year Plan propaganda. Letter writers described their daily routines as consumers for the benefit of distant officials, often to denounce commercial enemies and suggest more effective management of market forces. While some petitioners discussed pocketbook politics exclusively in individual or family terms, many considered threats to spending power in terms of larger political identities. Participants discussed access to commercial wares as individuals addressing matters of personal aspiration but also as spokespersons for the consumer interests of the working class, housewives, the pueblo, and other collectivities.

This widespread sense of entitlement to a better life that encompassed purchasing power, however, ran up against the reality of Argentina's faltering prosperity. The backdrop to frequent complaints about consumption in this correspondence was the rising cost of living, as retail inflation reached nearly 40 percent over the course of 1951. Throughout the lead-up to the presidential elections, Perón and other highly placed officials continued to extol the material comfort of the laboring majority (recall his election-year descriptions of "liberty and dignity" that began this book, in which he noted the ability of working people to eat plentifully, dress stylishly, and enjoy leisure). In the aftermath of Perón's victory, the participants in the letter-writing campaign provided a far less optimistic panorama of daily consumption, but without necessarily censuring the president or disparaging his ideal of popular abundance.

Opinions about remedies for escalating living costs took a range of forms. Some letter writers focused on the income side of the equation, arguing that their salaries were simply not keeping pace with prices. These commentators employed familiar conceptual tools to explain the slide in spending power. In addition to offering homespun blueprints for public works, those with purchasing power concerns spoke to state officials in the "technical" language of planning. For instance, a group letter from residents of General Ballivián, in the province of Salta, echoed the terminology of policymakers. It described how workers were suffering an "unbridled race [carrera] between the increase in wages and the rising cost of the standard de vida"—a problem originating, in their view, in poor enforcement of labor laws.[23] Letter writers shared Peronist planners' fondness for statistical surveys. Some offered their own estimations of endangered household budgets; a group of bakery workers from the suburb of Lomas de Zamora, for instance, quantified their main areas of monthly expenditure (commuting costs; rent and electricity bills; food, clothing, and other goods; and the 8 percent salary deduction for retirement). By their tally, food costs were the single largest area, constituting around 60 percent of their total expenses. Ultimately, their estimate reached the same gendered conclusions about the exposure of the working-class family as had social scientific reports from the mid-1930s: common expenditures outstripped the workers' incomes by a large margin, making it impossible for households to survive on one salary alone.[24]

In discussions of inadequate income, writers invoked the figure of the male breadwinner to play on the sympathies of Peronist authorities. A group of municipal workers and employees from the town of Laboulaye, Córdoba, painted a dire picture of families at risk. They described themselves as "men of mature age and fathers of large families" who had been forced to take odd jobs (*changas*) in their off hours to earn enough to "dress their children decently and provide a somewhat modest primary school education." Their regular wages were so low that some were thinking about sending their sons and daughters out to work. Recent salary raises were not enough, and the required contributions to the retirement system cut further into spending power. To defend male workers, the letter requested that wages be indexed to inflation. Evoking the leadership's own rhetoric, these men asserted: "We know that Perón wants for the workers of the country the well-being and tranquility of their families, that the laborer be remunerated in the manner he merits, so that he can confront life with dignity, with manliness, because living happily, he will work contently and contribute with his effort and dedication to the progress and greatness of his homeland."[25] In this case, the abstractions of national progress associated with public commentary on planning were defined more concretely by the men's masculine duties as family providers.

But it was not just these breadwinners who felt the pinch of rising costs. According to a resident of Rosario, high rent and food prices threatened all urban inhabitants, "especially the middle class and also the retired."[26] Similarly, individuals at a center for retired railway workers in Mendoza requested a boost in their pensions to deal with mounting inflation. Their letter described a basic threshold of consumption that was invoked by many petitioners: "It's not a question of us having money left over at the end of the month, no; we ask that in addition to paying for our daily stew [*puchero*], that from time to time we can buy a pair of shoes or a shirt." This entitlement to a modicum of consumer well-being was justified in terms of Perón's authority: "In this way we will live more decently," they wrote, "as we know is your wish."[27] For these retired workers, a decent life encompassed a basic basket of consumer goods that allowed them to join the mainstream of Argentine society. Solid meals on a regular basis and occasional purchases of clothing became one measure of citizenship as social belonging—and just the sort of everyday gains that many Argentines feared were slipping away in the early 1950s. Anxieties about declining living standards were softened by declarations of continued faith that partisan leaders could reverse the downward trend.

In other cases, however, letter writers presented themselves as shut out from the affluence relished by others. Individuals compared their positions to those of their peers in the New Argentina, and envy was often fueled by the extensive coverage of "social conquests." As a result, petitioners requested that they, too, be brought up to a higher standard, or as Rosario Iman, a female domestic servant, put it, "to enjoy the same rights of other workers," by which she specifically meant paid vacations, unemployment insurance, and health care. It was hard for these individuals to ignore the gaps in the benefactor state's web of protections. Pascual Romano, a fifty-six-year-old luggage carrier at the Retiro train station, described conditions typical for informal workers who lacked union representation. Not only did railway porters lack a fixed schedule, days off, and retirement benefits, but they were forced to live on tips—to "beg the good will of passengers to obtain remuneration for their labors, debasing themselves in their condition of dignified workers."[28] Complaints tinged with jealousy were also common in provincial areas, where the impact of federal social policies was sometimes dulled. Residents of

Catamarca, El Chaco, and other provinces lamented their plights, writing, "It is not possible that we are the only workers to not have year-end bonuses" and "I think that my union must be the only one that is still not well paid."[29]

Letter writers from hardscrabble rural communities took matters a step further and requested that state planners do something about the lack of well-paid employment. In particular, they offered grassroots perspectives on rural-urban migration, the major sociological trend of the era. This exodus accelerated under Peronist rule because of the allure of industrial and government jobs in larger provincial towns and Litoral cities. Metropolitan Buenos Aires alone received 117,000 provincial migrants in 1947, up from only 8,000 yearly in the mid-1930s.[30] The resident of a small town in La Pampa supplied his own microlevel migratory estimate: of his community's 120 homes, around 35 were now vacant. Even though the government had constructed a new hospital, post office, and power plant in the surrounding area, young people were leaving, driven by the "hope of good wages . . . earned in cities."[31] To stem the tide, petitioners called on state officials to redirect industrialization to provincial regions—a goal, incidentally, similar to that included later in the Second Five-Year Plan's call for economic decentralization.

Male representatives of civil and political society submitted proposals, but industrial employment struck a chord with individual rural women as well. In contrast to the Peronists, who emphasized male breadwinners, various female petitioners identified factory work as a way of improving the lot of "humble born women" and uplifting popular households. "Mr. President," opened one letter from rural Córdoba, "in this community there are many young women like ourselves with a desire to work and to be useful to the Homeland, but there are no jobs for women here." The construction of a new textile factory, suggested the ninety women who signed this petition, would offer them a chance to "help [their] fathers and brothers and thus stop being a burden on [their] families."[32] Without prospects of steady work or industrial salaries, rural residents of both sexes saw themselves as unable to take the first steps in achieving the Peronist vida digna.

Frustrations with inadequate incomes illustrate that the ideal living standards of the Nueva Argentina remained elusive for many. But another cohort of participants in the Perón Wants to Know campaign emphasized their vulnerability before the pressures of commercialization. Condemnations of merchant profiteering and other commercial crimes were commonplace in this body of correspondence. (Interestingly, these petitioners rarely identified specific merchants by name, even as they recounted local conditions in detail; it is possible that planners forwarded concrete accusations to the Federal Police and other agencies.) Consumers continued to assign blame for their privations to the machinations of commercial greed, suggesting again the inroads that Peronist antispeculation programs had made on cultural understandings of ethical exchange. Rather than simply toe the line, however, petitioners were also willing to think outside the guerra al agio. With a clear eye, they leveled critiques against government enforcement and analyzed their own consumer behavior. These accounts suggest a marketplace quite different from that portrayed by propagandists, one in which the state was only fitfully present, market forces often surpassed regulatory restraints, and consumers were left to confront merchant property holders.

Ordinary Argentines supplied narratives of their routines as shoppers in prosaic detail, providing virtual walking tours of local shops and markets. The illusion of direct communication with authorities was strong, and no fact was too insignificant to offer Perón or his representatives for their consideration. Individuals bemoaned the difficulty of finding an affordable wine to go with their Sunday meal of *tallarines* (pasta), and they complained about the price of potatoes, stallholders who sold watered-down milk, and bakers who passed off stale bread as fresh. Some included newspaper clippings on price controls to prove that neighborhood merchants were violating the law or demonstrate that the local almacenero was charging prices higher than those in the city of Buenos Aires.[33] There is a conversational, almost confessional quality to these descriptions quite distinct from the ecstatic mode of Peronist citizenship manifested in mass rallies, as if the letter writers sought to unburden themselves of personal travails to those in positions of power. This sense of intimate connection was combined, however, with a denunciatory tone regarding presumed illegalities. Letter writers documented commercial trickery for the benefit of the authorities, drawing on firsthand observation and local rumors. They targeted everyone from shopkeepers who tampered with price tags to importers who smuggled goods through customs and wholesalers who cooked their accounting books—all of whom were showered with epithets including "*inescrupulosos*," "agiotistas," and "vampires of commerce." In accordance with the populist nationalism of the day, some equated merchants with "imperialists" who threatened the "proletarian class" or with "*vendepatrias*" (literally, nation sellers) who lacked any patriotic sentiment.[34]

Petitioners bluntly assailed the police and other officials for failing to impose commercial order. Government price inspectors received surprisingly intense scorn and as objects of derision were second only to profiteering intermediaries. Outraged consumers inveighed against the laziness of local inspectors, who they felt dishonored Peronist leaders and subverted the quest for social justice. Mercedes

Juncos, a female worker from Devoto, Córdoba, captured this sense of betrayal in a request for a new post office and paved roads for her community, which ended with a condemnation of local antispeculation efforts: "It's the case that in many towns in this province, the merchant enjoys his vengeance by buying off the *señores* inspectors and certain municipal authorities, because unfortunately we workers give our life for Perón and others yell, 'Long live Perón' and make themselves seem big Peronists to secure personal benefits and stuff themselves full of money."[35] Similar complaints came from other corners of small-town Argentina. A sugar industry employee from rural Tucumán fumed about the ties of family, friendship, and influence that united merchants and inspectors; instead of serving hard time in jail, accused speculators in his town were coddled by the police, who detained suspects in a hotel. Even in areas where the federal government enforced commercial regulations, letter writers were disgusted with inept officials. One Buenos Aires resident remarked sardonically that his neighborhood inspectors seemed "to be more interested in the café than in completing their activities."[36]

These critics drew implicit contrasts between the virtues of high-ranking authorities and the incompetence of local officials. They assumed the problems with antispeculation measures to lie with enforcement, not with the creators of economic controls. On one level, this distinction is a variation on an age-old epistolary tactic—the king is good, but his representatives are bad—of which examples abound in Latin American history. In 1950s Argentina, petitioners explained ineffective policies partly as the consequence of corrupt officials masquerading as Peronists. A metalworker in the suburb of Avellaneda claimed that older webs of influence endured under Peronist rule: "the inspectors here are all the same Conservatives from the time of Barceló," he argued, referring to an infamous political boss from the 1930s.[37] There was an element of truth to these accusations. Perón's 1946 electoral coalition had forged alliances with preexisting political machines and provincial cliques, and these actors survived despite the creation of more vertically structured organizations. As did those in the region's other midcentury populisms, local political brokers and entrenched interests in Argentina dulled the impact of federal reformist initiatives that threatened their privileges or cronies.[38] Peronist sympathizers found these circumstances particularly galling, however, because they were forced to endure the disrespect of merchants. When these consumers complained to shopkeepers about overpriced goods, they were told, "Take it if you want, and if not let Perón give it to you." Others were met with mocking choruses of "Viva Peroncito" or recommendations that they vote for the Radical Party if they really wanted the economy to improve.[39]

The acrimony of these encounters and the deep frustrations with rising costs did not preclude some commentators from spreading the blame to their peers. Devious shopkeepers and reprobate inspectors were but part of the problem: consumers themselves also bore responsibility for the injustices of the marketplace. The main shortcoming of commercial regulations, a resident of Buenos Aires wrote, was that they placed the burden for action on the "*consumidor*." Since most lacked the initiative to "make their rights count," the result was all too predictable: "the merchant exploits him shamelessly and exaggeratedly, the agio inspectors are venal and fond of bribes, and the campaign against speculation is thus ineffective." Insightful observers pushed a step further to explain this seeming passivity of shoppers. A second letter from Laboulaye, Córdoba (this time from a CGT delegation), argued that consumers within the "laboring masses" were hampered by the social relations linking buyers to sellers, especially in small communities with a limited number of businesses. To survive between paychecks, workers with big families relied on the town bakers, butchers, and almaceneros to extend them store credit. Other wage earners had simply developed a neighborly bond with local shopkeepers over the years. In either case, residents were unwilling to accuse sellers, and matters were further complicated by ties of friendship between inspectors and business owners. The only solution, it seemed, was to bring in outside officials from the Federal Police who could remain independent from these webs of commercial dependence and small-town sociability.[40]

Whether they focused on consumer shortcomings, inadequate incomes, self-interested inspectors, or commercial misdeeds, these documents offer flashes of insight into the political outlook of popular sector Argentines at this historical moment. On the one hand, the correspondence clearly displays petitioners' sharp disappointment and even outrage. The virtuous cycle of productive labor, just remuneration, and ample consumption promised by Perón was simply not functioning in practice. Peronist authorities must have recognized the difficulty of ignoring popular frustrations, especially because economic conditions showed no immediate signs of getting better. On the other hand, the correspondence also reveals how participants viewed their struggles through the lens of Peronist citizenship. Aspirations for security, material comfort, and inclusion within the social mainstream underlay their requests, as evidenced in allusions to dignity and a decent life. For some, these conceptions were channeled into explicit rights talk as expressions of entitlement and assertions of rights to well-being. The good news, for the regime's leaders, was that letter writers presented the problems of the New Argentina in populist terms: as a battle between us and them in which Juan and Eva Perón were still on the side of the people. The letters indicate that most participants not only thought that improvements in living conditions were possible but also believed that the planning state was still able to deliver.

While the vast majority of these letters came from workers and consumers, the surviving documents contain a handful of intriguing exceptions. Scattered requests came into the planning agency from the targets of popular ire themselves: that is, from retail merchants and other property holders. Businesspersons, too, complained of high costs, but their troubles were of a slightly different order: high salaries and benefits for employees cut excessively into their profits, scarcities prevented meeting customer demands, and commercial laws were bothersome. As with trade groups when they ventilated complaints in publications, most entrepreneurs trod lightly with their critiques lest they attract unwanted government attention. Within these boundaries, merchants adroitly deployed Peronist discourses to advance their claims. The Federación Argentina de Centros de Almaceneros, for instance, requested government assistance in creating "distribution cooperatives" to speed the circulation of goods from producers to retailers, and it blamed rapacious wholesalers for rising prices. Likewise, an organization of butcher-shop owners from greater Buenos Aires argued that current profit margins did not allow them to provide an adequate standard de vida for their own families. Like working-class petitioners, they wielded charts and statistics to contend that Perón's government should also consider *their* unmet social needs.[41]

This observation captures the uneasy social position of small merchants, who were poised between their working-class customers and more affluent groups. They might be considered part of the pueblo, yet their status as businesspeople placed them, within the context of Peronist antispeculation rhetoric, in the category of potential agents of exploitation. In this political climate, some members of the petty bourgeoisie responded by presenting themselves as commercial workers rather than property holders. An association of cigarette retailers (essentially, street-corner and kiosk vendors) wrote to the government asking for an easing of caps on profit margins. Their letter grumbled about illegal intermediaries who undercut them by selling directly to consumers but noted that denunciations made to inspectors had gone unheeded. In addition, they proclaimed that they had taken Perón's call for unionization to heart and had organized themselves into a *sindicato* to accomplish higher goals: "to defend the professional interests of laborers, dignify work, humanize the workday, achieve economic well-being, and offer better services and amenities to the public, by means of cooperativism." In exchange, the tobacconists now asked Perón's administration for help in meeting personal aspirations. Not unlike informal workers in their requests, these small merchants coveted the social welfare enjoyed by labor unions: "We need and should have Vacation Colonies, our own Hotels to rest and recuperate energies lost during the year, Clinics and Medical Offices."[42] In sum, they requested that the Peronist regime open the doors of plenty to them as well.

For other merchants, however, the desire for state assistance was outweighed by resentment toward Peronist regulation and their enduring belief in the virtues of economic liberalism. In their letter, a group of Avellaneda shopkeepers enumerated the sacrifices made on behalf of customers, including eighteen-hour workdays. The almaceneros described themselves as a middle class on the verge of extinction, but they too took pride in their status as working folk—as "shop-counter workers, at the service of the pueblo." Although their letter praised the president and "Doña Eva Perón," it also rebuked authorities for not recognizing their contributions to social progress and for propagating the view that all merchants were criminals. As they daringly put it, retailers were subject to the "torture of inspections, fines, and detentions." Ultimately, they justified their role as businesspersons in commonsense terms: "it's not dishonest or speculative to sell something for four that one bought for three, that's commerce after all."[43] The fact that such a transaction—technically, making a 33 percent profit—was indeed a violation of commercial laws against speculation reveals the distance that separated regulators from ordinary retailers.

Antispeculation policy was but one of many sticking points among the merchant class most suited to Peronism's national-popular ideal. Throughout the remainder of the Peronist era, authorities made multiple attempts to build bridges between the administration and Argentina's business community (including the retail merchants whom Perón dubbed the "proletariat of commerce"). The early 1950s saw the formation of organizations inclined to cooperate more closely with the government, such as the Confederación Económica General (CGE), whose base comprised smaller industrial producers, commercial sectors, and provincial entrepreneurs from beyond the Litoral belt. Despite the corporatist designs of some public officials, however, relations with business remained fluid, and the CGE never developed the institutional solidity of the CGT and its Peronist-controlled labor unions.[44] The CGE emerged as an alternative to the traditional UIA but failed to develop into a vibrant branch of the Peronist movement prior to the regime's overthrow. The demands voiced by merchants and disgruntled customers suggest that the concept of the pueblo was powerfully flexible but ultimately had its limits: in order for the Peronist "us" to exist, some Argentines had to play the part of "them," a polarization made especially acute in the consumer marketplace by antispeculation campaigns. The 1951–1952 letters clearly show that certain social sectors fit comfortably within the Peronist camp (wage earners and consumers) while others (petty retailers and property holders) did so less well and with continued friction.

The People's Counterpolitics

Not satisfied with simply describing local conditions, petitioners offered planners clear recommendations by marshaling blueprints, privately collected statistics, and denunciations of criminal behavior. At first glance, these reactions may seem logical enough. But involvement in the Perón Wants to Know event should not be reduced to a narrow instrumentalism: individuals wanted paved roads, higher salaries, or a crackdown on merchants, so they asked for these things. After all, millions of other Argentines experienced similar material needs and chose not to participate in the epistolary campaign. The letter writers, however, shared an inclination to connect personal troubles with matters of state policy. In political science terms, they were "micro-macro linkers": that is, they envisioned their quotidian concerns as subjects worthy of consideration and action by the national government and its supreme political authorities.[45] This leap of the political imagination is by no means a given, especially for residents of impoverished communities with limited knowledge of the functioning of the state. The mass media played a role in raising expectations of the politically possible, and it was common for letter writers to reference radio speeches and newspaper reports in their commentaries. But to fully make sense of the letter writers' accounts, we must situate them within desires to cooperate in building the Nueva Argentina. Teasing out how letter writers envisioned Peronist cooperation requires us to tighten our focus once more, to examine discursive tactics and modes of self-representation. This approach offers additional insights into the changing views of citizenship, which blurred together with perceptions of partisan duty among many petitioners. Naturally, participants would tend to come from within the ranks of Peronist supporters (or at least present themselves as such). Yet partisan enthusiasm did not always match up with the leadership's model of the loyal supporter. Collective demands for economic justice outstripped the reformist orientation of policymakers, and letter writers expressed longings for an expanded, more intense form of collaboration with leaders. Hints of unease with the pace of state action and the mechanisms of mass politics reveal in turn how supporters at the grassroots themselves envisioned Peronism as a popular movement.

Eagerness to contribute to the Peronist cause was manifested in multiple ways. In addition to making general declarations of fervor, petitioners expressed gratitude for the social gains they had experienced since the mid-1940s and stressed their wonderment that the government was willing to listen to their problems. The opportunities for communication under Peronist rule were perceived as being of a different order than those of the past. A letter from Santos Olivera, of Buenos Aires, that offered suggestions for combating speculation closed with a description of the new freedoms working people enjoyed: "I am sure that you will find many spelling mistakes in this [letter], but as I offer it with a healthy and honest intention, I believe my suggestion will be taken into consideration. I am a worker and have not had the opportunity to study, because my situation was always precarious, but in this New Argentina Justicialista of Perón and our beloved Evita it has become possible that we humble-born be heard."[46] In this case, the writer's gestures of modesty were complemented with a favorable perception of the place of laborers under this political regime. Argentina was now a nation in which all *"humildes"* could voice their needs to caring rulers. Women, long excluded from the full rights of citizenship, also expressed feelings of empowerment mixed with deference. "It is my pleasure to present you," wrote María de Pereira in a letter on excessive milk prices, "with my respectful salute, as a representative of millions of housewives, who applaud in silence from their homes the magnificent work of the Plan Quinquenal that Your Excellency is attempting to complete."[47] To an extent, these declarations mirrored the propagandist depictions of Peronist Argentina as a new era, a sharp temporal break with the exploitation of the past. But this sense of being heard, of becoming socially visible to the powerful, often accompanied assertions of duty to repay benefactors. In supplying tips on improving enforcement of agio controls, another city resident proclaimed proudly: "I ask Mr. President to forgive me for this interference, but as an authentic Peronist I have listened to the words of our Líder who asked for collaboration in improving even more our standard de vida."[48]

Through these sorts of expressions, letter writers positioned complaints about failed state policies as forms of collaboration. This critical but loyalist reaction calls to mind Albert O. Hirschman's famous discussion of responses to decline in organizations.[49] Faced with worsening conditions, individuals with ties to some organization, such as the customers of a business or the subjects of a state, face choices along two poles: "exit," that is, severing their ties with the organization; or "voice," expressing their disapproval to management. Naturally, officials designed the Perón Wants to Know campaign to elicit voice from the population rather than exit. And voice they received. But in activating the loyalty of supporters, the architects of this political experiment took risks. The problem here lay not simply in satisfying raised expectations and meeting reformist demands (although this was a tricky issue in an era of economic downturn) but also in containing voice and loyalty within acceptable boundaries, especially as petitioners clamored to become more active participants in the movement. The risks of exit among members of the Peronist base were relatively small given the political alternatives available in 1950s Argentina. Pressure from within may not have presented as immediate a threat as did coup attempts from a disgruntled military faction, but it posed its own set of challenges to the leadership. From the perspective of the letter writers, assertions of voice and loyalty became crucial tools in justifying their demands, opinions, and recommendations before officials.

Letter writers took pains to demonstrate the intensity of their commitment to the Peronist cause, describing themselves in no uncertain terms as "authentic Peronists" and "authentic workers."[50] The contrast was, of course, with false supporters or those without sufficient commitment to the cause, and pointed criticisms of negligent inspectors, provincial elites masquerading as Peronists, and corrupt officials served to identify the true believers.[51] As in other mass movements, the impulse to distinguish pretenders from the faithful was a crucial internal characteristic of Peronism. Accusations against false Peronists were obscured by propaganda stressing a harmonious organized community, but the letters illustrate that these conflicts simmered among popular supporters early on. These dynamics would eventually escalate into open divisions within the Peronist camp, spilling over into violent confrontations among the movement's rival wings from the 1960s onward.[52]

In the aftermath of Perón's reelection, however, these centrifugal forces were contained within partisan organizations. Some sympathizers displayed their affiliations with pride, noting their membership in unidades básicas, CGT-affiliated unions, and other Peronist mediating institutions. These groups occasionally employed the printed request forms mailed out by the government in the letter campaign. But local chapters likely retained de facto autonomy to formulate policy recommendations. In addition, spontaneous partisan enthusiasm was evidenced by the fact that Peronists assembled into associations of their own that lacked party sanction. For instance, a self-described "group of citizens" from the Buenos Aires town of General San Martín founded a "Peronist fighter's house" (Casa del

Luchador Peronista) to address various issues. Individuals without clear affiliations chimed in as well, declaring their good standing as a Peronist of the first hour or an "Iron-Clad Peronist" (Peronista de fierro).[53] Although little is known about them, these "unofficial" sectors constituted a vocal part of Peronism's base.

Choices in written language, in the wording of recommendations and entreaties, offered another avenue for establishing an imagined bond with political authorities. At its most mechanistic, this set of discursive tactics involved echoing propaganda catchphrases back to state officials. Individuals identified themselves as descamisados, invoked the grandeur of the regime, and repeated worn mottos ("in Perón's Argentina, the only privileged ones are children"). Many addressed their missives directly to Perón with titles such as "My General," and "Your Excellency," in accordance with the paternalist terms of the letter-writing campaign. Supplication before the mighty was to be expected, but even abstract policy statements addressed to the planning agency sometimes closed with effusive prayers to the presidential couple—including wishes for Evita's quick recovery from her recently announced illness. Stock praise for leaders competed with more creative declarations of ardor. An association of truck loaders from Chivilcoy requested higher wages while eulogizing Perón with a poetic flourish as "the flagbearer of the justicialista movement who has dignified and redeemed our working class, like a bright lighthouse that illuminated the dark night in which we lived immersed by rulers without ideals and capital without scruples or conscience." In a letter to his "Beloved *Conductor*," Elias Tossounian of Buenos Aires placed Perón in august historical company. "In the same way that all the slaves of the world saw Lincoln as a Prometheus, who was the precursor of a World of Free Men, will all workers of the world see you as the precursor of their future emancipation?"[54]

But in offering adulation to the nation's "lighthouse" and Lincoln, writers did more than play to the expectations of officials. Supplication did not preclude petitioners from asserting their entitlements or offering pointed critiques. Fragments of propaganda could be refashioned to new ends by illuminating government inaction and unsatisfied needs. "Is it possible," asked a worker from Catamarca, "that one could die of hunger in an Argentina so Great, so rich, so Just, Free, and Sovereign?"[55] Individuals also stretched terms to encompass personal concerns typically not high on the agenda of planners. Rather than focus on the much-discussed needs of urban households, one letter suggested that indigenous peoples in Neuquén province required an elevation in the standard de vida.[56] At a deeper level, the practice of letter writing encouraged individuals to apply political discourses to make their own lived experiences intelligible. By "speaking Peronist," individuals imposed particular conceptual frameworks to explain the social world around them, straddling the gulf between a self-conscious pragmatism and the embrace of a propagandistic worldview. As I have shown, the regime's own terms, such as the "standard de vida" and "dignidad," appeared repeatedly in commentary on getting and spending. Whether these keywords and phrases served privately to give meaning to individual lives cannot be determined from these sources alone. But the letters suggest that ordinary Argentines viewed this language as a necessary tool for communicating with the state and a touchstone of public conversation.

In proclaiming their willingness to cooperate, letter writers advanced scores of recommendations to improve mass consumption. For all their idiosyncratic variety, most of the policy suggestions on consumer spending fall into three broad categories. The first (and fewest in number) came from petitioners who overwhelmingly agreed with the economic diagnoses of the Peronist leadership. For this minority, understandings of voice and loyalty went beyond accepting the logic of an antispeculation campaign. It translated as well into approval of the regime's parables of prodigality. Such petitioners agreed that excessively comfortable citizens were partially to blame for slipping living standards. These dutiful subjects suggested ways to limit frivolous purchasing and augment self-sufficiency. They thus floated ideas such as requiring commercial entertainments to shut down by midnight on Sunday and supplying rural laborers with garden plots to grow food. Others proposed ways to boost worker productivity ranging from profit sharing incentives to extending the workweek by four hours.[57] These diligent suggestions came from unidades básicas and other actors firmly within the Peronist base. Some accommodated more biting views of an indulgent working class within the regime's new emphasis on thrift and productivity, but individuals who recommended changing labor laws to make it easier to fire inefficient employees or who called for a "total nullification of worker demands" were an exception.[58] Most critics of prodigality presented themselves in a different light: as citizens working alongside officials for the nation's greater good, offering practical measures to restore economic order and sustain social conquests.

A second cohort placed the burden of action more firmly on the shoulders of government agents. This more numerous set of writers pressed for an expansion of Peronist alternatives to private retailing that would diminish the impact of commercial speculators. They called above all for the building of more Fundación Eva Perón stores, Grandes Almacenes Justicialistas, and municipal fairs. Similarly, political and civil organizations across Argentina announced their intentions to found consumer cooperatives destined for fellow neighbors, union workers, or state employees and appealed to planners for the financial and technical expertise to get their operations running. The differences between state-run stores and cooperatives were not clear to all (misunderstandings that are understandable since many had encountered alternative retailing only in media reports). By late 1951, FEP proveedurias existed only in the city of Buenos Aires, and union-run co-ops were clustered near urban areas. Yet consumers elsewhere in the country were often keenly aware of the benefits enjoyed by their porteño peers. A resident from Rosario asked Perón to build "great Justicialista stores, similar to those in the Federal Capital," for Argentina's second city. In greater Buenos Aires, barrio associations sought the expansion of the capital's street fairs and almacenes justicialistas to their suburban communities.[59] The frequency of these requests suggests that popular support for Peronist interventions in the distribution of consumer wares ran high, as did the realization of the unevenness of these experiments across the national territory. For some, commercial alternatives such as FEP-run stores represented a lifeline against high living costs but also a Peronist beacon of ethical exchange within the commercial marketplace, a partisan sanctuary where one could buy goods at a "precio justo y Justicialista," according to one letter writer's pithy slogan.[60]

The final (and perhaps most intriguing) category of recommendations came from individuals and organizations that wished to cooperate more actively in the war on speculation. In addition to lambasting "unscrupulous" merchants and inept inspectors, these motivated letter writers offered their services to Perón's government. The most common request was that the state authorize the "pueblo," whether interpreted as labor unions, state employees, unidades básicas, retirees, or housewives, to patrol businesses and enforce price controls. A letter from residents of Remedios de Escalada, in the province of Buenos Aires, exemplifies these assertions of patriotic and partisan duty:

> We offer ourselves as Volunteers, and in the free-time from our jobs wish to collaborate with Your Excellency to combat these Unscrupulous merchants, who forget that they are Argentines and do nothing else but think about the best way to steal. . . .
> As Argentines and firm Peronists we solicit you to issue us Identification Cards to combat these Individuals, who with the sole objective of obtaining bigger profits care not for the damage they cause to the working class of this community.[61]

Likeminded petitioners asked for additional authority to supervise local police inspectors in order to ensure that Perón's will was being enforced. Writers proposed all sorts of incentive schemes to improve commercial regulations, from giving would-be inspectors a percentage of the fines they assessed to mandating that all public officials daily monitor one store within a ten-block radius of their homes.[62] To enhance the efficiency of the marketplace, a suburban resident suggested that each barrio select a local representative or union worker who would report directly to the Fundación Eva Perón and Federal Police about shortages, infractions, and other conditions.[63] In short, these writers demanded that the state recognize them in some official capacity—hence the repeated mention of "identity cards"— and enable them to contribute in a more systematic fashion to the cause.

With their proposals for increased participation, Peronist supporters refashioned the leadership's own pleas for consumer solidarity in a more militant direction. Perón and Evita's calls for coordination between working households and the government suggested that all Argentines needed to monitor local businesses as did inspectors; nevertheless, few letters reference other priorities of the regime's consumer mobilization efforts, such as the adoption of home economics or thrift. Likewise, Peronist leaders stressed the importance of discipline and hierarchy in waging their antispeculation campaigns and insisted that consumers report merchants to the police rather than take matters into their own hands.[64] For their part, however, supporters latched onto themes of grassroots involvement in the management of commerce to pressure for greater popular action. Couched in the language of Peronist patriotism, these sectors pushed for a greater say in the implementation and even design of commercial policies. In the process, supporters envisioned a style of populist politics that would bypass intermediary officials, establishing a more direct connection between national authorities in the capital and their popular base in local communities.

Unions and other cost-of-living activists pressed for more vigorous involvement in antispeculation measures, but so too did women, a move that reflected the enhanced opportunities for political engagement available to females as consumers under Peronist rule. These petitioners typically assumed the mantle of housewives (amas de casas), further suggesting an acceptance of the conventional understandings of female authority offered by Peronist politics. For some, consumer activism was fused to an underlying social conservatism. The self-proclaimed "Association of Housewives" justified female guidance of commercial regulation through a strict division of labor: "Undeniably, the ideal within the family is that the man be in charge of the economic and moral maintenance of the home, and the woman fulfill her natural and specific function as wife and mother, contributing with her spiritual support to its equilibrium."[65] This gender traditionalism did not preclude this letter writer from envisioning an expanded public role for women, principally as inspectors of municipal stores and fairs. In other cases, women argued that the new female branches of the Peronist movement were best suited to managing commerce. Unidades básicas, with their "loyal directors and true Peronist conscience," would act as a support mechanism for individual housewives in their contentious disputes with profiteering merchants.[66]

Popular enthusiasm for strengthening the Peronist presence in the marketplace had a dark side as well. Investigations after the fall of Perón uncovered allegations concerning the illegal intimidation of merchants, including rumors that party members and officials from unidades básicas misrepresented themselves as price inspectors to extort money from merchants (in essence, acting on the demand to deputize the population as agents of antispeculation programs).[67] Resentment toward merchants was reflected in demands for ever-stronger punitive measures, such as seizures of businesses, long jail sentences, and massive fines for suspected lawbreakers. The correspondence reveals the predictable consequences of Juan and Eva Perón's aggressive harangues against the economic enemies of the people. Evoking the hawkish rhetoric of Argentina's leaders, letter writers called for the formation of "vigilance brigades" and "armies of inspectors" to crush hoarders, gougers, and other wrongdoers. One petitioner proposed deploying retired military personnel to ensure that guilty merchants would be "combated in war without mercy," while a resident of the Los Perales housing project wanted any foreigners among these "oligarchic traitors" to be deported.[68] A state employee from Rosario who proposed gathering crowds outside the shops of accused speculators reveals the fanaticism of some Peronist sympathizers at this moment: "The psychological impact on the exploiters, who will have to confront their exploited, will be more effective than fines and jail sentences. These eternal mockers of the law, these fifth columnists organized against the Justicialist Doctrine, will witness firsthand the surging crowd, and through police protection, the Lynch Law [*Ley de Lynch*] will be the ready weapon of the betrayed people and an object of obsession for the betrayers."[69]

Hatred of usurious shopkeepers certainly existed prior to this period, but these tirades illustrate how Perón's administration fanned the fires of merchant-consumer antagonisms through the war on speculation. Whether they echoed concerns about consumer wastefulness, called for more FEP stores, or fantasized about lynching, many letter writers shared not only an identification with the Peronist movement but also a sense that greater popular involvement was needed to fulfill the promise of the New Argentina. To these petitioners, participating meant more than simply writing a letter or voicing a request to officials. An ability to "speak Peronist" was useful in making personal needs and opinions visible to authorities, but supplication coexisted with assertions of duty, and petitioners displayed a simmering frustration at the pace of social change under Peronist rule. While pleas to pick up the pace of reform never materialized into widespread calls for revolution, demands for state authorization to impose "justice" on the marketplace suggest that some supporters equated populist rule with enhanced popular power. These letter writers did not necessarily contest the ideas of hierarchy and leadership at the heart of Perón's vision of an organized community. As self-identified members of a mass movement, however, they did express longings for greater coordination between the top and base of the Peronist political pyramid in achieving supposedly common aims.

Asking and Receiving?

Yielding everything from rabid attacks against merchants to meditations on social justice, Perón's call for planning suggestions through correspondence generated a flurry of requests and recommendations. But the purported goal of the December 1951 campaign was not just to canvass public opinion but also, and more important, to shape state planning in line with popular input. How did officials respond to the flood of correspondence, and what, if any, impact did these demands have? The dearth of sources on the internal workings of Perón's government makes it impossible to formulate comprehensive answers to these questions. Within weeks of mailing their letters, participants received stock responses from the government confirming the arrival of their suggestions. The historical record suggests that most requests went no further; although officials summarized and cataloged the letters, they apparently had a negligible impact on the Second Five-Year Plan. The economic constraints of 1952–1955 were partly to blame, for they hampered the state's ability to deliver. Yet the Perón Wants to Know campaign underscores the limitations of the regime's ideal of political participation. The vertical model of Peronism, in which followers performed demarcated roles and remained subordinated to leadership's decisions, remained strong—above all, for those at the pinnacle of the planning state.

At the conclusion of the letter-writing campaign, propaganda makers praised the cooperation of participants and the value of their contributions. Although media coverage given to this event was hardly extensive (suggesting that from the beginning officials sought to defuse the petitioners' anticipation of concrete results), references to the letters appeared in the Peronist media between December 1951 and the announcement of the Second Five-Year Plan, in December 1952. An article published in *Mundo Peronista* in July 1952 detailed what became of the "people's" letters.[70] Titled "¡Aquí está su proyecto!" (here is your project), the article offered the firsthand account of José López, a possibly fictitious individual who decided to visit the Dirección Nacional de Planificación to inquire about his letter. López described how he was taken through rooms and rooms of files until he was presented with his own proposal; this government agency functioned with machine-like efficiency, staffed by diligent bureaucrats who labored from 8 a.m. to 8 p.m. At the end of this impressive tour inside the nerve center of Peronist planning, López could not help but exclaim, as the magazine hoped its readers would, "¡Es grande Perón!"[72]

As one might expect, this public face differed notably from the government's internal response to correspondence. Brief memos appended to the letters by bureaucrats provide some insight into the problems officials faced in meeting popular demands. The Ministry of Technical Affairs acted as a clearinghouse, forwarding the correspondence to the appropriate national, provincial, or municipal agency. A handful of the surviving Perón Wants to Know letters have notes from these agencies still attached to them, but the majority, it appears, received no reply at all. In addition, it took anywhere from one to three years for these assessments to return to the MAT, well after the Second Five-Year Plan was adopted, indicating either the difficulties of processing the high volume of letters or their low priority for officials.

Formulaic in style, these internal memoranda illustrate a variety of state responses to the letter writers' requests. Memos sent to the MAT from the Ministry of Public Works issued terse judgments: a particular request fell under the jurisdiction of provincial rather than national authorities, was already under consideration by the ministry, or formed part of a project already under way. In the best-case scenario, a letter writer's request was met with the vague reply that the ministry would add the proposal to its list of future projects, which would be carried out when the agency received the proper funds. Yet bureaucrats also internally rejected many demands, often for apparently sound reasons. A request for a one-million-peso loan from a sports club was deemed too "excessive," and a female petitioner's personal plea for educational assistance was determined not to be "an initiative that should be considered for inclusion in the Second Five-Year Plan."[71] Budgetary restrictions were frequently cited as a reason for refusing requests, an internal acknowledgment that the economic downturn was curbing the Peronist planners' ambition. A memo from the "technical secretary" of La Rioja argued that a request for multiple urbanization projects did indeed fall under the provincial authority but that it lacked funds to implement its share of the plan.[72] The contrast between the letter writers' enthusiasm and the state's limitations was apparent. In a letter requesting telephone service, parks, and other public works, the Partido Peronista in the town of Estación Clark proclaimed triumphantly: "In Perón's Nueva Argentina the pueblo is joyful and the country progresses in giant leaps, and thus, we see new public works appear on a daily basis." Confronted with this demand, the Ministry of Communications concluded that although it had intended to extend phone service to the town, "financial needs" now precluded doing so.[73]

Recommendations on spending power and the consumer marketplace were met with similarly negative intrabureaucratic responses. State officials displayed little willingness to expand the terms of antispeculation programs as far as many participants wished. The more sweeping suggestions made by subaltern sectors—such as creating a legion of deputized price inspectors in communities across the nation—were dismissed as impractical or undesirable by Peronist authorities. Grassroots demands for zero tolerance against profiteers and roving bands practicing the ley de lynch complemented the militarism of the war on speculation, but these ideas also opposed the very core of the leadership's emphasis on political hierarchy and order. Rather than take matters in their own hands, the movement's base was expected to work through loyalist organizations and follow orders given from above by the leader. Discipline trumped enthusiasm when it came to giving rein to consumer desires for activism and increased cooperation with top leaders. At least in regard to quotidian commerce, officials chose not to unleash the zealotry of certain Peronist diehards.

Likewise, solicitations for greater state involvement in retailing also failed to shape planning priorities. Proposals that the government could combat agio by selling consumer staples directly to the public received the following type of judgment: "This Dirección Nacional does not believe it is advisable for the State to intervene directly in the sale of these articles. In this vein labor unions have advanced by establishing their own cooperatives, following the initiative of the Fundación Eva Perón's stores that sell to the public." The note asserted simply that the Ministry of Industry and Commerce held responsibility for fixing maximum prices and profit margins on consumer goods, while the Price Vigilance Agency and others enforced the laws.[74] This stock reply is suggestive for a number of reasons. Officials rejected popular demands that might take the regime further into the domain of state-based socialism; they resisted supplanting commercial networks with state distribution. Yet they were not opposed entirely to Peronist interventions in the marketplace—as long as they were left to ostensibly private, allied institutions, such as organized labor and the FEP. Regulated by multiple agencies, free enterprise would continue to exist in the New Argentina alongside these alternatives, which served a dual purpose: shielding purchasing power and converting frustrated consumers into Peronist loyalists.

Whereas planners looked favorably on these versions of "cooperative" retailing, however, other proposals along these lines were rebuffed. The director of a recently created meat-selling cooperative in a Santa Fe town wrote to explain his frustrations. Despite the popularity of his operation (it seems that 200 persons had joined during the first month), repeated attempts to get assistance from the state directorate of cooperatives had failed and his correspondence gone unanswered. Although the Second Five-Year Plan would affirm the importance of cooperatives, the reality of insufficient state support for these initiatives left some petitioners to their own devices. A letter from a neighborhood committee in Mendoza seeking help in establishing a "cooperativa justicialista" was met with the abrupt internal memo, "It is the interested parties that must constitute it and make it function."[75] This typical response seems to indicate a mood of exasperation among federal bureaucrats, a feeling that the pueblo was asking too much of the benefactor state.

As officials viewed it, the epistolary campaign constituted more an attempt to mobilize good will than a substantive innovation in planning. After processing, most letters simply gathered dust in storage rooms of the Ministry of Technical Affairs. Perón had warned his radio audience in December 1951 that not all recommendations could be put into action and that leaders would make decisions about the nation's true needs. As with its predecessor, the Second Five-Year Plan offered few details about the location of its projects and thus helped to diffuse specific complaints. Nevertheless, the problem of disenchantment loomed. Despite the president's triumphant reelection and the declarations of loyalty voiced in this correspondence, the lack of action could conceivably test sympathizers' faith in Peronism; exit, either through apathy or outright defection to political rivals, was still conceivably an option. Letter writers would realize that the government had failed to meet their requests for sewer systems, schools, or proveedurias.

In reality, some petitioners were already accustomed to such disappointments under Peronist rule. "It's already been four years," protested one petitioner in 1951, "that we neighbors have collected signatures to see if we can get electricity and some paths, not having obtained anything to date." Josefina Giovatto, a resident of greater Buenos Aires, claimed that municipal officials in her suburb had ignored her earlier correspondence; she reached the conclusion that "in order for those people to take action the order has to come at least from General Perón."[76] Irritation with the pace of the Peronist bureaucracy may explain in part why so many petitioners sought to communicate directly with Perón about their problems. In these cases, the fusing of populist politics and technical planning broke apart. Personal appeals to the nation's most influential patron seemed to offer a path around bureaucratic barriers. In the years that followed, one imagines, rebuffed petitioners must have felt forced to fall back on familiar tactics to achieve their goals. Some no doubt continued to work through the partisan channels of the Peronist movement. Others perceived the elusive path to progress to lie in personal striving and continuing local fomentismo efforts, which some pursued with remarkable resolve. A letter from a sociedad de fomento in greater Buenos Aires recounted the group's long struggle to get a public plaza built for its community. Members claimed to have sent twenty-seven petitions to various levels of government between 1928 and 1950 but found that that "all this was a useless, begging pilgrimage." In 1949 its members met with Domingo Mercante, the well-connected governor of the province of Buenos Aires, who referred their case favorably to Evita Perón. The project was considered by the federal Ministry of Transportation, which eventually rejected their request.[77] Rather than give up, this organization participated in Perón's call for planning suggestions, hoping to enlist his personal assistance in overcoming these obstacles. Perhaps not all petitioners were this tenacious, but this example points to the determination with which some advocates pursued their causes. It also suggests that for popular sector Argentines, the era of Peronist planning represented but one phase (albeit a highly significant one) in a much longer struggle for community improvement that continued under the surface of national political turmoil for decades to come.

❦

The Perón Wants to Know campaign was never again repeated. With Perón's overthrow in September 1955, his government lost the opportunity to develop a third five-year plan. But for the remainder of 1952–1955, the regime continued to encourage individuals to write in with demands for personal assistance, ideas for local projects, and general policy suggestions. Political participation with the planning state was not limited, of course, to epistolary campaigns. Letter writing coexisted with spectacles of partisan fervor enacted in city plazas, streets, and other public spaces; liberal traditions of electoral campaigning and voting became further opportunities for displays of majority support. Mass political gatherings such as the Cabildo Abierto were exceptional in their size but were mirrored in annual rallies and smaller gatherings at union halls, in unididad básica meetings, and at public works inaugurations. For historians, however, letter writing leaves behind a helpful record indicating how individuals and popular organizations experienced the terms of Peronist rule. As the correspondence suggests, these interactions were more than a simple bargain in which the state rewarded supporters in exchange for votes.

Gaining a better understanding of the relationship between planning and popular politics is important not only to the case of Peronist Argentina, for it offers a means of rethinking conventional notions of midcentury state power, which emphasize expanding command over territory and population. James C. Scott has characterized extreme forms of this statist impulse as "high modernism," defined as a "supreme self-confidence about continued linear progress, the development of scientific and technical knowledge, the expansion of production, the rational design of social order, the growing satisfaction of human needs, and, not least, an increasing control over nature (including human nature) commensurate with scientific understandings of natural laws."[78] Soviet examples immediately come to mind, but modernist impulses informed the practices of nonsocialist states in the developing world (e.g., massive "pharaonic" projects, such as the futuristic city of Brasília). In Argentina, one can see high modernist tendencies in the regime's pursuit of national organization through public works and other scattered interventions. Without reaching the violent depths of other countries, Peronist mass politics emphasized similar values of hierarchy, ideological consensus, and disregard for minority rights.

Scott's work offers a valuable critique of the political evils of this period, contrasting the damage inflicted by top-down, authoritarian techniques with a knowledge rooted in local practice (what he calls "mētis"). Yet not all planning experiments went to high modernist extremes or excluded local knowledge so directly. Across the midcentury world, the advances of the centralizing state were matched by modes of political participation that defy easy categorizations as authoritarian or democratic, a groundswell of enthusiasm that cannot be attributed *solely* to ritualized mobilizations and propagandizing. In Peronist Argentina, participation was based on a partial intersection of worldviews, one between statist visions of national development and the smaller-scale material aspirations of individuals and conceptions of urbanizing progress. These overlapping views existed in other, more tenuous forms prior to the Peronist era (and as I have shown, Argentine liberalism too was part of a hegemonic culture connecting rulers and the ruled). Nevertheless, the Peron Wants to Know campaign and other events created new mechanisms for communication and wider networks for political interaction that encouraged grassroots identification with the project of state planning. That even symbolic modes of participation could create real frictions between planners and insistent petitioners is clear; so, too, is the fact that the consolidation of centralized authority went hand-in-hand with praise for local knowledge.

Despite the restricted terms of participation, letter writers from across Argentina saw themselves as working with those at the highest level of the state. Talk of national inclusion through elevated living standards became not only an obsession of propagandists but also, by the early 1950s, part of the popular lexicon and framework for understanding citizenship. The petitioners' expressions of identification with the Peronist movement differed in key respects from the comunidad organizada of leaders and ideologues. As the petitioners saw it, Peronism was less a state campaign orchestrated from the top down than an open line of communication for addressing individual needs and a forum for expressing the popular will. The longings for collective improvement among subaltern sectors bubbled up from their own sources, hidden from the historian's sight, but glimpsed in popular documents such as the Perón Wants to Know letters. Religious notions of morality, peer expectations of respect and advancement, visions of abundance from the mass-media and commercial culture, personal experiences of daily struggles to get by— these were among the factors that shaped local understandings of justice, at times expressed in forms more radical and rough edged than official paradigms of justicia social might allow. In short, planning from above was not the same as planning from below. But while the five-years plans were responsible in part for summoning this enthusiasm for change at the grassroots level, the letter-writing campaign and other popular events also helped steer subaltern demands to hegemonic ends.

7

IRONIES OF ADJUSTMENT

As THE Perón Wants to Know letters flooded government offices with popular recommendations on national planning, state authorities embarked on their own revamping of the New Argentina. In the immediate postwar years, policymakers envisioned income redistribution and development as largely complementary aims. By the early 1950s, however, Perón's advisers began to conclude that the country had hit an economic wall: deteriorating conditions demanded policy changes to ward off full-blown crisis and, equally worrisome, to ensure their political survival. Rather than present redistribution and development as mutually exclusive, state officials identified the incommensurable elements of each. Mass consumption came under particular scrutiny, for high spending power was now considered at odds with the investments needed for recovery. In their eyes, preserving the revolución justicialista necessitated restraining those aspects of the vida digna now deemed threatening to national progress. Naturally, not all Peronists shared this outlook. As I have shown, many ordinary Argentines longed for an escalation, not moderation, of redistribution and market regulation. Political leaders, however, set other priorities. They reframed the national economy as a field of intervention and launched stronger campaigns to effect changes in the behavior of Argentina's population. They sought not just to contain consumption or overcome turbulent markets but also to finish transforming a "disorganized" populace into a more disciplined citizenry.

Officials had good reason to be concerned, and two problems stood out to them as especially troubling. The first was the country's deteriorating balance of payments. Agricultural output plummeted in the early 1950s following severe droughts. Earnings from Argentina's meat and grain exports failed to match demand for imported raw materials and industrial inputs. This bind, typical of Latin American countries in the era of import substitution, choked growth and deepened debt. These imbalances contributed to a second cause for unease: spiking inflation.[1] Despite antispeculation campaigns, policymakers tolerated mild inflation in the mid-1940s; after all, it acted as a mechanism for income redistribution when combined with higher union contracts, social benefits, and rent controls. But as production slackened and wages stagnated, the climb in prices went from being a daily worry for consumers to a major state preoccupation. Across the region, these conditions often sundered reformist coalitions and populist movements, because economic turbulence could all too easily energize opponents and widen internal divisions among former allies.

Against these odds, however, Perón's administration implemented policies that allowed it to weather the economic storm of the early 1950s. Although long-term dilemmas remained, the regime escaped the fate of the many others caught in balance of payment and inflationary quandaries. In fact, contrary to what one would expect, Peronist authorities succeeded in widening their political base during this difficult period. The movement's mediating networks staked their presence in local communities, while state-orchestrated mobilizations of support continued to expand on a massive scale. With these achievements, the regime seemed primed for a lasting consolidation of power. Yet here, too, Peronism defied expectations. Perón ultimately completed only half his second presidential term, for his government was overthrown by military coup on September 16, 1955. Suffering from neither economic calamity nor mass defections, the Nueva Argentina crumbled in just a few months when met by stiffening resistance from anti-Peronist groups.

Thus a perplexing combination of resilience and fragility characterized the final years of Peronist rule. Part of this story can be found in the way the recasting of consumption as an element of the vida digna reflected broader changes in social citizenship and state power. This "late period" (1952–1955) has received comparatively less scholarly attention, and it is too often collapsed into teleological narratives of an "exhausted" regime mired in inevitable decline. As a result, the paradoxical relationship between economic reorientation and political innovation remains poorly understood. It is clear that in response to mounting problems, state planners slowed income gains for the working class. These dynamics may seem at odds with the received wisdom about Peronism as a form of "populism," a political style commonly associated with reckless clientelism and spendthrift policies. But Peronist authorities, like other populists, were not uniformly focused on disbursing largesse. Rather, they demonstrated a preoccupation with restricting certain types of spending, especially those acquisitive practices deemed destabilizing, immoral, or wasteful. Naturally, subaltern actors pushed the limits of equilibrium, but perhaps more significantly, the downturn encouraged greater engagement with Peronist networks, which offered nonmarket alternatives to satisfy material needs and consumer wants in austere times. Within this context, frontal challenges to policymaking decisions were overshadowed by more circuitous tactics of negotiation that demanded at least outward signs of compliance and devotion.

If the Peronist regime bucked the pattern of populist redistribution followed by sudden collapse, there was one final irony in store. Perón was not overthrown because of an impending market crisis. Nevertheless, his demise originated, in part, in the political methods employed in guiding Argentina on the road to recovery. Mass-mobilization strategies and censorship further inflamed conflict with anti-Peronists. Even as state authorities reoriented the economy without major internal or external opposition, they found it ever harder to bend critics to their will. This weakness was indicative of a deeper flaw: the inability to create mechanisms for conflict resolution that accommodated rivals and that were widely perceived as legitimate within the nation's liberal republican traditions. The failure to build a hegemonic order with enough flexibility to contain the opposition created a series of ruptures that dispelled Perón's aura of total power and emboldened those seeking to force him from office.

A Peronist Ajuste

We should resist, for now at least, looking back from the 1955 coup, which reduces the period's history to mere outcomes, and instead consider how the regime first staved off economic calamity and retooled the Nueva Argentina. Concerns about potentially dangerous consumption were not entirely new. A decade earlier the Consejo Nacional de Posguerra had raised doubts about the inflationary consequences of labor reforms, and state planners had addressed signs of imbalance in the late 1940s by tightening public credit and encouraging savings. What changed, however, was the sense of urgency among Perón and his top advisers. Restricting domestic spending was a treacherous step for leaders who celebrated their ability to deliver and dignify. Avoiding adjustment measures was equally perilous, for the economy could spin further into an inflationary spiral or sink under the weight of mounting bankruptcies and deficits. Once Perón's reelection was secured, policymakers turned to the unpleasantness of austerity. Their package of reforms was dubbed the Plan Económico, echoing the rhetoric of the Plan Quinquenal but offering another mode of state intervention. It was, to use a more contemporary term, an *ajuste*—a "structural economic adjustment." Like the hundreds of ajustes that punctuate Latin American history—and whose full political and cultural history remains to be told—the Peronist plan was fairly conventional. It called for tightening consumption, reinvigorating agro-exports, and encouraging business investment. By 1954 it had achieved its major aims and restored growth. Despite its orthodoxy, the Plan Económico offered a rare exception by becoming one of the most successful stabilization programs in Argentina, if not in all of postwar Latin America.[2]

Prior to the plan's announcement, the government's Consejo Económico Nacional convened a series of closed-door meetings with labor and business organizations, ostensibly to gather their input, but primarily to secure their backing.[3] Over two weeks in January 1952, officials met with representatives from the CGT and CGE, the umbrella organization for mainly small- and medium-sized entrepreneurs founded just one month earlier.[4] Absent from these meetings was the Organización de Consumidores, headed by Evita's associate María Rosa Calviño de Gómez, confirming its marginal role. Instead, male-dominated business and labor groups put forth opposing views of Argentina's predicament. Within the privacy of their meeting room, conference participants debated the nation's ills with a frankness missing from the public sphere. All in attendance agreed that antispeculation campaigns had failed to prevent the erosion of purchasing power. In addition, they acknowledged the vast black market as a shadow economy that implicitly undermined state authority and distorted business relations.

Despite this initial degree of consensus, the attendees disagreed about ways to contain rising living costs. The CGE offered familiar business complaints about shortages of raw materials, declining worker productivity, and the burdensome guerra al agio. Without entirely rejecting the goals of national planning, its leaders argued that price controls and other regulations drove entrepreneurs away from manufacturing and other productive pursuits. The CGE advocated easing commercial controls and labor laws to create incentives for production while directing public credit to advance industrialization in the provinces.[5] Labor leaders greeted these grievances with open disdain. In their view, businesses had earned record profits by capturing a juicy share of working-class wages. Greater punishment for inefficient intermediaries and profiteers was required. As they saw it, consumer demand was not simply an abstract force but rather evidence of class empowerment, which they feared the economic downturn would erase. In the words of one CGT representative, enhanced spending power allowed laborers and their families to "live decently, or if one will, with comfort." Social aspirations had irrevocably changed: "for now we not only want enough to eat, but rather we have become dignified, we have another mentality and logically we do not want to retreat on all we have gained."[6] Accordingly, the CGT's wage-hike proposal took into account expenditures that went beyond mere subsistence. The organization's conception of the vida digna evoked male wage earners' enhanced abilities to provide for families and greater access to the fruits of consumer society, "conquests" that remained vulnerable in the face of proposals for macroeconomic stabilization.

The sessions ended without a clear resolution of these differences, but government officials tended to side with labor representatives. Minister Cereijo acknowledged that the current "disequilibrium" was caused partly by the "increased acquisitive power of the working masses" but stressed that businesses would make commercialization efficient or else the state would once again ratchet up regulations.[7] Notwithstanding the reassuring gestures to unions, the ajuste moved quickly in the opposite direction by restricting incomes and enhancing incentives for businesses.

Perón finally unveiled the Plan Económico in a radio address on February 18, 1952. The president contended that the "chaotic world situation" necessitated that citizens contribute to the defense of Argentina's economic independence: "each Argentine will know what to do, from this moment onward, to confront with solidarity a solution for all." Farmers received immediate relief. The IAPI would purchase the 1952–1953 harvest at prices 35 to 45 percent higher than the previous year's and pledged more credit and technical support. To check inflation, the government would rein in state expenditures and freeze salaries for two years, but after raising them between 40 and 80 percent.[8] To strengthen these policies, the president urged listeners to limit consumer spending and order their domestic economies. The public was asked to reduce unnecessary expenditures, put aside more savings, practice thrift when shopping, and (to use the president's favorite term) eliminate all types of "*derroche*" (wastefulness). Moving away from the optimism apparent in the visions of easy plenty invoked during the election campaign, Perón's tone became sober. His radio address made stern admonitions, including, "The welfare, abundance and even happiness of the pueblo is not the work of a government, or a certain group of persons, but rather the product of the action of the pueblo itself."[9] Authorities had called for responsible consumption and productivity in the past, but beginning in February 1952 these appeals inspired more ambitious campaigns to guide citizens as economic actors.

Propagandists minimized the coercive aspects of the Plan Económico by playing up the synchronization between patriots and the government. Various mediating institutions were deployed to broadcast instructions on measured spending habits. Federal agencies designated one thousand employees to canvass the nation and hold public session on the plan (including presentations for schoolchildren). Labor organizations staged similar educational sessions for workers and their families, and as president of the Partido Peronista Femenino, Evita instructed unidades básicas to lead consumer education drives.[10] Media coverage justified the temporary belt-tightening by stressing the abundance of life in previous years. For six years the pueblo had seen all its desires satisfied, claimed an editorial titled "Consumo y derroche" and signed by Perón. By his account, even humble workers had filled their closets with new clothes and "eaten at restaurants until they got tired." This spree was understandable, but now it was time to return to a "modest and moderate life."[11]

To complement the president's appeals, loyalists outlined the practical steps supporters could take to discipline spending. The pages of *Mundo Peronista* were filled with cost-cutting suggestions, complete with photographs of men and women in everyday shopping situations and "real-life" testimonials from proud descamisados. Articles profiled the "Peronist home economics" adopted by loyal followers of Perón and Evita. One such model family, Luis and Zulema Torres, made little changes to support the plan: patching up old clothes instead of buying new ones, finding creative recipes for leftovers, and planting a backyard garden to reduce food purchases. The Ministry of Public Health promoted these so-called health gardens by distributing free seeds, handing out thousands of packets in Buenos Aires and elsewhere. The economic imperatives of thrift complemented the ministry's ongoing "nutritional campaigns" that advocated altered eating habits, such as replacing beef with fish. Inspired by the findings of medical researchers, civil institutions close to the government (including female unidades básicas and the Grandes Alamacenes Justicialistas) offered "healthy cooking" classes pitched at popular sector women.[12] Yet within the context of the 1952 plan, healthfulness became another tool for justifying austerity. The techniques employed recall the mobilization measures of combatant nations during World War II and its aftermath, right down to the use of "victory gardens," albeit ones justified on nutritional rather than military grounds.[13]

Argentines were also told to seek out union cooperatives, FEP proveedurias, and other alternatives to private retailing that were committed to the recovery package. Local governments joined efforts to expand these commercial offerings.

Municipal officials under the Jorge Sabaté administration in Buenos Aires completed public works that enhanced the urban food supply and constructed a series of "model markets" in a streamlined, high modernist style. In contrast to traditional street markets, these spaces aimed to attract consumers with their sleek brightness and stress on hygiene, much as the gleaming FEP proveedurias sought to distinguish themselves from the grubby neighborhood almacenes. The model markets also experimented with novel commercial techniques including self-service food shopping, which was then spreading across the postwar world.[14] Peronist forays into modern retailing, however, were driven not by the search for profit or the emulation of foreign business practices but rather by the Plan Económico's efforts to persuade urban residents to take patriotic responsibility for their actions as shoppers.

Although authorities appealed to consumers of all types, publicity about the Plan Económico targeted housewives, or as Perón called them, the "nerve and motor" of the family economy. The language of efficiency and household rationalization seeped into the pages of women's magazines, including *Para Ti* and *Mundo Argentino* (still commercially produced but incorporated into the Peronist media consortium). Articles addressed the minutia of everyday life with practical tips: do not leave the radio on all day, eat less beef, limit visits to the movies and restaurants, and deposit savings in the bank. Some tips bordered on the absurd: loyalists were encouraged not to read in bed, as they might fall asleep with the lights on, and exhorted to resist taking hot showers by thinking how the power expended could instead run factory machinery. Reflecting the popularity of planning, the magazine argued that women should "direct home finances like a chief of state directs those of a country: with well-studied plans and an effective organization of earnings and expenses." Women could pitch in with the government campaign by employing their special skills as housewives, for example, mending clothes and learning techniques (e.g., hat repair) to stretch every peso.[15] Print media counseled female readers to combine thriftiness at home with public action in the streets, keeping a watchful eye on local stores and denouncing suspected agiotistas to the police. In these respects, the Plan Económico represented the pinnacle of Peronist efforts to define an explicit role for women as consumer citizens.

Evidence about the housewives' and others' reactions to these overtures is incomplete at best. The news media depicted scenes of collective compliance: supporters gathered at a cinema in the Buenos Aires neighborhood of Pompeya, listening to officials speak about the plan, or a smaller crowd of women in the suburb of San Justo, standing under umbrellas in the rain and holding aloft cutout portraits of Perón and Evita. Official statistics paint a similar picture: the Ministry of Public Health claimed that it distributed 685,000 packets of seeds by April 1952 and that some 47,500 health gardens had been planted in metropolitan Buenos Aires alone. Naturally, this "evidence," like the testimonials of "actual" Peronist couples, reveals more about government designs than about social responses. Adherence sometimes took idiosyncratic forms: one individual wrote to the Ministry of Technical Affairs with a homemade prototype for a sign with the slogan "Use this light only when necessary. / Your patriotism and cooperation with the Plan Económico 1952 demand it." The writer suggested that it be placed around every light switch in the country.[16] Moreover, the thousands of Perón Wants to Know letters that arrived in early 1952, just as the plan was taking hold, serve as a reminder that consumers expressed frustrations with high living costs and anger at the patchy enforcement of antispeculation measures rather than as a sign that they voluntarily complied with thriftiness campaigns.

For their part, economic policymakers did not rely solely on the goodwill of citizens and housewives. Most notably, the federal government prohibited the sale of beef in stores and restaurants on one day a week (Fridays in metropolitan Buenos Aires and Thursdays in the rest of the country). These unprecedented measures were designed to help Argentina meet an export contract with Britain for 200,000 tons of beef—a striking reversal for a government that celebrated the nationalization of British railroads as a victory over imperial dependency. Likewise, the imperative of augmenting exports led the government to approve in mid-1952 the sale of *pan negro,* a black bread made with millet and less processed flour. The Ministry of Public Health justified both these measures on nutritional grounds, a hard sell in a society where meat and white bread were eaten daily in vast quantities. The government's real goals were clear enough, and Perón publicly conceded the importance of beef and grain production to his administration's economic recovery.[17] For anti-Peronists, the meat restrictions and pan negro were clear signs of the depths to which Argentina, the agricultural powerhouse, had sunk. Editorials in *La Nación,* the most critical newspaper still in operation, welcomed the support now given to the mainstay of the old liberal economy. The regime's leaders responded to these arguments by blaming unforeseen droughts and unfavorable international prices, which did contribute to the agricultural crisis. But skeptics argued that years of clumsy government planning had damaged the nation's entrepreneurial spirit and fueled inflation. Seen from their vantage, pan negro symbolized the penury brought on by Peronist economic mismanagement.[18]

Within a year, however, the economy showed signs that the plan had accomplished its main objectives. Harvests improved, and the cost of living rose only slightly in 1952. By 1953 it had dropped dramatically to just 4 percent. Although the economy would never regain the robustness of the immediate postwar boom, its sustained recovery allayed fears of collapse.[19] The Plan Económico no doubt benefited from the lack of resistance by most anti-Peronist sectors, in part because the government adopted policies that placated some liberals. In a 1972 interview, one of the plan's architects, Alfredo Gómez Morales, maintained that its strength lay in the skillful coordination of wage and spending policies with protective price controls. The reorientation succeeded because supporters and officials endorsed it: consumers ate black bread, public agencies froze their budgets, and the military patriotically adopted belt-tightening measures, including the early dismissal of conscripts and the cultivation of crops on vacant lands. Even the president practiced creole-style thrift by entertaining visitors with *mate cocido* (a local tea) instead of imported coffee or whisky.[20]

Consumer solidarity with the demands of state-led austerity was no doubt crucial, but other evidence complicates this heroic picture of cooperation between subaltern actors and the planning state. In particular, government policies slashed worker spending power. In March 1952 the regime inaugurated the National Commission on Prices and Salaries, staffed by executive-branch officials and representatives from the CGT and CGE, to establish a so-called wage-price equilibrium. The administration had initially announced a 40 to 80 percent salary adjustment, but the two-year contracts signed between unions and employers in mid-1952 yielded meager gains. While farm workers fared slightly better, industrial laborers received an average increase of around 20 percent, only half the amount demanded by CGT leaders. A new round of price controls was supposed to defend the wage increase, but the need to jumpstart agriculture militated against consumer protection efforts; the IAPI even raised price ceilings on foodstuffs to promote farm production at the expense of urban buying power. Most important, austerity measures did not immediately end inflation, and thus rising prices wiped out official salary increases.[21]

The close ties between Perón's inner circle and unions facilitated the acceptance of these ephemeral wage hikes. Union cooperation was secured, apparently in part by state promises to ensure near full employment. Officials at the U.S. embassy reported that Perón's government took covert steps to contain unemployment, such as threatening industrialists with factory interventions and at least in one case purchasing a textile manufacturer's entire stock to prevent a plant from closing.[22] Equally important, the identification of rank-and-file workers with the justicialista movement helped to curtail bitter confrontations. The regime's track record of reform secured the compliance of organized labor (at least in the short term). The government eventually gave employers more leeway to negotiate staff reductions, but plans for large-scale layoffs met with union opposition. Responding to Perón's patriotic call, unions pursued no major strikes or popular protests during the crucial year of 1952. Ultimately, the Plan Económico's success was built on the intricate foundation of Peronist networks fostered since 1943 and the partisan bonds linking the president and the people.

Despite the urgent nature of this ajuste, there was little disguising the fact that the plan represented a move away from redistribution and a swing back to traditions of favoring rural producer-exporters over urban worker-consumers. Yet tensions over this shift in direction were contained, in large part because the plan coincided with the most significant event of 1952—the death of Eva Perón, which closed potential rifts with supporters. On July 26, 1952, Evita finally succumbed to cancer at the age of thirty-three. The public displays of grief that followed are legendary: for nearly two weeks, admirers formed lines up to thirty blocks long, often in the winter rain, to pay their last respects; columns of civilians, military troops, and government representatives marched through Buenos Aires in the funerary cortege that transported her body to the CGT's national headquarters. Along the way, hundreds of thousands of persons lined the streets to watch her casket being pulled by a team of workers in white shirtsleeves. Sympathizers recalled Evita's legacy in spontaneous ways, including barrio-level vigils, makeshift shrines erected in her memory, and public correspondence. Mario Abel Zandes, a young man from Misiones, wrote one such condolence letter, decorated with pictures of the president and First Lady, in which he described his sorrow to Perón directly: "As you can imagine sir, I feel greatly the disappearance of lady Evita 'The Flag Bearer of the humildes' because She has been my second mother. She was the one who fought for my future, for the position of aviation mechanic I now hold. For the innumerable benefits that she offered all the humildes, I will never stop crying for her, but I know that God will recompense her with the eternal rest that she deserves."[23] In coming to terms with the loss of a cherished leader, Zandes worked within the idiom of Peronist discourse, invoking its slogans and familiar tropes, notably, the emphasis on Evita as a saintly icon. In turn, the media celebrated Evita's devotion to the everyday problems of the poor and the individual acts of charity she personally administered. Newspapers and radio programs reminded the public of the FEP's social programs and the hundreds of clinics, orphanages, and old-age homes it built to care for Argentina's needy.[24] In the process of organizing the mourning and commemoration, Perón's government made appeals to sacrifice that resonated with the Plan Económico's campaigns for popular collaboration.

Evita's death may have stirred feelings of devotion among her enthusiasts, but it also raised uncertainties about the future given that Peronism's most vocal advocate for "dignificación" was gone. The impact of economic adjustments added to these concerns, especially for those Argentines who yearned to realize midcentury ideals of justice and comfort. With the Plan Económico, officials advanced an understanding of citizenship that linked the material circumstances of "ordinary" Argentines to the nation's future. Belt-tightening was presented as voluntary collaboration for the greater good, a move that not coincidentally shifted the focus of public debate from policymaking decisions to the household practices of working men and women. An implicit reciprocity undergirded this politics: authorities would safeguard popular well-being, and supporters would act as citizens by fulfilling their duties. Once again, officials acknowledged the importance of working-class and popular sectors to the nation, but the citizenry's scope of participation was tightly bounded. In explaining the plan to audiences, Perón used the metaphor of a nation swimming from choppy waters to the shores of recovery. Argentine citizens could help by paddling vigorously, but there were increasingly fewer ways for them to determine what course to take in reaching solid ground.

Dialectics of the Dignified Life

Thanks largely to the adjustment, the Argentine economy rebounded over the remainder of Perón's term: annual growth averaged 5 percent annually between 1953 and 1955, inflation was kept in the single digits, and agricultural activity surged upward (in part because of higher subsidies for producers). Real wages ended their decline, and salaries for industrial and agricultural laborers improved. Although these signs of recuperation were promising, the lingering effects of austerity conditioned state-citizen relations. Instead of setting the new equilibrium at peak 1949 wage levels, as they had promised, federal planners established a lower starting point to ease inflation and create greater incentives for private investment. After nearly a decade of ups and downs, the salary for an unskilled industrial worker (including social benefits) was about the same on the eve of Perón's overthrow in 1955 as it had been in 1947.[25] Authorities wrestled with a problem facing other midcentury reformers and revolutionaries in Latin America: how to manage followers' expectations during souring economic conditions without losing one's identity as an agent with a "credible vision" of change. In response, Perón and his assistants recast the socioeconomic components of citizenship in subtle but important ways. They counterbalanced talk of mass comfort with moralizing critiques of selfishness and laziness. Given this new political climate, popular actors pursued agendas within available opportunities, occasionally by taking to the streets in protest but more commonly by working within the system and engaging in the counterpolitics of voice.

As the recovery was underway, officials ramped up efforts to revise material expectations to the priorities of the Plan Económico. "To live with abundance does not necessarily mean to live well," opined Finance Minister Gómez Morales. Rejecting the twin evils of "disordered abundance" and "scarcity," he claimed that a return to the policies of Perón's first term would hurt wage earners. Only greater investment from the state and private sector would generate growth, the benefits of which would eventually trickle down to average households.[26] Appeals to patriotic discipline were matched with references to the continued ease of life in a bountiful nation, but leaders kept the perils of derroche in the public spotlight. Perón himself embraced the changing times at a 1954 conference of CGT and CGE representatives: "The first cycle that constituted the imposition, or better said, the drastic elevation of the standard of living up to a living level has already come to an end[;] it has been accomplished, and so drastic methods can no longer have an effect." Instead, future gains would depend on "rational systems" that would "lead to a gradual, progressive rise in the standard of living." The president was careful to note that working-class gains would be preserved: "It's not about having a submerged population, miserable and hungry, that does not consume." With the nation still relying on an expanding internal market for its industrial output, he proclaimed, "consumption is our wealth and our possibility for the future."[27]

Calls for disciplined acquisition became sharper in tone. Evita's death removed the matriarch of household thrift (as well as her displays of luxurious consumerist transgressions), but Perón occasionally adopted the mantle of the disappointed patriarch to scold members of the national family for their selfish appetites. Taking to the airwaves in April 1953, Perón expressed his personal "bitterness" at the lack of popular collaboration with the state, especially among consumers: "If one launches a campaign against agio nobody cares about paying a little more or less as long as they can fill their stomach, because it seems that for some the homeland is nothing but a question of the stomach." Perón suggested that the passive impulses of consumerism had contaminated attitudes toward social programs. He argued that even though the populace had lived in tenements in the past, crammed twenty to a room, now each citizen wanted a house—and even then they were unsatisfied: "they want us to provide them with the furniture and in addition bring them an automobile to the door." Perón contrasted the average Argentine with the stereotypical Italian immigrant, "*el tano*," figured as someone who worked tirelessly and sacrificed without complaint to build a home. "We are too lazy," Perón told his fellow Argentines: "when we don't have housing, comfortable and well-furnished housing, we think that the government is at fault. As if the government could resolve everyone's problems when they can't solve them themselves."[28] These statements may seem out of keeping for the continent's most famed populist; if anything, these attacks evoked elitist traditions of racial thought regarding the supposed indolence of creole populations and disciplined striving of European immigrants. While the bluntness of this particular rebuke was unusual, its view was consistent with the way the regime's leadership envisioned the dangers of mass consumption.

Perón's ear-pulling of an "excessively comfortable" populace complemented related campaigns to enhance worker productivity. Policymakers looked to the increased production of export commodities and consumer essentials for the domestic market as critical to a sustained recovery. The CGT and its member unions toed the official line by sponsoring newspaper advertisements that proclaimed: "Defend our economy by producing, producing, producing. Don't miss work for any reason that can be avoided." Partisan identity featured prominently in these appeals, and during the 1953 sugar harvest the CGT exhorted farmhands in Tucumán to labor diligently in the memory of the "Martyr of Work," Evita.[29] The efforts culminated in the March 1955 National Congress on Productivity and Social Welfare, a much-publicized summit of CGT, CGE, and federal officials.[30] Peronist authorities used admonishing slogans, such as "Live Better, Produce Better," to argue that future gains in the standard de vida depended more on worker productivity than on government programs. In his keynote address to Congress, Perón told workers in the audience, "What you do not produce today will never be consumed and you reduce the nivel de vida of all when you reduce your own production."[31] An internal CGT memorandum outlined similar arguments for union leaders to use on rank-and-file workers. "The increase in productivity results in a more fluid supply for the market. . . . It puts a greater quantity of goods and services at the consumer's disposal, at a lower price, because productivity always results in a reduction of costs, which in turn means greater spending power for the family budget." Evidence of the changing times, the insistence on productivity resembled the arguments of liberal business groups that had resisted Peronist commercial regulation.[32]

Labor representatives may have reluctantly supported productivity campaigns, but compliance with strategies of moral suasion was hard to secure. Authorities managed these tensions in part by integrating tutelary appeals within the larger drive to indoctrinate the nation's inhabitants. Throughout the early 1950s, the limitations on free speech worsened, as propaganda saturated the public sphere following the seizure of the opposition press and more severe intimidation.[33] By 1953 Argentina's formerly vibrant print culture had been, with few exceptions, replaced by apologists mouthing official rhetoric. Within its own ranks, the regime's ideologues conducted purges of the public administration, executive branch bureaucracies, and the court system, requiring officials to display allegiance to justicialista principles.[34] Government branches were also deployed to "order" the population. Most infamously, Peronist officials used the public schools to create the next generation of loyalists: millions of elementary school pupils were taught with texts that proclaimed "Perón loves us" and portrayed Evita as a saintly fairy godmother; older children were assigned the First Lady's biography and given lessons on the planning state's accomplishments; high-school and university students sat through classes on "citizenship culture." Official doctrine stressed blind allegiance. For instance, the "Twenty Truths of Justicialismo Peronista"—adages found in party literature, educational materials, and the popular press—included messages that emphasized solidarity, such as "For a Peronist, there is nothing better than another Peronist" and "In political action, the priorities of a Peronist are: first, the Patria; second, the movement; and third, mankind."[35]

This paradigm of national integration further fused state and civil society. On one level, these initiatives sought to "Peronize" populations marginalized from national politics in earlier eras (including women, the poor, children, and residents of interior provinces). But in practice ideals of a "people's democracy" could readily collapse into ritualized mourning for Evita's death and the wearing of Peronist insignia. Finding a space outside Peronism grew more difficult, for even the landscape bore its marks: incredibly, whole regions of the country were renamed, as in the case of the city of La Plata (which became Eva Perón) and the new provinces of Presidente Perón (El Chaco) and Eva Perón (La Pampa). These efforts to build a Peronist nation may seem farcical in hindsight, but they had a sinister side. The culture of obsequiousness stifled internal dissent within the Peronist ranks. At the same time, outspoken critics were forced into exile in neighboring countries or were imprisoned. Despite the lack of a full accounting of human rights abuses, it is clear that political prisoners were detained without charge and subjected to police interrogations. Moreover, repression was not entirely orchestrated by state cadres. Sympathizers at various levels of society were active enthusiasts in campaigns to "Peronize" their fellow citizens. Supporters accused co-workers, teachers, and neighbors for supposed immorality or treasonous behavior—denunciations that, as in the case of suspected merchant speculators, were not always ratified by public officials concerned with maintaining order.[36]

These modes of popular collaboration eroded the civil liberties of supporters and opponents alike. Indoctrination and repression, however, were counterbalanced by other strategies. In particular, Peronist institutions maintained openings for subaltern actors to address shortcomings in social citizenship. Perhaps the most visible contestation came, somewhat paradoxically, from one of Peronism's oldest allies: organized labor. Notwithstanding the state's influence over the CGT's members, factions within unions expressed their displeasure with the idea of equilibrium. Unionists adapted old traditions of cost-of-living activism by agitating for wage increases beyond the levels set by economic planners. The regime's leaders reacted, in turn, with strategies aimed to contain dissent. In particular, the administration viewed consumer politics as offering an attractive remedy. It responded to the consumer side of the cost-of-living issue by periodically intensifying antispeculation campaigns to forestall wage increases that might provoke the return of inflation.

One such episode occurred in early 1953, as rising prices and shortages stirred the Federación de Trabajadores de Luz y Fuerza and other unions to demand better salaries. The government replied with well-publicized measures targeting retail commerce and consumer staples imbued with strong cultural significance, such as beef, a food synonymous with the good life in Argentina. Shipments of meat earmarked for Britain and Europe were suspended temporarily to increase the supply in the butcher shops of Buenos Aires, an intervention that also demonstrated the flexing of nationalist politics over global market forces and old "imperial" patrons. That said, the leadership reminded audiences that speculators conspired against the self-sacrificing citizen. "Either we extirpate this cancer or this cancer will extirpate us," Perón told radio listeners in April 1953, a potent political metaphor given Evita's fatal struggle with cervical cancer. Days later, on April 15, grassroots expressions of enthusiasm for the Peronist ethics of exchange were on display at a mass rally staged in the Plaza de Mayo; one man carried an effigy with a noose around its neck and a sign reading "dishonest butcher."[37] This rally, however, would become famous for other incidents. During the gathering, two bombs planted by an anti-Peronist group exploded, leaving five dead and ninety-three injured. Perón fanned the stunned anger of his assembled followers by suggesting that they take justice into their own hands; that evening, bands carried out reprisals by sacking and burning the Jockey Club, Casa Radical, Socialist Casa del Pueblo, and other spaces associated with the opposition.

The violence was not directly linked to commercial policies, but the line between political and economic enemies was blurry at best and kept that way by public officials who spoke about both as guiding hidden conspiracies. (Perón declared on another occasion: "After the political opposition, the social blemish that follows is the crooks that speculate and cause anxiety and misery in the pueblo.")[38] In the weeks after the tragic rally, the federal government carried out its strongest clampdown on commerce to date. Police raids resulted in detentions and temporary business closings in metropolitan Buenos Aires; provincial counterparts from Mendoza to Santa Fe adopted similar measures, and in some localities sound trucks operated by the Ministry of Industry and Commerce cruised the streets broadcasting official price levels and instructing shoppers to report violations. Unions staged "loyalty meetings" to display support, and newspapers published lists of the unidades básicas, local governments, sociedades de fomento, and other community organizations that backed the crackdown. In all, over 10,500 cases against accused profiteers were opened between April and July 1953, with around 3,000 merchants detained and 247 stripped of their right to practice commerce.[39] This burst of activity illustrates how antispeculation considerations continued to resonate in mass politics despite the regime's economic reorientations. Public campaigns to impose justice on market forces retained broad appeal among leaders and grassroots sympathizers alike, even though these consumer protection measures shifted debate from wage demands to the machinations of internal enemies.

Labor organizations were not entirely distracted, and their push for greater redistribution won out on occasion. Tensions always ran high during renegotiations of union contracts, but never more so than in March 1954, when the two-year contracts that the Plan Económico set for most industrial, transportation, government, and service workers expired. This moment came just one month before national elections in which half the congressional seats and the vice presidency were at stake. In the lead-up to election day, Perón declared the end of the cycle of postwar redistribution. One week later, however, he reversed course and agreed to wage increases between 20 and 30 percent. This move caught members of the president's economic team off guard, for he had apparently made this pledge without their consultation.[40] Nevertheless, the state-sanctioned economic equilibrium survived this major test. The 1954 contracts finally raised salaries on average by about 15 to 20 percent (it was rumored that a subsequent relaxing in price controls provided hidden relief to employers, who were able to pass a portion of labor costs to customers).[41] The Peronist Party triumphed in the elections across the country, capturing approximately 63 percent of the vote and matching the level of support of the 1951 presidential elections.[42]

FIGURE 14. The closure of a corner market in a popular Buenos Aires neighborhood, with onlookers carefully posed to show the diversity of pueblo. *Archivo General de la Nación, Departamento Fotográficos, box 1307, envelope 24, doc. 201471 (Apr. 22, 1953); reproduced courtesy of the archive.*

But the Perón administration bent to popular demands only so far. State officials did not hesitate to punish recalcitrant union activists, and sporadic violence accompanied negotiations in the 1950s. One heated disagreement involved the metalworkers union, whose demands for its 1954 contract included a large wage raise; equal pay scales across gender and geographic lines; and most contentiously, greater control over internal factory commissions and union profit sharing. Faced with employer opposition and lukewarm state support, a wildcat faction of the union staged outdoor protests in Buenos Aires. These acts of defiance crossed the line and were met with overt repression: three metalworkers were killed in clashes with the police at a protest on June 5. Confederación General del Trabajo officials and the loyalist media blamed these incidents on communist agitators and quickly removed them from the public eye. In the aftermath of the violent crackdown, the state sought to appease protesters by raising wages and removing the metalworker union's secretary-general, Abdula Baluch.[43]

The mixture of mobilization, concession, and repression that shaped cost-of-living politics allowed the regime to maintain its dominance, though perhaps at the expense of heightening antagonisms with commercial interests and, to a lesser degree, within its own base of support. Yet other Peronist initiatives helped dampen conflict by addressing consumer needs through less fractious means. Tightening budgets and emphasizing austerity did not preclude the consolidation of Peronist social assistance in the 1950s. Although federal social spending was restricted, officials continued to experiment with bureaucratic and clientelistic modes of delivering assistance.[44] Membership in pension systems expanded to an estimated 6 million persons in 1953, up from 3.3 million in 1948, and the number of hospitals and health clinics run by the Fundación Eva Perón grew similarly. Innovations made up for tightening budgets. The Banco Hipotecario Nacional (BHN) implemented its so-called Plan Eva Perón (1952–1955), the federal government's most successful effort to provide housing for low-income families. Rather than construct public housing directly, the BHN supplied beneficiaries with blueprints for simple one- or two-bedroom houses that they could then present to construction companies or build themselves; mortgages set at gracious terms helped hundreds of thousands of working-class Argentines to enter the ranks of home owners.[45]

Nonmarket alternatives thus counterbalanced the impact that austerity measures had on consumer pocketbooks. Social citizenship continued to encompass both welfare and mass consumption, even as anti-inflationary policies made the latter unattractive for state officials. But if one side descended, then another rose: collective consumption programs mitigated the erosion of spending power (at least among those Argentines willing to access Peronist assistance). To a degree, the trends were propelled by grassroots demands, many of them directed by individuals through the community-level institutions and branches of the Peronist movement. Encounters between resource holders and petitioners were hardly idyllic, but conflicts were framed as more personal in nature and thus were rendered less politically challenging to Peronist hegemony. One unidad básica in Buenos Aires, for example, petitioned the Ministry of Technical Affairs with a cluster of requests from individual members: a job promotion, a position with the public gas agency, and an apartment in the public housing project of Barrio Curapaligue.[46] That the federal planning agency—and not just relevant welfare providers—received such requests suggests the ubiquity of these practices in 1950s Argentina. As other economic opportunities diminished, the state itself became a path to social mobility, and petitioners employed tactics that leveraged influence and navigated claims through bureaucracies.

Officials responded to the swell of individual demands by providing relief when possible while advancing Peronization campaigns. Personal connections and partisan loyalty had long mattered for securing public employment; by the early 1950s, this process had become formalized. Bureaucratic procedures even reached organizations, such as the Fundación Eva Perón, that had been characterized by a self-consciously empathetic and antibureaucratic approach. In late 1952, Minister Ramón Cereijo was assigned to manage the FEP, and under his tenure the agency refined its distribution of material goods and consumables. Take the case of Rosa Alonso, a sixty-two-year-old woman of Spanish nationality who wrote to the foundation asking for clothing and shoes for her family. An FEP letter informed her that she needed to obtain a "certificate of poverty" from a local justice of the peace and then write back with the sex, age, and size of each family member. Alonso convinced two of her neighbors from the Buenos Aires suburb of Villa Diehl to go before a justice and sign a form, attesting simply that she was poor.[47] The gatekeepers of social assistance tapped into the reservoir of goodwill built up in previous years, occasionally even instructing supplicants to write directly to Evita years after her death. Thus, Alonso was told to send her packet of documents to the address of the Presidential Residence, care of "Evita, Spiritual Chief of the Nation." The Ministry of Technical Affairs stipulated similar behavior. A man who wrote in May 1953 to secure a state job (or at least permission to sell Peronist insignias aboard trains) was commanded to address himself to Evita personally: "From her place of immortality, She watches as always over the Pueblo, to whom She devoted her life, through General PERÓN and the foundation that carries her name."[48] Peronist leaders were clearly not above manipulating Evita's enduring popularity as the poor's "spiritual mother" to manage grassroots demands.

These maneuvers illustrate the lengths taken to solidify the regime's standing and safeguard its revamped economic model. Clearly, the continuing identification of a majority of the Argentine population with Peronism cannot be attributed solely to actions of state administrators. For many, Peronism continued to embody varied ideals of social justice defined as everything from a heretical rejection of cultural hierarchies to desires for inclusion in a commercialized mainstream. These principles remained appealing despite circumstances less favorable to their realization. Peronist rule appeared to promise the best possibility for future improvements based on its past record. It would take more, of course, than anger at everyday consumption and the slower pace of changes in living standards to eliminate these sympathies entirely, especially in a time of mounting polarization, when the risks involved in jumping one partisan camp for another were not negligible. Yet solidarity involved more than just popular sentiment or the calculus of self-interest. The mixture of contract concessions, indoctrination campaigns, controls on public expression, and partisan mobilization served to channel frustrations within the Peronist ranks onto internal enemies (e.g., speculators) or into personal supplication through networks of social assistance.

From Equilibrium to Overthrow

Despite the importance of cultivating solidarity, Peronist leaders did not focus exclusively on efforts to consolidate, broaden, and mobilize their base. Their conception of power depended on establishing a façade of consensus and unanimity of national purpose—all had a role to play, aside from oligarchs, agiotistas, and other truly irredeemable social types. Wide sectors of the population, not just self-proclaimed Peronists, were subjected to state disciplinary campaigns, and public authorities were aware that coercive techniques went only so far. Repression was combined with renewed attempts to rally the population behind state-guided development. To this end, Perón and his collaborators aimed to convince skeptics that the Nueva Argentina had a future by highlighting prospects for investment and technological progress. Even as policymakers sought to contain popular spending power to solidify the recovery, Peronist officials gestured to the consumer bounty associated with the next stage of modernity that lay just over the horizon.

While these initiatives may have been welcomed by some, they were ultimately insufficient to stem the groundswell of sentiment for the overthrow of Perón. In staking an even greater presence in various areas of quotidian life, the central state and its allies exacerbated partisan strains felt since Peronism's birth. As before, anti-Peronism sprang from multiple sources, including resentments stirred by the economic impact of state planning, threats to status and order that the masses were thought to pose, frustrations with the monopolization of the state, and anger at erosion of individual rights. A full account of the winding process that culminated in the September 1955 coup is beyond the scope of this study, for the question of containing consumption had little direct connection to the Peronist regime's end. That said, the larger problems confronting officials during this period—above all, the challenge of reconciling popular demands for social justice with Argentina's economic limitations—would outlast the implosion of the regime. The unfinished business of the revolución justicialista would endure long after Perón fled the country.

The prospects for advancing consumer society under Peronist rule in the 1950s were by no means bleak. Popular grievances with bothersome marketplace conditions remained sources of worry, but certain businesses prospered. These included Peronist forays into commerce, such as the Commercial Employee Union's department store, Gran Just. According to the union's own reports, as the economy gained strength, so too did sales at the store (in June 1954 up 22 percent over the previous year).[49] Modernizing goods, such as refrigerators, washing machines, and electrical fans, remained in high demand, and the mass marketplace's offerings expanded to meet working- and middle-class consumer wants. For example, SIAM Di Tella signed an agreement with the Italian manufacturer of Lambretta motor scooters to produce vehicles in Argentina; the scooters rolled off the assembly lines in 1953 under the brand name Siambretta. For every success story, however, there were cases such as that of Fetoro, a small manufacturer of home appliances that foundered in the early 1950s and eventually petitioned the government for a bailout. Out-of-date machinery and the scarcity of raw materials hampered the light industries at the core of Peronist-era mass consumption. Textile manufacturers and retailers were particularly hard hit by shrinking demand, and in 1953–1955 they constituted nearly one-third of all bankrupt firms.[50]

Years before its demise, the Peronist regime redoubled efforts to dispel perceptions of weakness by projecting images of the bright future. Even amid the sacrifices of austerity and the sorrows of Evita's mourning, officials seized opportunities to stoke a sense of dynamism. The announcement of the Second Five-Year Plan in December 1952 offered just such an occasion to reinvoke the allure of state planning. Amid the fanfare, the new master plan for state-led development enumerated over 900 initiatives, mainly in areas of public works and social policy, that overlapped loosely with the priorities expressed in the Perón Wants to Know correspondence.[51] Yet the new five-year plan also departed in significant ways from these trends: it placed far greater emphasis on state support for agriculture, resource extraction, and heavy industry than had either its predecessor or the demands enunciated in the letter-writing campaign. Adapting notions of industrial-age progress, its policy statements reached out to business sectors frustrated with earlier regulatory interventions in the marketplace.

Throughout 1953–1955 administrators translated these general principles into specific measures to create a more investor-friendly climate. Most controversially, the government took steps to lure foreign businesses as part of developmental strategies. The Peronist-controlled Congress passed the Ley de Radicación de Capitales (1953) to facilitate overseas ventures, while the executive branch offered tax breaks and other perks for foreign corporations in fields the regime deemed important.[52] Behind these moves lay the changing relationship between the domestic economy and the international system. Despite Peronist appeals to sovreignty, the two five-year plans did little to alter Argentina's dependence on the foreign exchange gained from agricultural exports. If anything, the Plan Económico improved the position of rural producers as a route to financing future industrialization. But tighter credit policies designed to limit inflation forced officials to look abroad for the capital required for recovery. Principles of economic nationalism forged in the 1930s thus clashed with the realities of Argentina's place in a new world economy. As the reconstitution of international trade and finance around the Breton Woods accords took hold in the 1950s, U.S. businesses turned with keen interest to Latin America. In 1953 the Ministry of Foreign Relations set up a meeting between Perón and Milton Eisenhower, the U.S. president's brother, to discuss opportunities for entrepreneurs and to ease diplomatic strain with the United States. These moves by no means pleased diehard nationalists, who felt that Perón had retreated from the ardent anti-imperialism of his first term. The government went so far as publishing foreign-language pamphlets that stressed the benefits of doing business in the New Argentina, lauding Peronist "social peace" and an orderly union movement as a boon for would-be investors rather than as signs of victory over capitalist injustice.[53]

Yet the rapprochement with foreign capital did not signal a return to laissez-faire liberalism. The Ley de Radicación de Capitales proclaimed that foreign ventures "must not be designed—openly or covertly—to obtain the domination of national markets, the elimination of competition, or the usurious increase in profits."[54] In practice, state authorities did not surrender their ambitions to order the economy. Moreover, old populist tendencies outweighed new priorities (for instance, a proposed deal with Standard Oil of California over drilling rights fell through thanks to nationalist critiques). Although the Second Five-Year Plan highlighted heavy industry, Peronist officials had better luck attracting foreign capitalists interested in manufacturing consumer goods. In the mid-1950s the government negotiated with foreign automakers to set up factories in the suburbs of Córdoba and Buenos Aires. Perón's administration signed contracts with the multinational giant Fiat and lesser-known manufacturers including IKA (Industrias Kaiser Argentina), a company founded by the U.S. industrialist Henry Kaiser with the machinery used to build Jeeps during World War II.[55]

The Argentine state embarked on its own ventures in automobile production that catered to the aspirations of local consumers while confirming a commitment to state-led national development. Even as the Plan Económico's austerity measures took effect in 1952, Perón proudly introduced the government's own "Institec" line of cars, trucks, and motorcycles. The state had experimented with the construction of jet fighter airplanes (the so-called Pulqui I and II) in the late 1940s; now attention within the aeronautics agency, the IAME, turned to the era's ultimate consumer good, the motor vehicle. For Perón and his planners, high-end consumer goods fit into larger economic strategies. Cars provided a source of high-paying jobs and the means to industrialize Córdoba and other provincial cities. Vehicles made in Argentina constituted potent emblems of progress in a world where national might was defined increasingly by technological output. Automobiles were also much sought after in Peronist Argentina, partly because consumer expectations were rising but primarily because economic planners reduced their importation to save foreign exchange. By the early 1950s, the shortage of vehicles had become a political problem. Rumors circulated about officials who sold car import permits to the highest bidder or distributed them as favors to cronies. The Ministry of Technical Affairs frequently received letters from individuals across the country—from elected officials to physicians—requesting automobiles for work or private use.[56]

Although there had been other midcentury forays of this sort (Nazi Germany's Volkswagen being the most famous), the Institec line was the world's first line of vehicles built entirely by a national government for a mass commercial market.[57] The press lavished praise on the prototypes, and Perón himself was photographed taking the "Puma" motorcycle and other vehicles through their paces. In keeping with the drive to Peronize society (as if any doubt remained about who deserved the credit), the four-door sedan was named the "Justicialista." Its body design supposedly inspired by a classic 1951 Chevrolet, the car offered a potent symbol of the intersection of midcentury populism, trasnational consumer culture, and nationalist developmentalism.[58] In the end, however, the state's attempts to advance the frontiers of consumer society did not amount to much. Although private sector car manufacturing eventually took off in the late 1950s, government factories rolled out only a few thousand Institec cars and motorcycles before the 1955 coup. Peronist ventures in motor vehicle production sought to keep the New Argentina moving forward, but these measures did not transcend the more basic problems facing ordinary wage earners in the marketplace. The government's car program was designed to provide affordable vehicles for the average household. With the shift toward more gradual increases in the standard of living, it remained to be seen when, if ever, the average working family would ride around in its own Justicialista car.

These contradictions were more broadly characteristic of the Peronist government's desire to widen mass consumption through state intervention while creating a more business-friendly climate. Antispeculation measures were no exception: the regime carried out periodic crackdowns on profiteering in the 1950s, but internal records suggest a degree of laxness in levying economic penalties on business. By 1955 the state had collected some 23 million pesos in antispeculation fines, but over 50 million more remained unpaid by convicted businesses. It was a risky move, for speculators faced imprisonment and seizure of property, too; nevertheless, businesses large and small opted to drag their feet (in fact, sixty out of the

FIGURE 15. Visiting an expo for the Second Five-Year Plan, Perón and top advisers examine the Puma motorcycle, made in Argentina; the man to the far left is Interior Secretary Ángel Borlenghi, and the man in the dark suit on the right is propaganda czar Raúl Apold. *Archivo General de la Nación, Departamento Fotográficos, box 3179, envelope 7, doc. 203952 (July 31, 1953); reproduced courtesy of the archive.*

sixty-six companies assessed major fines of 100,000 pesos or more after 1950 simply waited for the state to demand payment).[59] The administration's failure to go after these scofflaws exemplifies the continued lack of coordination between branches of government, as well as the degree of merchant resistance to the regulations. Yet the tactic of issuing fines without ensuring their payment may have also reflected the state's growing pragmatism toward business: whether by accident or design, this approach to enforcement lessened the financial burdens on commercial interests while saving face with consumers committed to managed markets.

Ultimately, government efforts to mend fences with business failed to match high expectations. Overseas capital arrived in amounts smaller than desired, and attempts to draw the largest Argentine industrialists into Peronism's orbit fell short. The big firms and rural producers remained wary; most looked for generous public loans but tried to keep the state at arm's length. Even industrialists in metal manufacturing, whose economic interests coincided closely with state support for inward-oriented growth, were repelled by Peronist labor policies, commercial controls, and the courting of foreign competitors, among other factors.

The regime's leadership enjoyed the best relations with organizations, such as the CGE, whose members looked to Perón's government as an advocate for economic federalism and provincial investment.[60]

The setbacks in realizing the new vision of Peronist consumer society, however, were overshadowed from 1954 onward by the deepening political crisis. The biggest threat came not from mainstream parties or outside agitators but rather from factions within two major allies of the original Peronist coalition: the Roman Catholic Church and the military. Most historians agree that a rift with the Catholic Church acted as a catalyst precipitating the regime's collapse. In the early 1950s, groups within the Church attempted to assert greater organizational autonomy amid deepening Peronization. At the same time, state authorities moved to enhance control over Catholic youth organizations and anti-Peronist clerics while curtailing the perceived threat posed by a new (and minuscule) Christian Democratic party. These conflicts unexpectedly swelled into public confrontations as the government and Church competed for the sympathies of citizen-parishioners. Each side sniped at the other through the mass media and the pulpit. Federal officials imposed restrictions on Catholic processions and meetings. In 1954 continued opposition led the president to sign into law a package of progressive reforms —extending legal rights to illegitimate children, allowing divorce, and legalizing prostitution—that further incensed the devout.

As this dispute captured attention, the anger of other critics boiled closer to the top. More than a decade had passed since the 1943 June Revolution—a long time for the disgruntled third of the population to endure the irritations of Peronist rule. The regime tacked back and forth between concession and repression. Its leaders allowed some anti-Peronists openings for freer expression (largely in intellectual journals, such as *Contorno*) and held talks with members of opposition parties over a political amnesty (in part to divide these organizations internally).[61] At other moments they clamped down tightly on dissent. As the confrontations with old allies within the Catholic Church suggest, however, Peronist authorities displayed diminishing creativity in dealing with opposition. This wound was partially self-inflicted: Perón had replaced early collaborators in top government positions with yes-men who showed less skill for adapting to fluid political circumstances. For their part, anti-Peronists attributed the regime's wobbling to personal factors.[62] After Evita's death, Perón was rumored to be involved in a scandalous romantic relationship with a fifteen-year-old girl, Nelly Rivas. He was accused of spending too much time at the Presidential Residence, where the Union of Secondary Students (UES), a Peronist youth organization for high-school pupils, had relocated its headquarters. Gossip circulated that the organization's students were allowed to call the president by a childish nickname, "Pocho." In one celebrated 1954 incident, Perón joined a few hundred UES members in an impromptu ride through the streets of Buenos Aires on a fleet of brand-new Siambretta motor scooters, with the smiling president decked out in a white riding uniform and matching baseball cap. What propagandists might have viewed as a triumph of consumer modernity became the butt of jokes, with critics dubbing the scooters "Pochonettas" and mocking the aging Perón's fascination with youth.

While observers dissected the president's behavior, the political crisis with the Church reached a head in June 1955. The annual Corpus Christi procession in Buenos Aires culminated with clashes in the streets between Catholics and the police: the traditional religious festival devolved into a contest over command of the nation's most symbolic public spaces as devotees defied state measures to prohibit public gatherings. More important, these incidents inspired action from military conspirators encouraged by apparent signs of weakness.[63] A week after the Corpus Christi affair, military forces staged a coup. On June 16 naval warplanes bombarded the presidential offices and downtown Buenos Aires; the president survived, but 355 civilians were killed and hundreds more injured as they went about their daily routines. Coincidentally, the Vatican chose that day to announce the excommunication of all officials responsible for an earlier expulsion of two high-ranking clerics (a vaguely worded measure that implied Perón's own excommunication). His supporters retaliated that evening by setting fire to a handful of churches in the city center.

The government never fully recovered from these violent exchanges. Between June and September, Perón made conciliatory gestures by reaching out to opposition parties and reshuffling his cabinet. Neither his official declaration that the revolutionary phase of his government was over nor the drama of his temporary resignation in August did much to dissuade the opposition. Despite switching to rhetorical outbursts promising violent resistance, Perón was unwilling to arm his loyalists for civil war. In the end, this career military officer's conservatism outweighed his revolutionary impulses as a nationalist firebrand. On September 16, 1955, another coup attempt commenced, this one involving all branches of the armed forces and located in multiple points of the country. After a few days of intermittent fighting, Perón boarded a ship bound for Paraguay and fled into exile. The Nueva Argentina was over and the Revolución Libertadora had begun.

Its leader, General Eduardo Lonardi, spoke of reconciliation on assuming the presidency, and his slogan, "Ni vencedores, ni vencidos" (neither victors nor vanquished), offered the hope that the transition might be peaceful. The new government's manifesto promised the "recovery of equilibrium, harmony and mutual respect between different social and political groups."[64] This momentary optimism quickly evaporated. Two months later Lonardi was forced out by other coup plotters; his replacement, General Pedro Eugenio Aramburu, presided over a military government that pursued an aggressive brand of anti-Peronism. The most visible Peronist institutions (e.g., the Fundación Eva Perón and the IAPI) were dismantled, while military officers intervened in the unions. To extirpate Peronism, the state extended media controls and outlawed discussion of anything related to the "second tyranny" (Perón was envisioned as the second coming of the infamous nineteenth-century tyrant Juan Manuel de Rosas). The tables turned from the days of runway Peronization; now the mere mention of Perón or Evita in the media, the display of partisan symbols, and the playing of Peronist marches were specifically prohibited by Decree 4161. When confronted with opposition—in the form of labor protests, grassroots acts of sabotage, and most alarmingly, a failed uprising of a pro-Peronist military faction in 1956—the Aramburu regime responded with force that left scores dead and thousands imprisoned.[65]

It comes as little surprise that September 1955 stands out as a moment of rupture remembered by many Argentines for decades as a traumatic defeat.[66] For others, however, the coup was experienced as a moment of liberation, one that led them to reexamine the recent past and pass judgments on the deposed regime. In the years that followed the coup, the first generation of commentators tended to equate Peronism with methods of mass manipulation (or in the words of one observer, techniques of "systematic deception" that made justicia social into a "narcotic and tranquilizing slogan").[67] Comparisons to fascism retained their attraction, but commentators turned as well to the newer language of "totalitarianism" then sweeping across the cold war world, which highlighted Peronism's supposedly aberrant nature. Even the mass-media forum *El Hogar*, a women's magazine that had years earlier collaborated with the Plan Económico's call for consumer thrift, joined the chorus: its editors contrasted Perón's "totalitarian machine" with the return to the "*vida normal.*"[68] As the rancor of the preceding decade spilled into the open, working-class redistribution became a target. Industrialist organizations led the charge, arguing that greater worker sacrifice was required to restore prosperity. In a letter to President Aramburu, the Camara Argentina de Industrias Metalúrgicas asserted that while certain wage-earner gains should be maintained, it was time for the workforce to make amends: "the worker today is heavily in debt to not only the company but also the country, because his low productivity and in general low sense of responsibility threaten the Nation." Under the banner of productivity once carried aloft by Peronist authorities, employers and their government allies sought to roll back the power of unions and exert industrial discipline in the workplace.[69]

Despite launching campaigns to de-Peronize society, the architects of the Revolución Libertadora did not make a complete break. Beneath the surface of partisan clashes, they maintained certain priorities of the Peronist planning state. Union activists were repressed harshly, but features of Peronist economic morality survived the political rupture. While the Aramburu regime celebrated the virtues of economic liberalism, many commercial controls governing mass consumption remained in place. Periodic decrees froze consumer prices and set maximum profit levels. Responsibility for enforcement moved from the Federal Police to the Ministry of Commerce, a sign of slackening commitment to waging the antispeculation war. Still, the country's stern rulers were not above the occasional populist gesture of denouncing commercial speculation, an "act of sabotage that will not be tolerated under any pretext," according to one pronouncement.[70] In addition, the military government found itself in a situation similar to that facing Perón's administration in deploying national development to enhance its legitimacy. The Aramburu regime called on luminaries including Raúl Prebisch, a former Central Bank official in the 1930s and one of Latin America's leading economists, to chart a course for future progress. The Prebisch Report supplied a dire assessment of Argentina's economic obstacles, with blame placed heavily on Peronist state interference. But it did not depart entirely from earlier priorities, especially in linking redistribution and development. Mirroring rhetoric of the deposed rulers, the report claimed that the main problem facing Argentina and Latin America alike was how to "accelerate the rhythm of economic growth to raise rapidly the nivel de vida of the masses."[71]

Yet Argentina's military rulers failed to achieve their ideal of a post-Peronist order. Repressive efforts to break partisan solidarities only engendered defiance, and a shared hatred of the "second tyranny" did not stop many anti-Peronists from desiring civilian rather than military rule. Advisers and ministers passed through the military government via a revolving door without establishing any clear direction. Equally important, Perón was gone but not forgotten. From exile he encouraged supporters to resist alternative political projects and plotted to restore the movement to its former supremacy. If these sources of political instability were not enough, market forces added further volatility. Inflation returned with a vengeance: by the close of the 1950s, retail prices surged by the unprecedented annual rate of 130 percent, almost tripling the peak reached under justicialista rule. As a sign of the reversal of Peronist income redistribution, the industrial worker's share of the national income fell precipitously from 58 percent of the GDP in 1954 to 46 percent in 1959.[72] In 1958 the military decided to step aside by holding elections (with no Peronist candidates, of course); civilian politicians would be allowed to bear the brunt of these mounting burdens. For the next two decades, government after government tried its luck at transcending the political stalemate and finding a way out of the nation's economic impasses. As ordinary citizens struggled to make their way in increasingly chaotic times, the fundamental causes of Argentina's agony remained all too resistant to change.

❦

In retrospect, it is clear that the economic troubles of the early 1950s were not particularly unusual or acute; there had been more severe crises in Argentina's recent past (and there would be worse to come).[73] This moment's historical significance lies instead in what it reveals about Peronism's tremendous adaptability. Economic concern provoked political innovation, for officials retooled national planning in accordance with evolving ideas of development and the country's shifting position in the world economy. Peronist authorities flexed their power of command over citizens as consumers, workers, and household managers, initiatives that inspired a spectrum of reactions. The details of the Plan Económico mattered; officials acted before conditions deteriorated entirely and preserved employment to mitigate the sacrifices of wage earners. Similar preoccupations with "excessive" consumption surfaced across Latin America, even in cases where states embraced milder reforms favoring urban wage earners, rural proletarians, or workers in extractive industries. When faced with economic contraction, governments across the region have readily made popular consumption the main object of policy correction. Although other Latin American governments attempted similar ajustes, few were able to withstand the fallout from austerity.

Contrary to expectations, the Peronist case reveals as well the countryside's fundamental importance even in urban-centered projects of redistribution. Faced with declining agricultural exports, Peronist policymakers were forced to direct wealth back toward rural producers. Midcentury movements that privileged distribution through land reform faced different denouements: most either detonated in conflict as landowners and their foreign allies confronted rural laborers (as in Guatemala) or deflated because of faltering state support and redirection from local powerbrokers (as in Mexico, Bolivia, and Peru). Although conflicts unfolded differently in Argentina, Peronist authorities discovered that the burdensome constraints of agro-export legacies—what contemporaries would soon label "dependency"—necessitated difficult adaptations in nationalist developmental aims.

Looking back at the crisis of the early 1950s, it is easy to assume that working-class redistribution was the primary cause of deterioration. As I have shown, mythic depictions of this period as a popular spending spree were furthered by Peronists and anti-Peronists alike, either as evidence of a golden age or as the origins of the nation's bankrupting. Income gains in certain fields did outstrip improvements in productivity, a condition unsustainable in the long term. But productivity measured not just wage levels or workforce diligence but also employers' abilities to enhance efficiency, update plants, and lower production costs. With the benefit of hindsight, economic historians point to the structural impediments that hampered diversified, inward-oriented industrialization in a country of Argentina's population size and characteristics. However much redistribution may have contributed to imbalances, the reality is that state authorities identified household spending as a target of intervention. Within the constraints of the moment, Perón and his collaborators chose to contain consumption.

Once again, the standard de vida proved an essential tool for reimagining the relations among the state, the citizens, and the market. The idea that the government could raise needy populations to a threshold of well-being retained its centrality to Peronism. Planners assumed responsibility for determining how much and how quickly to adjust wages, price controls, and other economic levers. They proclaimed the end of an era: in the revolución justicialista's next stage, "social conquests" would be tied more closely to thrifty habits, private investment, and productivity. Obviously, moving in this direction involved more than making speeches or redrawing a line on a living standards chart; unions and other branches of the movement exerted pressure that limited the planning state's scope. Nevertheless, adjustments to the New Argentina advanced without major concessions to grassroots demands (at least not on a collective scale) during this Thermidor-style phase of consolidation. However, popular yearnings for Peronism's vida digna did not go away in 1955. In withstanding economic crisis, Peronist authorities bequeathed dilemmas of development and redistribution to subsequent rulers, but without having first established durable institutional arrangements to address the politics of social citizenship. Disciplinary campaigns begun under Perón were reworked by subsequent rulers, including those who saw the material aspirations of the "masses" as a far more dangerous obstacle to order and progress.

CONCLUSION

The Dignified Life and Beyond

MUCH HAS changed since Perón was deposed over five decades ago. Today the overwhelming majority of Argentines have no direct experience of life in the Nueva Argentina. With each passing year, less evidence of a once commanding regime remains, for subsequent administrations reduced its social programs, lifted commercial and labor regulations, dismantled the propaganda machine, and destroyed physical reminders of the era. The military rulers of the Revolución Libertadora went so far as leveling the Palacio Unzué, the belle-époque mansion where Juan and Evita had lived in Buenos Aires (and where she eventually died). After sitting vacant for years, the lot became home to the relocated National Library; few people strolling by this severe, brutalist-style building realize the site's former centrality to Perón's presidency (as, ironically I myself did not prior to beginning research on this book in the same library).[1] Other landmark projects—the vacation hotels, social assistance facilities, and union-run department stores—have fallen into ruin or been sold off to private investors. These examples serve as reminders that Peronist-era reforms were mostly transitory and this moment in time was short-lived.

Yet the era's brevity belies its traumatic intensity, which unleashed antagonisms that dominated national affairs for generations. Its legacies still weigh on the present, for in certain respects the Peronist era has never ended. Although the New Argentina may be in ruins, Peronism survives to this day, a remarkable feat when compared to similar mass political "-isms" that flowered and then faded in the mid-twentieth century. It has, to be sure, become an accepted feature of the landscape. Having survived periods of anti-Peronist backlash, the Justicialista Party is once again the country's principal political force. The most significant jockeying for state control occurs within its ranks rather than against external rivals, and Peronist organizations have coalesced into a new establishment. But they still operate as a nexus for disputes over redistribution and market regulation. Their patronage networks provide access to food and essential consumer staples among the country's poor while serving as channels to express frustrations during riots, boycotts, and other protests. The presidencies of Néstor Kirchner and Cristina Fernández de Kirchner (2003–present) have seen the revival of the controversies that animated midcentury politics. State proposals to boost social spending by taxing agro-exports, denunciations against profiteers who prey on consumers, frustrations with uncontrollable prices—all these issues have stirred debate again.

In one way or another, all works on Peronism try to explain why the movement has become such a fundamental, enduring feature of Argentine life. This problem remains vital not only to explaining the unfolding of the country's past but also to making sense of its present condition and future course. As I have shown, clues to Peronism's resonance may be found in the intensity of its formative years. One must be careful not to read too much back onto origins, however; doing so would ignore Argentina's twisting path to the present and the redirections within justicialismo itself. Yet the "classic" Peronist era (1943–1955) was undoubtedly *the* major turning point of twentieth-century Argentine history. In coming to terms with this transformative moment, I have focused on one of Peronism's most potent innovations: the articulation of an expansive sense of national belonging that spoke to the material needs and aspirations of popular households. Moreover, I have argued that contests over consumption provide us with a better understanding of Peronism's practices of social citizenship, insights that in turn can offer fresh answers to a variation of the question posed above: namely, why did Peronism strike such a chord in midcentury Argentine society?

Clearly, state power mattered. As Peronist institutions staked a presence across a vast territory, reforms targeting living standards went hand in hand with efforts to shape a partisan worldview. Officials flooded society with information to inculcate complementary ways of thinking and commanded the resources to rally potential supporters behind promises of plenty. Argentina's rulers rejected pluralism as a threat to the nation and defended a rigid model of ideological consensus. The intimidation of outspoken critics revealed the menacing side of populist nationalism; often overlooked, however, is the disciplinary attention that fell on the movement's working-class base. State campaigns sought to correct "unruly" behavior and instruct the citizens on their proper duties not only as laborers and voters but also as family members, students, and consumers. Yet these strategies of rule do not account fully for Peronism's profound appeal or the discord it sparked. Mid-century forms of mass politics cannot be reduced to crude manipulation; as one historian has written about the contemporaneous but unquestionably more extreme and repressive case of Stalinism: "To be effective, propaganda must offer a story that people are prepared at some level to accept; one that retains the capacity to capture their own imagination, and one that they can learn to express in their own words."[2] These principles were even more salient in Peronist Argentina, where, despite the weight of indoctrination and the material pressures of survival, the populace had far greater room to maneuver the terms of patronage and participation.

Peronism changed the very terrain of politics by connecting utopian ideals of national progress to yearnings for greater security, comfort, and plenty at the household level. This widened horizon of aspiration was undoubtedly an expression of state power, but as I have indicated, various records show Peronism to have had more spontaneous sources of enthusiasm at its base. For example, the era's public correspondence reveals not just how the public responded to propaganda but also, and more important, how sympathizers engaged with the opportunities open to them in this historical moment. In this context consumption became a crucial point of political inflection, for Peronism's story of justice was grounded in improved living conditions for the laboring majority, gains that encouraged individuals in these sectors to imagine their personal desires as enmeshed with those of the national government. Questions of everyday consumption—what people ate and wore; how they entertained themselves, shopped, and socialized; how they managed their domestic affairs and envisioned their future standing—put the utopian promise of the vida digna to the test. To be sure, the home and marketplace revealed both the New Argentina's achievements *and* its shortcomings. Disappointment with unmet needs simmered and at times was vented through pocketbook protests. But here, too, Peronism deepened its appeal, for most sympathizers voiced discontent against speculators and other enemies in the name of the movement instead of seeking to exit from it.

Consumption gained greater political significance in Peronist Argentina through a singular confluence of trends. Timing was critical. The Peronist alliance was a creature of the anxiety and confusion prevalent in the World War II era, but it was imbued with the faith that long-deferred reforms were possible in the post-war transition. Perón and his inner circle drew inspiration from these pent-up demands. Initially, the "deficiencies" of household consumption were framed in a restricted way—one conditioned by the social politics of the 1930s—as something potentially remedied by higher wages for male breadwinners and modest relief.

This orientation changed, however, with the unforeseen turn toward rapid income redistribution during the mid-1940s. As worker purchasing power surged, the challenge of defending their conquests from the dangers of the marketplace took on central importance. Social assistance, too, became more ambitious in a time of rising expectations; programs targeted basic needs and the comforts associated with a rapidly commercializing society. From Peronism's inception, political culture and political economy were thus deeply intertwined. Discourses and images of the vida digna had traction because they spoke to lived experiences of getting and spending. Without predetermining the choices of Peronist actors, the country's characteristics as an agricultural exporter and emerging consumer society imposed conditions that shaped how justice was understood culturally and how redistribution was enacted.

Argentina's wartime reorientation was in turn part of a larger wave of midcentury challenges to the orthodoxy of laissez-faire liberalism. State-led campaigns to defend citizens from the injustices of the marketplace struck a chord across the globe, engendering a comparable spectrum of reactions from popular enthusiasm to resistance from propertied interests. The tools for ordering market relations were often similar in all these cases, as were the accompanying attempts to establish a role for citizen consumers as patriotic collaborators. The postwar years saw a retreat from this posture in some countries, most notably the United States, which, as Lizbeth Cohen has suggested, witnessed the emergence of a "consumer's republic" centered on more business-friendly measures to ensure national abundance. By contrast, the ideal of the disciplined marketplace retained its combativeness in the Nueva Argentina, even if authorities moderated their policies over time. Peronist-style interventions signaled a regional trend in Latin America, for the pursuit of redistribution and regulation became increasingly ambitious in neighboring societies. In this sense, Peronism straddled the midcentury moment: it built upon Depression-era and wartime attempts to mitigate the chaotic disruptions of market forces while prefiguring the more radical economic nationalism of later populist and leftist movements in cold war Latin America.

In this moment of global experimentation, the Peronist alliance reformulated the terms of national politics in particularly distinct ways. To employ a musical metaphor, Peronism represented what Carl Schorske has called "politics in a new key." The Austrian factions that Schorske discusses bear little specific resemblance to the Peronists, but both groups shared an affinity for a politics that was "at once more abrasive, more creative, and more satisfying to the life of feeling than the deliberative style of the liberals."[3] This was partially a question of style, of ebullient mass rituals and brash attempts to impose a partisan subculture. Yet modulating to a new political key also meant changing the content of citizenship—that is, re-arranging the notes of liberal republicanism and introducing new themes. Through the expansion of collective entitlements, Peronist sympathizers reworked the language of *political* liberalism to critique the shortcomings of *economic* liberalism. This process involved more than simply adding rights onto an existing system, for in practice, justicialista rule restricted civil liberties (especially for non-Peronists). At the same time, however, rights blended with new conceptions of national inclusion. Peronist agents framed uplift in the developmental terms of managing a healthy, productive populace, and individualist notions of the rights-bearing citizen gave way to modernist-era concerns with vulnerable families, collectives, and masses. The language of living standards focused additional attention on popular consumption. So, too, did the populist impulses at the heart of Peronist mass politics. The logic of "giving the people what they want" meant that inclusion was defined in relation to Argentine consumer society. Despite the leadership's trepidations about the population's appetites, state policies reflected norms of comfort from the marketplace. Citizenship required achieving not just higher standards through poor relief but also the integration of working people in an already commercialized mainstream culture.

Peronism's new political key was not without its problems. A model of citizenship that merged liberalism with more expansive ideals of inclusion, such as the "right to well-being" and "right to a decent standard of living," was attractive to many, but it was plagued by inconsistencies. Fulfilling the high promise of citizenship was no easy feat, especially as postwar prosperity ran thin. Assertions of rights were often limited by the regime's hierarchical conception of the bond between leaders and followers. Supposedly universal entitlements rested on the personalistic, gift-giving mechanisms of assistance and patriarchal distinctions of respectability and gendered duty. The Peronist approach to regulating property relations was at times muddled; attacks on merchant speculators and other villains aside, the creation of further wealth depended primarily on the output of an economy based on private enterprise. By seeking to integrate the laboring households within this market-driven order while also critiquing its inherent immorality, Peronists appeared to want things both ways.

Yet these very contradictions gave justicialismo its massive appeal. Peronism ventilated frustrations with material inequality, exploitation, and unethical exchange even as its ideal of the just society held out a reassuring hope that these dilemmas could be resolved without destroying the existing order altogether. Peronist interventions fulfilled (at least in part) longings for security and respect among those kept at the margins of Argentina's abundance. Numerous other midcentury movements charted "third-way" paths between socialist and capitalist extremes, but none generated as great an outpouring of support. Although the alliance between the state and unions may have been the movement's spine, its body was far larger. Peronism literally spanned the nation: it made inroads among urban and rural populations alike; advanced a notion of the people that encompassed different ethnicities, occupations, and classes; and reached out to established political players while bringing new actors into mass politics. This diversity provided a major source of Peronism's persistent internal divisions. But guiding ideals such as the vida digna brought disparate factions together by convincing them of their cause's righteousness and the legitimacy of its authorities. Millions came to embrace a faith that, despite all the obstacles, they were unified in building the Nueva Argentina.

Peronism's hegemony, however, was ultimately flawed. The same political key that appealed to many was rejected by a sizable minority. The country's most entrenched economic interests expressed little enthusiasm for the Perón government; influential factions within the military and the Catholic Church broke off from the alliance over time. By mobilizing followers against internal enemies, populist politics took an enormous toll on national unity. Anti-Peronists contributed as well to polarization, for many condemned the movement with surprisingly intense vehemence. The 1955 coup thus marked the end of one Peronist era and the beginning of another. The decades that followed were dominated by futile attempts to found a post-Peronist order, yet neither outright repression nor tenuous overtures of accommodation made much headway. If anything, support deepened among Peronism's working-class base and branched out to new sectors (including the New Left and Catholic radicals). Some enthusiasts sought to return Perón from exile to reclaim the lost magic of the golden postwar years, and others saw the possibility of directing the movement on a more revolutionary path. The New Argentina's failure therefore paradoxically contributed to Peronism's reinvigorated ability to strike a chord among the country's majority after 1955.

As the opposition dug in its heels to prevent a restoration, civil strife worsened. Anti-Peronists disagreed about the best way to move forward: ten heads of state (five military and five civilian) passed through the Casa Rosada between September 1955 and October 1973. Political actors on all sides resorted to violence, dimming the possibilities for finding a peaceful means of transcending the mounting chaos. The country's uneasy economic situation aggravated these tensions. While other nations in the developing world appeared to accelerate with high rates of growth, contemporaries worried that volatile Argentina had fallen off the rails. Governments resorted periodically to restricting spending power as a means of calming inflation and boosting exports but lacked the justicialista regime's ability to manage popular counterreactions and only provoked more clamor for Perón's return. These conflicts revealed a problematic legacy of the vida digna. Under Peronist rule, social citizenship and partisanship were virtually one and the same. This fusion contributed to the movement's popularity but created the preconditions for a fractious denouement. Crusades to de-Peronize the nation all too readily became campaigns to reverse worker gains and roll back living standards.

Viewed from this vantage, the country's troubles contrast with most historical accounts of postwar mass consumption, which are based on a familiar story of political stability and expanding plenty. Midcentury Argentina failed to produce either a U.S.-style consumer's republic or the Fordist pacts seen in parts of Western Europe and East Asia. The reasons were many, but political antipathies thwarted alliances among business, workers, and the state. In other places, these competing interests were united by cold war conceptions of freedom, in which a general consumer bounty was presented as evidence of democratic capitalism's triumph over socialist authoritarianism. No such accord was reached under Peronist rule or its aftermath. Moreover, Argentina faced a different set of economic limitations than did the postwar exemplars of consumer society. Its foundation of prosperity was far narrower because of the country's dependency on agro-exports and barriers to deepening industrialization (most notably, a comparatively small population). These were not insurmountable obstacles, as the cases of postwar South Korea and Taiwan show, but Argentina lacked the benefit of patronage from the United States or other cold war superpower. Equally important, its homegrown political demons made reaching a common project of national development virtually impossible.

Argentina's post-Peronist crisis reached its anguishing nadir in the 1970s. The option all had either fantasized about or feared finally came to pass: after nearly eighteen years of exile, Perón returned to power. The third Perón presidency (1973–1974) was a debacle from the start, and the colossal gathering that awaited his arrival at Ezeiza airport erupted in internecine bloodletting. The aging Conductor could no longer hold together a divided movement, and he died in office. The military dictatorship that soon followed (1976–1983) earned worldwide infamy for its savagery. "Disappearances" and other crimes were carried out in the name of a "process of national reorganization" that employed the rhetoric of high modernist planning to justify unprecedented repression. Citizenship came under fire on two fronts. The first objective involved the persecution of so-called subversives, which created a climate of terror designed to crush any sense of entitlement and diminish mass participation. The most celebrated targets were middle-class youth, educators, and intellectuals, but the heaviest repression landed on "unredeemable" laborers, especially activists with Peronist loyalties. The second objective was less overtly defined but had equally destructive consequences. While military agents littered Argentina with torture camps, policymakers dismantled the nationalist edifice of state welfare and development erected since the 1930s. Purportedly seeking to move the country beyond stagnation, so-called liberalizing reforms added new burdens by aggravating poverty and worsening foreign indebtedness.

The dictatorship eventually succumbed to its chronic lack of legitimacy following the disaster of the Malvinas/Falklands War. From this low, the Argentine Republic entered the current era of civilian rule. "Democracy" became the political keyword of a system based on constitutionalism and electoral competition; Peronists and non-Peronists alike agreed, for the most part, to hash out their differences within this system rather than seek militarized solutions. Since the 1980s, citizenship has been fortified with the language of human rights, which stresses the respect for civil liberties, diversity of opinion, and the rule of law. These are welcome changes, but from the start, democracy was restricted in numerous ways. A robust emphasis on property rights superseded midcentury notions of national inclusion, now tainted by association with combative partisan politics. Military rule had stripped away the social content of citizenship, and the civilian governments of the post-1983 period proved unable or unwilling to reverse the trend. In another historical twist, the Peronist Party's leadership oversaw an economic restructuring in line with the global turn toward neoliberalism. While still mouthing Perón's rhetoric, President Carlos Menem (1989–1999) continued the assault on economic nationalism begun by the military. Investor-friendly reforms brought growth, but the frenzy of privatizations and borrowing devolved into a feast of corruption; meanwhile, the ranks of the unemployed swelled to nearly 20 percent of the total workforce. Menem's successors were left to pay the debts run up during his decade in office, an implosion that finally arrived in the 2001–2002 crisis that attracted worldwide attention to the republic's agony.

Events since the 1970s have thus irrevocably altered the political referents of the midcentury era. Successive reactions against populism's threats, both real and perceived, have reoriented the coordinates of nationalism. The "vida digna" and related terms no longer have the same resonance, for contemporary social trends have made the midcentury language of entitlement seem like a curious relic. The consumer marketplace has become ever-more bountiful, and each year brings a new cornucopia of commercial offerings to Argentina's shores—a seemingly inexhaustible flow of cars and clothes, electrical gadgets and household goods, originating in places from neighboring Brazil to far-off China. Market-driven culture may be more widespread than it was before, but Argentina's social inequalities and regional imbalances have hardened. For working households and the downwardly mobile middle class, the pressures of economic competition make it difficult to achieve a measure of security, let alone to realize a comprehensive elevation in living standards. These sectors too often focus on individual struggles to locate a job (typically, low paying and off the books) instead of demands for a share of abundance.

Given the scale of these transformations and the turmoil of nationalist politics in preceding decades, some contemporaries wish to turn the page on the midcentury moment. In their eyes, it is a time best forgotten or recalled only as a lesson on dangerous ideas. Yet misguided attempts to cordon off the past have enjoyed little success. At the most obvious level, a new generation of nationalist leaders in Latin America has retaken the path blazed by earlier experiments, a trend commonly equated with Hugo Chávez in Venezuela. (And there is more than a passing similarity between Chávez and Perón, not only in their military background, but also in their populist attacks on speculation, their personal touch in delivering assistance, and their troubles in managing the marketplace.) Nonetheless, the reinvigoration of reformist politics and self-proclaimed nationalist revolutions are not limited to this one figure, and it is too early to determine where this tendency will lead. What is clear is that repeated efforts to expel issues of redistribution from political consideration, to declare them distastefully naïve or passé, have failed. Although critics have chastened the faith in the state's ability to deliver solutions, the fundamental questions posed by midcentury movements continue to resurface—central among them, how to balance collective entitlements and individual rights, reduce the threats posed by needless social suffering, and ensure that all citizens have the resources to live decently.

Rather than look at the history of Peronist Argentina for models to emulate or lessons to avoid, we do better to consider these guiding questions. They require protection as well from attempts to silence Latin America's past, a project pursued on many fronts but that in the United States and elsewhere has involved trivializing the era's populist movements.[4] We are all familiar with the stereotypes of Latin passion trotted out whenever Juan and Eva enter the scene of mainstream culture, the overblown representations that belittle Peronism's agenda and bid us to view their followers as mindless masses. Getting serious about Peronism hardly means retreating to a posture of quantitative rationality; as I have shown, the movement's political culture was indeed purposefully dramatic, poignantly jubilant, and at times undoubtedly absurd. Yet the sense of self-superiority generated by mocking depictions of populism comes at a higher cost, for it prevents audiences abroad from seeing that Argentina's unresolved problems are also, to a degree, their own. Peronism's midcentury moment forces us to consider both how national politics can inspire a greater sense of individual purpose and solidarity and how high ideals of freedom and inclusion can become tools of domination. Above all, it reveals the difficulties in accommodating reformist desires for egalitarianism in market-driven societies, in balancing longings for ethical exchange with demands for access to capitalism's plenty. The pursuit of a truer democracy in the present, however, need not require repeating midcentury errors; one need not be prisoner to this past in pondering its unmet promise.

In contemporary Argentina, nostalgia for the glory days of Peronism understandably lingers in some quarters. But the landscape of political possibilities has been so altered (or better put, flattened) that few major actors advocate sudden redistribution on a postwar scale. Moreover, there is much about which one ought *not* to be nostalgic. After the last military dictatorship, most Argentines would not welcome a return to the bloody confrontations of recent memory or even the restrictions of the Comunidad Organizada. Peronism endures through it all—the years of proscription and repression, the cynical reversals of its leaders, the battering of periodic crises—even if its ambitions are reduced, and its sympathizers cannot agree how to reconcile founding principles with the logic of a globalized age. Much as in the postwar heyday, its institutions both extend pathways for easing misery and erect mechanisms for conserving the status quo. Yet for a majority of the population, Peronism remains identified with popular entitlement to a better life, one that includes the right to work, the satisfaction of material wants, and aspirations of collective justice. Although distrust of justicialismo shows no signs of abating, the fact that some skeptics outside the movement's ranks share these yearnings may serve as a bridge forward. The midcentury Nueva Argentina may no longer inspire confidence as blueprint for the future, and the alternative directions may still be uncertain, but the hope for a new Argentina persists.

Notes

Introduction: Peronism and the Midcentury Moment

1. Subsecretaría de Informaciones, *Tres charlas radiofónicas del General Perón* (Buenos Aires, 1951), 7–8.

2. Letter from Hilda Benítez de Maldonado, n.d., doc. 12806, legajo 331, Archivo General de la Nación, Ministerio de Asuntos Técnicos Collection (hereinafter AGN-MAT); the events it describes suggest the letter was probably written sometime in late 1951 or early 1952. In translating these letters, I have standardized spellings.

3. Since beginning this project in the late 1990s, I have been joined by a wonderful cohort of historians—among them Rebekah Pite, Natalia Milanesio, and Kathleen Fuller-French—who work on other aspects of Peronism and consumption.

4. This approach is inspired by recent reconsiderations of mass politics and populism; see, for example, Stephen Kotkin's *Magnetic Mountain: Stalinism as Civilization* (Berkeley: University of California Press, 1995), which explores the "partially intersecting dreams" (23) of political authorities and ordinary people in Soviet Russia. Among Latin Americanists, the "new political history" of the past generation probes similar dynamics, although often by stressing resistance or processes of "everyday state formation" highlighting cultural policies (see, e.g., Gilbert M. Joseph and Daniel Nugent, eds. *Everyday Forms of State Formation: Revolution and the Negotiation of Rule in Modern Mexico* [Durham, N.C.: Duke University Press, 1994]). Creative treatments of populist forms of authoritarianism include Richard Lee Turits, *Foundations of Despotism: Peasants, the Trujillo Regime, and Modernity in Dominican History* (Stanford, Calif.: Stanford University Press, 2003); Lauren Derby, *The Dictator's Seduction: Politics and the Popular Imagination in the Era of Trujillo* (Durham, N.C.: Duke University Press, 2009). On the politics of the "capacity for aspiration," see Arjun Appadurai, "Deep Democracy: Urban Governmentality and the Horizon of Politics," *Public Culture* 14, no. 1: 21–47.

5. Eric Hobsbawm, *The Age of Extremes: A History of the World, 1914–1991* (New York: Vintage, 1994), 112; Mark Mazower, *Dark Continent: Europe's Twentieth Century* (New York: Vintage, 2000).

6. I side with those who espouse a conception of populism not as a political style fixed to a specific developmental "stage" or geographical area but rather as a tradition characterized by discursive appeals that emphasize the righteousness and moral authority of the social majority. My use of related terms, such as "the people" or "popular," reflects the flexibility (and vagueness) with which they were deployed by Peronist actors rather than a rigorous attempt on my part to pinpoint an exact stratum of the population. As Laclau has noted, Latin American populism has a strong statist component that channels demands for redistribution and popular rule in opposition to liberal-oligarchic orders; these characteristics set it apart somewhat from the ethnic populism of Eastern Europe and other regions. For more on this subject, see Alan Knight, "Populism and Neo-populism in Latin America, especially Mexico," *Journal of Latin American Studies* 30 (1998): 223–48; Ernesto Laclau, *Populism and Ideology in Marxist Theory* (London: New Left Books, 1977), 143–98; Michael L. Conniff, "Introduction: Toward a Comparative Definition of Populism," in *Populism in Latin America*, ed. Michael Conniff (Tuscaloosa: University of Alabama Press, 1999), 3–30; Michael Kazin, *The Populist Persuasion:*

An American History (New York: Basic Books, 1998); Steve Stein, *Populism in Peru: The Emergence of the Masses and the Politics of Social Control* (Madison: University of Wisconsin Press, 1980); Herbert Braun, *The Assassination of Gaitán: Public Life and Urban Violence in Colombia* (Madison: University of Wisconsin Press, 1985).

7. Michel-Rolph Trouillot, *Silencing the Past: Power and the Production of History* (Boston: Beacon, 1995); Dipesh Chakrabarty, "Postcoloniality and the Artifice of History," in *Provincializing Europe: Postcolonial Thought and Historical Difference* (Princeton, N.J.: Princeton University Press, 2000), 27–46. The problem of translation figures as a central dynamic in Argentine cultural history; see Ricardo Piglia, *Crítica y ficción* (Buenos Aires: Seix Barral, 2000).

8. Historians in other Latin American fields have probed the winding, often paradoxical, evolution of citizenship in their respective national, provincial, and urban settings. See, among other works, Claudio Lomnitz, "Modes of Mexican Citizenship," in *Deep Mexico, Silent Mexico* (Minneapolis: University of Minnesota Press, 2001), 58–80; José Murilo de Carvalho, *Cidadania no Brasil* (Rio de Janeiro: Civilização Brasileira, 2001); Hilda Sábato, ed., *Ciudadanía política y formación de las naciones: Perspectivas históricas de América Latina* (Mexico, D.F.: Colegio de México, Fondo de Cultura Económica, 1999); Brodwyn Fischer, *A Poverty of Rights: Citizenship and Inequality in Twentieth-Century Rio de Janeiro* (Stanford, Calif.: Stanford University Press, 2008).

9. Hilda Sábato, *La política en las calles: Entre el voto y la movilización, 1862–1880* (Buenos Aires: Editorial Sudamericana, 1998); Leandro H. Gutiérrez and Luis Alberto Romero, *Sectores populares, cultura y política: Buenos Aires en la entreguerra* (Buenos Aires: Editorial Sudamericana, 1995); Luciano de Privitellio, *Vecinos y ciudadanos: Política y sociedad en la Buenos Aires de entreguerras* (Buenos Aires: Siglo Veintiuno, 2003); Matthew Karush, *Workers or Citizens: Democracy and Identity in Rosario, Argentina (1912–1930)* (Albuquerque: University of New Mexico Press, 2002).

10. T. H. Marshall, *Citizenship and Social Democracy* (New York: Doubleday, 1964); James Holston, *Insurgent Citizenship: Disjunctions of Democracy and Modernity in Brazil* (Princeton, N.J.: Princeton University Press, 2008). Similar problems arise in other "non-Western" fields. In a recent essay, Frederick Cooper criticizes the tendency of postcolonial studies of Africa to "leapfrog" the midcentury era of mass mobilization, developmentalism, and shifting citizenship. He draws attention to this flaw in Mahmood Mamdani's otherwise brilliant book *Citizen and Subject*, which links 1980s apartheid to early twentieth-century colonial rule but largely bypasses the midcentury era (Frederick Cooper, "Postcolonial Studies and the Study of History," in *Postcolonial Studies and Beyond*, ed. Ania Loomba et al. [Durham, N.C.: Duke University Press, 2005], 401–22; see also Mahmood Mamdani, *Citizen and Subject: Contemporary Africa and the Legacy of Late Colonialism* [Princeton, N.J.: Princeton University Press, 1996]).

11. Daniel James, *Resistance and Integration: Peronism and the Argentine Working Class, 1946–1976* (Cambridge: Cambridge University Press, 1988), 7–40. Alternative notions of social citizenship have sprouted in other studies of populist-era politics in Mexico and Brazil, apparently from independent origins. See, for example, Mary Kay Vaughan, *Cultural Politics in Revolution: Teachers, Peasants, and Schools in Mexico, 1930–1940* (Tucson: University of Arizona Press, 1997); Bryan McCann, *Hello, Hello Brazil: Popular Music and the Making of Modern Brazil* (Durham, N.C.: Duke University Press, 2004).

12. On the subject of language, it is important to note that the term "development" began to come into its own as a sociopolitical keyword only in the Peronist era. Its protagonists often used the older term "*progreso*" rather than "*modernización*" or "*desarrollo*" even as the latter

two acquired currency across the postwar world. Nevertheless, their stress on the progressive elevation of living standards as part of a broader process of national improvement reveals an underlying developmentalist impulse characteristic of this global moment. On the rise and fall of development as a category, see Barbara Weinstein, "Developing Inequality," *American Historical Review*, 113, no. 1 (Feb. 2008): 1–18; James Ferguson, "Decomposing Modernity: History and Hierarchy after Development," in *Global Shadows: Africa in the Neoliberal World Order*, ed. Ferguson (Durham, N.C.: Duke University Press, 2006), 176–93.

13. John D. Wirth, *The Politics of Brazilian Development* (Stanford, Calif.: Stanford University Press, 1970), 6.

14. Mary Kay Vaughan, "Modernizing Patriarchy," in *Hidden Histories of Gender and the State in Latin America*, ed. Elizabeth Dore and Maxine Molyneux (Durham, N.C.: Duke University Press, 2000), 195–214; Heidi Tinsman, "A Paradigm of Our Own: Joan Scott in Latin American History," *American Historical Review* 113, no. 5 (Dec. 2008): 1357–74; Sandra McGee Deutsch, "Gender and Sociopolitical Change in Twentieth-Century Latin America," *Hispanic American Historical Review* 71, no. 2 (1991): 259–306.

15. Reevaluations of civil society under Peronist rule include Eduardo Elena, "What the People Want: State Planning and Political Participation in Peronist Argentina, 1946–1955," *Journal of Latin American Studies* 37, no. 1 (Feb. 2005): 81–108; Omar Acha, "Sociedad civil y sociedad política durante el primer peronismo," *Desarrollo Económico* 44, no. 174 (Jul.–Dec. 2004): 199–230.

16. It would be impractical to enumerate the hundreds of works on Peronism. Relevant works will be cited in the chapters that follow. For historiographical surveys, see Mariano Plotkin, "The Changing Perceptions of Peronism," in *Peronism and Argentina*, ed. James P. Brennan (Wilmington, Del.: SR Books, 1998), 29–54; Emilio de Ipola, "Ruptura y continuidad: Claves parciales para un balance de las interpretaciones del peronismo," *Desarrollo Económico* 29, no. 115 (Oct.–Dec. 1989): 331–59.

17. Arnold Bauer, *Goods, Power, History: Latin America's Material Culture* (Cambridge: Cambridge University Press, 2001); Gilbert M. Joseph, Anne Rubenstein, and Eric Zolov, eds., *Fragments of a Golden Age: The Politics of Culture in Mexico since 1940* (Durham, N.C.: Duke University Press, 2001); Néstor García Canclini, *Consumidores y ciudadanos: Conflictos multiculturales de la globalización* (Mexico City: Grijalbo, 1995); Benjamin Orlove, ed., *The Allure of the Foreign: Imported Goods in Postcolonial Latin America* (Ann Arbor: University of Michigan Press, 1997); Thomas O'Brien, *The Century of U.S. Capitalism in Latin America* (Albuquerque: University of New Mexico Press, 1999); Heidi Tinsman, "Politics of Gender and Consumption in Authoritarian Chile, 1973–1900," *Latin American Research Review* 41, no. 3 (Oct. 2006): 7–31; Alexis McCrossen, ed., *Land of Necessity: Consumer Culture in the United States–Mexico Borderlands* (Durham, N.C.: Duke University Press, 2009); Greg Grandin, *Fordlandia: The Rise and Fall of Henry Ford's Forgotten Jungle City* (New York: Picador, 2010).

18. Brian Owensby, *Intimate Ironies: Modernity and the Making of Middle-Class Lives in Brazil* (Stanford, Calif.: Stanford University Press, 1999) 7–8; Marshall Berman, *All That Is Solid Melts into Air: The Experience of Modernity* (New York: Simon and Schuster, 1982). Rather than see midcentury political efforts to grapple with commerce and consumption through a flexing of regulatory and tutelary forms of power as signs of modernity, neoliberals and other critics have assailed them as backward-thinking and short-sighted, irresponsible politicking. See, e.g., Rudiger Dornbusch and Sebastian Edwards, eds., *The Macroeconomics of Populism in Latin America* (Chicago: University of Chicago Press, 1991); Francis Fukuyama, ed., *Falling Behind: Explaining the Development Gap between Latin America and the United States* (Oxford: Oxford University Press, 2008).

19. My use of the concept of double movement is a loose adaptation of Karl Polanyi's terminology. In his classic treatment of the historical evolution of liberalism, Polanyi stressed the state's role in the formation of liberal orders and market economies (notwithstanding the discourse of laissez-faire capitalism). Political attempts to carve out autonomy for markets were met, however, by counterreactions from within society to limit capitalist injustices—hence a double movement of action and reaction. My usage of the term implies the coexistence of both impulses within populist efforts to regulate market liberalism. See Karl Polanyi, *The Great Transformation* (Boston: Beacon, 1957 [1944]).

20. On collective consumption, see Manuel Castells, *City, Class, and Power* (New York: St. Martin's, 1978); David Harvey, *Consciousness and the Urban Experience: Studies in the History and Theory of Capitalist Urbanization* (Baltimore, Md.: John Hopkins University Press, 1985).

21. On the merits and pitfalls of the "consumerism" tradition, see Jackson Lears, *Fables of Abundance: A Cultural History of Advertising in America* (New York: Basic Books, 1994); Frank Trentmann, "Beyond Consumerism: New Historical Perspectives on Consumption," *Journal of Contemporary History* 39, no. 3 (2004): 373–401; Jean-Christophe Agnew, "Coming Up for Air: Consumer Culture in Historical Perspective," in *Consumer Society in American History*, ed. Lawrence B. Glickman (Ithaca, N.Y.: Cornell University Press, 1999), 373–97.

22. Notable examples of works that adopt transnational approaches include Daniel T. Rodgers, *Atlantic Crossings: Social Politics in a Progressive Age* (Cambridge, Mass.: Belnap, 1998); Thomas Bender, *A Nation among Nations: America's Place in World History* (New York: Hill and Wang, 2006); Jesse Hoffnung-Garskof, *A Tale of Two Cities: Santo Domingo and New York after 1950* (Princeton, N.J.: Princeton University Press, 2008). See also Partha Chatterjee, *Nationalist Thought and the Colonial World: A Derivative Discourse?* (London: Zed Books, 1986).

Chapter 1: An Imperfect Abundance

1. Roberto Arlt, *Obra Completa*, vol. 2 (Buenos Aires: Carlos Lohlé, 1981), 160–61.

2. Ibid., 58–59, 76–78, 136–38, 164–66, 195.

3. José Martínez Orozco, *Quince centavos: Un día de vida en Buenos Aires* (New York: Henry Holt, 1945), 51–57.

4. André Siegfried, *Impressions of South America*, trans. H. H. Hemming and Doris Hemming (New York: Harcourt, Brace, 1933), 90.

5. Quoted in Christiane Crasemann Collins, "Urban Interchange in the Southern Cone: Le Corbusier (1929) and Werner Hegemann (1931) in Argentina," *Journal of the Society of Architectural Historians*, 54, no. 2 (June 1995): 208–27. See also Adrián Gorelik, *La grilla y el parque: Espacio público y cultura urbana en Buenos Aires, 1887–1936* (Buenos Aires: Universidad Nacional de Quilmes, 1998).

6. Ruth Greenup and Leonard Greenup, *Revolution before Breakfast* (Chapel Hill: University of North Carolina Press, 1947), 25–38.

7. Luis Alberto Romero, *A History of Argentina in the Twentieth Century*, trans. James P. Brennan (University Park: Pennsylvania State University Press, 2002), 10–11.

8. Fernando Rocchi, *Chimneys in the Desert: Industrialization in Argentina during the Export Boom Years, 1870–1930* (Stanford, Calif.: Stanford University Press, 2006), 50–52.

9. Despite a commitment to doctrines of comparative advantage that privileged rural exports, national governments erected tariff barriers to shield local manufacturers and in some cases directed public credit to well-connected groups. See Rocchi, *Chimneys*; Jorge Schvarzer, *La industria que supimos conseguir: Una historia político-social de la industria argentina* (Buenos Aires: Planeta, 1996).

10. María Inés Barbero and Fernando Rocchi, "Industry," in *A New Economic History of Argentina*, ed. Gerardo della Paolera and Alan M. Taylor (Cambridge: Cambridge University Press, 2003), 275.

11. Schvarzer, *Industria*, 159.

12. Pablo Gerchunoff and Lucas Llach, *El ciclo de la ilusión y el desencanto: Un siglo de políticas económicas argentinas* (Buenos Aires: Ariel, 1998), 120. For example, the size of audiences for the cinema and public performances in the capital city shrank from 30 to 19 million between 1928 and 1932.

13. Gerchunoff and Llach, *Ciclo de la ilusión*, 139–46; Schvarzer, *Industria*, 151–85.

14. James Cane-Carrasco, *The Fourth Enemy* (University Park: Pennsylvania State University Press, forthcoming).

15. Gutiérrez and Romero, *Sectores populares*; De Privitellio, *Vecinos y ciudadanos*.

16. Some observers were convinced that ordinary Argentines emulated the habits of those "above" them, a view best captured in the stereotype of the well-dressed worker. In the words of one Argentine businessman from 1910, "One does not see workers without ironed shirts, without ties, and very few who do not have a watch, frequently of gold; and it is common to see young factory girls, as well as family house cooks and maids, wearing varnished shoes, and sometimes even showing fishnet stockings" (qtd. in Rocchi, *Chimneys*, 66).

17. Eduardo Aunós, *Viaje a la Argentina* (Madrid: Editorial Nacional, 1943), 115.

18. Gerchunoff and Llach, *Ciclo de la ilusión*, 145.

19. Francis Herron, *Letters from the Argentine* (New York: G. P. Putnam, 1943), 83–87.

20. *Kilómetro 111*, feature film, dir. Mario Soffici (1938).

21. Departamento Nacional de Trabajo, *Condiciones de vida de la familia obrera* (Buenos Aires, 1937), 56–68.

22. Armour Research Foundation, *Technological and Economic Survey of Argentine Industries with Industrial Research Recommendations* (Ann Arbor, Mich.: Edwards Brothers, 1943), 28.

23. For similar problems in consumer surveys of Western Europe, see Victoria de Grazia, *Irresistible Empire: America's Advance Through Twentieth-Century Europe* (Cambridge, Mass.: Harvard University Press, 2005), 75–129.

24. Armour Foundation, *Technological and Economic Survey*, 70–79.

25. Thomas Cochran and Ruben Reina, *Entrepreneurship in Argentine Culture: Torcuato Di Tella and S.I.A.M.* (Philadelphia: University of Pennsylvania Press, 1962); Marcelo Rougier and Jorge Schvarzer, *Las grandes empresas no mueren de pie: El (o)caso de SIAM* (Buenos Aires: Grupo Editorial Norma, 2006). Statistical estimates of class are, of course, impressionistic at best. According to the leading sociological estimate, the one-third figure for the middle class in the 1947 Argentine census could be subdivided into the *clase media asalariada* (18.7 percent) and the *clase media autonoma* (13.4 percent, with merchants large and small forming part of that group). The categories constituting the working class—the *clase obrera asalariada* (45.8 percent) and the *clase obrera autonoma* (16.3 percent)—added up to around 62 percent of the total (see Susana Torrado, *Estructura social de la Argentina, 1945–1983* [Buenos Aires: Ediciones de la Flor, 1992], 145–53).

26. Aunós, *Viaje,* 150–51.

27. Greenup and Greenup, *Revolution,* 120.

28. *Mundo Argentino,* July 10, 1946. For advertisers' views on consumer psychology and gender, see Asociación de Jefes de Propaganda, *Cursos de enseñanza de propaganda (1940–41)* (Buenos Aires, 1941); idem, *Síntesis Publicitaria* (1943–46) (Buenos Aires: Talleres Kraft, 1944–47).

29. *Rosalinda,* January 1941.

30. *Rosalinda,* September 1941.

31. Zulma Recchini de Lattes, *La participación económica feminina en la Argentina desde la segunda posguerra hasta 1970* (Buenos Aires: Centro de Estudios de Población, 1980), 11.

32. Sue Maxwell and Golda Larkin O'Callahan, *South American Fiesta* (Boston: Bruce Humphries, 1950), 93.

33. A few institutions, including the *Museo Social,* the Argentine version of the famed French social policy clearinghouse, acted as forums for the exchange across ideological lines. Policy journals, such as the *Revista de Economía Argentina, Revista de Ciencias Económicas,* and *Boletín del Museo Social,* were channels through which Argentine experts learned of social policy initiatives in other nations. On social politics in early twentieth-century Argentina, see Eduardo A. Zimmerman, *Los liberales reformistas: La cuestión social en la Argentina, 1890–1916* (Buenos Aires: Editorial Sudamericana, 1995); Juan Suriano, ed., *La cuestión social en Argentina, 1870–1943* (Buenos Aires: Editorial La Colmena, 2000); José Panettieri, ed., *Argentina: Trabajadores entre dos guerras* (Buenos Aires: Eudeba, 2000).

34. Rodgers, *Atlantic Crossings,* 209.

35. De Grazia, *Irresistible Empire,* 75–129; Judith G. Coffin, "A 'Standard' of Living? European Perspectives on Class and Consumption in the Early Twentieth Century," *International Labor and Working-Class History* 55 (Spring 1999): 16. As Coffin notes, the concept of the "standard of living" itself had taken on various guises as a "technical measurement of purchasing power, an aspiration, [and] an entitlement" in ways that spanned subsistence minima and broader ideals of development (6).

36. Juan Bialet Massé, *Informe sobre el estado de la clase obrera,* vol. 2 (Buenos Aires: Hyspamerica, 1985 [1904]), 487–88. His massive report did include a sample budget for one provincial family (215), but little attention was given to consumer behavior or purchasing decisions.

37. Alejandro Bunge, *Una nueva Argentina* (Buenos Aires, Hyspamerica, 1984 [1940]), 388. Bunge did consider the high cost of shelter to be a major problem, and in response he drew up plans for public subsidized housing construction.

38. Ibid., 221–22 (Bunge appears to have used the terms "standard" and "nivel" almost interchangeably in this book).

39. Ibid., 235.

40. Investigations into ethnicity and race in Argentina during this time are fraught with major complications given the subjective, historically contingent nature of all racial categories. Despite social discrimination against darker-skinned individuals from the "provinces" seen as having "Indian" ancestry, these two broad groups—recent immigrants and criollos—were each internally diverse and intermixed with one another, and members of both could be found living in all corners of the nation. In provinces with less variety of economic opportunity and fewer recent European arrivals, the racial boundaries of social status were often more firmly entrenched. But even in urban areas, depending on the context, physical appearance and ethnic background took on racial characteristics that overlapped with class distinctions to fix an individual's place in the hierarchy. For more on provincial racial politics, see Oscar Chamosa,

The Argentine Folklore Movement: Sugar Elites, Criollo Workers, and the Politics of Cultural Nationalism, 1900–1950 (Tucson: University of Arizona Press, 2010).

41. Emilio Llorens, *Encuesta continental sobre el consumo de productos de alimentación y vestido y sobre la vivienda popular* (Montevideo: 1944), 22–26, 79–99 (Llorens's norms were based upon nutritional standards devised at the famed 1943 Hot Springs conference). See also Nick Cullather, "The Foreign Policy of the Calorie," *American Historical Review* 112, no. 2 (Apr. 2007): 337–64.

42: Bunge, *Nueva Argentina*, 222.

43. Raanan Rein, *In the Shadow of Perón: Juan Atilio Bramuglia and the Second Line of Argentina's Populist Movement* (Stanford, Calif.: Stanford University Press, 2008), 56. Figuerola had served under Eduardo Aunós, labor minister for the Primo de Rivera regime in Spain, who later visited Argentina and offered opinions regarding the calle Florida and consumption cited earlier in this chapter.

44. For an example of the sort of pieces he wrote, see José Figuerola, "Organización Social," *Revista de Economía Argentina* (Mar. 1939): 83–87. In 1943 Figuerola wrote a book that expounded his own corporatist philosophy, which called for the integration of labor and business organizations under state structures to quell the dangers of class conflict: *La colaboración social en Hispanoamérica* (Buenos Aires: Editorial Sudamericana, 1943).

45. Departamento Nacional de Trabajo, *Condiciones de vida*, 30. The DNT's first major study was conducted in 1935 among industrial workers in Buenos Aires and nearby suburbs; published two years later, it highlighted overall patterns in the spending habits of blue-collar families, noting in precise quantities the scores of goods and services purchased monthly.

46. Secretaría de Trabajo y Previsión, *Condiciones de vida de la familia obrera, 1943–1945* (Buenos Aires, 1946), 64.

47. Ibid., 19–21.

48. Departamento Nacional de Trabajo, *Condiciones de vida*, 30–312. See also DNT, *Adaptación de los salarios a las fluctuaciones del costo de la vida* (Buenos Aires, 1943), 3–25.

49. Barbara Weinstein, *For Social Peace in Brazil: Industrialists and the Remaking of the Working Class in São Paulo, 1920–1964* (Chapel Hill: University of North Carolina Press, 1996); Thomas Miller Klubock, *Contested Communities: Class, Gender, and Politics in Chile's El Teniente Copper Mine, 1904–1951* (Durham, N.C.: Duke University Press, 1998); Karin Alejandra Rosemblatt, *Gendered Compromises: Political Cultures and the State in Chile, 1920–1950* (Chapel Hill: University of North Carolina Press, 2000).

50. *El Obrero Ferroviario*, Jan. 1, 1939, 6.

51. In "The Moral Economy of the English Crowd in the Eighteenth Century," *Past and Present* 50 (Feb. 1971): 76–136, E. P. Thompson argued that food riots could not be explained only as the product of hunger or rising prices but rather were shaped by "a consistent traditional view of social norms and obligations, of the proper economic functions of several parties within the community, which, taken together, can be said to constitute the moral economy of the poor" (79).

52. The historian Ricardo Salvatore, in "The Normalization of Economic Life: Representations of the Economy in Golden-Age Buenos Aires, 1890–1913" (*Hispanic American Historical Review* 81, no. 1 [2001]: 1–44), has suggested that what changed was the scope of this critique: by the early twentieth century, "people directed their attention to the distributional effects of economic growth, especially to the inequalities of efforts and benefits in the struggle for life" (40). If anything, Salvatore's analysis underestimates the continued appeal of Argentina's traditions of utopian, anticapitalist thinking well into the twentieth century. On the moral economy of twentieth-century liberalism (and neoliberalism), see Frank Trentmann,

Free Trade Nation: Commerce, Consumption, and Civil Society in Modern Britain (Oxford: Oxford University Press, 2008); Daniel Fridman, "A New Mentality for a New Economy: Performing the *Homo Economicus* in Argentina (1976-83)," *Economy and Society* 39, no. 2 (May 2010): 271-302.

53. In the mid-1930s the bulk of organized laborers were members of the socialist-controlled railway worker and transportation unions, whose officials also dominated the leadership of the CGT. Communist labor activists, however, made great strides among previously nonunionized workers in manufacturing, meatpacking, construction, and rural harvesting, among other fields. A wave of highly publicized strikes by construction workers and others between 1935 and 1937 marked the sudden ascendancy of Communist Party organizers. Still, only a fraction of workers joined labor organizations in this period. See Roberto Korzeniewicz, "Labor Unrest in Argentina, 1930-1943," *Latin American Research Review* 28, no. 1 (1993): 7-40.

54. *La Vanguardia*, the socialist's daily newspaper, alone boasted a circulation of 70,000 copies a day by 1945 (not counting periods of political crisis when the paper, like other leftist outlets, was closed by the police); see Cane-Carrasco, *Fourth Enemy*.

55. *CGT*, May 17, 1935, 1.

56. Alfredo Palacios, *Pueblos desamparados: Solución de los problemas del noroeste argentino* (Buenos Aires: Guillermo Kraft, 1944), 60, 80.

57. Joel Horowitz, *Argentina's Radical Party and Popular Mobilization, 1916-1930* (University Park: Pennsylvania State University Press, 2008); David Rock, *Politics in Argentina, 1890-1930: The Rise and Fall of Radicalism* (Cambridge: Cambridge University Press, 1975), 115-24, 203-9.

58. Juan Cafferata, "Algunas condiciones sobre el problema de la vivienda popular en la república," *Boletín del Honorable Consejo Deliberante* (Sept.-Oct. 1939): 171-74.

59. On film as a window onto popular mentalities, see Matthew B. Karush, "The Melodramatic Nation: Integration and Polarization in the Argentine Cinema of the 1930s," *Hispanic American Historical Review* 87, no. 2 (May 2007): 293-326.

60. Directors of popular commercial films often used their work to cast light on social problems ranging from the power of foreign railroad companies (*Kilometro 111*) and the neglect of children in rural public schools (*Maestro Levita*) to the struggle for respectability faced by a single working mother with an "illegitimate" child (*Gente Bien*). Their works commented obliquely on the downside of commercialization as well: in the film *Chingolo*, an affable bum turns against his benefactor, a factory owner whose fortune was based on selling canned peaches and other foods known to be contaminated. Other films (e.g., *La maestrita de los obreros*) were set against a social realist background of working-class life with ordinary men and women caught between low wages and high living costs. See *Maestro Levita*, feature film, dir. Luis César Amadori (1938); *Gente Bien*, feature film, dir. Manuel Romero (1939); *Chingolo*, feature film, dir. Lucas Demare (1940); *La maestrita de los obreros*, feature film, dir. Alberto de Zavalía (1942). See also Domingo Di Nubila, *La época de oro: Historia del cine argentino I* (Buenos Aires: Ediciones del Jilguero, 1998).

61. *Mujeres que trabajan*, feature film, dir. Manuel Romero (1938).

62. Joel Horowitz, "Occupational Community and the Creation of a Self-Styled Elite: Railroad Workers in Argentina," *The Americas* 1 (July 1985): 55-82.

63. Alejandro Cattaruzza, *Marcelo T. de Alvear: El compromiso y la distancia* (Buenos Aires: Fondo de Cultura Económica, 1997), 95-96.

64. Jorge Nállim, "Between Free Trade and Economic Dictatorship: Socialists, Radicals, and the Politics of Economic Liberalism in Argentina, 1930-1943," *Canadian Journal of Latin*

American and Caribbean Studies 33, no. 65 (2008): 139–74; Jeremy Adelman, "Socialism and Democracy in Argentina in the Age of the Second International," *Hispanic American History Review* 72, no. 2 (May 1992): 211–38; Richard Walter, *The Socialist Party of Argentina, 1890–1930* (Austin, Tex.: Institute of Latin American Studies, 1977).

65. Thoughtful considerations of this problem include de Grazia, *Irresistible Empire*, 110–18; Noel Thompson, "Social Opulence, Private Asceticism: Ideas of Consumption in Early Socialist Thought," in *The Politics of Consumption: Material Culture and Citizenship in Europe and America*, ed. Martin Daunton and Matthew Hilton (Oxford: Berg, 2001), 51–68.

66. *La Fraternidad*, April 20, 1940, n.p. Many of these advertisements were placed by only a handful of furniture factories and stores, all based in Buenos Aires; these businesses noted that catalogs were available for customers located in the interior. For similar advertisements of home appliances and furnishings, see *La Fraternidad*, April 5, 1941, 7; *El Obrero Ferroviario*, May 1, 1935, 10; and November 1, 1938, 9.

67. *La Fraternidad*, April 20, 1933, 86; April 20, 1941, n.p.; and May 5, 1938, 29.

Chapter 2: Standards for a New Argentina

1. Rodgers, *Atlantic Crossings*, 5–6.

2. Fermín Bereterbide, "El problema de la vivienda popular en Buenos Aires," *Boletín del Honorable Consejo Deliberante* 1, nos. 6–7 (Sept.–Oct. 1939): 112–60.

3. Ibid., 160.

4. Gerchunoff and Llach, *Ciclo de la ilusión*, 130–39.

5. Ibid.; Javier Villanueva, "Economic Development," in *Prologue to Perón: Argentina in Depression and War, 1930–1943*, ed. Mark Falcoff and Ronald H. Dolkart (Berkeley: University of California Press, 1975), 57–82; José Villarruel, "Los conflictos entre el estado," in *Representaciones inconclusas: Las clases, los actores y los concursos de la memoria, 1912–1946*, ed. Waldo Ansaldi, Alfredo R. Pucciarelli, and José C. Villarruel (Buenos Aires: Biblos, 1995), 317.

6. Junta Nacional para Combatir la Desocupación, *Memoria elevada al Ministro del Interior* (Buenos Aires, 1936) (recipients of aid received little in the way of compassion: with the completion of one shelter in Buenos Aires, the police razed the camps set up by the unemployed, forcing the residents to locate elsewhere or stay temporarily at the official shelter). Aside from the public works projects and road-building campaigns championed by the Justo administration, plans for airports, dams, and other infrastructure were drawn up but remained largely on the drawing board; see Anahi Ballent and Adrián Gorelik, "País urbano o país rural: La modernización territorial y su crisis," in *Nueva historia Argentina*, vol. 7, *Crisis económica, avance del Estado e incertidumbre política (1930–1942)*, ed. Alejandro Cattaruzza (Buenos Aires: Editorial Sudamericana, 2001), 143–200.

7. Gobierno de la Provincia de Córdoba, *Junta de trabajo* (Córdoba, 1934) (additional social legislation was adopted in Córdoba during the administration of Governor Amadeo Sabattini in the late 1930s); César Tcach Asad, *Amadeo Sabattini: La nación y la isla* (Buenos Aires: Fondo de Cultura Económica, 1997). On Santa Fe, see *Revista de Ciencias Económicas* (Feb. 1942), 164–66.

8. Speech by Nobel in Provincia de Buenos Aires, *Política obrera y legislación del trabajo del gobierno de Buenos Aires* (La Plata, Argentina: Talleres de Impresiones Oficiales, 1937), 8, 29; María Dolores Béjar, "La política laboral del gobierno de Manuel Fresco," in *Argentina: Trabajdores entre dos guerras*, ed. José Panettieri (Buenos Aires: Eudeba, 2000), 155–89.

9. Richard Walter, *The Province of Buenos Aires and Argentine Politics, 1912–1943* (Cambridge: Cambridge University Press, 1985), 160–61. See also Manuel Fresco, *Mi verdad* (Buenos Aires: Talleres de Pellegrini, 1966); Rafael Bitrán and Alejandro Schneider, "Coersión y consenso: La política obrera de Manuel Fresco, 1936–1940," in *Argentina en la paz de dos guerras, 1914–1945*, ed. Waldo Ansaldi, Alfredo R. Pucciarelli, and José C. Villarruel (Buenos Aires: Biblos, 1993), 255–94.

10. Between 1913 and 1917 Argentina's GDP shrank by 19.6 percent, whereas it shrank 9.7 percent in 1929–33. Likewise, unemployment figures shot up from 5 percent in 1913 to around 20 percent in 1914 (José Villarruel, "El futuro como incertidumbre: Los industrialistas y la tutela del estado," in *Argentina en la paz de dos guerras, 1914–1945*, ed. Waldo Ansaldi, Alfredo R. Pucciarelli, and José Villarruel [Buenos Aires: Biblos, 1993], 193–230).

11. Villarruel, "El futuro," 199. The years 1939–1943 would see periodic attempts to tighten price controls and respond to consumer demands. For instance, in 1943 officials within the Castillo administration devised a plan for lowering the price of meat in areas of the country with low spending power; see Daniel Campione, *Orígenes estatales del peronismo* (Buenos Aires: Miño y Dávila, 2007), 175.

12. *CGT: Periodico de la Confederación General del Trabajo*, July 10, 1942, n.p.; January 8, 1943, 5; and January 15, 1943, 5; *La Vanguardia* (Socialist Party daily newspaper), April 25, 1942, 1; and May 24, 1943, 1; *Noticias Gráficas*, March 1, 1943. According to these critics, the cost of shelter, food, and clothing increased by one-third between 1939 and 1945 in Buenos Aires, while the residents of provincial cities experienced a nearly 50 percent growth (Secretaría de Trabajo y Previsión, *Investigaciones sociales, 1943–1945* [Buenos Aires, 1946], 269).

13. Ministerio de la Hacienda, *El plan de reactivación económica ante el honorable senado* (Buenos Aires, 1940). As Juan José Llach has convincingly argued, the failure of this planning proposal resulted mainly from partisan conflicts over federal interventions in provincial governments and electoral corruption, not from intrinsic opposition toward Pinedo's economic strategies (see Juan José Llach, "El Plan Pinedo de 1940, su significado histórico y los origenes de la economía politica del peronismo," *Desarrollo Económico* 23, no. 92 [Jan.–Mar. 1984]: 515–57; see also Horacio José Pereyra, "Pinedo y El Plan Económico de 1940," in *Representaciones inconclusas: Las clases, los actores y los concursos de la memoria, 1912–1946*, ed. Waldo Ansaldi, Alfredo R. Pucciarelli, and José C. Villarruel (Buenos Aires: Biblos, 1995), 257–88; Gisela Cramer, "Argentine Riddle: The Pinedo Plan of 1940 and the Political Economy of the Early War Years," *Journal of Latin American Studies* 30 [1998]: 519–50).

14. *Revista de Economía Argentina* (May 1943): 175–77, (Oct. 1943): 416–17; Torcuato S. Di Tella, *Torcuato Di Tella: Industria y política* (Buenos Aires: Tesis/Grupo Editorial Norma, 1993), 119–20, 126–38. The congress was soon thereafter renamed the "Congreso Permanente de Fuerzas Productoras." Bunge participated frequently in UIA discussions until his death in 1943. At the same time, the UIA organizations sought to balance the influence of the right-leaning Bunge with experts from other political backgrounds.

15. Most experiments in "corporate welfare" were motivated by a sense of pro-family Catholic piety, but in his case inspiration came apparently from Di Tella's youthful dalliance with socialism in his homeland of Italy (Di Tella, *Torcuato Di Tella*, 1–35). See also María Inés Barbero and Mariela Ceva, "La vida obrera en una empresa paternalista," in *Historia de la vida privada en la Argentina*, vol. 3, *La Argentina entre multitudes y soledades: De los años treinta a la actualidad*, ed. Fernando Devoto and Marta Madero (Buenos Aires: Taurus, 1999), 141–68.

16. SIAM Di Tella Ltd., *La contribución de la gran industria a la mejora de la vivienda obrera* (Buenos Aires, 1941). Workers at SIAM lived in both Buenos Aires and Avellaneda, so clear distinctions as to where living conditions were worse are hard to make.

17. Torcuato Di Tella, *Dos temas de legislación del trabajo: Proyectos de ley de seguro social obrero y asignaciones familiares* (Buenos Aires, 1961 [1941]); Cochran and Reina, *Entrepreneurship*, 159–65; Di Tella, *Torcuato*, 110–15.

18. Torcuato Di Tella, *Problemas de la posguerra: Función económica y destino social de la industria argentina* (Buenos Aires: Libreria Hachette, 1943), 16–17, 60–63.

19. These remarks were printed in the UIA's trade magazine, *Argentina Fabril*, April 1943, 16.

20. *Revista de Economía Argentina* (May 1943): 176; *La Vanguardia*, September 27, 1942, 1.

21. Llach, "El Plan Pinedo"; Schvarzer, *Industria*, 188–96.

22. Robert A. Potash, *The Army and Politics in Argentina, 1928–1945* (Stanford, Calif.: Stanford University Press, 1969), 182–200; Potash, *Perón y el GOU: Los documentos de una logia secreta* (Buenos Aires: Editorial Sudamericana, 1984); Alain Rouquié, *Poder militar y sociedad política en la Argentina* (Buenos Aires: Emece, 1982); Constantino Fernández, *La revolución del 4 de junio, por qué y para qué se hizo* (Buenos Aires: Talleres Gráficos Optimus, 1944). For business frustrations, see Villarruel, "Los conflictos," 323–34.

23. Loris Zanatta, *Del estado liberal a la nación católica: Iglesia y ejército en los orígenes del peronismo, 1930–1943* (Buenos Aires: Universidad Nacional de Quilmes, 1996); Lila M. Caimari, *Perón y la iglesia católica: Religión, estado y sociedad en la Argentina (1943–1955)* (Buenos Aires: Ariel, 1985); Richard J. Walter, "The Right and the Peronists, 1943–1955," in *Argentine Right*, ed. Sandra McGee Deutsch and Ronald Dolkart (Wilmington, Del.: SR Books, 1993), 99–118; Cristián Buchrucker, *Nacionalismo y peronismo: La Argentina en la crisis ideológica mundial (1927–1955)* (Buenos Aires: Editorial Sudamericana, 1987).

24. Campione, *Orígenes*, 52–55, 61–63, 99–109.

25. Ibid., 100.

26. Rouquié, *Poder militar*, 29–30; Schvarzer, *Industria*, 196–201, 207–10; *Revista de Economía Argentina* (Aug. 1943): 757–58.

27. The most comprehensive biography remains Joseph A. Page's *Perón: A Biography* (New York: Random House, 1983). See also Tomás Eloy Martínez, *Las memorias del general* (Buenos Aires: Planeta, 1996).

28. The journalist Hugo Gambini interviewed Figuerola for the magazine *Primera Plana* in July 1966; see Hugo Gambini, *Historia del peronismo*, vol. 1, *El poder total (1943–1951)* (Buenos Aires: Editorial Planeta, 1999), 115.

29. The agency's reports, many with commentary from Figuerola, include Departamento Nacional del Trabajo (DNT), *La desocupación en la Argentina* (Buenos Aires, 1940); DNT, *Investigaciones sociales* (Buenos Aires, 1942); DNT, *Adaptación de los salarios a las fluctuaciones del costo de la vida* (Buenos Aires, 1943); Secretaría de Trabajo y Previsón (STP), *Nivel de vida de la familia obrera, evolución durante la segunda guerra mundial* (Buenos Aires, 1945); STP, *Condiciones de vida de la familia obrera*; STP, *Investigaciones sociales, 1943–1945* (Buenos Aires, 1946).

30. Martínez, *Memorias del general*, 44. Walter Little, "La organización obrera y el estado peronista," in *La formación del sindicalismo peronista*, ed. Juan Carlos Torre, 221–320 (Buenos Aires: Editorial Legasa, 1988). Provincial labor bureaus were incorporated within the secretariat, as were the retirement programs for transportation unions and government employees managed by the federal government (cajas de jubilación), reorganized as the National Social Insurance Institute. In this case as well, the agency enveloped preexisting government institutions and amassed new ones: the Comisión de Desempleo, Tribunal de Rentas, Caja Nacional de Ahorro Postal, Comisión de Casas Barratas, División de Trabajo Femenino, and others (Germán Soprano, "El DNT y su proyecto de regulación estatal de las relaciones Capital-

Trabajo en Argentina, 1907–1943," in *Argentina: Trabajdores entre dos guerras,* ed. Jose Panettieri [Buenos Aires: Eudeba, 2000], 31–53).

31. Labor historians have studied at length the negotiations between Perón's secretariat and individual unions. See Samuel Baily, *Labor, Nationalism, and Politics in Argentina* (New Brunswick, N.J.: Rutgers University Press, 1967); Miguel Murmis and Juan Carlos Portantiero, *Estudios sobre los orígenes del peronismo* (Buenos Aires: Siglo Veintiuno, 1971); Hiroshi Matsushita, *Movimiento obrero argentino, 1930–1945* (Buenos Aires: Siglo Viente, 1983); Juan Carlos Torre, ed., *La formación del sindicalismo peronista* (Buenos Aires: Editorial Legasa), 1988; Torre, "Interpretando (una vez más) los orígenes del peronismo," *Desarrollo Económico* 28, no. 112 (Jan.–Mar. 1989): 525–48; David Tamarin, *The Argentine Labor Movement 1930–1945: A Study in the Origins of Peronism* (Albuquerque: University of New Mexico Press, 1985); Joel Horowitz, *Argentine Unions, the State, and the Rise of Perón, 1930–1945* (Berkeley, Calif.: Institute of International Studies, 1990); Torcuato S. Di Tella, *Perón y los sindicatos: El inicio de una relación conflictiva* (Buenos Aires: Ariel, 2003).

32. The son of a train engineer and union member, Mercante held a nationalist outlook on unmet working-class needs that resembled Perón's own views. Mercante became Perón's principal liaison with the railroad workers unions, which represented nearly half the pre-1943 unionized workforce; he attended meetings and collected valuable information on specific demands and internal power struggles within unions. For an analysis of Mercante's role in the formation of Peronism, written by Mercante's son, see Domingo Alfredo Mercante, *Mercante: El corazón de Perón* (Buenos Aires: Ediciones de la Flor, 1995). On other key collaborators, see Rein, *In the Shadow.*

33. Tamarin, *Argentine Labor Movement,* 191; Ricardo Gaudio and Jorge Pilone, "Estado y relaciones laborales en el periodo previo al surgimiento del peronismo," in *La formación del sindicalismo,* ed. Torre, 44.

34. Luis B. Cerrutti Costa, *El sindicalismo, las masas y el poder* (Buenos Aires: Trafac, 1957), 174–75. These efforts extended to provincial areas with scant presence of unions. In Tucumán, for instance, government aid helped to create a new sugar cane workers organization, which in just three years after its creation in 1944 had unionized nearly 90 percent of the workforce (ibid.).

35. Juan Domingo Perón, *Obras completas* (Buenos Aires: Proyector Hernandarias, 1984–), 7:153, 445. For more on the Unión Ferroviaria and its place within Peronist labor politics, see Louise Doyon, "El crecimiento sindical bajo el peronismo," in *La formación del sindicalismo,* ed. Torre, 169–75; Horowitz, "Occupational Community."

36. For instance, all measures adopted by the Secretariat of Industry and Commerce that had a potential inflationary impact were required, in theory, to be first approved by the Consejo Nacional de Posguerra.

37. On Peronism and state planning, see Patricia Berrotarán, *Del plan a la planificación: El estado durante la época peronista* (Buenos Aires: Imago Mundi 2004); Campione, *Orígenes*; Alberto Ciria, *Política y cultura popular: La Argentina peronista, 1946–1955* (Buenos Aires: Ediciones de la Flor, 1983), 13–24.

38. Vicepresidencia de la Nación, Consejo Nacional de Posguerra (CNP), *Ordenamiento económico-social* (Buenos Aires, 1945); *Revista de Economía Argentina* (July 1945): 351–63.

39. CNP, *Ordenamiento,* 39–41.

40. Ibid., 56.

41. This compilation forms the basis for J. Perón, *Obras completas,* vol. 7.

42. Ibid., 367, 246.

43. Ibid., 405, 534–35.

44. Ibid., 8:300.

45. Works on the origins of Peronism, gender, and the working class include Karina Inés Ramacciotti and Adriana María Valobra, eds., *Generando el peronismo: Estudios de cultura, política y género (1946–1955)* (Buenos Aires: Proyecto Editorial, 2004); Susana Bianchi, "Catolicismo y peronismo: La familia entre la religión y la política (1946–1955)," *Boletín del Instituto de Historia Argentina y Americana "Dr. Emilio Ravignani"* 19 (First Semester, 1999): 115–37; Dora Barrancos, "Moral sexual, sexualidad, y mujeres trabajadoras en el período de entreguerras," in *Historia de la vida privada en la Argentina*, vol. 3, ed. Fernando Devoto and Marta Madero (Buenos Aires: Taurus, 1999), 199–226; Recchini de Lattes, *Participación económica femenina*, 11.

46. J. Perón, *Obras completas*, 7:427–30, 439. The division's chiefs were Lucila de Gregorio Lavié and María Tizón, a teacher and inspector of the Consejo Nacional de Educación.

47. Ibid., 361, 332.

48. Ibid., 125, 192, 231–32.

49. Ernesto Laclau and other theorists have explored the centrality of this rhetorical strategy to populist politics, in particular the process by which this appeal to the popular can both build on and supersede class identities. See Laclau, *Politics and Ideology*; Emilio de Ipola, "Populismo e ideología"; Silvia Sigal and Eliseo Verón, *Perón o Muerte: Los fundamentos discursivos del fenómeno peronista* (Buenos Aires: Legasa, 1986).

50. Fernández, *La revolución*, 64.

51. On the earthquake and its aftermath, see Mark Alan Healey, *The Ruins of the New Argentina: Peronism and the Remaking of San Juan after the 1944 Earthquake* (Durham, N.C.: Duke University Press, forthcoming).

52. On business relations with Perón, see James P. Brennan and Marcelo Rougier, *The Politics of National Capitalism: Peronism and the Argentine Bourgeoisie, 1945–1976* (University Park: Pennsylvania State University Press, 2009); James P. Brennan, "Industrialists and Bolicheros: Business and the Peronist Populist Alliance, 1943–1976," in *Peronism and Argentina*, ed. James P. Brennan (Willmington, Del.: SR Books, 1998), 79–124; Christina Luccini, *Apoyo empresarial en los origenes del peronismo* (Buenos Aires: Centro Editor de América Latina, 1990); Judith Teichman, "Interest Conflict and Entrepreneurial Support for Perón," *Latin American Research Review* 16, no. 1 (1981): 144–55; Jorge Schvarzer, *Empresarios del pasado: La Unión Industrial Argentina* (Buenos Aires: CISEA/Imago Mundi, 1991); Peter Birle, *Los empresarios y la democracia en la Argentina* (Buenos Aires: Editorial de Belgrano, 1997).

53. Campione, *Orígenes*, 148.

54. *Argentina Fabril*, January 1945, 42–43.

55. Much of the recent historiography on Peronism is critical of this position. It is true that opponents clung to the argument that Peronism equaled homegrown fascism far too long —well into the 1960s in some cases. See Marcela García Sebastiani, *Los antiperonistas en la Argentina peronista: Radicales y socialistas en la política argentina entre 1943 y 1951* (Buenos Aires: Prometeo, 2005); Plotkin, "Changing Perceptions."

56. Ronald C. Newton, *The Nazi Menace in Argentina, 1931–1947* (Stanford, Calif.: Stanford University Press, 1992); Buchrucker, *Nacionalismo*; Federico Finchelstein, *Transatlantic Fascism: Ideology, Violence, and the Sacred in Argentina and Italy, 1919–1945* (Durham, N.C.: Duke University Press, 2010).

57. Page, *Perón*, 106–11; Gambini, *Historia del peronismo*, 1:24–25.

58. The decree also expanded federal authority over organized labor by allowing the secretariat to legally recognize (or ignore) individual unions (Jeremy Adelman, "Reflections

on the Rise of Argentine Labour and the Rise of Perón," *Bulletin of Latin American Research* 11, no. 3 [1992]: 243–59).

69. Cipriano Reyes, *Yo hice el 17 de octubre* (Buenos Aires: Centro Editor de América Latina, 1984); Daniel James, "October 17th and 18th, 1945: Mass Protest, Peronism, and the Argentine Working Class," *Journal of Social History* 21 (Spring 1988): 441–61; Juan Carlos Torre, ed., *El 17 de Octubre de 1945* (Buenos Aires: Ariel, 1995).

60. Gambini, *Historia del peronismo,* 1:24–25.

61. James, "October 17th"; Raúl Scalabrini Ortiz, *Hechos e Ideas,* February 1946, excerpted in *La jornada del 17 de Octubre por cuarenta y cinco autores,* ed. Fermín Chavez (Buenos Aires: Ediciones Corregidor, 1996), 29–30.

62. *Argentina Fabril,* January 1946, 2–17. Likewise, Perón turned to his advantage a report published by the U.S. State Department in February 1946 that outlined the "Nazi-Fascist" character of Farrell's regime. The brainchild of Spruille Braden, a former ambassador to Argentina, this so-called Blue Book was released three weeks before the elections to deliver a final blow to Perón. Its effect was quite the opposite; Perón contended that the Blue Book revealed the sinister alliance between his opponents and foreign imperialists who interfered in Argentina's internal affairs. At his culminating rally, he declared that voters truly had only one choice: Braden or Perón.

63. The Democratic Union was certainly not helpless, for it was well funded and relied on established party networks. But as the Socialist Party put it after Perón's electoral victory: "Twenty-four hours of order on election day do not erase the fraud of thirty months of dictatorship" (*La Vanguardia,* March 5, 1946).

64. Juan Perón, *El pueblo ya sabe de que se trata* (Buenos Aires: n.p., 1946), 229–33.

65. Gerchunoff and Llach, *Ciclo de la ilusión,* 181; Peter Ross, "Justicia social: Una evaluación del los logros del peronismo clásico," *Anuario de IEHS* 8 (1993): 112. Ross discusses the problems with statistical estimates of real wage levels in the Peronist era, including the difficulties of determining an "average" worker and how to account for the impact of social benefits. See also Guy Bourdé, *La classe ouvrière argentine (1929–1969),* 3 vols. (Paris: Editions L'Harmattan, 1987), 2:846–61.

66. Pablo Gerchunoff and Damián Antúnez, "De la bonanza peronista a la crisis de desarrollo," in *Nueva Historia Argentina,* vol. 8, *Los Años Peronistas (1943–1955),* ed. Juan Carlos Torre (Buenos Aires: Editorial Sudamericana, 2002), 146.

67. Eugene Joseph Weber, *The Hollow Years: France in the 1930s* (New York: Norton, 1994), 150–53.

68. Jim Handy, *Revolution in the Countryside: Rural Conflict and Agrarian Reform in Guatemala, 1944–1954* (Chapel Hill: University of North Carolina Press, 1994); Cindy Forester, *The Time of Freedom: Campesino Workers in Guatemala's October Revolution* (Pittsburgh, Pa.: University of Pittsburgh Press, 2001); Merilee Grindle and Pilar Domingo, eds., *Proclaiming Revolution: Bolivia in Comparative Perspective* (London: Institute of Latin American Studies, 2003).

69. Poder Ejecutivo, *Plan Quinquenal de Gobierno del Presidente Perón, 1947–1951* (Buenos Aires, 1946); Ministerio de Obras Públicas, *El Plan Quinquenal y las Obras Públicas* (Buenos Aires: Talleres Gráficos del Ministerio, 1946).

70. Perón, *El pueblo ya sabe,* 229–33.

71. On Miranda's biography, see Rein, *In the Shadow,* 48–55.

72. *Hechos e Ideas* 6, no. 42 (Aug. 1947): 62–74.

73. *Hechos e Ideas* 6, no. 43 (Sept. 1947): 3–7. This editorial, titled "La responsabilidad de la masa trabajadora frente a las conquistas económico-sociales," was presumably written by the journal's director, Enrique Eduardo García.

74. Birle, *Los empresarios,* 77–78.

75. Gerchunoff and Llach, *Ciclo de la ilusión,* 155–66; Schvarzer, *Industria,* 171–82; Margarita Gutman and Jorge Enrique Hardoy, *Buenos Aires: Historia urbana de la área metropolitana* (Madrid: Editorial Mapfre, 1992), 265–86, 220–21.

76. Schvarzer, *Industria,* 192–94; Carlos Escudé, "U.S. Political Destabilization and Economic Boycott of Argentina during the 1940s," in *Argentina between the Great Powers, 1939–1946,* ed. Guido Di Tella and D. Cameron Watt (Pittsburgh, Pa.: University of Pittsburgh Press, 1990), 56–76.

77. Doyon, "Creciminento sindical," 174–75.

78. Leslie Bethell and Ian Roxborough, "Latin America between the Second World War and the Cold War," *Journal of Latin American Studies* 20, no. 1 (May 1988): 167–89. See also Greg Grandin, *The Last Colonial Massacre: Latin America in the Cold War* (Chicago: University of Chicago Press, 2004), 169–98.

Chapter 3: The War on Speculation

1. *El Mundo,* June 12, 1947, 6.

2. In mid-1940s Chile, for instance, state officials created "vigilance juntas" to crack down on profiteering, while civil associations on the Left organized to defend consumers from the dangers of "speculation" (Rosemblatt, *Gendered Compromises,* 115–121).

3. See Meg Jacobs, "How about Some Meat? The Office of Price Administration, Consumption Politics, and State Building from the Bottom Up, 1941–1946," *Journal of American History* 84, no. 3 (Dec. 1997): 910–41. On consumer politics at midcentury, see Victoria de Grazia and Ellen Furlough, eds., *The Sex of Things: Gender and Consumption in Historical Perspective* (Berkeley: University of California Press, 1996); Susan Strasser, Charles McGovern, and Mathias Judt, eds., *Getting and Spending: European and American Consumer Societies in the Twentieth Century* (Cambridge: Cambridge University Press, 1998); Lizabeth Cohen, *A Consumers' Republic: The Politics of Mass Consumption in Postwar America* (New York: Knopf, 2003); Meg Jacobs, *Pocketbook Politics: Economic Citizenship in Twentieth-Century America* (Princeton, N.J.: Princeton University Press, 2005); Kate Soper and Frank Trentmann, *Citizenship and Consumption* (Houndmills, N.Y.: Palgrave Macmillan, 2008).

4. Félix Luna, *Perón y su tiempo,* vol. 1, *La Argentina era una fiesta* (Buenos Aires: Editorial Sudamericana, 1991 [1984]).

5. Secretaría de Asuntos Técnicos, *Comercio Minorista en la Capital Federal* (Buenos Aires, 1954), 5–15; idem, *Comercio Minorista en los 17 partidos del Gran Buenos Aires* (Buenos Aires, 1954), 6–19.

6. Foreign travelers often remarked on the beef-centric diet of middle-class Argentines; see, e.g., Greenup and Greenup, *Revolution,* 25–38. On the cultural and political significance of beef in this era, see Natalia Milanesio, "Food Politics and Consumption in Peronist Argentina," *Hispanic American Historical Review* 90 (Feb. 2010): 75–108.

7. James Bruce, *Those Perplexing Argentines* (New York: Longmans, Green, 1953), 240; Bourdé, *La classe ouvrière,* 2:792–93.

8. *Noticias Gráficas,* November 4, 1948.

9. Juan Luis de Lannoy, *Los niveles de vida en América Latina* (Fribourg, Switzerland, and Bogotá: Oficina Internacional de Investigaciones Sociales de FERES, 1963), 134. Again, these are crude statistical averages, not necessarily an accurate description of life in all popular households.

10. Confederación General Económica, *Informe económico* (Buenos Aires, 1955), 121; Secretaría de Asuntos Técnicos, *Comercio Minorista en Capital Federal*, 4–6; idem, *Comercio Minorista en los 17 partidos*, 6–8.

11. Caja Nacional de Ahorro Postal, *El ahorro en la enseñanza media, programa y desarrollo* (Buenos Aires: Editorial Polo, 1947). Savings deposits in Argentina increased from 2.7 to 6 billion pesos between 1943 and 1948, in figures unadjusted for inflation; deposits in the Caja Nacional grew from 190 to 800 million pesos in the same period (ibid.). See also Marcelo Rougier and Martín Fiszbein, "De Don Derrochín a Maese Ahorrín: El fomento del ahorro durante la economía peronista," in *Sueños de bienestar en la Nueva Argentina: Estado y políticas públicas durante el peronismo, 1946–1955*, ed. Patricia Berrotarán, Aníbal Jáuregui, and Marcelo Rougier (Buenos Aires: Imago Mundi, 2004), 107–44.

12. Juan Carlos Torre and Eliza Pastoriza, "La democratización del bienestar," in *Nueva Historia Argentina*, vol. 8, *Los Años Peronistas (1943–1955)*, ed. Juan Carlos Torre (Buenos Aires: Editorial Sudamericana, 2002), 257–312; Isabella Cosse, *Estigmas de nacimiento: Peronismo y orden familiar, 1946–1955* (Buenos Aires: Universidad San Andrés/Fondo de Cultura Económica Argentina, 2006).

13. Horacio Gaggero and Alicia Garro, *Del trabajo a la casa: La política de vivienda del gobierno peronista, 1946–1955* (Buenos Aires: Editorial Biblos, 1996), 68–73; Anahi Ballent, *Las huellas de la política: Vivienda, ciudad, peronismo en Buenos Aires, 1943–1955* (Buenos Aires: Universidad Nacional de Quilmes/Prometeo, 2005). Peter Ross ("Justicia social") suggests that white-collar public employees were the greatest beneficiaries of BHN loans, although the agency did attempt to reach out to lower-income groups with the 1954 Plan Evita. On home ownership and suburbanization, see Horacio A. Torre, "Cambios en la estructura socioespacial de Buenos Aires a partir de la decada de 1940," in *Después de Germani: Exploraciones sobre la estructura social en la Argentina*, ed. Jorge Raúl Jorrat and Ruth Sautu (Buenos Aires: Paidos, 1992), 158–75.

14. *Noticias Gráficas*, March 6, 1950; *Mundo Argentino*, July 10 and August 14, 1946.

15. Eduardo Coghlan, *La condición de la vivienda en la Argentina a través del censo de 1947* (Buenos Aires: Rosso, 1959), 90–100; Gerchunoff and Antúnez, "De la bonanza," 146.

16. Carlos Ulanovsky and Marta Merkin, *Dias de radio: Historia de la radio argentina* (Buenos Aires: Espasa Calpe, 1995), 121–76; Ernesto Goldar, *Buenos Aires: Vida cotidiana en la década del 50* (Buenos Aires: Plus Ultra, 1980), 144–52.

17. Brennan and Rougier, *Politics of National Capitalism*.

18. Gary W. Wynia, *Argentina in the Postwar: Politics and Economic Policymaking in a Divided Society* (Albuquerque: University of New Mexico Press, 1978), 49–52; Susana Novick, *IAPI: Auge y decadencia* (Buenos Aires: Centro Editor de América Latina, 1986); Daniel Muchnik, "El IAPI: Balance y memoria de una experiencia," *Todo Es Historia* 229 (May 1986): 74–85.

19. Novick, *IAPI*, 39, 72–73. On beef policies after 1943, see Peter Smith, *Politics and Beef in Argentina: Patterns of Conflict and Change* (New York: Columbia University Press, 1969); 231–46; Milanesio, "Food Politics."

20. Adriana Marshall, "La composición del consumo en los obreros industriales de Buenos Aires, 1930–1980," *Desarrollo Económico*, 21, no. 83 (Oct.–Dec. 1981): 351–74; Torrado, *Estructura social*, 272–74.

21. Confederación General Económica, *Informe económico*, 121–22. These retail sales figures were apparently not adjusted for inflation. A more mixed picture is provided by statistics on the physical volume of retail sales per inhabitant, which nationwide increased by 30 percent between 1946 and 1948, only to then decline over the ensuing years. By 1953 they had fallen 17 percent below 1946 levels.

22. *El Mundo,* April 25, 1947, 4. See also *Noticias Gráficas,* October 11, 1946; and April 24, 1947.

23. *El Pueblo,* June 13, 1946, 9.

24. Miguel Miranda, "Cómo se dirigió nuestra economía y retrasó el progresso industrial del país," *Hechos e Ideas* 6, no. 42 (Aug. 1947): 71–74.

25. Perón in Ministerio de Interior, *Leyes, decretos y revoluciones para normalizar precios y reprimir la especulación* (Buenos Aires, 1947), 4–5.

26. *Noticias Gráficas,* June 11 and August 14, 1946; *El Pueblo,* June 19, 1946, 3; and August 14, 1946, 6–7; *La Voz del Interior,* June 20, 1946, 5.

27. On Evita's speech, see Eva Perón, *Discursos completos* (Buenos Aires: Editorial Megafón, 1985), 1:9–12; Estela dos Santos, *Las mujeres peronistas* (Buenos Aires: Centro Editor de América Latina, 1983), 33.

28. *Para Ti,* January 7, 1947.

29. Like the new ministerial agencies created or revamped since 1943, the Federal Police itself was less than a decade old at this time. See Lila Caimari, *Apenas un delincuente: Crimen, castigo y cultura en Buenos Aires, 1880–1955* (Buenos Aires: Siglo Veintiuno, 2004).

30. Subsecretaría de Informaciones, Dirección General del Registro Nacional, *Abastecimiento y represión del agio* (Buenos Aires, 1950), 1:9; Ministerio del Interior, *Conferencia de gobernadores de provincias y territorios nacionales, para la represión del agio, la especulación y los precios abusivos* (Buenos Aires: Imprenta del Congreso, 1947), 85–87.

31. Decree 18,640/47, October 16, 1947, legajo 426, AGN-MAT; *El Mundo,* October 18, 1947, 7. A June 1947 decree, for instance, granted government the power of *incautación* (seizure) of textile goods; the executive branch threatened to confiscate all clothing and sell it directly to the public unless merchants sold inventory immediately to consumers at official prices (Comunicado de Secretaría de Informaciones, June 11, 1947, legajo 425, AGN-MAT).

32. The maximum markup on goods at each stage of commercialization varied from around 7 to 20 percent, depending on the trade and product. For instance, a retailer of housewares might be allowed 12 percent, and a manufacturer of rayon, 20 percent (*El Mundo,* October 18, 1947). For decrees affecting the clothing industry, see *Gaceta Textil,* August 1950, 14–17; October 1950, 11; and May 1951, 13; *Mundo Argentino,* October 4, 1950, 3. See also price freeze decree from 1952, 5245/52, legajo 181, AGN-MAT.

33. Ministerio del Interior, *Conferencia de gobernadores,* 39–45, 58; Subsecretaría de Informaciones, *Abastecimiento,* 1:45, 61; Confederación General del Trabajo, *Anuario del trabajo* (Buenos Aires, 1948), 33–34.

34. J. Perón, speech to Consejo Económico Social, June 11, 1947, legajo 425, AGN-MAT.

35. Reports from Comisión de Investigaciones de Agio y Especulación, November 1–December 1, 1955, 14, memorias, box 6, Fondo Comisión Nacional de Investigaciones, Archivo Intermedio, Archivo General de la Nación (hereinafter abbreviated AGN-FCNI). The military government that overthrew Perón created this series of internal reports and memoranda to document supposed wrongdoing by the justicialista regime. Despite its obvious biases, this unpublished documentation of antiagio activities provides important insights on the Peronist marketplace.

36. Mark Edmunson, *Nightmare on Main Street: Angels, Sadomasochism, and the Culture of the Gothic* (Cambridge, Mass.: Harvard University Press, 1997).

37. Subsecretaría de Informaciones, *Abastecimiento,* 1:71.

38. George J. Eder, a U.S. employee of International Telegraph and Telephone in Buenos Aires, provided a detailed description of the procedures of antispeculation enforcement, at least based on his own experiences and those of fellow businesspeople. See Despatch on Price Control Decrees, *Confidential U.S. State Department Central Files. Argentina, 1945–1949,*

September 8, 1947, reel 4, pt. 2, doc. 835.5017/9-847, U.S. State Department Central Files. The number of *sumarios* varied considerably each year but reached a peak in 1950 with 15,891 formal cases opened; see Reports from Comisión de Investigaciones de Agio y Especulación, November 1–December 1, 1955, 72, memorias, box 6, AGN-FCNI.

39. *Memoria de la Dirección Nacional de Vigilancia de Precios y Abastecimiento correspondente al año 1949* (Buenos Aires, 1950), 95–97; Dirección Nacional de Estadística y Censos, *Censo de Comercio 1954*, vol. 1 (Buenos Aires, 1959), 10–11, 17–19. Decree 17,852 (June 1947) charged the police with enforcement of Law 12,830 and 12,983.

40. Letter from the Unión de Repartidores y Comerciantes en Fideos, Dec. 26, 1951, doc. 1873, legajo 331, AGN-MAT.

41. Sudamtex case, November 1947, legajo 425, AGN-MAT; letter from Ducci and Sabrelli, July 16, 1948, legajo 426, AGN-MAT; Despatch on Price Control Decrees, September 8, 1947, U.S. State Department Central Files.

42. List of accused speculators (February 1948), legajo 427, AGN-MAT. The seventy cases of accused speculators for this month are as follows: eighteen butchers, twelve fruit and vegetable stands, ten restaurants, eight pastry shops, five bars and cafés, three construction material stores, three groceries, three bakeries, three ice sellers, two delicatessens (*fiambrerías*), one fur wholesaler, one general wholesaler, and one general store. Geographically, sixty of the cases were from Buenos Aires and ten were from the city's suburbs.

43. Summary of judgments, doc. 35071, November 8, 1947, legajo 425, AGN-MAT.

44. *Noticias Gráficas,* November 10, 1948.

45. Decree 35,198, November 12, 1947, legajo 425, AGN-MAT. For reports on hoarding, see *El Mundo,* February 1, 1948, 9; *Noticias Gráficas,* June 6, 1951; *Argentina,* January 1949, 5–8.

46. *Argentina,* January 1949, 5–8.

47. *Noticias Gráficas,* September 17, 1951; and March 2, 1950; *Mundo Argentino,* June 4, 1952, 19.

48. Gambini, *Historia del peronismo,* vol. 2, *La obsecuencia* (Buenos Aires: Editorial Planeta, 2001), 174–82; Félix Luna, *Perón y su tiempo,* vol. 3, *El régimen exhausto, 1953–1955* (Buenos Aires: Editorial Sudamericana 1991 [1986]), 694–705; Vicepresidencia de la Nación, Comisión Nacional de Investigaciones, *Documentación, autores y cómplices de las irregularidades cometidas durante la segunda tiranía,* 5 vols. (Buenos Aires, 1958).

49. Reports from Comisión de Investigaciones de Agio y Especulación, November 1–December 1, 1955, 61–65, memorias, box 6, AGN-FCNI. Records show that almost all the accused police and price inspectors were later acquitted.

50. Historians of the Soviet Union have, not surprisingly, looked carefully at the political dynamics of the black market. See Kotkin, *Magnetic Mountain,* 238–79; Sheila Fitzpatrick, *Everyday Stalinism: Ordinary Life in Extraordinary Times: Soviet Russia in the 1930s* (New York: Oxford, 1999); Amy E. Randall, *The Soviet Dream World of Retail Trade and Consumption in the 1930s* (New York: Palgrave Macmillan, 2008).

51. Letter from Vicente Santos, January 16, 1948, legajo 426, AGN-MAT.

52. Telegram from Villa Devoto prisoners, February 1948, legajo 428, AGN-MAT. On fear of Villa Devoto among merchants, see Despatch on Price Control Decrees, September 8, 1947, U.S. State Department Central Files; Goldar, *Buenos Aires,* 28–29.

53. See note 52 in chapter 2.

54. Despatch on Price Control Decrees, September 8, 1947, U.S. State Department Central Files.

55. Letter from Cámara Argentina de Comerciantes, *Gaceta Textil,* May 1950, 21–26; letter from Cámara de Grandes Tiendas y Anexos, doc. 642, legajo 596, AGN-MAT. For similar

complaints made by the Federación Argentina de Centros de Almaceneros, see *El Mundo,* May 7, 1947, 6.

56. Confederación Económica Argentina, *Memorial de la Confederación Económica Argentina sobre los costos de la comercialización* (Buenos Aires, 1950), 7–28; Birle, *Los empresarios,* 84–85.

57. Confederación Económica Argentina, *Memorial* (1950) 14. Verifying these claims is virtually impossible, as few businesses made public their balance sheets.

58. Ministerio de Economía, Secretaría de Comercio, *Estadísticas comerciales* (Buenos Aires, 1983), 24–26; Dirección Nacional de Estadística y Censos, *Censo de Comercio 1954,* 17–19; Secretaría de Asuntos Técnicos, *Comercio Minorista en los 17 partidos,* 14–16, 19.

59. *El Pueblo,* June 12, 1947, 3; *La Voz del Interior,* September 1, 1946, 8.

60. *Noticias Gráficas,* March 6, 1950; *Mundo Argentino,* July 10 and August 14 (quotation), 1946. Consumer demand for modernizing products, such as electric refrigerators, can be seen in SIAM's sales figures: the company went from selling 11,693 refrigerators in 1948 to 73,928 in 1955 (Cochran and Reina, *Entrepreneurship,* 210–52).

61. Brennan and Rougier, *Politics of National Capitalism,* 17–61.

62. In a typical editorial of this period, *La Prensa* acknowledged the existence of profiteering and worldwide inflationary conditions but concluded that in Argentina, "one of the most powerful causes of inflation . . . [was] the increase in State expenditures" (*La Prensa,* May 13, 1947, 4).

63. *El Pueblo,* June 8, 1946.

64. Partido Socialista, *Hacia la bancarrota* (Buenos Aires: Editorial La Vanguardia, 1949), n.p. See also Romulo Bogliolo, *Salarios y nivel de vida* (Buenos Aires: Editorial La Vanguardia, 1946).

65. *Obrero Ferroviario,* May 16, 1947, 1, 5.

66. Letter from Federación de Sindicatos Unidos de Obreros (Mendoza), 1946, legajo 583, AGN-MAT.

67. *La Gaceta* (Tucumán), January 27, 1947, 5; June 14, 1948, 9; and June 18, 1948, 5.

68. *Noticias Gráficas,* May 4, 1947, n.p.; *Norte* (Quilmes, Buenos Aires), June 27, 1946; April 9, 1947, 1; and May 6, 1947, 1, 7.

69. Letter from Agustín Giovanelli, president of the Bloque Peronista of the Consejo Deliberante of Avellaneda, November 16, 1948, legajo 462, AGN-MAT.

70. *El Pueblo,* November 27, 1948, 7; *El Mundo,* August 9, 1947, 5. On Evita, see *El Obrero Metalúrgico,* September 15, 1948, 24.

71. On Peronism and the mobilization of female consumers, see Natalia Milanesio, "The Guardian Angels of the Domestic Economy: Housewives' Responsible Consumption in Peronist Argentina," *Journal of Women's History* 18: 3 (September 2006): 91–117. On gender and consumer politics, see the essays in de Grazia and Furlough's collection *The Sex of Things,* particularly de Grazia's article "Nationalizing Women: The Competition between Fascist and Commercial Cultural Modes in Mussolini's Italy," 337–58. See also Jacobs, *Pocketbook Politics;* Cohen, *Consumers' Republic.*

72. Peronist efforts to attract a female political following have received much scholarly attention. See Marysa Navarro, *Evita* (Buenos Aires: Ediciones Corregidor, 1981); Susana Bianchi and Norma Sanchis, *El partido peronista femenino* (Buenos Aires: CEAL, 1988); Mariano Plotkin, *Mañana es San Perón: Propaganda, rituales políticos y educación en el régimen peronista (1946–1955)* (Buenos Aires: Ariel Historia Argentina, 1993), 256–74; Silvana A. Palermo, "El sufragio femenino en el Congreso Nacional: Ideologías de género y ciudadanía en la Argentina (1916–1955)," *Boletín del Instituto de Historia Argentina y Americana "Dr.*

Emilio Ravignani" 16–17 (1997): 151–78; Dos Santos, *Mujeres peronistas*; Ramacciotti and Vaolobra, *Generando el peronismo.*

73. *Noticias Gráficas,* July 26, 1946.

74. On the modernization of patriarchy, see note 14 to the introduction and note 49 to chapter 1.

75. Celina Martínez de Paiva, interview by Luis Alberto Romero, October 18, 1972, Instituto Di Tella and Columbia University Oral History Project, New York, N.Y.

76. Eva Perón cited in Carolina Barry, *Evita capitana: El Partido Peronista Femenino, 1949–1955* (Buenos Aires: EDUNTREF, 2009), 161.

77. Navarro, *Evita,* 212–13; Bianchi and Sanchis, *Partido,* 66–84; Ciria, *Política y cultura popular,* 186.

78. Martínez de Paiva interview, 8–10; Barry, *Evita capitana,* 179–204.

79. *Noticias Gráficas,* May 3 and 5, 1947.

80. Photographs, April 22, 1953, doc. 201471, envelope 24; n.d., doc. 188496, envelope 6; May 9, 1947, doc. 172881, envelope 4, all in box 1307, AGN, Departamento de Fotografía.

81. *Arrabalera,* feature film, dir. Tulio Demicheli (1950). Another Tita Merello film, *Mercado de Abasto* (dir. Lucas Demare [1954]), dealt more extensively with the world of everyday commerce; although this film made familiar criticisms of commercial greed, it offered a surprisingly positive portrait of merchants in the late Peronist years.

82. Letter from Salvador Rodríguez García, January 18, 1947, legajo 597, AGN-MAT.

83. Letter from resident of Buenos Aires, July 1946, doc. 771, legajo 771, AGN-MAT.

Chapter 4: Needs, Wants, and Comforts

1. *Señalando rumbos,* Sucesos Argentinos no. 574, 16-mm film, November 1949, AGN, Departamento de Cine, Audio y Video.

2. On domestic space, appliances, and cooking see, Rebekah Pite, "Creating a Common Table: Doña Petrona, Cooking, and Consumption in Argentina, 1928–1983," Ph.D. diss., University of Michigan (2007).

3. Marcela Gené, *Un mundo feliz: Imágenes de los trabajadores en el primer peronismo, 1946–1955* (Buenos Aires: Universidad de San Andres, 2005); Ballent, *Las huellas,* 19–20; Gutiérrez and Romero, *Sectores populares,* 168.

4. Useful overviews include Patricia Berrotarán, Aníbal Jáuregui, and Marcelo Rougier, eds., *Sueños de bienestar en la Nueva Argentina: Estado y políticas públicas durante el peronismo, 1946–1955* (Buenos Aires: Imago Mundi, 2004); Torre and Pastoriza, "La democratización del bienestar."

5. Linda Gordon, *Pitied but Not Entitled: Single Mothers and the History of Welfare* (Cambridge, Mass.: Harvard University Press, 1994), 1–13; Rodgers, *Atlantic Crossings,* 28–32; Michel Foucault, *Power/Knowledge: Selected Interviews and Other Writings, 1972–1977,* ed. Colin Gordon (New York: Pantheon, 1980), 63–166. Historical studies of state planning, regulation, and governmentality include James C. Scott, *Seeing Like a State: How Certain Schemes to Improve the Human Condition Have Failed* (New Haven, Conn.: Yale University Press, 1998); Paul Rabinow, *French Modern: Norms and Forms of the Social Environment* (Cambridge, Mass.: MIT Press, 1989); Gyan Prakash, *Another Reason: Science and the Imagination of Modern India* (Princeton, N.J.: Princeton University Press, 1999); James Holston, *The Modernist City: An Anthropological Critique of Brasília* (Chicago: University of Chicago Press, 1989).

6. Servicio Internacional de Publicaciones Argentinas (SIPA), *La asistencia social justicialista* (Buenos Aires, 1952), 22. The Servicio Internacional de Publicaciones Argentinas was a federal agency that published scores of pamphlets about social assistance and other subjects. These were distributed in Argentina, and many were translated into foreign languages and shipped abroad. As with those produced by other agencies, these pamphlets were short (around forty or so unnumbered pages each) and illustrated with photographs, charts, and drawings.

7. Donna Guy, *Women Build the Welfare State: Performing Charity and Creating Rights in Argentina, 1880–1955* (Durham, N.C.: Duke University Press, 2009); Laura Golbert, "Las políticas sociales antes y después de la Fundación Eva Perón," in *La Fundación Eva Perón y las mujeres: Entre la provicación y la inclusión*, ed. Carolina Barry, Karina Ramacciotti, and Adriana Valobra (Buenos Aires: Editorial Biblos, 2008), 19–50.

8. SIPA, *La asistencia*, 12; Ramón Carrillo, *Política sanitaria argentina*, 2 vols. (Buenos Aires: Ministerio de Salud Pública, 1949). On public health programs, see Karina Ramacciotti, *La política sanitaria del peronismo* (Buenos Aires: Editorial Biblos, 2009); Ramacciotti, "Las voces que cuestionaron la política sanitaria del peronismo (1946–1949)," in *Las políticas sociales en perspectiva histórica*, ed. Daniel Lvovich and Juan Suriano (Buenos Aires: Prometeo, 2006), 169–96; Eric Carter, "'God Bless General Perón': DDT and the Endgame of Malaria Eradication in Argentina in the 1940s," *Journal of the History of Medicine and Allied Sciences* 64, no. 1 (2009): 78–122.

9. Patricia Berrotarán et al., *Sueños de bienestar*; Gaggero and Garro, *Del trabajo*; Rosa Aboy, *Viviendas para el pueblo: Espacio urbano y sociabilidad en el barrio Los Perales, 1946–1955* (Buenos Aires: San Andres/Fundo de Cultura Económica, 2005); Eugenia Scarzanella, "El ocio peronista: Vacaciones y 'turismo popular' en la Argentina (1943–1955)," *Entrepasados, Revista de Historia* 7, no. 14 (first half, 1998): 65–86.

10. At one end of the spectrum, the governor of Buenos Aires province, Domingo Mercante, spearheaded a "three-year plan" (1947–50) that mirrored the priorities of the national Plan Quinquenal. Argentina's largest and most populated province constructed approximately 146 "*barrio obrero*" housing projects, as well as initiating other public works ventures, including schools, roads, sewer systems, and tourist facilities; see Gobernación de la Provincia de Buenos Aires, Ministerio de Obras Públicas, *Plan general de trabajos públicos* (Buenos Aires: Guillermo Kraft, 1948); Mercante, *Mercante*. For public housing policies in another provincial context, see Healey, *Ruins*.

11. *Obrero Ferroviario*, January 1, 1947; October 1950, 104–5; October 1953, 1; December 1953; and April 14, 1954; *Revista de Trabajo y Previsión* (Feb. 1953): 132; Confederación General del Trabajo, *Anuario*, 106–9, 120. The Unión Ferroviaria operated approximately twenty *policlinicas* and medical centers, many in interior towns located far from major hospitals, as well as dozens of consumer cooperatives and housing projects. By 1953 the medium-sized paper and printers union had a portfolio of facilities that included a new headquarters, four policlinicas, fourteen consumer cooperatives, a worker barrio in the Buenos Aires suburb of Beccar, and a "vacation colony" in the hill town of La Falda, Córdoba. For other examples of union obra social, see Federación de Obreros y Empleados de la Industrial de Papel, Cartón, Quimicos y Afines, *Manual del trabajador papelero* (Buenos Aires: Gráficos ALEA, 1953), 69; Confederación General de Empleados de Comercio, *Memoria del Consejo Directivo* (Buenos Aires, 1953), 126.

12. Peter Ross, "Justicia social." On Peronist social insurance see, Torre and Pastoriza, "Democratización," 288–89, 295–99; Colin M. Lewis, "Social Insurance: Ideology and Policy in the Argentine, c. 1920–1966," in *Welfare, Poverty, and Development in Latin America*, ed. Christopher Abel and Colin M. Lewis (London: Macmillan, 1993), 175–85; Ricardo Riguera,

Seguro social integral (Buenos Aires: INPS, 1946); José González Galé, *Previsión social* (Buenos Aires: Losada, 1946).

13. Plotkin, *Mañana es San Péron*, 227–34; Fraser and Navarro, *Evita*, 116–22; Néstor Ferioli, *La Fundación Eva Perón* (Buenos Aires: Centro Editor de América Latina, 1990), vol. 2; Mónica Campins, Horacio Gaggero, and Alicia Garro, "La Fundación Eva Perón," in *Estado, corporativismo y acción social en Brasil, Argentina y Uruguay*, ed. Mónica Campins, Ana Frega Novales, and Angela María de Castro Gomes (Buenos Aires: Editorial Biblos/Fundación Simón Rodríguez, 1992), 49–108; Martín Stawski, "El populismo paralelo," in *Sueños de bienestar*, ed. Berrotarán, Jáuregui, and Rougier, 193–228; Carolina Barry, Karina Ramacciotti, and Adriana Valobra, eds., *La Fundación Eva Perón y las mujeres: Entre la provocación y la inclusión* (Buenos Aires: Editorial Biblos, 2008).

14. Campins, Gaggero, and Garro, "La Fundación," 85–88, 92–96; SIPA, *La asistencia social argentina*; Fundación Eva Peron/Servicio Internacional de Publicaciones Argentinas, *Colonias de vacaciones* (Buenos Aires, 1950); Subsecretaría de Informaciones, *Eva Perón y su obra social* (Buenos Aires, 1951).

15. Campins, Gaggero, and Garro, "La Fundación," 88–92, 94–96; Plotkin, *Mañana es San Perón*, 256–96.

16. Campins, Gaggero, and Garro, "La Fundación," 50; Fraser and Navarro, *Evita*, 118.

17. Managers possessed competing understandings of what types of services to provide, and debates raged in each field around everything from the aesthetics of public housing architecture to the structure of health care access. On the diverse output in the field of Peronist housing, urbanism, and public works, see Ballent, *Las huellas*.

18. Much has been written about the issue of business donations, and stories about Evita's skill in forcing "gifts" from the wealthy continue to circulate to this day. But recent studies have turned up little concrete evidence, and military investigations conducted immediately after Perón's fall did no better. Mariano Plotkin's study into the FEP finances has suggested a more nuanced picture in which business donations were given under threat of reprisal but also more freely in the hopes of securing special perks (procurement contracts, tax breaks, etc.) from the government. Worker contributions were at least equal to and mostly likely greater than the amount provided by businesses. For more on the FEP's finances, see Plotkin, *Mañana es San Perón*, 335–48; Campins, Gaggero, and Garro, "La Fundación," 70–80.

19. In some cases, a percentage of wage increases was deducted by the government or FEP and set aside for special projects, such as the building of a union hotel. The FEP, in turn, provided unions with additional funding; for example, the construction workers union obtained a 100,000-peso grant to build new headquarters in 1948. See Confederación General del Trabajo, *Anuario*, 120; *Obrero Ferroviario*, October 1950, 10; Federación de Obreros de Papel, *Manual del papelero*, 69.

20. Recent English-language works on ameliorative social programs in Latin America include Ann Zulawski, *Unequal Cures: Public Health and Political Change in Bolivia* (Durham, N.C.: Duke University Press, 2007); Katherine Elaine Bliss, *Compromised Positions: Prostitution, Public Health, and Gender Politics in Revolutionary Mexico City* (University Park: Pennsylvania State University Press, 2001); Marcos Cueto, *Cold War, Deadly Fevers: Malaria Eradication in Mexico, 1955–1975* (Washington, D.C.: Woodrow Wilson Center Press; Baltimore, Md.: Johns Hopkins University Press, 2007).

21. The term "organized community" itself came out of a 1949 philosophy conference tasked with doctrinal matters; see Carlos Altamirano, "Ideologías políticas y debate cívico," in

Nueva Historia Argentina, vol. 8, *Los Años Peronistas (1943–1955),* ed. Juan Carlos Torre (Buenos Aires: Editorial Sudamericana, 2002), 231–39.

22. Pablo Sirven, *Perón y los medios de comunicación (1943–1955)* (Buenos Aires: Centro Editor de América Latina, 1984), 251–60; Gambini, *Historia del peronismo,* 1:403–13; Doris Fagundes Haussen, *Rádio e política: Tempos de Vargas e Perón* (Porto Alegre, Brazil: EDIPU-CRS, 1997), 61–102; María Helena Capelato, *Multidões em cena: Propaganda política no var-guismo e no peronismo* (São Paulo: FAPESP, 1998).

23. Cane-Carrasco, *The Fourth Enemy*; Raanan Rein and Claudio Panella, eds., *Pe-ronismo y prensa escrita: Abordajes, miradas e interpretaciones nacionales y extranjeras* (La Plata, Argentina: Editorial de la Universidad Nacional de La Plata, 2008). On contemporary criti-cisms of censorship, see Américo Ghioldi, *La Argentina tiene miedo* (Montevideo, Uruguay: Talleres La Vanguardia en Exilio, 1954).

24. Plotkin, *Mañana es San Perón*; Gené, *Un mundo feliz*; Ciria, *Política y cultura popular.*

25. Luna, *Perón y su tiempo,* 1:323–62.

26. *Conoscamos nuestra constitución* (Buenos Aires: Talleres Gráficos Kraft, 1950), 22–23; Subsecretaría de Informaciones, *Declaración de los derechos del trabajador* (Buenos Aires, 1950).

27. Jeremy Adelman, *Republic of Capital: Buenos Aires and the Legal Transformation of the Atlantic World* (Stanford, Calif.: Stanford University Press, 1999), 293.

28. Photograph of float, May 1, 1948, doc. 174846, envelope 8, box 2931, AGN, Departa-mento de Fotografía.

29. Sirven, *Perón y los medios,* 122–27; Gambini, *Historia del peronismo,* 1:408–10; Ciria, *Política y cultura popular,* 261; Gené, *Un mundo felíz,* 29–64. State propaganda makers are rarely savory individuals, and Apold was apparently much feared by fellow Peronists for his collection of incriminating files about his peers. By 1955 this agency had accumulated vast financial resources and a staff of over a thousand employees.

30. Vicepresidencia de la Nación, Comisión Nacional de Investigaciones, *Libro negro de la segunda tiranía* (Buenos Aires, 1958), 83–84.

31. *Mundo Argentino,* September 21, 1955. Calendars and handkerchiefs can be found in the Hoover Institution's Perón collection.

32. On the political trope of the "construction of the new" and Peronism, see Capelato, *Multidões,* 114; Ciria, *Política y cultura popular,* 261–63.

33. *Justica social,* 16-mm film, 1948, AGN, Departamento de Cine, Audio y Video.

34. Subsecretaría de Informaciones, *Eva Perón y su obra social.*

35. Ulanovsky and Merkin, *Dias de radio.* The audio excerpts were transcribed from the book's accompanying compact disk.

36. Ballent, *Las huellas*; Aboy, *Viviendas*; Healey, *Ruins.*

37. Torre and Pastoriza, "Democratización," 301; Scarzanella, "El ocio peronista"; Elisa Pastoriza and Juan Carlos Torre, "Mar del Plata, un sueño de los argentinos," in *Historia de la vida privada en la Argentina,* vol. 3, *La Argentina entre multitudes y soledades: De los años treinta a la actualidad,* ed. Fernando Devoto and Marta Madero (Buenos Aires: Taurus, 1999): 49–78.

38. Dirección General de Relaciones Culturales y Difusión, *Turismo para el pueblo* (Buenos Aires, 1950), 1–48; Fundación Eva Perón/SIPA, *Colonias de vacaciones*; Confederación General de Empleados de Comercio, *Memoria del Consejo Directivo,* 126; Confederación Gen-eral del Trabajo, *Anuario,* 172–73.

39. Torre and Pastoriza, "Democratización."

40. Confederación General del Trabajo, *Anuario,* 172–73.

41. Direción General de Relaciones Culturales y Difusión, *Turismo.*

42. Gené, *Un mundo feliz,* 51–62.

43. Secretaría de Prensa y Difusión, *Nuestro hogar,* 35-mm film, 1952, at AGN, Departamento de Cine, Audio y Video. This depiction of tenement life had by the mid-1940s become a stock scene in film and theater, standing as a metaphor of the social problems facing popular sectors in the early twentieth century. By including this type of familiar scene, Soffici and other propagandists drew from mass cultural tropes to invigorate their partisan documents and celebrate the grandeur of the New Argentina.

44. Ibid.

45. Gené, *Mundo feliz.*

46. Ibid.; Gutiérrez and Romero, *Sectores populares,* 134; James, *Resistance and Integration,* 7–40.

47. Secretaría de Prensa y Difusión, *Fraternidad justicialista,* 35-mm film, date unknown, AGN, Departamento de Cine, Audio y Video. In a propaganda film produced by the Secretaría de Prensa y Difusión titled "Justicialist Fraternity," the FEP's "*tren sanitario*" was held up as an example of technological advancements in public health. The film profiled the inaugural trip of the "Tren Sanitario Eva Perón"—a train with hospital-like facilities built into each car. The train's mission was to wage the "battle for health, for dignification, for welfare"; a community of sugar workers in rural Tucumán was the first stop. The camera lavished attention on the medical equipment inside the train—the shiny X-ray machines, microscopes, dentist's chairs—as well as the white-frocked physicians and nurses going about their business. The film noted proudly that in just two weeks the staff had provided over 39,000 services to patients. These images of medical expertise contrasted with the views of the thousands of poor country folk in tattered clothes waiting outside the train (*Obrero Ferroviario,* April 1954, 1).

48. José M. Freire, *Nuevos vientos en la política social argentina* (Buenos Aires, 1950), 19–20.

49. On kitsch, gender, and the FEP's luxurious style, see Anahi Ballent, "El lenguaje del bibelot," in *La Fundación Eva Perón y las mujeres,* ed. Barry, Ramacciotti, and Valobra, 179–200; Ballent, *Las huellas.*

50. Fundación Eva Perón/Servicio Internacional de Publicaciones Argentinas, *Os lares de tránsito* (Buenos Aires, 1951); Campins, Gaggero, and Garro, "La Fundación," 85–86; Dos Santos, *Las mujeres peronistas,* 121.

51. Carolina Barry, "Mujeres en tránsito," in *La Fundación Eva Perón y las mujeres,* ed. Barry, Ramacciotti, and Valobra, 77–117. See also Mirta Zaida Lobato, ed., *Cuando las mujeres reinaban: Belleza, virtud y poder en la Argentina del siglo XX* (Buenos Aires: Editorial Biblos, 2005).

52. Fundación Eva Perón/Servicio Internacional de Publicaciones, *El hogar de la empleada* (Buenos Aires, 1952); *Mundo Argentino,* May 3, 1950, 34–35; Campins, Gaggero, and Garro, "La Fundación," 86–87; Omar Acha, "Dos estrategias de domesticación de la mujer joven trabajadora: La Casa y el Hogar de la Empleada," in *La Fundación Eva Perón y las mujeres,* ed. Barry, Ramacciotti, and Valobra, 151–78.

53. FEP/SIPA, *El hogar,* 36–37.

54. Robert Frost, "Machine Liberation: Inventing Housewives and Home Appliances in Interwar France," *French Historical Studies* 18, no. 1 (Spring 1993): 109–30.

55. *La Carta,* undated, University of Miami, Perón Collection.

56. Dos Santos, *Las mujeres peronistas,* 39. A similar anecdote regarding the generosity of public housing was recounted by María Elena Warner, a longtime resident of Barrio Evita, in a U.S. documentary; see *Evita, the Woman behind the Myth,* videocassette, History Television Network, 1996. On the sparseness of public housing amenities, see Aboy, *Viviendas,* 75–114.

57. Eva Perón, *La razón de mi vida y otros escritos* (Buenos Aires: Planeta, 1996), 159–60. There is some question as to how many of the views expressed in this book are Evita's rather than those of her handlers.

58. Ibid., 160–61.

59. Navarro and Fraser, *Evita,* 114–33; Alicia Dujovne Ortiz, *Eva Perón,* trans. Shawn Fields (New York: St Martin's, 1996), 207–43.

60. Gaggero and Garro, *Del trabajo,* 68–69.

61. Barry, "Mujeres en tránsito," 90–91.

62. On the "tactics of the habitat," see Michel de Certeau, *The Practice of Everyday Life* (Berkeley: University of California Press, 1984); Pierre Bourdieu, *Outline of a Theory of Practice* (Cambridge: Cambridge University Press, 1977); Kotkin, *Magnetic Mountain,* 21–23.

63. Torre and Pastoriza, "Democratización," 296–97.

64. Dos Santos, *Las mujeres peronistas,* 35; Fraser and Navarro, *Evita,* 117.

65. Statistics on the total increase of state employees are unavailable. Scholars comparing the 1946 and 1960 national censuses have suggested that white-collar public employment was one of the occupational categories that grew the most in this period. By way of comparison, the total spending of federal agencies increased in real terms nearly threefold between 1941 and 1949 (Gerchunoff and Llach, *Ciclo de la ilusión,* 179). For the sociology of occupational trends, see Torrado, *Estructura social,* 263–310.

66. David Rock, "Radical Populism and the Conservative Elite, 1912–1930," in *Argentina in the Twentieth Century,* ed. Rock (Pittsburgh, Pa.: University of Pittsburgh Press, 1975), 75–81.

67. Letter, Oct. 23, 1946, legajo 583, AGN-MAT. In subsequent citations I will identify the document number assigned to the letter or, if this is lacking, the date and/or name of the correspondent.

68. Fraser and Navarro, *Evita,* 137–40; Dujovne Ortiz, *Eva Perón,* 252–55, 280–89; Gambini, *Historia del peronismo,* 2:84–85; Barry, *Evita Capitana,* 186.

69. For example, Américo, a rural worker from the town of Felicia, Santa Fe, found work as a farmhand at an experimental agricultural facility, thanks to the MAT's intervention (his good luck ran out, as he was soon laid off); see his letter, April 1950, doc. 75, legajo 584, AGN-MAT. On Esperanza's size, see J. Walter Thompson Company, *The Latin American Markets* (New York: McGraw-Hill, 1956), 14.

70. Letter from Amalia Erminda Goicochea, September 1951; letter from Dolores García, May 21, 1951, both legajo 579, AGN-MAT.

71. Letter from Tulia Gaute, n.d., legajo 579, AGN-MAT.

72. Letter from María Teresa Marti, September 3, 1951; letter from Josefina Valía de Gaccetta, August 16, 1951, both legajo 579, AGN-MAT. For more on Evita and religion, see Fraser and Navarro, *Evita,* 148–92; J. M. Taylor, *Eva Perón: The Myths of a Woman* (Chicago: University of Chicago Press, 1979); Tomás Eloy Martínez, *Santa Evita* (Buenos Aires: Planeta, 1997). Propaganda makers often presented Evita in mystical, religious terms, especially in texts directed at children. For an early example, see Fundación de Ayuda Social Maria Eva Duarte de Perón, *Por la ruta de los cuentos mágicos* (Buenos Aires, 1948). See also Frank Graziano, *Cultures of Devotion: Folk Saints of Spanish America* (Oxford: Oxford University Press, 2007).

73. Letter from Eduardo A. L. Chesaux, May 26, 1951, legajo 579, AGN-MAT.

74. Letters from Federico Cano, January 18, 1951; letter from Miguel Espíndola, December 21, 1951, both legajo 579, AGN-MAT.

75. Letter from Susana González, July 1950, doc. 240, legajo 584; see also MAT response, December 1953, doc. 2817, legajo 587, AGN-MAT.

76. Letter from Elena D'Alessandri de Létora, April 1951, legajo 579, AGN-MAT.

77. Barry, *Evita Capitana*, 186–88. In her study of the PPF, Barry examines the log books from a unidad básica that suggest the type of direct social assistance requests channeled through these organizations to the FEP. They resemble in general terms the demands from letter writers surveyed in this chapter: for housing, work, medicines, sewing machines, and basic consumables.

78. Letter from Fernando Di Matteo, August 1951, legajo 579, AGN-MAT.

79. Letter from Mario Vaudagna, July 23, 1951, legajo 579, AGN-MAT.

80. "Una carta para la compañera Evita," *Mundo Peronista*, January 15, 1952, 18–22.

81. I thank Donna Guy for drawing this comparison to my attention. Recent studies of these transnational circuits of consumer culture in Latin America include Micol Seigel, *Uneven Encounters: Making Race and Nation in Brazil and the United States* (Durham, N.C.: Duke University Press, 2009), 13–66; McCrossen, ed., *Land of Necessity*; Maureen O'Dougherty, *Consumption Intensified: The Politics of Middle-Class Daily Life in Brazil* (Durham, N.C: Duke University Press, 2002); Orlove, *Allure of the Foreign*.

Chapter 5: Parables of Prodigality

1. *El Trabajador de la Carne,* July 1948, 3.

2. Histories of consumption in this vein include T. H. Breen, *The Marketplace of Revolution: How Consumer Politics Shaped American Independence* (Oxford: Oxford University Press, 2004); de Grazia and Furlough, eds., *The Sex of Things*; Arjun Appadurai, ed., *The Social Life of Things: Commodities in Global Perspective* (Cambridge: Cambridge University Press, 1986); O'Dougherty, *Consumption Intensified*.

3. See note 3 to chapter 3.

4. Documenting class resentment is a tricky business. For impressions of middle-class views in this period, see Luna, *Perón y su tiempo*, 1:466–507; Goldar, *Buenos Aires*. A series of anti-Peronist tracts published after 1955 sheds light on these attitudes. See E. F. Sanchez Zinny, *El culto de la infamia: Historia documentada de la segunda tiranía argentina* (Avellaneda, Argentina: Artes Gráficas Bartolomé V. Chiesino, 1958); Raúl Damonte Taborda, *Ayer fue San Perón: 12 años de humillación Argentina* (Buenos Aires: Ediciones Gure, 1955). On anti-Peronist stereotyping, class, and consumption, see Natalia Milanesio, "Peronists and *Cabecitas*: Stereotypes and Anxieties at the Peak of Social Change," in *New Cultural History of Peronism*, ed. Matthew Karush and Oscar Chamosa (Durham, N.C.: Duke University Press, 2010), 53–84.

5. Goldar, *Buenos Aires,* 55–60.

6. Luna, *Perón y su tiempo*, 1:467; Goldar, *Buenos Aires*, 168.

7. Historians are beginning to explore Peronism's impact on the formation of middle-class identities as defined in opposition to the emergent working class of this era; see Sergio Visacovsky and Enrique Garguin, eds., *Moralidades, economías, e identidades de clase media: Estudios historicos y etnograficos* (Buenos Aires: Antropologia, 2009). On the racial politics of

the Peronist era, see Oscar Chamosa, "Criollo and Peronist: The Argentine Folklore Movement during the First Peronism, 1943–1955," in *New Cultural History of Peronism*, ed. Matthew Karush and Oscar Chamosa (Durham, N.C.: Duke University Press, 2010), 113–42; Chamosa, "Indigenous or Criollo: The Myth of White Argentina in Tucumán's Calchaquí Valley," *Hispanic American Historical Review* 88 (Feb. 2008): 71–106; Chamosa, *Argentine Folklore Movement*.

8. Francisco Domínguez, *El apóstol de la mentira: Juan Perón* (Buenos Aires: Ediciones La Reja, 1956 [1951]), 76.

9. On the legacies of Evita's "black legend," see Taylor, *Eva Perón: Myths,* 78–85, 97–104.

10. Flavia Fiorucci, "Between Institutional Survival and Intellectual Commitment: The Case of the Argentine Society of Writers during Perón's Rule, 1945–1955," *The Americas* 62, no. 4 (Apr. 2006): 591–622; Garcia Sebastiani, *Los antiperonistas*; Federico Neiburg, *Los intelectuales y la invención del peronismo* (Buenos Aires: Alianza Editorial, 1998).

11. Jorge Luis Borges and Adolfo Bioy Casares, "La fiesta del monstruo," in *Nuevos Cuentos de Bustos Domecq* (Buenos Aires: Libreria la Ciudad, 1977), 87–103. Borges, at least, had good reason to be angry. Peronist officials had reappointed him from library director to subinspector of poultry in the municipal markets.

12. Américo Ghioldi, *Alpargatas y libros en la historia argentina* (Buenos Aires: La Vanguardia, 1946).

13. Georges de Hemricourt, *J'ai vu l'Argentine de Perón* (Brussels: Charles Dessart, 1953), 115.

14. Greenup and Greenup, *Revolution*, 25–38.

15. Bruce, *Those Perplexing Argentines*, 49–50.

16. Teasing out the reactions of consumers to these political appeals is highly problematic. The available, if largely indirect, evidence suggests that the pronouncements of Perón and his advisers resonated with at least some individuals sympathetic to the regime, for whom personal acts of consumption became infused with political meaning. In his book *Doña Maria's Story,* the historian Daniel James presents the life story of María Roldán, a worker and union activist from the meatpacking town of Berisso. Roldán recalled the immediate postwar years as a time of widespread joy—"Berisso was one of the happiest places on the face of the earth"— memories colored, no doubt, by the tough times facing workers in subsequent decades. For Roldán, Peronist rule brought labor legislation, the right to vote, and union social services but also movies and cheap credit to buy kitchen appliances: "Under Perón we discovered many things. A pair of nylons, a nice dress. Life changed. We could buy things like refrigerators. I bought my first in 1947. We could buy sheets, mattresses. . . . In Berisso four schools were built by Perón's government, and the possibilities of our children improved." Her story presents individual consumer improvements as part of a collective advance of the working class, as the opening up of new opportunities and comforts previously out of reach (Daniel James, *Doña Maria's Story: Life History, Memory, and Political Identity* [Durham, N.C.: Duke University Press, 2000], 70–71).

17. Milanesio, "Peronists and *Cabecitas*," 65–68.

18. Susana Saulquin, *La moda en la Argentina* (Buenos Aires: Emecé, 1990), 118–22; Fraser and Navarro, *Evita*, 88–101.

19. J. Perón, *Obras completas*, 8:122, 153–58, 231–36.

20. Freire, *Nuevos vientos*, 69.

21. Ibid., 67–70.

22. *Mundo Argentino,* March 12, 1947.

23. *Mundo Argentino,* January 3, 1951; *Para Ti,* March 11, 1947.

24. *Revista de Economía Argentina* (Mar. 1946): 71–76, (May 1946): 144.

25. *Noticias Gráficas,* July 26, 1946, n.p.

26. Ministerio de Interior, *Leyes,* 7.

27. Anson Rabinbach, *The Human Motor: Energy, Fatigue, and the Origins of Modernity* (New York: Basic Books, 1990).

28. Dornbusch and Edwards, *Macroeconomics of Populism,* 7–44.

29. Gerchunoff and Llach, *Ciclo de la ilusión,* 206.

30. Louise M. Doyon, "Conflictos obreros durante el régimen peronista (1946–1955)," in *La formación del sindicalismo,* ed. Torre, 223–63; Michael Snodgrass, "Topics Not Suitable for Propaganda: Working-Class Resistance under Peronism," in *Workers' Control in Latin America,* ed. Jonathan C. Brown (Chapel Hill: University of North Carolina Press, 1997), 159–88; Baily, *Labor, Nationalism,* 121–61.

31. Alfredo Gómez Morales, interview by Leandro Gutiérrez, May 17 and 19, 1972, Instituto Di Tella and Columbia Oral History Project, 60–68; Gambini, *Historia del peronismo,* 1:21, 148–51; Luna, *Perón y su tiempo,* 1:113–25.

32. Gerchunoff and Antúnez, "De la bonanza," 159–72.

33. Subsecretaría de Informaciones, *Guerra a muerte a los especuladores dijo Perón* (Buenos Aires, 1950); Organización de Consumidores, *Defienda sus Pesos! Vigile los precios! No pague un centavo más!* (Buenos Aires, 1950).

34. Subsecretaría de Informaciones, *Guerra a muerte,* 4–11.

35. Confederación General de Empleados de Comercio, *Memoria,* 46.

36. *Noticias Gráficas,* September 29, 1950, n.p.

37. Barry, *Evita capitana,* 164.

38. Subsecretaría de Informaciones, *Guerra a muerte,* 11–13. See also Milanesio, "Guardian Angels."

39. Recchini de Lattes, *La participación,* 11; Cosse, *Estigmas de nacimiento*; Ramacciotti and Valobra, *Generando el peronismo.*

40. Barbara Weinstein has explored similar dynamics in Brazil. In São Paulo, state and business officials teamed up through vocational programs to mold the proper roles for male and female workers. See Barbara Weinstein, "Unskilled Worker, Skilled Housewife: Constructing the Working-Class Woman in São Paulo, Brazil," in *The Gendered Worlds of Latin American Women Workers,* ed. John D. French and Daniel James (Durham, N.C.: Duke University Press, 1997), 72–99.

41. Caja Nacional de Ahorro Postal, *Economía familiar* (Buenos Aires, 1950). Consumer education propaganda was also disseminated through the labor press; see, e.g., *Obrero Ferroviario,* Oct. 1950, 12; and Nov. 1950, 11.

42. Plotkin, *Mañana es San Perón,* 211–96.

43. Barry, *Evita Capitana,* 269–70.

44. Ferioli, *Fundación Eva Perón,* 139; Campins, Gaggero, and Garro, "Fundación," 98–99.

45. Caja Nacional de Ahorro Postal, *Economía familiar.*

46. Ibid., *El ahorro,* 11–38.

47. Rougier and Fiszbein, "De Don Derochín," 115–19, 132–35.

48. Enrique Santos Discepolo, *Mordisquito, a mí no me vas a contar* (Buenos Aires: Ediciones Realidad Política, 1986).

49. Selva Zulema Durán de González to Ministry of Technical Affairs, 1951, doc. 13024, legajo 307, AGN-MAT. For an alternative reading of this same letter, see Elena, "What the People Want," 81.

50. Jacobs, *Pocketbook Politics*; Cohen, *Consumer's Republic*; Ina Zweiniger-Bargielowska, *Austerity in Britain: Rationing, Controls, and Consumption 1939–1955* (Oxford: Oxford University Press, 2000); Laura C. Nelson, *Measured Excess: Status, Gender, and Consumer Nationalism in South Korea* (New York: Columbia University Press, 2000).

51. For Mexico, see Enrique C. Ochoa, *Feeding Mexico: The Political Uses of Food since 1910* (Wilmington, Del.: SR Books, 2000). Lázaro Cárdenas created the State Food Agency in 1937 to distribute subsidized goods to urban consumers in Mexico, and he complained about merchants "who generally speculate[d] with the basic needs of the poor." The PRI struggled to balance the political imperative of satisfying popular sector consumers with increasingly liberal economic policies. For Peru, see Paulo Drinot, "Food, Race and Working-Class Identity: Restaurantes Populares and Populism in 1930s Peru," *The Americas* 62, no. 2 (Oct. 2005): 245–70.

52. Jorge del Rio, Ministerio de Trabajo y Previsión, Instituto Nacional de Previsión Social, *La defensa del consumidor* (Buenos Aires, 1951), 22–26; Congreso Nacional de Planificación, Anteproyecto Segundo Plan Quinquenal, 20, legajo 395, AGN-MAT.

53. *Norte* (Quilmes), April 25, 1947, 1, 4; May 12, 1947, 7, 9; Del Rio, *Defensa del consumidor*.

54. Juan C. Juárez, *Los trabajadores en función social* (Buenos Aires: Libro de Edición Argentina, 1947) 97–100; Federación de Obreros de Papel, *Manual*; *Mundo Argentino*, April 25, 1951, 10.

55. Confederación General de Empleados de Comercio, *Memoria*, 89–93. Sucessos de las Américas, "Inauguración de Almacenes Justicialistas," 35-mm newsreel, AGN, Departamento de Cine, Audio y Video. On Borlenghi's place in the regime, see Rein, *In the Shadow*, 24–38.

56. Accounts differ as to the name of the former store, called either Tienda Ciudad de Mexico or Granmex. For a report on the inauguration and business reactions, see "New Cooperative Store Opened in Buenos Aires," *Confidential U.S. State Department Central Files. Argentina, 1950–1954*, May 14, 1951, reel 12, doc. 835.052/5-1451, U.S. State Department Central Files.

57. Eva Perón, *Discursos Completos*, 2:315–16.

58. Ferioli, *Fundación Eva Perón*, 139. Campins, Gaggero, and Garro, "La Fundación," 98–99; *Mundo Peronista*, April 1, 1952, 10–11.

59. *Mundo Peronista*, April 1, 1952, 10–11.

60. Servicio Internacional de Publicaciones Argentinas, *The Eva Perón Provision Stores* (Buenos Aires, 1954), n.p.; *Noticias Gráficas*, June 10, 1951; *Mundo Peronista*, "Nuevos Barrios de Buenos Aires," February 15, 1952, 22–24; idem, "Este es mi barrio," March 15, 1952, 21–23.

61. Eva Perón, *Discursos Completos*, 1:182–85; Ferioli, *Fundación Eva Perón*, 105–08; *Noticias Gráficas*, September 3 and June 10, 1951.

62. For an extended analysis, see Eduardo Elena, "Peronism in 'Good Taste': Culture and Consumption in the Magazine *Argentina*," in *New Cultural History of Peronism*, ed. Matthew Karush and Oscar Chamosa (Durham, N.C.: Duke University Press, 2010), 209–38.

63. Plotkin, *Mañana es San Perón*, 95–99; Page, *Perón*, 225, 235–37. Gustavo Martínez Zuviría served as the editor-in-chief and appears to have managed the magazine's monthly production; he was one of Argentina's best-selling authors of fiction (published under the pseudonym Hugo Wast) and a celebrated member of right-wing nationalist circles. His long-

time position as the director of the National Library (1931-55) gave him a degree of influence within the broader intellectual community and, eventually, a platform within the Peronist government. Other contributors to *Argentina*—Carlos Ibarguren, Manuel Gálvez, Delfina Bunge de Gálvez—came from similar nationalist and Catholic backgrounds; see Juan Carlos Moreno, *Gustavo Martínez Zuviría* (Buenos Aires: Ediciones Culturales Argentinas, 1962); Flavia Fiorucci, "La cultura, el libro y la lectura bajo el peronismo: El caso de las bibliotecas," unpublished paper.

64. Oscar Ivanissevich, *Rindo Cuenta, 1893-1973* (Buenos Aires: Talleres Gráficos del Ministerio de Cultura y Educación, 1973), 2:319-20.

65. On the diversity of print culture, see Carlos Ulanovsky and Marta Merkin, *Paren las rotativas: Una historia de grandes diarios, revistas y periodistas argentinos* (Buenos Aires: Espasa, 1997).

66. *Argentina*, July 1950, 33; and February 1949, 70.

67. *Argentina*, January 1950, 22-24.

68. *Argentina*, July 1949, 56; and June 1949, 56.

69. *Argentina*, September 1949, 70-72. This conclusion was confirmed by the employment profile of the audience, who worked in a variety of working- and middle-class jobs as public employees, professionals, and merchants, but with clerks (*empleados de comercio*, 15 percent) and workers (*obreros*, 13 percent) as the largest categories. In addition, more than one-third of *Argentina*'s readers did not earn a salary, including housewives (14 percent) and students and recruits (21 percent).

70. If one compares it to media circulation figures from 1945 (the last date for which reliable statistics exist), a more modest picture emerges: in that year the Socialist Party newspaper *La Vanguardia* sold 70,000 copies a day, and two Yiddish papers (*Di Presse* and *El Diario Israelita*) sold around 45,000 each. See Cane-Carrasco, *The Fourth Enemy*.

71. *Argentina*, August 1949, 54.

72. There are other theories why Ivanissevich was forced out. In addition to performing his ministerial duties, he served as personal physician to Juan and Eva Perón and was among the first to become aware of the First Lady's cervical cancer. He advocated a hysterectomy, a procedure that Evita rejected and, so the theory goes, caused her to turn against this staunch Peronist. See Page, *Perón*, 235.

73. Daryl Williams, *Culture Wars in Brazil* (Durham, N.C.: Duke University Press, 2001); García Sebastiani, *Los antiperonistas*.

74. Naturally, many of these actors broke with tradition by creating new political "subcultures," and they sought to imprint their own socialist, fascist, or partisan characteristics onto existing cultural practices. But like their Argentine counterparts, they tapped into the legitimacy of established hierarchies of taste in seeking to create a new hegemony. Historians have suggested that the pursuit of cultural orthodoxy served different political purposes: in some cases, it offered a means for a new state elite to shore up ties with an intellectual and managerial stratum (as in the 1930s Soviet Union and Vargas-era Brazil), and in others, it provided leaders with a means to protect "national values" against threats to sovereignty posed by mass cultural imports (as in postwar Mexico and Fascist Italy). See Williams, *Culture Wars*; Joseph, Rubenstein, and Zolov, eds., *Fragments*; Sheila Fitzpatrick, *The Cultural Front: Power and Culture in Revolutionary Russia* (Ithaca, N.Y.: Cornell University Press, 1992); de Grazia, "Nationalizing Women."

75. Julio Moreno, *Yankee Don't Go Home! Mexican Nationalism, American Business Culture, and the Shaping of Modern Mexico, 1920-1950* (Chapel Hill: University of North Carolina Press, 2003); O'Brien, *Century of U.S. Capitalism*.

76. De Grazia, *Irresistible Empire*, 118-29.

Chapter 6: The Counterpolitics of Voice

1. "Un día en la vida de un obrero argentino," *Argentina,* September 1949, 22–24.

2. The most ambitious such oral history project has been carried out by Daniel James and Mirta Zaida Lobato on the predominately working-class community of Berisso. See James, *Doña María's Story*; Mirta Zaida Lobato, *La vida en las fábricas: Trabajo, protesta y política en una comunidad obrera, Berisso (1904–1970)* (Buenos Aires: Entrepasados/Prometeo, 2001).

3. For an insightful analysis of the genres of public letter writing, see Sheila Fitzpatrick, "Supplicants and Citizens: Public Letter-Writing in Soviet Russia in the 1930s," *Slavic Review* 55, no. 1 (Spring 1996): 78–105. On letter writing in midcentury Latin America, see W. John Green, *Gaitanismo, Left Liberalism, and Popular Mobilization in Colombia* (Gainsville: University of Florida Press, 2003); Joel Wolfe, "Father of the Poor or Mother of the Rich? Getúlio Vargas, Industrial Workers, and Constructions of Class, Gender, and Populism in São Paulo, 1930–1954," *Radical History Review* 58 (Winter 1994): 80–111; Robert M. Levine, *Father of the Poor? Vargas and His Era* (Cambridge: Cambridge University Press, 1998).

4. The term "counterpolitics" is borrowed from Foucauldian approaches, though it has a potentially wider applicability. For further definitions, see Colin Gordon, "Government Rationality: An Introduction," in *The Foucault Effect: Studies in Governmentality,* ed. Graham Burchell, Colin Gordon, and Peter Miller (Chicago: University of Chicago Press, 1991), 5.

5. On Peronist letter writing, see Elena, "What the People Want"; Acha, "Sociedad Civil."

6. Scott, *Seeing.*

7. Even if one allows for propagandistic excess and accepts a more modest estimate of half this number, this crowd's size is startling considering the total Argentine population was around 16 million at the time. For estimates and general narratives of the Cabildo Abierto, see Luna, *Perón y su tiempo,* vol. 2, *La comunidad organizada, 1950–1952* (Buenos Aires: Editorial Sudamericana, 1985), 180–91; Page, *Perón,* 240–46.

8. For analysis of electoral results in the Peronist era, see the collected essays in Manuel Mora y Araujo and Ignacio Llorente, eds., *El voto peronista* (Buenos Aires: Editorial Sudamericana, 1980).

9. *La Nación,* December 4, 1951, 1.

10. Poster, doc. 197326, envelope 62, box 1307, AGN, Departamento de Fotografía; Ministerio de Obras Públicas, *Labor realizada y en ejecución, Deciembre 1943–Junio 1947* (Buenos Aires, 1947).

11. Ballent, *Las huellas,* 259–65.

12. For an account of these contests and the context of radio under Perón, see Ulanovsky and Merkin, *Dias de radio,* 121–76. On the subsecretariat, see Gené, *Un mundo feliz,* 29–64.

13. Beatriz Sarlo, *La imaginación técnica: Sueños modernos de la cultura argentina* (Buenos Aires: Ediciones Nueva Visión, 1992).

14. Elena, "What the People Want," 91–93. All the letters examined in this chapter arrived at the Ministry of Technical Affairs between December 1951 and March 1952.

15. Ibid. Letters classified as concerning "public works in general" and "sanitary works" make up approximately 27 percent of all the Perón Wants to Know letters in the archive. These estimates are based on the categories used by the National Archive to classify the correspondence. My sense is that the basic geographic and demographic distributions for the petitioners hold true, with some variation, for other topics. See Archivo General de la Nación, *Fondo Documental Secretaría Técnica 1º y 2º Presidencia del Teniente General Juan Domingo Perón (1936–1955)* (Buenos Aires: Archivo General de la Nación, 1995).

16. Letter from María del Carmen Albuerne, doc. 6607, legajo 307, AGN-MAT.

17. Letter from Sociedad de Fomento "Villa Spinola," doc. 8664, legajo 12, AGN-MAT. It is important to note that the term "villa" in this time period did not necessarily mean a *villa miseria* (shantytown); it could equally denote a neighborhood of recent settlement. In some cases petitioners made reference to buying plots of land through real estate agents, suggesting that villa residents were not primarily squatters.

18. Ibid.

19. Using Partha Chatterjee's concept of "political society," Omar Acha has examined the MAT letters in order to suggest a way beyond a rigid dichotomy of state and civil society; see Acha, "Sociedad civil." See also Partha Chatterjee, "Two Poets and Death: On Civil and Political Society in the Non-Christian World," in *Questions of Modernity,* ed. Timothy Mitchell (Minneapolis: University of Minnesota Press, 2000), 35–48.

20. Letters from residents of La Puerta, Córdoba, doc. 1497, legajo 320; letter from residents of El Fortín, Córdoba, doc. 8154, legajo 254, AGN-MAT.

21. Gutiérrez and Romero, *Sectores populares*; de Privitellio, *Vecinos y ciudadanos.*

22. Research on clientelism and participation in Latin America has widened our outlook on participation, in the process highlighting the often hidden interactions between the average citizen and political authorities. See John A. Booth and Mitchell Seligson, eds., *Political Participation in Latin America,* vol. 1, *Citizen and State* (New York: Holmes and Meier, 1978); Javier Auyero, *Poor People's Politics: Peronist Survival Networks and the Legacy of Evita* (Durham, N.C.: Duke University Press, 2000); Nancy R. Powers, *Grassroots Expectations of Democracy and Economy: Argentina in Comparative Perspective* (Pittsburgh: University of Pittsburgh Press, 2001).

23. Letter from residents of General Ballivián, December 10, 1951, doc. 6475, legajo 301, AGN-MAT.

24. Letter from Federación Argentina, Unión Personal Panaderias Pastelerias y Afines, doc. 6657, legajo 146, AGN-MAT. The union offered the following estimate of monthly expenditures: commuting costs, 30.00 pesos; rent for a one-room home, 200.00; electrical bill, 8.00; food, 600.00; clothes and other, 100.00; 8 percent deduction for retirement fund, 43.60; "*Changa solidaria,*" 23.00. The spending totaled 1,004.80 pesos, and income was 545.00 pesos, which left a deficit of 459.80 pesos.

25. Letter from Unión de Obreros y Empleados Municipales, "17 de Octubre," December 20, 1951, doc. 7592, legajo 43, AGN-MAT.

26. Letter from Miguel Eguiazú, January 28, 1952, doc. 17721, legajo 181, AGN-MAT.

27. Letter from Jubilados Ferroviarios de Mendoza, December 24, 1951, doc. 11030, legajo 184, AGN-MAT.

28. Letter from Rosario Iman, doc. 5873, legajo 106; letter from Pascual Romano, doc. 17101, legajo 327, AGN-MAT.

29. Letter from Unión Hacheros y Peones Rurales, Villa Berthet, El Chaco, December 21, 1951, doc. 8074; letter from Cecilio Roberto Carballo, n.d., doc. 8668, both legajo 43, AGN-MAT.

30. Torre and Pastoriza, "Democratización," 262.

31. Letter from Pablo Ricardo Castaldo, n.d., doc. 15018, legajo 223, AGN-MAT.

32. Letter from residents of Las Perdices, Córdoba, December 1951, doc. 12158, legajo 36, AGN-MAT. See also letter from residents of Balcarce, Buenos Aires, December 17, 1951, doc. 7783; letter from residents of Paraná, Entre Rios, December 12, 1951, doc. 12180, both legajo 36, AGN-MAT.

33. Letter from G. Rodríguez, n.d., doc. 17424, legajo 79; letter from residents of Salta, n.d., doc. 12302, legajo 41, AGN-MAT. Consumers in other nations also turned to letter

writing as a means to communicate this type of microlevel detail about market conditions to authorities at the apex of the state, including Franklin Roosevelt; see Jacobs, *Pocketbook Politics*, 124.

34. Letter from José Cabrera, December 29, 1951, doc. 17172, legajo 365, AGN-MAT.

35. Letter from Mercedes Juncos, January 28, 1952, doc. 12545, legajo 331, AGN-MAT. The original Spanish of this letter gives some sense of the flavor and tone of these documents: "Se puede constar que en muchos pueblos de esta provincia, el comerciante disfruta con su venganza comprandose con su dinero a los señores hinspectores [sic], a cierta autoridades comunales porque desgraciadamente havemos [sic] obreros que damos la vida por Peron y otro [sic] dan un grito Viva Peron y hasiendonse [sic] ver grandes Peronistas para buscar sus comodidades y cargarse de dinero."

36. Letter from Mario Oscar López, n.d., doc. 17673, legajo 365; letter from Armando García, April 7, 1952, doc. 9668, legajo 41, AGN-MAT.

37. Letter from Alvaro Podesta, December 25, 1951, doc. 11510, legajo 181, AGN-MAT.

38. Darío Macro and César Tcach, eds., *La invención del peronismo en el interior del país* (Santa Fe, Argentina: Universidad Nacional del Litoral, 2003); James P. Brennan and Ofelia Pianetto, eds., *Region and Nation: Politics, Economics, and Society in Twentieth-Century Argentina* (New York: St. Martin's, 2000). The tension between reformist desires and entrenched political traditions is a major theme in histories of Latin American populism and the Left. See Alan Knight, "Cardenismo: Juggernaut or Jalopy?" *Journal of Latin American Studies* 26, no. 1 (1994): 73–109.

39. Letter from Termas de Río Hondo, Santiago del Estero, January 16, 1952, doc. 7554, legajo 331 (quotation); letter from José Bellido, December 1, 1951, doc. 12630, legajo 365; letter from Flor de Oro, Santa Fé, December 1951, , doc. 13617, legajo 41, AGN-MAT.

40. Letter from Luís Munita, December 31, 1951, doc. 8485, legajo 331; letter from CGT in Laboulaye, Córdoba, April 8, 1952, doc. 9603, legajo 41, AGN-MAT.

41. Letter from Federación Argentina de Centros Almaceneros, December 10, 1951, doc. 8699, legajo 41; letter from Asociación de Patrones Carniceros de Capital and Gran Buenos Aires, December 27, 1951, doc. 6528, legajo 331, AGN-MAT.

42. Letter from Sindicáto Argentino de Cigarreros Minoristas, January 3, 1952, doc. 17192, legajo 181, AGN-MAT.

43. Letter from Centro de Almaceneros de Avellaneda, December 31, 1951, doc. 8499, legajo 331, AGN-MAT.

44. On the creation of the CGE, see Brennan and Rougier, *Politics of National Capitalism*; Maria Seoane, *El burgués maldito* (Buenos Aires: Planeta, 1998).

45. Powers, *Grassroots Expectations*, 13–33.

46. Letter from Santos Olivera, n.d., doc. 16501, legajo 214, AGN-MAT.

47. Letter from María de Pereira, December 29, 1951, doc. 7363, legajo 133, AGN-MAT.

48. Letter from Amadeo Tresseras, January 25, 1952, doc. 17881, legajo 365, AGN-MAT.

49. Albert O. Hirschman, *Exit, Voice, and Loyalty: Responses to Decline in Firms, Organizations, and States* (Cambridge, Mass.: Harvard University Press, 1970).

50. Letter from Amadeo Tresseras; letter from Agrupación Peronista Ferroviaria, December 27, 1951, doc. 9314, legajo 79, AGN-MAT.

51. Letter from Libertad Ravizzini, n.d., doc. 12882, legajo 88, AGN-MAT.

52. James, *Resistance and Integration*; Steven Levitsky, *La transformación del justicialismo: Del partido sindical al partido clientelista, 1983–1999*, trans. Leandro Wolfson (Buenos Aires: Siglo Veintiuno, 2005); James W. McGuire, *Peronism without Perón: Unions, Parties, and Democracy in Argentina* (Stanford, Calif.: Stanford University Press, 1997).

53. Letter from Pro Casa de Luchador Peronista, December 1951, doc. 7142, legajo 351; letter from Juan Alfano, January 21, 1952, doc. 16247, legajo 41, AGN-MAT.

54. Letter from Sindicato de Cargadores de Camiones, n.d., doc. 10670; letter from Elias Tossounian, December 13, 1951, doc. 15167, both legajo 106, AGN-MAT.

55. Letter from Cecilio Roberto Carballo, n.d., doc. 8688, legajo 43, AGN-MAT.

56. Letter from Neuquén, December 1951, doc. 17160, legajo 351, AGN-MAT.

57. Letter from Enrique Piñero, January 1952, doc. 16381, legajo 331; letter from Pedro Echarren, December 1951, doc. 10830, legajo 106; letter from unidad básica, Buenos Aires, January 22, 1952, doc. 16396, legajo 331; letter from Pedro Callero, December 21, 1951, doc. 15353, legajo 106, AGN-MAT.

58. Letter from Emiliano Zucano, April 10, 1952, doc. 18872, legajo 79; letter from Joaquín Oscar Vicedo and Antonio Adolfo García Areso (quotation), December 6, 1951, doc. 5382, legajo 106, AGN-MAT.

59. Letter from Julián Guillermo Heredia, December 28, 1951, doc. 10186, legajo 331, AGN-MAT.

60. Letter from Unión Obrera de Construcción, March 1952, doc. 9496, legajo 133, AGN-MAT.

61. Letter from Ricardo Silvani and other residents of Remedios de Escalada, December 15, 1951, doc. 9407, legajo 181, AGN-MAT.

62. Letter from Unidad Básica, Buenos Aires, January 30, 1952, doc. 17296, legajo 79; letter from Agrupación Peronista Ferroviaria; letter from Rodolfo de Rocha, December 14, 1951, doc. 10510, legajo 365; letter from Juan Alfano, AGN-MAT.

63. Letter from Lanus, April 7, 1952, doc. 9410, legajo 181, AGN-MAT.

64. Barry, *Evita capitana*, 269–70.

65. Letter from Asociación Amas de Casa, January 30, 1952, doc. 14003, legajo 133, AGN-MAT.

66. Letter from Angela Fraquella (quotation), December 6, 1951, doc. 14288, legajo 133; letter from female municipal employees, January 8, 1952, doc. 12453, legajo 181, AGN-MAT.

67. Reports from Comisión de Investigaciones de Agio y Especulación, November 1–December 1, 1955, 15, memorias, box 6, AGN-FCNI.

68. Letter from Oscar Limarino, November 17, 1952, doc. 14441, legajo 365; letter from Juan García de Rios, January 8, 1952, doc. 12469, legajo 181, AGN-MAT.

69. Letter from Ramón Riba, January 26, 1952, doc. 17876, legajo 365, AGN-MAT.

70. *Mundo Peronista*, July 1, 1952, 8–11. The article claimed that some 24,000 letters from individuals and 7,000 response forms from organizations had been received by that time—surprisingly, a figure less than the ministry's own internal estimate of 43,100.

71. Memo from Ministry of Public Works, n.d., doc. 8676, legajo 12, AGN-MAT; memo from Ministry of Public Works, n.d., doc. 10144, legajo 205, AGN-MAT.

72. Memo from technical secretary, n.d., doc. 8082, legajo 12, AGN-MAT.

73. Letter from Partido Peronista of Estación Clark, n.d., doc. 11409, legajo 161, AGN-MAT.

74. Memo from MAT, September 12, 1952, doc. 10804, legajo 41, AGN-MAT. In a similar example, the Ministry of Industry and Commerce responded that direct state intervention in the buying and sale of goods was "not advisable" (memo, Jan. 19, 1951, doc. 16269, legajo 365, AGN-MAT).

75. Letter from Manuel Giménez, January 4, 1952, doc. 17490, legajo 79; memo from MAT, December 21, 1951, doc. 17846, legajo 331, AGN-MAT.

76. Letter from Anonieta di Leonardo de Monaco, December 11, 1951, doc. 6401; letter from Josefina Giovatto, January 6, 1952, doc. 11623, both legajo 205, AGN-MAT. The second

petitioners' requests were eventually added to the province of Buenos Aires's planning registry, according to an internal memo from November 1953.

77. Letter from Asociación Fomento de Caseros, December 27, 1951, doc. 9886, legajo 62, AGN-MAT.

78. Scott, *Seeing*, 89–90.

Chapter 7: Ironies of Adjustment

1. Gerchunoff and Llach, *Ciclo de la ilusión*, 208. On the period's economic history, see Gerchunoff and Llach, *Ciclo de la ilusión*, 201–31; Pablo Gerchunoff, "Peronist Economic Policies, 1946–1955," in *The Political Economy of Argentina, 1946–83*, ed. Guido Di Tella and Rudiger Dornbusch (Pittsburgh: University of Pittsburg Press, 1989, 59–85; Mario Rapoport et al., *Historia económica, política y social de la Argentina (1880–2003)* (Buenos Aires: Ariel, 2006); Carlos F. Díaz Alejandro, *Essays on the Economic History of the Argentine Republic* (New Haven, Conn.: Yale University Press, 1970).

2. Africanist scholars are leading the way in more expansive inquires on the politics and culture of structural adjustment. See James Ferguson, *Global Shadows: Africa in the Neoliberal World Order*, ed. Ferguson (Durham, N.C.: Duke University Press, 2006), 69–89; Ferguson, *Expectations of Modernity Myths and Meanings of Urban Life on the Zambian Copperbelt* (Berkeley: University of California Press, 1999); J. A. Mbembé, *On the Postcolony* (Berkeley: University of California Press, 2001).

3. A transcript of these meetings can be found in the AGN's Biblioteca Perón as Consejo Económico Social, *Equilibrio de Precios y Salarios*, 9 vols. (Buenos Aires, 1952). The consejo was led by ministers Alfredo Gómez Morales (finance), Ramón Cereijo (treasury), Roberto Ares (economy), and José Constantino Barro (industry and commerce).

4. The CGE was by no means a cohesive institution at this stage, but it was willing at least to adopt a more open position toward the Perón government than were most other business organizations. In the words of one representative, "The Confederación General Económica is in diapers. Better said, it was not been organized yet. Those of us who are here represent the three big pillars of the country that are industry, commerce, and production" (Consejo Económico Social, *Equilibrio de Precios*, 1:19).

5. Ibid., 1:1–10, 4:18–20.

6. Ibid., 2:10.

7. Ibid., 9:25.

8. Subsecretaría de Informaciones, *Perón anuncia el Plan Económico de 1952 y los precios de la cosecha* (Buenos Aires, 1952), 7 (quotation); *La Nación*, February 19, 1952, 1–2; February 22, 1952, 1; February 23, 1952, 1; March 17, 1952, 1; and May 18, 1952, 1; Luna, *Perón y su tiempo*, 2:281–85.

9. Subsecretaría de Informaciones, *Perón anuncia*, 8.

10. *El Obrero Ferroviario*, March 1952, 3; *La Nación*, February 22, 1952, 1; March 1952, 6, 1–2; and March 25, 1952, 1; *La Epoca*, July 26, 1952, 5. On campaigns to mobilize female consumers, see Milanesio, "Guardian Angels."

11. *Mundo Peronista*, February 15, 1952, 1.

12. *Mundo Peronista*, April 1, 1952, 22–23; *La Nación*, March 6, 1952, 2; Goldar, *Buenos Aires*, 19; Ramacciotti, *La política sanitaria*, 156–65.

13. On the politics of wartime austerity and postwar recovery in other midcentury nations, see Zweinger-Bargielowska, *Austerity in Britain*; Jacobs, *Pocketbook Politics*, 179–220; Cohen, *A Consumers' Republic*, 62–109.

14. Ballent, *Las huellas,* 247–50.

15. *Mundo Argentino,* March 15, 1952, n.p.; April 9, 1952, 10; April 16, 1952, 10; April 30, 1952, 10; May 7, 1952, 10; May 14, 1952, 10; and July 16, 1952, n.p. (quotation).

16. *La Época,* April 1, 1952, 3; May 11, 1952, 3; and June 1, 1952, 5; letter from a resident of Barrio Perón, June 1952, doc. 2800, legajo 594, AGN-MAT.

17. Economic and Financial Review, *Confidential U.S. State Department Central Files. Argentina, 1950–1954,* July 14, 1952, reel 12, doc. 835.00/7-1452, U.S. State Department Central Files; Goldar, *Buenos Aires,* 17–21. Because of increasing government control of the media, this chapter draws from U.S. State Department reports compiled by embassy officials, including a specially assigned labor attaché. Despite the obvious problems and potential biases of these sources, they provide insight behind the official façade of propaganda.

18. *La Nación,* March 5, 1952, 2.

19. Gerchunoff, "Peronist Economic Policies," 59–85.

20. In a long interview from 1972, Perón's minister of finance and head of the Central Bank described the steps taken to "rationalize" wage and price policies. See Alfredo Gómez Morales, interview by Leandro Gutiérrez (May 17, 19, 1972), Instituto Di Tella and Columbia Oral History Project, New York, 60–68.

21. Novick, *IAPI,* 72–73, 130; Economic and Financial Review, July 14, 1952; "Inflationary Trends and Checks in Argentina," *Confidential U.S. State Department Central Files. Argentina, 1950–1954,* November 3, 1952, reel 12, doc. 835.00/11-352, U.S. State Department Central Files. Subsidies to rural producers and traders increased dramatically after 1952, and the majority of the subsidies—around 90 percent in 1954—went to the commercialization and processing of beef, grains, oil and other raw material.

22. Economic and Financial Review, July 14, 1952, reel 12, U.S. State Department Central Files; Economic and Financial Review, *Confidential U.S. State Department Central Files. Argentina, 1950–1954,* October 13, 1952, reel 12, unclassified, U.S. State Department Central Files. Employers found ways around the regulations and laid off workers, although unemployment did not become critical.

23. Letter from Mario Abel Zandes, December 1952, doc. 2540, legajo 581, AGN-MAT.

24. On Evita's death, see Fraser and Navarro, *Evita,* 148–67; Tomás de Elia and Juan Pablo Queiroz, eds., *Evita: El retrato de su vida* (Buenos Aires: Bramblia, 1997).

25. Bourdé, *La classe ouvrière,* 2:846–51; Gerchunoff and Llach, *Ciclo de la ilusión,* 181, 211.

26. Ministerio de Asuntos Económicos, *La organización de las fuerzas económicas y la función del gobierno* (Buenos Aires, 1954).

27. *Gaceta Textil,* March 1954, 10–11.

28. *La Gaceta,* April 9, 1953.

29. *La Gaceta,* May 12, 1953, 3.

30. Marcos Giménez Zapiola and Carlos M. Leguizamón, "La concertación peronista de 1955: El Congreso de la Productividad," in *La formación del sindicalismo,* ed. Torre, 323–58; Rafael Bitrán, *El Congreso de la Productividad* (Buenos Aires: El Bloque Editorial, 1994); Report on Argentine Labor, *Confidential U.S. State Department Central Files. Argentina, 1950–1954,* November 2, 1951, reel 13, doc. 835.06/11-1551, U.S. State Department Central Files.

31. Secretaría de Asuntos Técnicos, *¿Qué es . . . la productividad social?* (Buenos Aires, 1955); Juan D. Perón, "El Congreso Nacional de Productividad y Bienestar Social," *Hechos e Ideas* 15, no. 129 (Jan. 1955): 7–14.

32. *CGT Circular No. 127,* December 13, 1954, doc. 881, folder 10A, Instituto Di Tella Archive; *Metalurgía,* January–February 1955, 3.

33. Cane-Carrasco, *The Fourth Enemy*; Sirven, *Perón y los medios*, 251–60.

34. Plotkin, *Mañana es San Perón*; Gambini, *Historia del peronismo*, 2:133–71; Miguel Somoza Rodríguez, *Educación y política en Argentina (1946–1955)* (Buenos Aires: Miño y Dávila Editores, 2006); Marta Barbieri-Guardia, *Aportes para el estudio sobre las políticas educativas durante el primer peronismo, Tucumán 1946–1955* (Tucumán, Argentina: Universidad Nacional de Tucumán, 2005); Héctor Rubén Cucuzza et al., *Estudios de historia de la educación durante el primer peronismo, 1943–1955* (Buenos Aires: Editorial Los Libros del Riel, 1997).

35. *Mundo Peronista*, July 15, 1951, 11.

36. Flavia Fiorucci, "La denuncia bajo el peronismo: Conflicto y consenso en el caso del campo escolar," unpublished essay; Robin Derby, "In the Shadow of the State: The Politics of Denunciation and Panegyric during the Trujillo Regime in the Dominican Republic," *Hispanic American Historical Review* 83, no. 2 (May 2003): 295–344.

37. *La Gaceta*, April 2, 1953, 1 (quotation); *Democracia*, April 10–16, 1953; Report on Argentine Labor, *Confidential U.S. State Department Central Files. Argentina, 1950–1954*, July 27, 1953, reel 13, doc. 835.06/7-1853, U.S. State Department Central Files; Luna, *Perón y su tiempo*, 3:28–30.

38. Gambini, *Historia del peronismo*, 2:187.

39. Reports from Comisión de Investigaciones de Agio y Especulación, November 1–December 1, 1955, 12–13, 72, memorias, box 6, AGN-FCNI.

40. Gómez Morales interview, 72–74.

41. *Metalurgía*, April 1954, 3–13; Quarterly Economic Report, *Confidential U.S. State Department Central Files. Argentina, 1950–1954*, July 22, 1954, reel 12, doc. 835.00/7-2254, U.S. State Department Central Files.

42. Ignacio Llorente, "La composición social del movimiento peronista hacia 1954," in *El voto peronista*, ed. Mora y Araujo and Llorente, 369–96.

43. Baily, *Labor, Nationalism*, 153–56; Luna, *Perón y su tiempo*, 3:153–55.

44. Gerchunoff and Llach, *Ciclo de la ilusión*, 223. According to the Second Five-Year Plan, social policy expenditures declined from 18.3 to 12.5 percent.

45. Report on Argentine Labor, *Confidential U.S. State Department Central Files. Argentina, 1950–1954*, November 4, 1954, reel 13, doc. 835.06/11-1611, U.S. State Department Central Files; Banco Hipotecario Nacional, *Plan Eva Perón* (Buenos Aires, 1953); Servicio Internacional de Publicaciones Argentinas, *Houses for All in Argentina: Solution to the Problem of the Housing Shortage in Argentina* (Buenos Aires: 1953) 1–50; Ballent, *Las huellas*, 86–95; Gaggero and Garro, *Del trabajo*, 362–70. In December 1954 Congress passed laws to create two new retirement programs, one for rural workers, who had lagged well behind their urban, industrial counterparts in "social conquests," and another for entrepreneurs, professionals, and independent workers (e.g., merchants).

46. Letter from unidad básica, Buenos Aires, May 1953, doc. 854, legajo 587, AGN-MAT.

47. Letter from Rosa Alonso, April 1953, legajo 581, AGN-MAT.

48. Letter from MAT, May 11, 1953, doc. 185, legajo 587, AGN-MAT. Even in the final days of the regime, state agencies continued to produce propaganda on Evita that celebrated her humanitarian deeds; see Fundación Eva Perón/Secretaría de Prensa y Difusión, *Presencia de Eva Perón* (Buenos Aires, 1955).

49. Confederación de Empleados de Comercio, *La opinión de Perón sobre los empleados de comercio* (Buenos Aires: Castromán y Orbiz, 1954).

50. Cochran and Reina, *Entrepreneurship*, 236–44; letter from Fetoro, S.A., December 1953, doc. 582, legajo 582, AGN-MAT; Secretaría de Asuntos Técnicos, *Comercio Minorista*

en la Capital Federal, 5–15; idem, *Comercio Minorista en los 17 Partidos,* 6–19; Confederación General Económica, *Informe económico,* 115–26; *Gaceta Textil,* April 1953, 3; January 1954, 5; and May 1954, 4.

51. *Democracia,* December 2, 1952, 2–4; and December 8, 1952, 3; Subsecretaría de Informaciones, *Segundo Plan Quinquenal* (Buenos Aires, 1952). The government also printed manuals that instructed schoolteachers and other functionaries on explaining the plan to their pupils and constituents: Ministerio de Educación, *Justicialismo (Cuadernos para el maestro argentino),* 2 vols. (Buenos Aires, 1953); Ministerio de Asistencia Social y Salud Publica, *2o Plan Quinquenal, manual doctrinario y practico* (Buenos Aires, 1954); Banco Hipotecario Nacional, *El Segundo Plan Quinquenal y el Banco Hipotecario Nacional* (Buenos Aires, 1953).

52. Schvarzer, *La industria,* 221–24; Gerchunoff and Antúnez, "De la bonanza," 166–97.

53. Ministerio de Relaciones Exteriores, *Economic Possibilities in the New Argentina: Investment of Foreign Capital* (Buenos Aires, 1953), 1–40.

54. Ibid, 5.

55. James P. Brennan, *The Labor Wars in Córdoba, 1955–1976: Ideology, Work, and Labor Politics in an Argentine Industrial City* (Cambridge, Mass.: Harvard University Press, 1994).

56. See, for instance, letter from Pablo Heisser, July 1954, legajo 582, AGN-MAT.

57. On the politics of automotive modernity in midcentury Brazil, see Joel Wolfe, *Autos and Progress: The Brazilian Search for Modernity* (New York: Oxford, 2010); Grandin, *Fordlandia.*

58. *Noticias Gráficas,* October 2, 1954; Goldar, *Buenos Aires,* 84; Page, *Perón,* 281–88.

59. Reports from Comisión de Investigaciones de Agio y Especulación, November 1– December 1, 1955, 15–16, 74–75, memorias, box 6, AGN-FCNI.

60. Brennan and Rougier, *Politics of National Capitalism,* 85–106.

61. Fiorucci, "El antiperonismo intelectual"; Jorge Nállim "Del antifacismo al antiperonismo: *Argentina Libre,* . . . *Antinazi* y el surgimiento del antiperonismo político e intelectual," in *Fascismo y antifascismo, peronismo y antiperonismo,* ed. Marcela García Sebastiani (Madrid: Iberoamericana, 2006), 77–105; William Katra, *Contorno: Literary Engagement in Post-Peronist Argentina* (Rutherford, N.J.: Fairleigh Dickinson University Press, 1988); Neiburg, *Los intelectuales.*

62. Gambini, *Historia del peronismo,* 2:133–42.

63. On the conflicts leading up to Perón's fall, see Potash, *Army and Politics,* 170–213; Caimari, *Perón y la iglesia católica,* 249–314; Luna, *Perón y su tiempo,* 3:235–336.

64. Rouquié, *Poder militar,* 129. See also Secretaría de Prensa de la Presidencia de la Nación, *Declaración de principios de la Revolución Libertadora* (Buenos Aires, 1955).

65. Roberto Baschetti, *Documentos de la resistencia peronista, 1955–1970* (La Plata, Argentina: Editorial de la Campana, 1997).

66. César Seveso, "Political Emotions and the Origins of the Peronist Resistance," in *New Cultural History of Peronism,* ed. Matthew Karish and Oscar Chamosa (Durham, N.C.: Duke University Press, 2010), 239–69.

67. Sanchez Zinny, *El culto,* 253.

68. *El Hogar,* September 20, 1957, 1.

69. *Metalurgía,* December 1955, 5; see also Daniel James, "Racionalización y respuesta de la clase obrera: Contexto y limitaciones de la actividad gremial en la Argentina," *Desarrollo Económico* 21, no. 83 (Oct.–Dec. 1981): 321–49.

70. *Gaceta Textil,* December 1955, 3. See also *Revista de la Cámara Argentina de Sociedades Anónimas* (June 1956): 22–25; Reports from Comisión de Investigaciones de Agio y Especulación, November 1–December 1, 1955, 62, memorias, box 6, AGN-FCNI; Gerchunoff and Llach, *Ciclo de la ilusión,* 238–39.

71. Cámara Argentina de Comercio, *La libre empresa y el progreso económico* (Buenos Aires: Imprenta López, 1955), 29; Raúl Prebisch, *Informe preliminar acerca de la situación económica* (Buenos Aires: Secretaría de Prensa y Actividades Culturales de la Presidencia de la Nación, 1955).

72. Gerchunoff and Llach, *Ciclo de la ilusión*, 264; Baily, *Labor, Nationalism*, 175.

73. For an insightful analysis of these recurrent conflicts in Argentina, see William C. Smith, *Authoritarianism and the Crisis of the Argentine Political Economy* (Stanford, Calif.: Stanford University Press, 1989).

Conclusion: The Dignified Life and Beyond

1. Passersby paying closer attention may now notice efforts to commemorate the Peronist past—including a horridly allegorical statue of Evita Perón—that have appeared around the library since the late 1990s.

2. Kotkin, *Magnetic Mountain*, 358.

3. Carl E. Schorske, *Fin-de-Siècle Vienna: Politics and Culture* (New York: Vintage, 1981), 119.

4. On power and history, see Trouillot, *Silencing the Past*.

Bibliography

Archives and Libraries Consulted

Buenos Aires, Argentina

Archivo General de la Nación (AGN)
        Fondo Comisión Nacional de Investigaciones; FCNI
    Archivo Intermedio
    Biblioteca Juan D. Perón
    Colección del Ministerio de Asuntos Técnicos (MAT)
    Departamento de Cine, Audio y Video
    Departamento de Fotografía
Banco Central de la República Argentina
    Biblioteca Prebisch
    Biblioteca Tornquist
Biblioteca del Congreso
    Colección Peronista
Biblioteca de la Universidad Di Tella
Biblioteca del Ministerio de Economía
Biblioteca Nacional
    Hemeroteca Nacional
Centro de Documentación e Investigación de la Cultura de Izquierdas en la Argentina
    (CEDINCI)

United States

Boston Public Library
    Perón Era Pamphlets Collection
Columbia University, New York, N.Y.
    Columbia University and Instituto Di Tella Oral History Project
Library of Congress, Washington, D.C.
New York Public Library, New York, N.Y.
Princeton University Library, Princeton, N.J.
Stanford University, Palo Alto, Calif.
    Hoover Institution on War, Peace, and Revolution
    Latin American Collection
United States State Department, Washington, D.C.
    Confidential U.S. State Department Central Files. Argentina. Microfilm Collection.
University of Miami, Coral Gables, Fla.
    Peronist Era Collection

Newspapers and Periodicals *(place of publication is Buenos Aires unless noted)*

Argentina
Argentina Fabril
Boletín del Honorable Consejo Deliberante
Boletín del Museo Social Argentino
La Capital (Rosario)
CGT
Clarín
Democracia
El Día
La Época
La Fraternidad
La Gaceta (Tucumán)
Gaceta Textil
Hechos e Ideas
El Hogar
Metalurgía
El Mundo
Mundo Argentino
Mundo Peronista
Norte (Quilmes, Buenos Aires)
Noticias Gráficas
El Obrero Ferroviario
El Obrero Metalúrgico
Para Ti
El Pueblo
La Razón
Revista de Ciencias Económicas
Revista de Economía Argentina
Revista de la Cámara Argentina de Sociedades Anónimas
Revista de Trabajo y Previsión
Rosalinda
El Trabajador de la Carne
La Vanguardia
La Voz del Interior (Córdoba)
La Voz del Pueblo (Vicente López, Buenos Aires)

Primary Sources

Arlt, Roberto. *Obra Completa.* Vol. 2. Buenos Aires: Carlos Lohlé, 1981.
Armour Research Foundation, *Technological and Economic Survey of Argentine Industries with Industrial Research Recommendations.* Ann Arbor: Edwards Brothers, 1943.
Arrabalera. Feature film. Dir. Tulio Demicheli. 1950.
Asociación de Jefes de Propaganda. *Cursos de enseñanza de propaganda (1940-41).* Buenos Aires: 1941.
———. *Síntesis Publicitaria* (1943-1946). Buenos Aires: Talleres Kraft, 1944-47.

Aunós, Eduardo. *Viaje a la Argentina*. Madrid: Editorial Nacional, 1943.

Banco Hipotecario Nacional. *Plan Eva Perón*. Buenos Aires, 1953.

——. *El Segundo Plan Quinquenal y el Banco Hipotecario Nacional*. Buenos Aires, 1953.

Bereterbide, Férmin. "El problema de la vivienda popular en Buenos Aires." *Boletín del Honorable Consejo Deliberante* 1, nos. 6–7 (Sept.–Oct. 1939): 112–60.

Bialet Massé, Juan. *Informe sobre el estado de la clase obrera*. Vol. 2. Buenos Aires: Hyspamerica, 1985 [1904].

Bogliolo, Romulo. *Salarios y nivel de vida*. Buenos Aires: Editorial La Vanguardia, 1946.

Borges, Jorge Luis, and Adolfo Bioy Casares. "La fiesta del monstruo." In *Nuevos Cuentos de Bustos Domecq*. Buenos Aires, Librería la Ciudad, 1977.

Bruce, James. *Those Perplexing Argentines*. New York: Longmans, Green, 1953.

Bunge, Alejandro. *Una nueva Argentina*. Buenos Aires: Hyspamerica, 1984 [1940].

Cafferata, Juan. "Algunas condiciones sobre el problema de la vivienda popular en la república." *Boletín del Honorable Consejo Deliberante* (Sept.–Oct. 1939): 171–74.

Caja Nacional de Ahorro Postal. *El ahorro en la enseñanza media, programa y desarrollo*. Buenos Aires: Editorial Polo, 1947.

——. *Economía familiar*. Buenos Aires, 1950.

Cámara Argentina de Comercio. *La libre empresa y el progreso económico*. Buenos Aires: Imprenta López, 1955.

Carrillo, Ramón. *Política sanitaria argentina*. 2 vols. Buenos Aires: Ministerio de Salud Pública, 1949.

Cerrutti Costa, Luis. *El sindicalismo, las masas y el poder*. Buenos Aires: Trafac, 1957.

Chingolo. Feature film. Dir. Lucas Demare. 1940.

Coghlan, Eduardo. *La condición de la vivienda en la Argentina a través del censo de 1947*. Buenos Aires: Rosso, 1959.

Confederación Económica Argentina. *Memorial de la Confederación Económica Argentina sobre los costos de la comercialización*. Buenos Aires, 1950.

Confederación General de Empleados de Comercio. *Memoria del Consejo Directivo*. Buenos Aires: Castromán y Orbiz, 1953.

——. *La opinión de Perón sobre los empleados de comercio*. Buenos Aires: Castromán y Orbiz, 1954.

Confederación General del Trabajo. *Anuario del trabajo*. Buenos Aires, 1948.

Confederación General Económica. *Informe económico*. Buenos Aires, 1955.

Conoscamos nuestra constitución. Buenos Aires: Talleres Gráficos Kraft, 1950.

Consejo Económico Social. *Equilibrio de precios y salarios*. 9 vols. Buenos Aires, 1952.

Damonte Taborda, Raúl. *Ayer fue San Perón: 12 años de humillación argentina*. Buenos Aires: Ediciones Gure, 1955.

Del Rio, Jorge. *La defensa del consumidor*. Buenos Aires: Ministerio de Trabajo y Previsión, Instituto Nacional de Previsión Social, 1951.

Departamento Nacional de Trabajo. *Adaptación de los salarios a las fluctuaciones del costo de la vida*. Buenos Aires, 1943.

——. *Condiciones de vida de la familia obrera*. Buenos Aires, 1937.

——. *La desocupación en la Argentina*. Buenos Aires, 1940.

——. *Investigaciones sociales*. Buenos Aires, 1942.

Dirección General de Relaciones Culturales y Difusión. *Turismo para el pueblo*. Buenos Aires, 1950.

Dirección Nacional de Estadística y Censos. *Censo de Comercio 1954*. 2 vols. Buenos Aires, 1959.

Di Tella, Torcuato. *Dos temas de legislación del trabajo: Proyectos de ley de seguro social obrero y asignaciones familiares.* Buenos Aires, 1961 [1941].

———. *Problemas de la posguerra: función económica y destino social de la industria argentina.* Buenos Aires: Libreria Hachette, 1943.

Domínguez, Francisco. *El apóstol de la mentira: Juan Perón.* Buenos Aires: Ediciones La Reja, 1956 [1951].

Federación Argentina de la Industria Metalúrgica. *Industria Metalúrgica, Memoria 1950–1951.* Buenos Aires, 1951.

Federación de Obreros y Empleados de la Industrial de Papel, Cartón, Químicos y Afines. *Manual del trabajador papelero.* Buenos Aires: Gráficos ALEA, 1953.

Fernández, Constantino. *La revolución del 4 de junio, por qué y para qué se hizo.* Buenos Aires: Talleres Gráficos Optimus, 1944.

Figuerola, José. *El gran movimiento social argentino.* Buenos Aires: Editorial La Huella, 1961.

———. *La colaboración social en hispanoamerica.* Buenos Aires: Editorial Sudamericana, 1943.

———. "Organización Social." *Revista de Economía Argentina* (Mar. 1939): 83–87.

Freire, José M. *Nuevos vientos en la política social argentina.* Buenos Aires, 1950.

Fresco, Manuel. *Mi verdad.* Buenos Aires: Talleres de Pellegrini, 1966.

Frondizi, Arturo. *Petróleo y política.* Buenos Aires: Raigal, 1955.

Fundación de Ayuda Social María Eva Duarte de Perón. *Por la ruta de los cuentos mágicos.* Buenos Aires, 1948.

Fundación Eva Perón/Secretaría de Prensa y Difusión. *Presencia de Eva Perón.* Buenos Aires, 1955.

Fundación Eva Perón/Servicio Internacional de Publicaciones Argentinas. *Colonias de vacaciones.* Buenos Aires, 1950.

———. *El hogar de la empleada.* Buenos Aires, 1952.

———. *Os lares de tránsito.* Buenos Aires, 1951.

Gente Bien. Feature film. Dir. Manuel Romero. 1939.

Ghioldi, Américo. *Alpargatas y libros en la historia argentina.* Buenos Aires: La Vanguardia, 1946.

———. *La argentina tiene miedo.* Montevideo: Talleres La Vanguardia en Exilio, 1954.

Gobernación de la Provincia de Buenos Aires, Ministerio de Obras Públicas. *Plan general de trabajos públicos.* Buenos Aires: Guillermo Kraft, 1948.

Gobierno de la Provincia de Córdoba. *Junta de trabajo.* Córdoba, 1934.

González Galé, José. *Previsión social.* Buenos Aires: Losada, 1946.

Greenup, Ruth, and Leonard Greenup. *Revolution before Breakfast.* New York: University of North Carolina Press, 1947.

Hemricourt, Georges de. *J'ai vu l'Argentine de Perón.* Brussels: Charles Dessart, 1953.

Herron, Francis. *Letters from the Argentine.* New York: G. P. Putnam, 1943.

Ivanissevich, Oscar. *Rindo cuenta, 1893–1973.* 2 vols. Buenos Aires: Talleres Gráficos del Ministerio de Cultura y Educación, 1973.

J. Walter Thompson Company. *The Latin American Markets.* New York: McGraw-Hill, 1956.

Juárez, Juan C. *Los trabajadores en función social.* Buenos Aires: Libro de Edición Argentina, 1947.

Junta Nacional para Combatir la Desocupación. *Memoria elevada al Ministro del Interior.* Buenos Aires, 1936.

Kilómetro 111. Feature film. Dir. Mario Soffici. 1938.

Lannoy, Juan Luis de. *Los niveles de vida en América Latina.* Fribourg, Switzerland, and Bogotá: Oficina Internacional de Investigaciones Sociales de FERES, 1963.

Llorens, Emilio. *Encuesta continental sobre el consumo de productos de alimentación y vestido y sobre la vivienda popular.* Montevideo, 1944.

La maestrita de los obreros. Feature film. Dir. Alberto de Zavalía. 1942.

Maestro Levita. Feature film. Dir. Luis César Amadori. 1938.

Martínez Orozco, José. *Quince centavos: Un día de vida en Buenos Aires.* New York: Henry Holt, 1945.

Maxwell, Sue, and Golda Larkin O'Callahan. *South American Fiesta.* Boston: Bruce Humphries, 1950.

Memoria de la Dirección Nacional de Vigilancia de Precios y Abastecimiento correspondiente al año 1949. Buenos Aires, 1950.

Mercado de abasto. Feature film. Dir. Lucas Demare. 1954.

Ministerio de Asistencia Social y Salud Publica. *Segundo Plan Quinquenal, manual doctrinario y práctico.* Buenos Aires, 1954.

Ministerio de Asuntos Económicos. *La organización de las fuerzas económicas y la función del gobierno.* Buenos Aires, 1954.

Ministerio de Economía, Secretaría de Comercio. *Estadísticas comerciales.* Buenos Aires, 1983.

Ministerio de Educación. *Justicialismo (Cuadernos para el maestro argentino).* 2 vols. Buenos Aires, 1953.

Ministerio de la Hacienda. *El plan de reactivación económica ante el honorable senado.* Buenos Aires, 1940.

Ministerio del Interior. *Conferencia de gobernadores de provincias y territorios nacionales, para la represión del agio, la especulación y los precios abusivos.* Buenos Aires: Imprenta del Congreso, 1947.

———. *Leyes, decretos y revoluciones para normalizar precios y reprimir la especulación.* Buenos Aires, 1947.

Ministerio de Obras Públicas. *Labor realizada y en ejecución, Diciembre 1943–Junio 1947.* Buenos Aires, 1947.

———. *El Plan Quinquenal y las obras públicas.* Buenos Aires: Talleres Gráficos del Ministerio, 1946.

Ministerio de Relaciones Exteriores. *Economic Possibilities in the New Argentina: Investment of Foreign Capital.* Buenos Aires, 1953.

Ministerios de Hacienda y Agricultura. *Plan de Acción Económica Nacional.* Buenos Aires, 1934.

Mujeres que trabajan. Feature film. Dir. Manuel Romero. 1938.

Organización de Consumidores. *Defienda sus pesos! Vigile los precios! No pague un centavo más!* Buenos Aires 1950.

Palacios, Alfredo. *Pueblos desamparados: Solución de los problemas del noroeste argentino.* Buenos Aires: Guillermo Kraft, 1944.

Partido Socialista. *Hacia la bancarrota.* Buenos Aires: Editorial La Vanguardia, 1949.

Perón, Eva. *Discursos completos.* 3 vols. Buenos Aires: Editorial Megafón, 1985–87.

———. *La razón de mi vida y otros escritos.* Buenos Aires: Planeta, 1996.

Perón, Juan Domingo. "El Congreso Nacional de Productividad y Bienestar Social." *Hechos e Ideas* 15, no. 129 (Jan. 1955): 7–14.

———. *Obras Completas.* 27 vols. to date. Buenos Aires: Proyector Hernadarias, 1984–.

———. *El pueblo ya sabe de qué se trata.* Buenos Aires, 1946.

Poder Ejecutivo. *Plan Quinquenal de gobierno del Presidente Perón, 1947–1951.* Buenos Aires, 1946.

Prebisch, Raúl. *Informe preliminar acerca de la situación económica.* Buenos Aires: Secretaría de Prensa y Actividades Culturales de la Presidencia de la Nación, 1955.

Provincia de Buenos Aires. *Política obrera y legislación del trabajo del gobierno de Buenos Aires.* La Plata: Talleres de Impresiones Oficiales, 1937.

Reyes, Cipriano. *Yo hice el 17 de octubre.* Buenos Aires: Centro Editor de América Latina, 1984.

Riguera, Ricardo. *Seguro social integral.* Buenos Aires: Instituto Nacional de Previsión Social, 1946.

Sanchez Zinny, E. F. *El culto de la infamia: Historia documentada de la segunda tiranía argentina.* Avellaneda, Argentina: Artes Gráficas Bartolomé V. Chiesino, 1958.

Santos Discepolo, Enrique. *Mordisquito, a mí no me vas a contar.* Buenos Aires: Ediciones Realidad Política, 1986.

Secretaría de Asuntos Técnicos. *Comercio Minorista en la Capital Federal.* Buenos Aires, 1954.

———. *Comercio Minorista en los 17 Partidos del Gran Buenos Aires.* Buenos Aires, 1954.

———. *¿Qué es . . . la productividad social?* Buenos Aires, 1955.

Secretaría de Prensa de la Presidencia de la Nación. *Declaración de principios de la Revolución Libertadora.* Buenos Aires, 1955.

Secretaría de Prensa y Difusión. *Fraternidad justicialista.* 35-mm film, n.d.

———. *Justicia social.* 16-mm film, 1948.

———. *Nuestro hogar.* 35-mm film, 1952.

Secretaría de Trabajo y Previsión. *Condiciones de vida de la familia obrera, 1943-1945.* Buenos Aires, 1946.

———. *Investigaciones sociales, 1943-1945.* Buenos Aires, 1946.

———. *Nivel de vida de la familia obrera, evolución durante la segunda guerra mundial.* Buenos Aires, 1945.

Señalando Rumbos. Sucesos Argeninos no. 574. 16-mm film. November 1949.

Servicio Internacional de Publicaciones Argentinas. *La asistencia social justicialista.* Buenos Aires, 1952.

———. *The Eva Perón Provision Stores.* Buenos Aires, 1954.

———. *Houses for All in Argentina: Solution to the Problem of the Housing Shortage in Argentina.* Buenos Aires, 1953.

———. *La justicia social es realizada por el pueblo.* Buenos Aires, 1950.

———. *Policlinico Evita: Partido 4 de junio.* Buenos Aires, 1952.

SIAM Di Tella Ltd. *La contribución de la gran industria a la mejora de la vivienda obrera.* Buenos Aires, 1941.

Siegfried, André. *Impressions of South America.* Trans. H. H. Hemming and Doris Hemming. New York: Harcourt, Brace, 1933.

Subsecretaría de Informaciones. *Declaración de los derechos del trabajador.* Buenos Aires, 1950.

———. *Eva Perón y su obra social.* Buenos Aires, 1951.

———. *Guerra a muerte a los especuladores dijo Perón.* Buenos Aires, 1950.

———. *Perón anuncia el Plan Económico de 1952 y los precios de la cosecha.* Buenos Aires, 1952.

———. *Segundo Plan Quinquenal.* Buenos Aires, 1952.

———. *Tres charlas radiofónicas del General Perón.* Buenos Aires, 1951.

Subsecretaría de Informaciones, Dirección General del Registro Nacional. *Abastecimiento y represión del agio.* 2 vols. Buenos Aires, 1950.

Vicepresidencia de la Nación, Comisión Nacional de Investigaciones. *Documentación, autores y cómplices de las irregularidades cometidas durante la segunda tiranía.* 5 vols. Buenos Aires, 1958.

———. *Libro negro de la segunda tiranía*. Buenos Aires, 1958.

Vicepresidencia de la Nación, Consejo Nacional de Posguerra. *Ordenamiento económico-social*. Buenos Aires, 1945.

Secondary Sources

Aboy, Rosa. *Viviendas para el pueblo: Espacio urbano y sociabilidad en el barrio Los Perales, 1946–1955*. Buenos Aires: San Andrés/Fundo de Cultura Económica, 2005.

Acha, Omar. "Dos estrategias de domesticación de la mujer joven trabajadora: La Casa y el Hogar de la Empleada." In Barry, Ramacciotti, and Valobra, *La Fundación Eva Perón y las mujeres*, 151–78.

———. "Sociedad civil y sociedad política durante el primer peronismo. *Desarrollo Económico* 44, no. 174 (July–Dec. 2004): 199–230.

Adelman, Jeremy. "Reflections on the Rise of Argentine Labour and the Rise of Perón." *Bulletin of Latin American Research* 11, no. 3 (1992): 243–59.

———. *Republic of Capital: Buenos Aires and the Legal Transformation of the Atlantic World*. Stanford, Calif.: Stanford University Press, 1999.

———. "Socialism and Democracy in Argentina in the Age of the Second International." *Hispanic American History Review* 72, no. 2 (May 1992): 211–38.

Agnew, Jean-Christophe. "Coming Up for Air: Consumer Culture in Historical Perspective." In *Consumer Society in American History*, edited by Lawrence B. Glickman, 373–97. Ithaca, N.Y.: Cornell University Press, 1999.

Altamirano, Carlos. "Ideologías políticas y debate cívico." In *Nueva Historia Argentina*. Vol. 8, *Los Años Peronistas (1943–1955)*, edited by Juan Carlos Torre, 231–39. Buenos Aires: Editorial Sudamericana, 2002.

Appadurai, Arjun. "Deep Democracy: Urban Governmentality and the Horizon of Politics." *Public Culture* 14, no. 1:21–47.

———, ed. *The Social Life of Things: Commodities in Global Perspective*. Cambridge: Cambridge University Press, 1986.

Archivo General de la Nación. *Fondo Documental Secretaría Técnica 1 y 2 Presidencia del Teniente General Juan Domingo Perón (1936–1955)*. Buenos Aires: Archivo General de la Nación, 1995.

Auyero, Javier. *Poor People's Politics: Peronist Survival Networks and the Legacy of Evita*. Durham, N.C.: Duke University Press, 2000.

Baily, Samuel. *Labor, Nationalism, and Politics in Argentina*. New Brunswick, N.J.: Rutgers University Press, 1967.

Ballent, Anahi. *Las huellas de la política: Vivienda, ciudad, peronismo en Buenos Aires, 1943–1955*. Buenos Aires: Universidad Nacional de Quilmes/Prometeo, 2005.

———. "El lenguaje del bibelot." In Barry, Ramacciotti, and Valobra, *La Fundación Eva Perón y las mujeres*, 179–200.

Ballent, Anahi, and Adrián Gorelik. "País urbano o país rural: La modernización territorial y su crisis." In *Nueva historia Argentina*. vol. 7, *Crisis económica, avance del Estado e incertidumbre política (1930–1942)*, edited by Alejandro Cattaruzza, 143–200. Buenos Aires: Editorial Sudamericana, 2001.

Barbero, María Inés, and Mariela Ceva. "La vida obrera en una empresa paternalista." *Historia de la vida privada en la Argentina*. Vol. 3, *La Argentina entre multitudes y soledades:*

De los años treinta a la actualidad, edited by Fernando Devoto and Marta Madero, 141–68. Buenos Aires: Taurus, 1999.

Barbero, María Inés, and Fernando Rocchi. "Industry," in *A New Economic History of Argentina,* edited by Gerardo della Paolera and Alan M. Taylor, 261–94. Cambridge: Cambridge University Press, 2003.

Barbieri-Guardia, Marta. *Aportes para el estudio sobre las políticas educativas durante el primer peronismo, Tucumán 1946–1955.* Tucumán, Argentina: Universidad Nacional de Tucumán, 2005.

Barrancos, Dora. "Moral sexual, sexualidad, y mujeres trabajadoras en el período de entreguerras." In *Historia de la vida privada en la Argentina.* Vol. 3, *La Argentina entre multitudes y soledades: De los años treinta a la actualidad,* edited by Fernando Devoto and Marta Madero, 199–226. Buenos Aires: Taurus, 1999.

Barry, Carolina. *Evita capitana: El Partido Peronista Femenino, 1949–1955.* Buenos Aires: EDUNTREF, 2009.

———. "Mujeres en tránsito." In Barry, Ramacciotti, and Valobra, *La Fundación Eva Perón y las mujeres,* 77–117.

Barry, Carolina, Karina Ramacciotti, and Adriana Valobra, eds. *La Fundación Eva Perón y las mujeres: Entre la provocación y la inclusión.* Buenos Aires: Editorial Biblos, 2008.

Baschetti, Roberto. *Documentos de la resistencia peronista, 1955–1970.* La Plata, Argentina: Editorial de la Campana, 1997.

Bauer, Arnold. *Goods, Power, History: Latin America's Material Culture.* Cambridge: Cambridge University Press, 2001.

Béjar, María Dolores. "La política laboral del gobierno de Manuel Fresco." In *Argentina: Trabajdores entre dos guerras,* edited by José Panettieri, 155–89. Buenos Aires: Eudeba, 2000.

Bender, Thomas. *A Nation among Nations: America's Place in World History.* New York: Hill and Wang, 2006.

Berman, Marshall. *All That Is Solid Melts into Air: The Experience of Modernity.* New York: Simon and Schuster, 1982.

Berrotarán, Patricia. *Del plan a la planificación: El estado durante la época peronista.* Buenos Aires: Imago Mundi 2004.

Berrotarán, Patricia, Aníbal Jáuregui, and Marcelo Rougier, eds. *Sueños de bienestar en la Nueva Argentina: Estado y políticas públicas durante el peronismo, 1946–1955.* Buenos Aires: Imago Mundi, 2004.

Bethell, Leslie, and Ian Roxborough. "Latin America between the Second World War and the Cold War." *Journal of Latin American Studies* 20, no. 1 (May 1988): 167–89.

Bianchi, Susana. "Catolicismo y peronismo: La familia entre la religión y la política (1946–1955)." *Boletín del Instituto de Historia Argentina y Americana "Dr. Emilio Ravignani"* 19 (First Semester, 1999): 115–37.

Bianchi, Susana, and Norma Sanchis. *El partido peronista femenino.* Buenos Aires: CEAL, 1988.

Birle, Peter. *Los empresarios y la democracia en la Argentina.* Buenos Aires: Editorial de Belgrano, 1997.

Bitrán, Rafael. *El Congreso de la Productividad.* Buenos Aires: El Bloque Editorial, 1994.

Bitrán, Rafael, and Alejandro Schneider. "Coersión y consenso: La política obrera de Manuel Fresco, 1936–1940." In *Argentina en la paz de dos guerras, 1914–1945,* edited by Waldo Ansaldi, Alfredo R. Pucciarelli, and José C. Villarruel, 255–94. Buenos Aires: Biblos, 1993.

Bliss, Katherine Elaine. *Compromised Positions: Prostitution, Public Health, and Gender Politics in Revolutionary Mexico City.* University Park: Pennsylvania State University Press, 2001.

Booth, John A., and Mitchell Seligson, eds. *Political Participation in Latin America*. Vol. 1, *Citizen and State*. New York: Holmes and Meier, 1978.

Bourdé, Guy. *La classe ouvrière argentine (1929–1969)*. 3 vols. Paris: Editions L'Harmattan, 1987.

Bourdieu, Pierre. *Outline of a Theory of Practice*. Cambridge: Cambridge University Press, 1977.

Braun, Herbert. *The Assassination of Gaitán: Public Life and Urban Violence in Colombia*. Madison: University of Wisconsin Press, 1985.

Breen, T. H. *The Marketplace of Revolution: How Consumer Politics Shaped American Independence*. Oxford: Oxford University Press, 2004.

Brennan, James P. "Industrialists and *Bolicheros*: Business and the Peronist Populist Alliance, 1943–1976." In *Peronism and Argentina*, edited by James P. Brennan, 79–124. Wilmington, Del.: SR Books, 1998.

———. *The Labor Wars in Córdoba, 1955–1976: Ideology, Work, and Labor Politics in an Argentine Industrial City*. Cambridge, Mass.: Harvard University Press, 1994.

Brennan, James P., and Ofelia Pianetto, eds. *Region and Nation: Politics, Economics, and Society in Twentieth-Century Argentina*. New York: St. Martin's, 2000.

Brennan, James P., and Marcelo Rougier. *The Politics of National Capitalism: Peronism and the Argentine Bourgeoisie, 1945–1976*. University Park: Pennsylvania State University Press, 2009.

Buchrucker, Cristián. *Nacionalismo y peronismo: La Argentina en la crisis ideológica mundial (1927–1955)*. Buenos Aires: Editorial Sudamericana, 1987.

Caimari, Lila M. *Apenas un delincuente: Crimen, castigo y cultura en Buenos Aires, 1880–1955*. Buenos Aires: Siglo Veintiuno, 2004.

———. *Perón y la iglesia católica: Religión, estado y sociedad en la Argentina (1943–1955)*. Buenos Aires: Ariel, 1994.

Campins, Mónica, Horacio Gaggero, and Alicia Garro. "La Fundación Eva Perón." In *Estado, corporativismo y acción social en Brasil, Argentina y Uruguay*, edited by Mónica Campins, Ana Frega Novales, and Angela María de Castro Gomes, 49–108. Buenos Aires: Editorial Biblos/Fundación Simón Rodríguez, 1992.

Campione, Daniel. *Orígenes estatales del peronismo*. Buenos Aires: Miño y Dávila, 2007.

Cane-Carrasco, James. *The Fourth Enemy*. University Park: Pennsylvania State University Press, forthcoming.

Capelato, María Helena. *Multidões em cena: Propaganda política no varguismo e no peronismo*. São Paulo: FAPESP, 1998.

Carter, Eric D. "'God Bless General Perón'": DDT and the Endgame of Malaria Eradication in Argentina in the 1940s." *Journal of the History of Medicine and Allied Sciences* 64, no. 1 (2009): 78–122.

Castels, Manuel. *City, Class, and Power*. New York: St Martin's, 1978.

Cattaruzza, Alejandro. *Marcelo T. de Alvear: El compromiso y la distancia*. Buenos Aires: Fondo de Cultura Económica, 1997.

Centeno, Miguel A., and Patricio Silva, eds. *The Politics of Expertise in Latin America*. New York: St. Martin's, 1998.

Certeau, Michel de. *The Practice of Everyday Life*. Berkeley: University of California Press, 1984.

Chakrabarty, Dipesh. "Postcoloniality and the Artifice of History." In *Provincializing Europe: Postcolonial Thought and Historical Difference*, 27–46. Princeton, N.J.: Princeton University Press, 2000.

Chamosa, Oscar. *The Argentine Folklore Movement: Sugar Elites, Criollo Workers, and the Politics of Cultural Nationalism, 1900–1950.* Tucson: University of Arizona Press, 2010.

———. "Criollo and Peronist: The Argentine Folklore Movement during the First Peronism, 1943–1955." In *New Cultural History of Peronism,* edited by Matthew Karush and Oscar Chamosa, 113–42. Durham, N.C.: Duke University Press, 2010.

———. "Indigenous or Criollo: The Myth of White Argentina in Tucumán's Calchaquí Valley." *Hispanic American Historical Review* 88 (Feb. 2008): 71–106.

Chatterjee, Partha. *Nationalist Thought and the Colonial World: A Derivative Discourse?* London: Zed Books, 1986.

———. "Two Poets and Death: On Civil and Political Society in the Non-Christian World." In *Questions of Modernity,* edited by Timothy Mitchell, 35–48. Minneapolis: University of Minnesota Press, 2000.

Chávez, Fermín, ed. *La jornada del 17 de Octubre por cuarenta y cinco autores.* Buenos Aires: Ediciones Corregidor, 1996.

Ciria, Alberto. *Política y cultura popular: La Argentina peronista, 1946–1955.* Buenos Aires: Ediciones del Flor, 1983.

Cochran, Thomas, and Ruben Reina. *Entrepreneurship in Argentine Culture: Torcuato Di Tella and S.I.A.M.* Philadelphia: University of Pennsylvania Press, 1962.

Coffin Judith G. "A 'Standard' of Living? European Perspectives on Class and Consumption in the Early Twentieth Century." *International Labor and Working-Class History* 55 (Spring 1999): 6–26.

Cohen, Lizabeth. *A Consumers' Republic: The Politics of Mass Consumption in Postwar America.* New York: Knopf, 2003.

———. *Making a New Deal: Industrial Workers in Chicago, 1919–1939.* Cambridge: Cambridge University Press, 1990.

Collins, Christiane Crasemann. "Urban Interchange in the Southern Cone: Le Corbusier (1929) and Werner Hegemann (1931) in Argentina." *Journal of the Society of Architectural Historians* 54, no. 2 (June 1995): 208–27.

Conniff, Michael L., ed. *Populism in Latin America.* Tuscaloosa: University of Alabama Press, 1999.

Cooper, Frederick. "Postcolonial Studies and the Study of History." In *Postcolonial Studies and Beyond,* edited by Ania Loomba et al., 401–22. Durham, N.C.: Duke University Press, 2005.

Cosse, Isabella. *Estigmas de nacimiento: Peronismo y orden familiar, 1946–1955.* Buenos Aires: University San Andrés/Fondo de Cultura Económica Argentina, 2006.

Cramer, Gisela. "Argentine Riddle: The Pinedo Plan of 1940 and the Political Economy of the Early War Years." *Journal of Latin American Studies* 30 (1998): 519–50.

Cucuzza, Héctor Rubén, and Cristina Acevedo, eds. *Estudios de historia de la educación durante el primer peronismo, 1943–1955.* Buenos Aires: Editorial Los Libros del Riel, 1997.

Cueto, Marcos. *Cold War, Deadly Fevers: Malaria Eradication in Mexico, 1955–1975.* Washington, D.C.: Woodrow Wilson Center Press; Baltimore, Md.: Johns Hopkins University Press, 2007.

Cullather, Nick. "The Foreign Policy of the Calorie." *American Historical Review* 112, no. 2 (Apr. 2007): 337–64.

Daunton, Martin, and Matthew Hilton, eds. *The Politics of Consumption: Material Culture and Citizenship in Europe and America.* Oxford, U.K.: Berg, 2001.

De Elia, Tomás, and Juan Pablo Queiroz, eds. *Evita: El retrato de su vida.* Buenos Aires: Bramblia, 1997.

De Grazia, Victoria. *Irresistible Empire: America's Advance Through Twentieth-Century Europe.* Cambridge, Mass.: Harvard University Press, 2005.

De Grazia, Victoria, and Ellen Furlough, eds. *The Sex of Things: Gender and Consumption in Historical Perspective.* Berkeley: University of California Press, 1996.

De Ipola, Emilio. "Populismo e ideología." *Revista Mexicana de Sociología* 4, no. 31 (July–Sept. 1979): 331–59.

———. "Ruptura y continuidad: Claves parciales para un balance de las interpretaciones del peronismo." *Desarrollo Económico* 29, no. 115 (Oct.–Dec. 1989): 331–59.

De la Torre, Carlos. *Populist Seduction in Latin America: The Ecuadorian Experience.* Columbus: Center for International Studies, Ohio State University, 2000.

De Privitellio, Luciano. *Vecinos y ciudadanos: Política y sociedad en la Buenos Aires de entreguerras.* Buenos Aires: Siglo Veintiuno, 2003.

Derby, Lauren. *The Dictator's Seduction: Politics and the Popular Imagination in the Era of Trujillo.* Durham, N.C.: Duke University Press, 2009.

———. "In the Shadow of the State: The Politics of Denunciation and Panegyric during the Trujillo Regime in the Dominican Republic." *Hispanic American Historical Review* 83, no. 2 (May 2003): 295–344.

Deutsch, Sandra McGee. "Gender and Sociopolitical Change in Twentieth-Century Latin America." *Hispanic American Historical Review* 71, no. 2 (1991): 259–306.

Deutsch, Sandra McGee, and Ronald Dolkart, eds. *Argentine Right: Its History and Intellectual Origins, 1910 to the Present.* Wilmington, Del.: SR Books, 1993.

Díaz Alejandro, Carlos F. *Essays on the Economic History of the Argentine Republic.* New Haven, Conn.: Yale University Press, 1970.

Di Nubila, Domingo. *La epoca de oro: Historia del cine argentino I.* Buenos Aires: Ediciones del Jilguero, 1998.

Di Tella, Guido, and Rudiger Dornbusch, eds. *The Political Economy of Argentina, 1946–83.* Pittsburgh, Pa.: University of Pittsburgh Press, 1989.

Di Tella, Torcuato S. *Perón y los sindicatos: El inicio de una relación conflictiva.* Buenos Aires: Ariel, 2003.

———. *Torcuato Di Tella: Industria y política.* Buenos Aires: Tesis/Grupo Editorial Norma, 1993.

Dornbusch, Rudiger, and Sebastian Edwards, eds. *The Macroeconomics of Populism in Latin America.* Chicago: University of Chicago Press, 1991.

Dos Santos, Estela. *Las mujeres peronistas.* Buenos Aires: Centro Editor de América Latina, 1983.

Doyon, Louise. "Conflictos obreros durante el régimen peronista (1946–1955)." In Torre, *La formación del sindicalismo peronista,* 223–63.

———. "El crecimiento sindical bajo el peronismo." In Torre, *La formación del sindicalismo peronista,* 169–75.

Drinot, Paulo. "Food, Race and Working-Class Identity: *Restaurantes Populares* and Populism in 1930s Peru." *The Americas* 62, no. 2 (Oct. 2005): 245–70.

Dujovne Ortiz, Alicia. *Eva Perón.* Translated by Shawn Fields. New York: St. Martin's, 1996.

Edmunson, Mark. *Nightmare on Main Street: Angels, Sadomasochism, and the Culture of the Gothic.* Cambridge, Mass.: Harvard University Press, 1997.

Elena, Eduardo. "Peronism in 'Good Taste': Culture and Consumption in the Magazine *Argentina.*" In *New Cultural History of Peronism,* edited by Matthew Karush and Oscar Chamosa, 209–38. Durham, N.C.: Duke University Press, 2010.

———. "Peronist Consumer Politics and the Problem of Domesticating Markets in Argentina, 1943–1955." *Hispanic American Historical Review* 87, no. 1 (Feb. 2007): 111–49.

———. "What the People Want: State Planning and Political Participation in Peronist Argentina, 1946–1955." *Journal of Latin American Studies* 37, no. 1 (Feb. 2005): 81–108.

Eloy Martínez, Tomás. *Las memorias del general.* Buenos Aires: Planeta, 1996.

———. *Santa Evita.* Buenos Aires: Planeta, 1997.

Escudé, Carlos. "US Political Destabilization and Economic Boycott of Argentina During the 1940s." In *Argentina between the Great Powers, 1939–1946,* edited by Guido Di Tella and D. Cameron Watt, 56–76. Pittsburgh, Pa.: University of Pittsburgh Press, 1990.

Evita, the Woman behind the Myth. Television program. Produced by History Television Network. 1996.

Fagundes Haussen, Doris. *Rádio e Política: Tempos de Vargas e Perón.* Porto Alegre, Brazil: EDIPUCRS, 1997.

Ferguson, James. "Decomposing Modernity: History and Hierarchy after Development." In Ferguson, *Global Shadows,* 176–93.

———. *Expectations of Modernity: Myths and Meanings of Urban Life on the Zambian Copperbelt.* Berkeley: University of California Press, 1999.

———, ed. *Global Shadows: Africa in the Neoliberal World Order.* Durham, N.C.: Duke University Press, 2006.

Ferioli, Néstor. *La Fundación Eva Perón.* Vol. 2. Buenos Aires: Centro Editor de América Latina, 1990.

Fitzpatrick, Sheila. *The Cultural Front: Power and Culture in Revolutionary Russia.* Ithaca, N.Y.: Cornell University Press, 1992.

———. *Everyday Stalinism: Ordinary Life in Extraordinary Times: Soviet Russia in the 1930s.* New York: Oxford, 1999.

———. "Supplicants and Citizens: Public Letter-Writing in Soviet Russia in the 1930s." *Slavic Review* 55, no. 1 (Spring 1996): 78–105.

Finchelstein, Federico. *Transatlantic Fascism: Ideology, Violence, and the Sacred in Argentina and Italy, 1919–1945.* Durham, N.C.: Duke University Press, 2010.

Fiorucci, Flavia. "El antiperonismo intelectual: De la guerra ideológica a la guerra espiritual." In *Fascismo y antifascismo, peronismo y antiperonismo,* edited by Marcela García Sebastiani. Madrid: Iberoamericana, 2006, 161–93.

———. "Between Institutional Survival and Intellectual Commitment: The Case of the Argentine Society of Writers during Perón's Rule, 1945–1955." *The Americas* 62, no. 4 (Apr. 2006): 591–622.

———. "La cultura, el libro y la lectura bajo el peronismo: El caso de las bibliotecas." Unpublished essay.

———. "La denuncia bajo el peronismo: Conflicto y consenso en el caso del campo escolar. Unpublished essay.

Fischer, Brodwyn. *A Poverty of Rights: Citizenship and Inequality in Twentieth-Century Rio de Janeiro.* Stanford, Calif.: Stanford University Press, 2008.

Forester, Cindy. *The Time of Freedom: Campesino Workers in Guatemala's October Revolution.* Pittsburgh, Pa.: University of Pittsburgh Press, 2001.

Foucault, Michel. *Power/Knowledge: Selected Interviews and Other Writings, 1972–1977.* Edited by Colin Gordon. New York: Pantheon, 1980.

Fraser, Nicolas, and Marysa Navarro. *Evita.* New York: Norton, 1996 [1980].

French, John D., and Daniel James, eds. *The Gendered World of Latin American Women Workers: From Household and Factory to Union Hall and Ballot Box.* Durham, N.C.: Duke University Press, 1997.

Fridman, Daniel. "A New Mentality for a New Economy: Performing the *Homo Economicus* in Argentina (1976–83)." *Economy and Society* 39, no. 2 (May 2010): 271–302.

Frost, Robert. "Machine Liberation: Inventing Housewives and Home Appliances in Interwar France." *French Historical Studies* 18, no. 1 (Spring 1993): 109–30.

Fukuyama, Francis, ed. *Falling Behind: Explaining the Development Gap between Latin America and the United States.* Oxford: Oxford University Press, 2008.

Gaggero, Horacio, and Alicia Garro. *Del trabajo a la casa: La política de vivienda del gobierno peronista, 1946–1955.* Buenos Aires: Editorial Biblos, 1996.

Gambini, Hugo. *Historia del peronismo.* 2 vols. Buenos Aires: Editorial Planeta, 1999–2001.

García Canclini, Néstor. *Consumidores y ciudadanos: Conflictos multiculturales de la globalización.* Mexico City: Grijalbo, 1995.

García Sebastiani, Marcela. *Los antiperonistas en la Argentina peronista: Radicales y socialistas en la política argentina entre 1943 y 1951.* Buenos Aires: Prometeo, 2005.

Gaudio, Ricardo, and Jorge Pilone. "Estado y relaciones laborales en el periodo previo al surgimiento del peronismo." In Torre, *La formación del sindicalismo peronista,* 55–98.

Gené, Marcela. *Un mundo feliz: Imágenes de los trabajadores en el primer peronismo, 1946–1955.* Buenos Aires: Universidad de San Andres, 2005.

Gerchunoff, Pablo. "Peronist Economic Policies, 1946–1955." In *The Political Economy of Argentina, 1946–83,* edited by Guido Di Tella and Rudiger Dornbusch, 59–85. Pittsburgh, Pa.: University of Pittsburg Press, 1989.

Gerchunoff, Pablo, and Damián Antúnez. "De la bonanza peronista a la crisis de desarrollo." In *Nueva Historia Argentina.* Vol. 8, *Los Años Peronistas (1943–1955),* edited by Juan Carlos Torre, 125–206. Buenos Aires: Editorial Sudamericana, 2002.

Gerchunoff, Pablo, and Lucas Llach. *El ciclo de la ilusión y el desencanto: Un siglo de políticas económicas argentinas.* Buenos Aires: Ariel, 1998.

Germani, Gino. *Authoritarianism, Fascism, and National Populism.* New Brunswick, N.J.: Transaction Books, 1978.

Giménez Zapiola, Marcos, and Carlos M. Leguizamón. "La concertación peronista de 1955: El Congreso de la Productividad." In Torre, *La formación del sindicalismo peronista,* 323–58.

Golbert, Laura. "Las políticas sociales antes y después de la Fundación Eva Perón." In Barry, Ramacciotti, and Valobra, *La Fundación Eva Perón y las mujeres,* 19–50.

Goldar, Ernesto. *Buenos Aires: Vida cotidiana en la década del 50.* Buenos Aires: Plus Ultra, 1980.

Gordon, Colin. "Government Rationality: An Introduction." In *The Foucault Effect: Studies in Governmentality,* edited by Graham Burchell, Colin Gordon, and Peter Miller, 1–51. Chicago: University of Chicago Press, 1991.

Gordon, Linda. *Pitied but Not Entitled: Single Mothers and the History of Welfare.* Cambridge, Mass.: Harvard University Press, 1994.

Gorelik, Adrian. *La grilla y el parque: Espacio público y cultura urbana en Buenos Aires, 1887–1936.* Buenos Aires: Universidad Nacional de Quilmes, 1998.

Grandin, Greg. *Fordlandia: The Rise and Fall of Henry Ford's Forgotten Jungle City.* New York: Picador, 2010.

———. *The Last Colonial Massacre: Latin America in the Cold War.* Chicago: University of Chicago Press, 2004.

Graziano, Frank. *Cultures of Devotion: Folk Saints of Spanish America.* Oxford: Oxford University Press, 2007.

Green, W. John. *Gaitanismo, Left Liberalism, and Popular Mobilization in Colombia.* Gainesville: University of Florida Press, 2003.

Grindle, Merilee, and Pilar Domingo, eds. *Proclaiming Revolution: Bolivia in Comparative Perspective.* London: Institute of Latin American Studies, 2003.

Gutiérrez, Leandro, and Luis Alberto Romero. *Sectores populares, cultura y política: Buenos Aires en la entreguerra.* Buenos Aires: Editorial Sudamericana, 1995.

Gutman, Margarita, and Jorge Enrique Hardoy. *Buenos Aires: Historia urbana de la área metropolitana.* Madrid: Editorial Mapfre, 1992.

Guy, Donna. *Women Build the Welfare State: Performing Charity and Creating Rights in Argentina, 1880–1955.* Durham, N.C.: Duke University Press, 2009.

Handy, Jim. *Revolution in the Countryside: Rural Conflict and Agrarian Reform in Guatemala, 1944–1954.* Chapel Hill: University of North Carolina Press, 1994.

Harvey, David. *Consciousness and the Urban Experience: Studies in the History and Theory of Capitalist Urbanization.* Baltimore, Md.: John Hopkins University Press, 1985.

Healey, Mark Alan. *The Ruins of the New Argentina: Peronism and the Remaking of San Juan after the 1944 Earthquake.* Durham, N.C.: Duke University Press, forthcoming.

Hirschman, Albert O. *Exit, Voice, and Loyalty: Responses to Decline in Firms, Organizations, and States.* Cambridge, Mass.: Harvard University Press, 1970.

Hobsbawm, Eric. *The Age of Extremes: A History of the World, 1914–1991.* New York: Vintage, 1994.

Hoffnung-Garskof, Jesse. *A Tale of Two Cities: Santo Domingo and New York after 1950.* Princeton, N.J.: Princeton University Press, 2008.

Holston, James. *Insurgent Citizenship: Disjunctions of Democracy and Modernity in Brazil.* Princeton, N.J.: Princeton University Press, 2008.

———. *The Modernist City: An Anthropological Critique of Brasília.* Chicago: University of Chicago Press, 1989.

Horowitz, Joel. *Argentina's Radical Party and Popular Mobilization, 1916–1930.* University Park: Pennsylvania State University Press, 2008.

———. *Argentine Unions, the State, and the Rise of Perón, 1930–1945.* Berkeley, Calif.: Institute of International Studies, 1990.

———. "Occupational Community and the Creation of a Self-Styled Elite: Railroad Workers in Argentina." *The Americas* 1 (July 1985): 55–82.

Jacobs, Meg. "How about Some Meat? The Office of Price Administration, Consumption Politics, and State Building from the Bottom Up, 1941–1946." *Journal of American History* 84, no. 3 (Dec. 1997): 910–41.

———. *Pocketbook Politics: Economic Citizenship in Twentieth-Century America.* Princeton, N.J.: Princeton University Press, 2005.

James, Daniel. *Doña María's Story: Life History, Memory, and Political Identity.* Durham, N.C.: Duke University Press, 2000.

———. "October 17th and 18th, 1945: Mass Protest, Peronism, and the Argentine Working Class." *Journal of Social History* 21 (Spring 1988): 441–61.

———. "Racionalización y respuesta de la clase obrera: Contexto y limitaciones de la actividad gremial en la Argentina." *Desarrollo Económico* 21, no. 83 (Oct–Dec.1981): 321–49.

———. *Resistance and Integration: Peronism and the Argentine Working Class, 1946–1976.* Cambridge: Cambridge University Press, 1988.

Joseph, Gilbert M., and Daniel Nugent, eds. *Everyday Forms of State Formation: Revolution and the Negotiation of Rule in Modern Mexico.* Durham, N.C.: Duke University Press, 1994.

Joseph, Gilbert M., Anne Rubenstein, and Eric Zolov, eds. *Fragments of a Golden Age: The Politics of Culture in Mexico Since 1940*. Durham, N.C.: Duke University Press, 2001.

Karush, Matthew B. "The Melodramatic Nation: Integration and Polarization in the Argentine Cinema of the 1930s." *Hispanic American Historical Review* 87, no. 2 (May 2007): 293–326.

———. *Workers or Citizens: Democracy and Identity in Rosario, Argentina (1912–1930)*. Albuquerque: University of New Mexico Press, 2002.

Katra, William. *Contorno: Literary Engagement in Post-Peronist Argentina*. Rutherford, N.J.: Fairleigh Dickinson University Press, 1988.

Kazin, Michael. *The Populist Persuasion: An American History*. New York: Basic Books, 1998.

Klubock, Thomas Miller. *Contested Communities: Class, Gender, and Politics in Chile's El Teniente Copper Mine, 1904–1951*. Durham, N.C.: Duke University Press, 1998.

Knight, Alan. "Cardenismo: Juggernaut or Jalopy?" *Journal of Latin American Studies* 26, no. 1 (1994): 73–109.

———. "Populism and Neo-populism in Latin America, especially Mexico." *Journal of Latin American Studies* 30 (1998): 223–48.

Korzeniewicz, Roberto. "Labor Unrest in Argentina, 1930–1943." *Latin American Research Review* 28, no. 1 (1993): 7–40.

Kotkin, Stephen. *Magnetic Mountain: Stalinism as Civilization*. Berkeley: University of California Press, 1995.

———. "Modern Times: The Soviet Union and the Interwar Conjuncture." *Kritika* 2, no. 1 (Winter 2001): 111–64.

Laclau, Ernesto. *Politics and Ideology in Marxist Theory*. London: NLB, 1977.

Lears, Jackson. *Fables of Abundance: A Cultural History of Advertising in America*. New York: Basic Books, 1994.

Levine, Robert M. *Father of the Poor? Vargas and His Era*. Cambridge: Cambridge University Press, 1998.

Levitsky, Steven. *La transformación del justicialismo: Del partido sindical al partido clientelista, 1983–1999*. Translated by Leandro Wolfson. Buenos Aires: Siglo Veintiuno, 2005.

Lewis, Colin M. "Social Insurance: Ideology and Policy in the Argentine, c. 1920–1966." In *Welfare, Poverty, and Development in Latin America*, edited by Christopher Abel and Colin M. Lewis, 175–85. London: Macmillan, 1993.

Little, Walter. "La organización obrera y el estado peronista." In Torre, *La formación del sindicalismo peronista*, 221–330.

Llach, Juan José. "El Plan Pinedo de 1940, su significado histórico y los orígenes de la economía política del peronismo." *Desarrollo Económico* 23, no. 92 (Jan.–Mar. 1984): 515–57.

Llorente, Ignacio. "La composición social del movimiento peronista hacia 1954." In Mora y Araujo and Llorente, *El voto peronista*, 369–96.

Lobato, Mirta Zaida, ed. *Cuando las mujeres reinaban: Belleza, virtud y poder en la Argentina del siglo XX*. Buenos Aires: Editorial Biblos, 2005.

———. *La vida en las fábricas: Trabajo, protesta y política en una comunidad obrera, Berisso (1904–1970)*. Buenos Aires: Entrepasados/Prometeo, 2001.

Lomnitz, Claudio. *Deep Mexico, Silent Mexico*. Minneapolis: University of Minnesota Press, 2001.

Luccini, Christina. *Apoyo empresarial en los orígenes del peronismo*. Buenos Aires: Centro Editor de América Latina, 1990.

Luna, Félix. *Perón y su tiempo*. 3 vols. Buenos Aires: Editorial Sudamericana, 1991 [1984–86].

Macro, Darío, and César Tcach, eds. *La invención del peronismo en el interior del país*. Santa Fe, Argentina: Universidad Nacional del Litoral, 2003.

Mamdani, Mahmood. *Citizen and Subject: Contemporary Africa and the Legacy of Late Colonialism*. Princeton, N.J.: Princeton University Press, 1996.

Marshall, Adriana. "La composición del consumo en los obreros industriales de Buenos Aires, 1930–1980." *Desarrollo Económico* 21, no. 83 (Oct.–Dec. 1981): 351–74.

Marshall, T. H. *Citizenship and Social Democracy*. New York: Doubleday, 1964.

Matsushita, Hiroshi. *Movimiento obrero argentino, 1930–1945*. Buenos Aires: Siglo Viente, 1983.

Mazower, Mark. *Dark Continent: Europe's Twentieth Century*. New York: Vintage, 2000.

Mbembé, J. A. *On the Postcolony*. Berkeley: University of California Press, 2001.

McCann, Bryan. *Hello, Hello Brazil: Popular Music and the Making of Modern Brazil*. Durham, N.C.: Duke University Press, 2004.

McCrossen, Alexis, ed. *Land of Necessity: Consumer Culture in the United States–Mexico Borderlands*. Durham, N.C.: Duke University Press, 2009.

McGuire, James W. *Peronism without Perón: Unions, Parties, and Democracy in Argentina*. Stanford, Calif.: Stanford University Press, 1997.

Mercante, Domingo Alfredo. *Mercante: El corazón de Perón*. Buenos Aires: Ediciones de la Flor, 1995.

Milanesio, Natalia. "Food Politics and Consumption in Peronist Argentina." *Hispanic American Historical Review* 90 (Feb. 2010): 75–108.

———. "The Guardian Angels of the Domestic Economy: Housewives' Responsible Consumption in Peronist Argentina." *Journal of Women's History* 18, no. 3 (Sept. 2006): 91–117.

———. "Peronists and *Cabecitas*: Stereotypes and Anxieties at the Peak of Social Change." In *New Cultural History of Peronism*, edited by Matthew Karush and Oscar Chamosa, 53–84. Durham, N.C.: Duke University Press, 2010.

Molina y Vedia, Juan. *Fermín Bereterbide: La construcción de lo imposible*. Buenos Aires: Ediciones Colihue, 1997.

Mora y Araujo, Manuel, and Ignacio Llorente, eds. *El voto peronista: Ensayos de sociología electoral argentina*. Buenos Aires: Editorial Sudamericana, 1980.

Moreno, Juan Carlos. *Gustavo Martínez Zuviría*. Buenos Aires: Ediciones Culturales Argentinas, 1962.

Moreno, Julio. *Yankee Don't Go Home! Mexican Nationalism, American Business Culture, and the Shaping of Modern Mexico, 1920–1950*. Chapel Hill: University of North Carolina Press, 2003.

Muchnik, Daniel. "El IAPI: Balance y memoria de una experiencia." *Todo es historia* 229 (May 1986): 74–85.

Murilo de Carvalho, José. *Cidadania no Brasil*. Rio de Janeiro: Civilização Brasileira, 2001.

Murmis, Miguel, and Juan Carlos Portantiero. *Estudios sobre los orígenes del peronismo*. Buenos Aires: Siglo Veintiuno, 1971.

Nállim, Jorge. "Between Free Trade and Economic Dictatorship: Socialists, Radicals, and the Politics of Economic Liberalism in Argentina, 1930–1943." *Canadian Journal of Latin American and Caribbean Studies* 33, no. 65 (2008): 139–74.

———. "Del antifacismo al antiperonismo: *Argentina Libre,* . . . *Antinazi* y el surgimiento del antiperonismo político e intelectual." In *Fascismo y antifascismo, peronismo y antiperonismo*, edited by Marcela García Sebastiani, 77–105. Madrid: Iberoamericana, 2006.

Navarro, Marysa. *Evita*. Buenos Aires: Ediciones Corregidor, 1981.

Neiburg, Federico. *Los intelectuales y la invención del peronismo.* Buenos Aires: Alianza Editorial, 1998.

Nelson, Laura C. *Measured Excess: Status, Gender, and Consumer Nationalism in South Korea.* New York: Columbia University Press, 2000.

Newton, Ronald C. *The Nazi Menace in Argentina, 1931–1947.* Stanford, Calif.: Stanford University Press, 1992.

Novick, Susana. *IAPI: Auge y decadencia.* Buenos Aires: Centro Editor de América Latina, 1986.

O'Brien, Thomas. *The Century of U.S. Capitalism in Latin America.* Albuquerque: University of New Mexico Press, 1999.

Ochoa, Enrique C. *Feeding Mexico: The Political Uses of Food since 1910.* Wilmington, Del.: SR Books, 2000.

O'Dougherty, Maureen. *Consumption Intensified: The Politics of Middle-Class Daily Life in Brazil.* Durham, N.C.: Duke University Press, 2002.

Orlove, Benjamin, ed. *The Allure of the Foreign: Imported Goods in Postcolonial Latin America.* Ann Arbor: University of Michigan Press, 1997.

Owensby, Brian. *Intimate Ironies: Modernity and the Making of Middle-Class Lives in Brazil.* Stanford, Calif.: Stanford University Press, 1999.

Page, Joseph A. *Perón: A Biography.* New York: Random House, 1983.

Palermo, Silvana A. "El sufragio femenino en el Congreso Nacional: Ideologías de género y ciudadanía en la Argentina (1916–1955)." *Boletín del Instituto de Historia Argentina y Americana "Dr. Emilio Ravignani"* 16–17 (1997): 151–78.

Panettieri, José, ed. *Argentina: Trabajadores entre dos guerras.* Buenos Aires: Eudeba, 2000.

Pastoriza, Elisa, and Juan Carlos Torre. "Mar del Plata, un sueño de los argentinos." In *Historia de la vida privada en la Argentina.* Vol. 3, *La Argentina entre multitudes y soledades: De los años treinta a la actualidad,* edited by Fernando Devoto and Marta Madero, 49–78. Buenos Aires: Taurus, 1999.

Pereyra, Horacio José. "Pinedo y El Plan Económico de 1940." In *Representaciones inconclusas: Las clases, los actores y los concursos de la memoria, 1912–1946,* edited by Waldo Ansaldi, Alfredo R. Pucciarelli, and José C. Villarruel, 257–88. Buenos Aires: Biblos, 1995.

Piglia, Ricardo. *Crítica y ficción.* Buenos Aires: Seix Barral, 2000.

Pite, Rebekah. "Creating a Common Table: Doña Petrona, Cooking, and Consumption in Argentina, 1928–1983." Ph.D. diss., University of Michigan, 2007.

Plotkin, Mariano. *Mañana es San Perón: Propaganda, rituales políticos y educación en el régimen peronista (1946–1955).* Buenos Aires: Ariel Historia Argentina, 1993.

———. "The Changing Perceptions of Peronism." In *Peronism and Argentina,* edited by James P. Brennan, 29–54. Wilmington, Del.: SR Books, 1998.

Polanyi, Karl. *The Great Transformation.* Boston: Beacon, 1957 [1944].

Potash, Robert A. *The Army and Politics in Argentina, 1928–1945.* Stanford, Calif.: Stanford University Press, 1969.

———. *Perón y el GOU: Los documentos de una logia secreta.* Buenos Aires: Editorial Sudamericana, 1984.

Powers, Nancy R. *Grassroots Expectations of Democracy and Economy: Argentina in Comparative Perspective.* Pittsburgh, Pa.: University of Pittsburgh Press, 2001.

Prakash, Gyan. *Another Reason: Science and the Imagination of Modern India.* Princeton, N.J.: Princeton University Press, 1999.

Rabinbach, Anson. *The Human Motor: Energy, Fatigue, and the Origins of Modernity.* New York: Basic Books, 1990.

Rabinow, Paul. *French Modern: Norms and Forms of the Social Environment.* Cambridge, Mass.: MIT Press, 1989.

Ramacciotti, Karina. *La política sanitaria del peronismo.* Buenos Aires: Editorial Biblos, 2009.

———. "Las voces que cuestionaron la política sanitaria del peronismo (1946–1949)." In *Las políticas sociales en perspectiva histórica,* edited by Daniel Lvovich and Juan Suriano, 169–96. Buenos Aires: Prometeo, 2006.

Ramacciotti, Karina Inés, and Adriana María Valobra, eds. *Generando el peronismo: Estudios de cultura, política y género (1946–1955).* Buenos Aires: Proyecto Editorial, 2004.

Randall, Amy E. *The Soviet Dream World of Retail Trade and Consumption in the 1930s.* New York: Palgrave Macmillan, 2008.

Rapoport, Mario, Eduardo Madrid, Andrés Musacchio, and Richardo Vicente. *Historia económica, política y social de la Argentina (1880–2003).* Buenos Aires: Ariel, 2006.

Recchini de Lattes, Zulma. *La participación económica feminina en la Argentina desde la segunda posguerra hasta 1970.* Buenos Aires: Centro de Estudios de Población, 1980.

Rein, Raanan. *In the Shadow of Perón: Juan Atilio Bramuglia and the Second Line of Argentina's Populist Movement.* Stanford, Calif.: Stanford University Press, 2008.

Rein, Raanan, and Claudio Panella, eds. *Peronismo y prensa escrita: Abordajes, miradas e interpretaciones nacionales y extranjeras.* La Plata, Argentina: Editorial de la Universidad Nacional de La Plata, 2008.

Rocchi, Fernando. *Chimneys in the Desert: Industrialization in Argentina during the Export Boom Years, 1870–1930.* Stanford, Calif.: Stanford University Press, 2006.

Rock, David. *Politics in Argentina, 1890–1930: The Rise and Fall of Radicalism.* Cambridge: Cambridge University Press, 1975.

———. "Radical Populism and the Conservative Elite, 1912–1930." In *Argentina in the Twentieth Century,* edited by David Rock, 75–81. Pittsburgh, Pa.: University of Pittsburgh Press, 1975.

Rodgers, Daniel T. *Atlantic Crossings: Social Politics in a Progressive Age.* Cambridge, Mass.: Belknap, 1998.

Romero, Luis Alberto. *A History of Argentina in the Twentieth Century.* Translated by James P. Brennan. University Park: Pennsylvania State University Press, 2002.

Rosemblatt, Karin Alejandra. *Gendered Compromises: Political Cultures and the State in Chile, 1920–1950.* Chapel Hill: University of North Carolina Press, 2000.

Ross, Peter. "Justicia social: Una evalución de los logros del peronismo clásico." *Anuario de IEHS* 3 (1993): 105–24.

Rougier, Marcelo, and Martín Fiszbein. "De Don Derrochín a Maese Ahorrín: El fomento del ahorro durante la economía peronista." In Berrotarán, Jáuregui, and Rougier, *Sueños de bienestar en la Nueva Argentina,* 107–44.

Rougier, Marcelo, and Jorge Schvarzer. *Las grandes empresas no mueren de pie: El (o)caso de SIAM.* Buenos Aires: Grupo Editorial Norma, 2006.

Rouquié, Alain. *Poder militar y sociedad política en la Argentina.* Buenos Aires: Emece, 1982.

Sábato, Hilda, ed. *Ciudadanía política y formación de las naciones: Perspectivas históricas de América Latina.* Mexico, D.F.: Colegio de México, Fondo de Cultura Económica, 1999.

———. *La política en las calles: Entre el voto y la movilización, Buenos Aires 1862–1880.* Buenos Aires: Editorial Sudamericana, 1998.

Salvatore, Ricardo D. "The Normalization of Economic Life: Representations of the Economy in Golden-Age Buenos Aires, 1890–1913." *Hispanic American Historical Review* 81, no. 1 (2001): 1–44.

Sarlo, Beatriz. *La imaginación técnica: Sueños modernos de la cultura argentina*. Buenos Aires: Nueva Visión, 1992.

Saulquin, Susana. *La moda en la Argentina*. Buenos Aires: Emecé, 1990.

Scarzanella, Eugenia. "El ocio peronista: Vacaciones y 'turismo popular' en la Argentina (1943–1955)." *Entrepasados, Revista de Historia* 7, no. 14 (1st half 1998): 65–86.

Schorske, Carl E. *Fin-de-Siècle Vienna: Politics and Culture*. New York: Vintage, 1981.

Schvarzer, Jorge. *Empresarios del pasado: La Unión Industrial Argentina*. Buenos Aires: CISEA/Imago Mundi, 1991.

———. *La industria que supimos conseguir: Una historia político-social de la industria argentina*. Buenos Aires: Planeta, 1996.

Scott, James C. *Seeing Like a State: How Certain Schemes to Improve the Human Condition Have Failed*. New Haven, Conn.: Yale University Press, 1998.

Seigel, Micol. *Uneven Encounters: Making Race and Nation in Brazil and the United States*. Durham, N.C.: Duke University Press, 2009.

Seoane, Maria. *El burgués maldito*. Buenos Aires: Planeta, 1998.

Seveso, César. "Political Emotions and the Origins of the Peronist Resistance." In *New Cultural History of Peronism*, edited by Matthew Karush and Oscar Chamosa, 239–69. Durham, N.C.: Duke University Press, 2010.

Sigal, Silvia, and Eliseo Verón. *Perón o Muerte: Los fundamentos discursivos del fenómeno peronista*. Buenos Aires: Legasa, 1986.

Sirven, Pablo. *Perón y los medios de comunicación (1943–1955)*. Buenos Aires: Centro Editor de América Latina, 1984.

Smith, Peter. *Politics and Beef in Argentina: Patterns of Conflict and Change*. New York: Columbia University Press, 1969.

Smith, William C. *Authoritarianism and the Crisis of the Argentine Political Economy*. Stanford, Calif.: Stanford University Press, 1989.

Snodgrass, Michael "Topics Not Suitable for Propaganda: Working-Class Resistance under Peronism." In *Workers' Control in Latin America*, edited by Jonathan C. Brown, 159–88. Chapel Hill: University of North Carolina Press, 1997.

Somoza Rodríguez, Miguel. *Educación y política en Argentina (1946–1955)*. Buenos Aires: Miño y Dávila Editores, 2006.

Soper, Kate, and Frank Trentmann. *Citizenship and Consumption*. Houndmills, N.Y.: Palgrave Macmillan, 2008.

Soprano, Germán. "El DNT y su proyecto de regulación estatal de las relaciones Capital-Trabajo en Argentina, 1907–1943." In Panettieri, *Argentina: Trabajdores entre dos guerras*, 31–53.

Stawski, Martín. "El populismo paralelo." In Berrotarán, Jáuregui, and Rougier, *Sueños de bienestar en la Nueva Argentina*, 193–228.

Stein, Steve. *Populism in Peru: The Emergence of the Masses and the Politics of Social Control*. Madison: University of Wisconsin Press, 1980.

Strasser, Susan, Charles McGovern, and Mathias Judt, eds. *Getting and Spending: European and American Consumer Societies in the Twentieth Century*. Cambridge: Cambridge University Press, 1998.

Suriano, Juan, ed. *La cuestión social en Argentina, 1870–1943*. Buenos Aires: Editorial La Colmena, 2000.

Tamarin, David. *The Argentine Labor Movement 1930–1945: A Study in the Origins of Peronism*. Albuquerque: University of New Mexico Press, 1985.

Taylor, J. M. *Eva Perón: The Myths of a Woman*. Chicago: University of Chicago Press, 1979.

Teach Asad, César. *Amadeo Sabattini: La nación y la isla*. Buenos Aires: Fondo de Cultura Económica, 1997.

Teichman, Judith. "Interest Conflict and Entrepreneurial Support for Perón." *Latin American Research Review* 16, no. 1 (1981): 144–55.

Thompson, E. P. "The Moral Economy of the English Crowd in the Eighteenth Century." *Past and Present* 50 (Feb. 1971): 76–136.

Thompson, Noel. "Social Opulence, Private Asceticism: Ideas of Consumption in Early Socialist Thought." In Daunton and Hilton, *The Politics of Consumption*, 51–68.

Tinsman, Heidi. "A Paradigm of Our Own: Joan Scott in Latin American History." *American Historical Review* 113, no. 5 (Dec. 2008): 1357–74.

———. "Politics of Gender and Consumption in Authoritarian Chile, 1973–1900." *Latin American Research Review* 41, no. 3 (Oct. 2006): 7–31.

Torrado, Susana. *Estructura social de la Argentina, 1945–1983*. Buenos Aires: Ediciones de la Flor, 1992.

Torre, Horacio A. "Cambios en la estructura socioespacial de Buenos Aires a partir de la década de 1940." In *Después de Germani: Exploraciones sobre la estructura social en la Argentina*, edited by Jorge Raul Jorrat and Ruth Sautu, 158–75. Buenos Aires: Paidos, 1992.

Torre, Juan Carlos, ed. *La formación del sindicalismo peronista*. Buenos Aires: Editorial Legasa, 1988.

———. "Interpretando (una vez más) los orígenes del peronismo." *Desarrollo Económico* 28, no. 112 (Jan.–Mar. 1989): 525–48.

———, ed. *El 17 de Octubre de 1945*. Buenos Aires: Ariel, 1995.

Torre, Juan Carlos, and Eliza Pastoriza. "La democratización del bienestar." In *Nueva Historia Argentina*. Vol. 8, *Los Años Peronistas (1943–1955)*, edited by Juan Carlos Torre, 257–312. Buenos Aires: Editorial Sudamericana, 2002.

Trentmann, Frank. "Beyond Consumerism: New Historical Perspectives on Consumption." *Journal of Contemporary History* 39, no. 3 (2004): 373–401.

———. *Free Trade Nation: Commerce, Consumption, and Civil Society in Modern Britain*. Oxford: Oxford University Press, 2008.

Trouillot, Michel-Rolph. *Silencing the Past: Power and the Production of History*. Boston: Beacon, 1995.

Turits, Richard Lee. *Foundations of Despotism: Peasants, the Trujillo Regime, and Modernity in Dominican History*. Stanford, Calif.: Stanford University Press, 2003.

Ulanovsky, Carlos. *Paren las rotativas: Una historia de grandes diarios, revistas y periodistas argentinos*. Buenos Aires: Espasa Calpe, 1997.

Ulanovsky, Carlos, and Marta Merkin. *Días de radio: Historia de la radio argentina*. Buenos Aires: Espasa Calpe, 1995.

Vaughan, Mary Kay. *Cultural Politics in Revolution: Teachers, Peasants, and Schools in Mexico, 1930–1940*. Tucson: University of Arizona Press, 1997.

———. "Modernizing Patriarchy." In *Hidden Histories of Gender and the State in Latin America*, edited by Elizabeth Dore and Maxine Molyneux, 195–214. Durham, N.C.: Duke University Press, 2000.

Villanueva, Javier. "Economic Development." In *Prologue to Perón: Argentina in Depression and War, 1930–1943*, edited by Mark Falcoff and Ronald H. Dolkart, 57–82. Berkeley: University of California Press, 1975.

Villarruel, José C. "El futuro como incertidumbre: Los industrialistas y la tutela del estado." In *Argentina en la paz de dos guerras, 1914–1945*, edited by Waldo Ansaldi, Alfredo R. Pucciarelli, and José C. Villarruel, 193–230. Buenos Aires: Biblos, 1993.

————. "Los conflictos entre el estado." In *Representaciones inconclusas: Las clases, los actores y los concursos de la memoria, 1912–1946,* edited by Waldo Ansaldi, Alfredo R. Pucciarelli, and José C. Villarruel, 303–50. Buenos Aires: Biblos, 1995.

Visacovsky, Sergio, and Enrique Garguin, eds. *Moralidades, economías, e identidades de clase media: Estudios historicos y etnograficos.* Buenos Aires: Antropologia, 2009.

Walter, Richard J. *The Province of Buenos Aires and Argentine Politics, 1912–1943.* Cambridge: Cambridge University Press, 1985.

————. "The Right and the Peronists, 1943–1955." In Deutsch and Dolkart, *The Argentine Right,* 99–118.

————. *The Socialist Party of Argentina, 1890–1930.* Austin, Tex.: Institute of Latin American Studies, 1977.

Weber, Eugene Joseph. *The Hollow Years: France in the 1930s.* New York: Norton, 1994.

Weinstein, Barbara. "Developing Inequality." *American Historical Review* 113, no. 1 (Feb. 2008): 1–18.

————. *For Social Peace in Brazil: Industrialists and the Remaking of the Working Class in São Paulo, 1920–1964.* Chapel Hill: University of North Carolina Press, 1996.

————. "Unskilled Worker, Skilled Housewife: Constructing the Working-Class Woman in São Paulo, Brazil." In French and James, *The Gendered Worlds of Latin American Women Workers,* 72–99.

Williams, Daryl. *Culture Wars in Brazil.* Durham, N.C.: Duke University Press, 2001.

Wirth, John D. *The Politics of Brazilian Development.* Stanford, Calif.: Stanford University Press, 1970.

Wolfe, Joel. *Autos and Progress: The Brazilian Search for Modernity.* New York: Oxford, 2010.

————. "Father of the Poor or Mother of the Rich? Getúlio Vargas, Industrial Workers, and Constructions of Class, Gender, and Populism in São Paulo, 1930–1954." *Radical History Review* 58 (Winter 1994): 80–111.

Wynia, Gary W. *Argentina in the Postwar: Politics and Economic Policymaking in a Divided Society.* Albuquerque: University of New Mexico Press, 1978.

Zanatta, Loris. *Del estado liberal a la nación católica: Iglesia y ejército en los orígenes del peronismo, 1930–1943.* Buenos Aires: Universidad Nacional de Quilmes, 1996.

Zimmerman, Eduardo A. *Los liberales reformistas: La cuestión social en la Argentina, 1890–1916.* Buenos Aires: Editorial Sudamericana, 1995.

Zulawski, Ann. *Unequal Cures: Public Health and Political Change in Bolivia.* Durham, N.C.: Duke University Press, 2007.

Zweiniger-Bargielowska, Ina. *Austerity in Britain: Rationing, Controls, and Consumption 1939–1955.* Oxford: Oxford University Press, 2000.

Index

advertising, 25, 28, 32; aimed at women, 33, 90, 171; depictions of male consumers, 49; Eva Perón Foundation stores, 179; manufactured goods, 90, 105, 165; similarities between Peronist propaganda and private sector, 95, 134, 138–39, 165, 183; in union newspapers, 48–50. *See also* propaganda

agriculture, 12; and domestic market, 45, 51, 91, 167; exports, 24, 167–68, 249, 252, 254; and industrialization, 23–24; and Marshall Plan, 79–81; Peronist regulation of, 61–62, 66, 76–79, 91–92; and Plan Económico, 221–22, 225–26, 228–29, 249; regional variety of, 27, 36–39; state management before Perón, 55–56; subsidies for, 55, 91, 115, 231. *See also* food; land reform

Africa: scholarship on midcentury politics in, 15, 262n10, 295n2

appliances, 90, 91, 240–41; electric fans, 18, 240; electric irons, 32, 49, 90; kitchen stoves, 32, 49, 90, 120, 287n16; Peronist distribution of sewing machines, 120, 124, 139–40, 145, 150; and Peronist social assistance, 120, 140, 287; refrigerators, 1, 90, 120, 164, 167, 240; sewing machines, 31, 90; vacuum cleaners, 90; washing machines, 240

anti-Peronism, 3, 9; criticism of Peronist consumers, 155–60, 166, 173, 184; decline and fall of Peronist regime, 222–23, 228, 235, 245–47; and letter writing, 151; March for the Constitution and Liberty, 73, 83; and opposition to antispeculation campaigns, 106–7, 202; reactions to 1949 constitutional reform, 128; wartime origins of, 72–74. *See also* business organizations; military; Radical Party; Socialist Party

antispeculation campaigns: business reactions to, 102–6, 204–6; businesses' refusal to pay fines, 243–44; and corruption, 101–2; enforcement during Perón's first term, 98–102; enforcement during Perón's second term, 235–37; ethnic and racial dimensions of, 97, 114; legal and discursive foundations of, 84–86, 93–98; letter writer views on, 115–16, 200–14; opposition to, 106–7; popular collaboration with, 107–17, 171–72; roots in pre-Peronist era, 44, 57, 62; violence accompanying, 213. *See also* commerce; consumption, mass; morality

Apold, Raúl, 130, 244, 283n29

Aramburu, Pedro Eugenio, 247–48

Arbenz, Jacobo, 5, 76

Argentina: definition of litoral region, 16, 27–28, 37; foreign travelers' impressions of, 21–23, 26, 31–32, 160–61; instability in recent decades, 256–58; literacy rates, 143; mythic wealth, 1, 12, 19–20, 79, 162; population size, 23, 30, 77, 291n7; regional differences, 16, 26–29, 37–38, 51, 92–93; social opportunity in, 25–26, 135; social structure, 265n25

Argentina (magazine), 180–84, 187–88, 289n63

Arlt, Roberto, 18–19, 21, 32, 34, 50

Armour Research Foundation, 30–32, 34

Arrabalera (film, 1950), 114

Atlantic World: Argentina's place within, 15, 22–24, 36

Aunós, Eduardo, 26, 31–32, 267n43

Australia, 88

Avellaneda, Buenos Aires (city), 59, 109, 165, 202, 205

Balbín, Ricardo, 191–92

Benítez de Maldonado, Hilda, 2–3, 17

Bereterbide, Fermín, 54–55, 58, 81

Bialet Massé, Juan, 36–38, 163

Blum, Léon, 76

Bolivia, 76, 249

Bolsa de Comercio, 58, 68, 93

Borges, Jorge Luis 159, 287n11

Borlenghi, Ángel Gabriel, 169, 177, 244

Braden, Spruille, 274n62

Brazil: consumer society, 51, 101, 185, 259; "disjunctive democracy," 6; midcentury politics, 5, 54, 288n40, 290n74

Bretton Woods Conference, 242

Bruce, James, 160–61

Buenos Aires, city of, 12, 16, 79, 119, 227; commercial conditions in the 1930s, 18–19, 21–22, 26–29, 45, 51; commercial conditions under Peronism, 1–2, 87–90, 92, 157, 160, 177–80; Corrientes avenue, 18, 22; Florida street, 21, 26, 138, 177, 193; impact of antispeculation campaigns in, 95, 98–102, 113–14; letters from residents of, 201–3, 207, 209, 211, 238; model markets, 226–27; population, 23; rallies and protests, 57, 73–74, 191–92, 230, 235–37, 246; residents' living standards, 37, 39, 57, 62, 130

Buenos Aires, greater (suburban region), 72, 89, 105, 109, 187; letters from residents of, 145, 176, 194–95, 204, 211, 217–18, 239. *See also* urbanization (suburbanization)

Buenos Aires province, 27, 56, 64, 123, 192; letters from residents of, 149, 211, 218; social programs, 1, 133, 137–39, 148, 177

Bunge, Alejandro, 36–38, 41, 51, 58; circle of followers, 62, 65, 167

business organizations: reactions to antispeculation, 102–6, 204–6; relations with Peronist regime, 91, 98–101, 107, 241–45; responses to Perón's rise, 72–74; role in postwar planning, 55–60. *See also* Confederación General Económica; Unión Industrial Argentina

Cafferata, Juan, 45, 47, 51

Calviño de Gómez, María Rosa, 170, 172, 224

Cárdenas, Lázaro, 5, 54, 289n51

Casares, Bioy, 159

Castillo, Ramón, 60–61

Catamarca province, 37, 200, 209

Catholicism, 10, 61, 138; attitudes toward mass consumption, 42–43, 45, 95, 106; Church's role in the fall of the Peronist regime, 245–46, 256; and the intellectuals of *Argentina* magazine, 159, 181–82; influence on 1930s social politics, 35, 37, 41, 45–48, 70, 270n15; and Peronist conceptions of justice, 94–95, 97–98, 220; and popular religiosity, 2, 146–47, 150, 220, 230; and saintly portrayals of Evita, 147, 150, 230, 233–34; and social assistance programs, 135–36, 138

Cereijo, Ramón, 104, 225, 239, 295n3

Chávez, Hugo 83, 259

Chile, 54, 63, 83

China, 259

citizenship: and antispeculation campaigns, 107–17; and austerity, 221, 225–33; and civil liberties restrictions, 7, 126–27, 234–35; and consumer thrift, 154–56, 166–75, 180; Constitution of 1949, 7–9 128–29, 144; in contemporary Argentina, 257–59; in early Peronist discourse, 52–53, 68–71, 81–83; letter writers' views on, 151, 189, 203–4, 206–14, 218–20; and midcentury "consumer citizenship," 85–86, 117–18, 155–56, 186, 254; Peronist paradigm of, 2–3, 7–10, 254–56; "populist constitutionalism," 128, 151; scholarship on, 4–7; and social assistance, 120–21, 129–31, 151–53; and social rights, 7, 127–29, 255; and state planning, 196–97, 218–20

civil society: alliances with Peronist political organizations, 195–96, 200, 208–9; continuity of older forms under Peronist rule, 190–91, 194–97; neighborhood improvement organizations, 6, 195–96, 218, 236; and Peronist indoctrination, 126–27, 195, 234; Peronist partisan institutions, 155–56, 170–72, 200, 226–28, 230; role in antispeculation campaigns, 107–12; scholarly models of,

6–7, 9; *See also* labor unions; Peronist Party; anti-Peronism

clothing, 24, 87–88; 98; alpargatas (cord-soled shoes), 30, 160; household production of, 112, 137, 169–71, 226–27; imported, 165, 259; letter writer commentary on, 145, 149, 174, 198–99, 239; as marker of Peronist social justice, 1, 131, 137, 140, 178, 226; norms of proper attire, 183; Peronist distribution of, 139–40, 149–50; Peronist-era styles of, 157–59, 161–62; shortages of, 168; working-class consumption of, 31–32, 36, 39–41. *See also* consumer goods

Cohen, Lizabeth, 254

cold war, 5, 15, 82, 247, 254, 257

Colombo, Luis, 60, 72

Colombia, 5

commerce: black market, 94, 100–2, 168, 170, 224; juntas reguladoras, 55–56, 62; marketplace conditions in the 1930s, 18–19, 21–24, 29, 45–47; marketplace conditions under Peronist rule, 86–95, 99–100, 164–65; middlemen and wholesalers, 97–99; Peronist regulation of marketplace, 91–92, 94–107; street fairs, 29, 92, 114, 227. *See also* antispeculation campaigns; department stores; economy; retail stores

commercial culture: definition of, 25; in 1930s Argentina, 25, 27–29; emulation by Peronist regime, 165, 173, 177–86; media depictions of injustice, 46–47, 49–50, 114; and popular entertainment in Peronist era, 87–90, 165, 169, 210; write-in contests, 193. *See also* advertising; film; music; print media; radio

communism: anticommunism, 56, 68, 273; Communist Party of Argentina, 43, 46, 73–74, 268n53; and Soviet Union, 4, 13, 253, 261n4. *See also* cold war

Confederación Económica Argentina, 104

Confederación General Económica (CGE), 205, 224–25, 229, 232–33, 245, 295n4

Confederación General del Trabajo (CGT), 57, 268n53; contracts, strikes, and consumer politics, 108–10, 224–25, 229–35; membership, 80; social programs, 123, 134; role as Peronist mediating institution, 80–81, 148, 191–92, 195, 203, 208. *See also* unions, labor

Consejo Económico Nacional, 168, 224–25

Consejo Nacional de Posguerra, 65–67, 76, 223

Constitution of 1949, 7–9 128–29, 144

consumer goods: and constitutional rights, 128; floor rags, 112–14; as gifts, 2, 124, 163, 255; household production of, 112, 137, 169–71, 226–27; imported, 1, 23–24, 165, 173, 229; Latin America as producer of, 11; Perón cheese, 116; Peronist memorabilia, 130; subsidies for, 55–56, 91–92, 231; Peronist distribution of, 120, 124–25, 130–31, 139–40,

149–50. *See also* appliances; clothing; food; radio; vehicles, motor

consumerism: definition of 11, 14

consumption, collective: definition of, 13–14. *See also* consumption, mass; housing; social assistance programs

consumption, mass: and anti-Peronist stereotypes, 155–61; and Argentina's status as consumer society, 10–11, 18–34; and austerity measures, 223–29, 231; business views on encouraging, 103–4; and collective consumption, 13, 75, 121, 126–27, 238; and consumer credit, 29, 31–32, 44, 49, 164, 203; consumer protests before Perón, 47–48, 57; consumer protests in contemporary era, 252; definition of, 13–14; and democratic social relations, 25–27; and gender relations in the 1930s, 32–34, 40–42; home delivery of goods, 33; and home economics, 170–71, 226–27; impact of income redistribution on, 75; influence of European models on, 23–24, 161–62; in midcentury Latin America, 11–13, 51; in Peronist Argentina and the world, 85–86, 117–18, 152–53; Peronist celebrations of spending power, 161–64, 169; and Peronist model of consumer society, 83, 91, 118, 141–42; and Peronist commercial experiments, 175–86; and postwar economic boom, 84–95; and problem of infraconsumo, 37, 50, 53, 66, 167; regional variations in 1930s Argentina, 26–30, 37–38, 44, 50, 92–93; scholarship on, 10–11, 14; and social assistance programs, 119–21, 132–42, 151–53; and social rights, 12, 127–29; state policies designed to boost, 75–81, 91–92; state views on excessive spending, 166–67, 169–74, 221–31, 249–50; United States as model of, 10–11, 22–23, 30–32; and waste, 154–60, 166–71, 226–27. *See also* antispeculation campaigns; consumer goods; gender; thrift

cooperatives, consumer, 47–49; and austerity measures, 226–27; Peronist versions of, 175–80, 240, 281n11; popular demands for, 210–12, 216–17

Córdoba province, 27, 56, 71, 92, 133, 242; letters from residents of, 195, 198, 200, 202–3

cost of living: after Perón's overthrow, 248–49; and encouragement of consumer thrift, 155, 161–75; newspaper coverage of, 93, 100–2, 114; and Plan Económico, 221–22, 228–31, 235–37; popular frustrations with inflation in early 1950s, 2, 197–99; and the postwar boom, 87–95; statistics, 93, 168, 197. *See also* antispeculation campaigns; standard of living

Cuba: as consumer society, 51, 185; revolution, 6, 83

De Chikoff, Eugenia, 183

Del Rio, Jorge, 176

democracy: in Argentina since 1980s, 258–60; in Latin American history, 6–7; and Peronist "democratization of wellbeing," 134, 137; postwar moment of expansion, 82; relationship to mass consumption, 26, 34, 107; and state planning, 196, 219. *See also* citizenship; civil society

Democratic Union, 74, 106, 274n63

Departamento Nacional de Trabajo: and origins of Peronist movement, 63–64; surveys of household budgets, 38–41, 54, 63. *See also* Secretaría de Trabajo y Previsión

department stores, 12, 32–34, 45; film representations of, 46–47; and the Hogar de la Empleada simulacrum, 138–39; Harrods, 21, 138; Peronist experiments with, 14, 175–80, 240, 251; and postwar consumer boom, 87–88, 98, 157, 160–62. *See also* cooperatives, consumer; Foundation, Eva Perón

development, national: and dependency, 249–50; midcentury ideas of, 15, 83, 219, 262n12; obstacles in Latin America, 168; Peronist conceptions of, 2–4, 7, 94, 240–43, 255; problems after Perón's overthrow, 248–49, 257–58; and redistribution, 221–22; and social assistance, 133. *See also* economy; planning

Di Tella, Torcuato, 59–60, 65, 81

dignified life. *See* vida digna

Dirección Nacional de Vigilancia de Precios, 98, 117, 192, 216

Dominican Republic, 261n4

"Don't Cry for Me Argentina" (song), 5

double movement: and consumption, 94; definition, 13–14, 264n19; and social assistance, 120–21

Duarte, Juan, 101–2

Durán de González, Selva Zulema, 174–75

economy: disruptions in international trade, 24–25, 52, 79, 254; home economics, 170–71, 226–27; impact of First World War, 52, 56–57, 78; impact of Great Depression, 5, 24–5, 56–57; inflationary crisis of early 1950s, 221–23; and Peronist attempts to attract foreign investment, 241–45; and Peronist economic policy during first term, 78–81, 91–94, 110; Peronist industrial policy, 240, 242–45; and Peronist model of wage-price equilibrium, 229–33, 235–40; and Peronist price controls, 84–86, 92–102; Plan Económico structural adjustment, 223–31; recurrent crises in Argentine history, 249–50; structural adjustments in Latin America, 223, 224, 249–50; third way between capitalism and socialism, 13, 256; wartime price controls, 57, 62. *See also* development, national; planning; redistribution, income

education: Peronist influence over, 172–73, 234, 245 56

Egypt, 15
Eisenhower, Milton, 242
El Chaco province, 163, 200, 234
elections: congressional (1954), 236; and extension of female franchise, 7, 128; presidential (1946), 74–75; presidential reelection (1951), 1, 191–92
Entre Rios province, 27, 96
Esperanza, Santa Fe (town), 144–45, 148
Estatuto del Peón, 65, 72
Europe, Western: business practices of, 104; consumer society in, 10–11, 117; and Fordism, 257; and immigration to Argentina, 23, 37–38, 233; influence of commercial culture from, 28, 152; and postwar reconstruction, 79, 88, 91, 169, 185; rise of midcentury authoritarianism in, 4; as social policy inspiration, 36, 54, 82; and trade with Argentina, 24–25, 235; and worker spending power, 30–31, 36. *See also* France; Germany; Great Britain; Italy; Soviet Union; Spain

family: letter writers reflections on, 145–49, 199, 212, 239; Peronist authorities' views on, 8, 63–64, 69–70, 170–75, 182, 187, 255; and propaganda on household management, 172, 226–27, 233; postwar marriage rates, 171; reformer concerns with vulnerability of, 3, 8, 19–21, 34–42, 53, 66; as target of Peronist social assistance, 119–21, 128–29, 134–36, 138–40; unidades básicas as second family homes, 112; views of accused speculator on, 102–3. *See also* gender; working class
Farrell, Edelmiro, 64–65, 74
fascism: impact on Argentina, 35, 54, 56, 63; and mass consumption in Italy, 185; in midcentury Europe, 4; Nazism, 59, 73, 243, 274n62; Peronism as a form of, 9, 65, 73, 160, 247
Federal Police: and antispeculation campaigns, 96–99, 109, 200, 248; letter writer views on, 203, 212
Figuerola y Tressols, José Miguel: genesis of Peronist movement, 63–67, 69, 82; role in state planning, 76, 78, 144; surveys of worker spending habits, 39–41, 54–55
film: Argentine cinema of the 1930s, 15, 18, 28–29, 34, 46–47, 268n60; depictions of merchants, 114–15, 268n60; Hollywood and foreign film, 28, 134, 142, 152, 157; Peronist-era newsreels and shorts, 119–21, 127–30, 134–37, 152, 193; and postwar consumption, 1, 87–89, 98, 118, 157, 227
Five-Year Plan, First, 76–77: and mass consumption, 80–81, 167, 176; media coverage of, 193; and social assistance, 123
Five-Year Plan, Second, 241–42, 244; and letter writers' suggestions for, 188–94, 197, 200, 214–17

food: and anti-Peronist stereotypes, 158, 162; and austerity measures, 226–28, 235; beef as marker of plenty, 87, 162, 168; consumer waste of, 169; consumption during postwar boom, 87–88, 114, 162–63; consumption in Argentina compared to other countries, 30–32; distribution through social assistance programs, 120, 124, 139, 252; exports, 23, 91, 167–68, 228; and household budgets, 37–41; letter writer commentary on, 116, 149, 198–99, 201; manufacturing and processing, 24–25, 64, 79; nutritional campaigns, 137, 171, 179, 226, 228; pan negro, 228; Peronist cider and pan dulce, 2, 124, 163; restaurants, 22–23, 46, 88, 99–100; retail sale, 29, 164–65, 227; sale in Peronist cooperatives, 177–80; scarcity of, 42, 44, 51, 93, 168; state subsidies and regulation, 55, 57, 91–92, 96–100, 229; variety and quantity in 1930s Argentina, 22–23, 39
Fordism: and postwar planning, 55, 59–60, 66; Peronist version of, 79, 257
France: commercial landscape of Paris, 18, 22, 24, 36; fashion, 161; popular front government, 76
Franco, Francisco, 161
Freire, José María, 136, 162–64, 167
Fresco, Manuel, 56–57, 82
Foundation, Eva Perón: after Evita's death, 238–39, 247; finances, 99, 124–26, 282n18; hogar de la empleada, 138–40; hogares de tránsito, 137–38; letter writer commentary on, 210–12, 216–17; and Plan Económico, 226–27, 238; as provider of social assistance, 122–25, 140–42, 144–51; retail stores (proveedurías), 175, 178–80, 211, 217, 226–27

Gaitán, Jorge Eliécer, 5
Gatica, José María "El Mono," 165
gender: and antispeculation campaigns, 110–11, 112–14; anxieties about male breadwinner, 40–41, 63, 86, 198–200; assumptions about male and female spending, 40, 172; and consumer protest traditions, 48; domestic duty and social assistance, 119–21, 136–41; Eva Perón Foundation's norms of femininity, 137–42, 178; fashion and the female body, 159, 183; housewife as agent of thrift, 170–73, 212–13, 226–28; "modernization of patriarchy," 9, 111, 123; and Perón's discourse of vida digna, 8, 68–71, 76; Peronist ideals of gender roles, 8–9, 119–21, 187, 197; and shopping routines, 32–34, 90, 160–61, 170–74, 182–83; undisciplined male worker, 154–56, 169–72, 174. *See also* family; women; working class
Germany, 30, 59, 73, 243
Ghana, 15

Ghioldi, Américo, 159–60
Goldar, Ernesto, 157–58
Gómez Morales, Alfredo, 168, 229, 232, 295n3
governmentality, 121–22, 126, 167
Grandes Almacenes Justicialistas, 177–78, 210, 226, 240
Great Britain, 24, 36, 42; Anglo-U.S. civil society, 6; economic relations with Argentina, 79, 91, 228, 235; living standards, 30–31; midcentury social programs, 56, 60
Greenup, Ruth and Leonard, 22–23, 32, 160
Guatemala, 5, 76, 249

Haya de la Torre, Victor, 5
Hechos e Ideas (journal), 79
Hirschman, Albert O., 207–8
El Hogar (magazine), 247
housing: Banco Hipotecario Nacional, 89, 238; Eva Perón Foundation as provider of, 137–38, 140; letter writer requests concerning, 145, 148, 194, 233, 238; Peronist aesthetics and design, 119–21, 132–36; Peronist public housing projects, 119–21, 123, 142, 213; Plan Pinedo, 57; popular demands, 233; postwar homeownership, 89–90; reformist proposals during 1930s, 54, 70; rent control, 47, 62, 100; and social rights, 128; working-class conditions of, 29–30, 42, 45, 59; working-class expenditures on, 39, 92, 126, 198

India, 15
Infamous Decade: definition, 20–21
inflation, *See* cost of living
Instituto Argentino de Promoción del Intercambio (IAPI), 91, 225, 229, 247
International Labour Office, 36, 59
International Telephone and Telegraph, company, 103
Italy, 23, 150, 241; Fascist, 54, 56, 63, 73, 185, 290n74; immigrants from, 114, 233, 270n15
Ivanissevich, Oscar, 181, 183, 290n72

Jacobs, Meg, 86
Jamandreu, Paco, 161
James, Daniel, 7, 287n16
June Revolution (1943), 60–67, 72–74; continuities with Perón government, 92, 122
Justicialismo, 7, 234, 255, 260. *See also* Peronism
Justo, Agustín, 55–56, 269n6

Keynesianism, 55, 66
Kilómetro 111 (film, 1938), 28
Kirchner, Néstor and Cristina Fernández de, 252

La Pampa province, 200, 234
land reform, 12, 76, 249–50
Latin America: consumer society, 11–13, 51, 85, 88, 176, 185; contemporary politics in, 258–59;

midcentury nationalist reform, 6–8, 12, 54, 76, 82–83, 231, 249–50; obstacles to development in, 168, 222, 224; populism, 5–6, 8, 83, 254, 273n49; race relations, 9; scholarship on citizenship in, 6–7; as part of Third World, 15; urbanization, 12
Le Corbusier, 22
letter writing: as part of antispeculation campaigns, 102–3, 108–9, 115–16; and businessowner requests, 102–3, 204–5; and criticism of merchants, 211–13, 173–75; expressing collaboration with Plan Económico, 228; to Eva Perón, 142–51, 239; as historical documents, 16, 188–89; identity of "Perón Wants to Know" petitioners, 188, 193–94, 206–9; as non-electoral political participation, 189–91; 196–97; and obstacles to vida digna, 195–205; the "Perón Wants to Know" event, 188–94; and popular identification with Peronist movement, 206–14; requests for motor vehicles, 243; requests for public works, 194–97; state responses to correspondence, 214–18; as strategy for circumventing austerity measures, 238–39
liberalism: and Argentina's republican traditions, 218, 223; business defense of, 103–5, 204–5; wartime critiques of, 50, 52, 56, 72; cultural hegemony of, 41, 43, 219; midcentury global crisis of, 4–5, 254; neoliberalism, 6, 13, 258–60, 267n52, 263n18; and Peronist national planning, 78, 85–86, 228–29, 233, 242, 248; relationship to Peronist citizenship, 52, 255–56; third way alternatives to, 13, 254–55
Llorens, Emilio, 38
Lomas de Zamora, Buenos Aires (suburb), 82, 198
Lonardi, Eduardo, 246–47

magazines. *See* print media
manufacturing, 11–12; challenges under Peronist rule, 93, 100, 105, 168, 224, 229; dependence on imported raw materials, 25, 80; economic regulations affecting, 84, 94–96, 98; employment and economic size in wartime era, 79; food processing, 24–25, 64, 79; growing Argentine industrialization in 1930s, 21, 22–24, 34; import substitution, 24; and Miguel Miranda's economic policies, 78; Peronist motor vehicles, 14, 242–43; Peronist state support for, 229, 242, 244; and postwar planning, 57–59, 61; SIAM Di Tella, 31, 59, 105, 241; as target of antispeculation campaigns, 97–99, 103; textile, 25, 31, 79, 99, 200, 229, 241; U.S. operated, 31, 103, 242
Marshall, T. H., 6
Mendé, Raúl, 144–50
Mendoza province, 27, 68, 112, 133, 236; letters from residents of, 2, 108, 199, 217

Menem, Carlos, 258
Menéndez, Benjamín, 191
Mercante, Domingo, 64, 109, 218, 272n32, 281n10
Mexico: consumer society, 51, 176, 185; midcentury politics, 5, 54, 249
middle class: attitudes toward Peronism, 102, 106, 156–58, 205–6, 256; as consumers, 25–26, 31–33, 90–93; and impact of inflation on living standards, 92–93, 199, 205; and Peronist emulation of "bourgeois" lifestyle, 120, 135–36, 152, 181–84; Peronist regime's courtship of, 68, 70, 97, 240–41; size of, 265n25. *See also* anti-Peronism
migration: anti-immigrant sentiment, 47, 97; immigration, 23–5, 37–39, 233; rural-urban, 27–29, 89–90, 200
military: coup attempts against Perón, 191, 222, 245–46; involvement in wartime politics, 5, 20, 60–74; Proceso dictatorship, 258; role in postwar planning, 55–60. *See also* June Revolution; Revolución Libertadora
Ministry of Industry and Commerce, 216, 236. *See also* Secretariat of Industry and Commerce
Ministry of Public Health, 123, 226, 228
Ministry of Public Works, 119, 121, 123, 132, 215
Ministry of Technical Affairs: archival collection of letters, 16, 143, 188–90, 193; Dirección Nacional de Planificación, 192, 215–16; and Peronist patronage networks, 143–44, 148, 215, 238–39, 243; role in antispeculation campaigns, 96, 104, 109, 115, 174; role in state planning, 144, 193, 217, 228
Miranda, Miguel: architect of Peronist economic policy, 78–81, 91–94, 110; dismissal of, 167–68
morality: condemnation of commercial culture, 181–84; ethics of exchange in the 1930s, 20, 42–51; figure of the speculator, 42–44, 57, 86, 68–70, 235–36; letter writer views on unethical merchants, 115–16, 174, 201–2, 211–14; liberalism and moral economy, 42–43; Peronist views on just marketplace, 85–86, 94–98, 107–18, 253; and state corruption, 56, 101–2, 202, 208, 258. *See also* antispeculation campaigns; Catholicism; social justice; vida digna
Mujeres que trabajan (film, 1938), 46–47, 49
El Mundo (newspaper), 18
Mundo Argentina (magazine), 181, 227
Mundo Peronista (magazine), 150, 184, 215, 226
music: jazz and tango in midcentury Argentina, 46, 89, 101, 157–58; tango and Peronism, 68, 173, 181
Mussolini, Benito, 56, 73

La Nación (newspaper), 93, 106, 228
Nasser, Gamal Abdel, 15

National Economic Council, 168, 224
National Library, 251, 299n1
National Office of Price Surveillance, 98–99, 101–2, 177
nationalism: economic nationalism during Second World War, 58, 61–63, 66; erosion of faith in economic nationalism, 257–59; experiments with Peronist cultural nationalism, 181–86; in midcentury Latin America, 6–8, 17, 54, 82, 254; and modernist state planning, 190–94, 218–20; Perón's conception of, 70, 74, 246; and Peronism in Third World context, 15; and Peronist consumer society, 85–86, 91, 184; and Peronist economic policy, 76–81, 241–42; right-wing varieties in 1930s Argentina, 35–41, 45, 47; scholarship on, 15
Nehru, Jawaharlal, 15
newspapers. *See* print media
New Zealand, 88
Nkrumah, Kwame, 15
Nuestro Hogar (film, 1952), 134–35
Una nueva Argentina (book), 37–38, 58

Organización de Consumidores, 170, 224

Palacios, Alfredo, 44–45, 51, 163
Para Ti (magazine), 33, 227
Paraguay, 246
Perón, Eva Duarte de: approach to social assistance, 123–24, 131–32, 137–42; celebrity as radio and film star, 67, 184; critiques of, 161–62; death and commemoration, 230–31, 234, 239; defense of luxury, 14, 132, 137–42, 151; early life, 29, 158–59, 184; and Foundation retail stores, 178; ideals of feminine sexuality, 137–38, 161; and integration of women into Peronist Party, 111–12, 170–72; personal fashion and shopping habits, 158–59, 161–62; relationship to letter writers, 2, 143–51, 205, 239; role in consumer politics, 1, 95, 110–11, 167, 170–72; role in Plan Económico, 224, 226–28; role in wartime politics, 67, 71, 123; *La razón de mi vida* autobiography, 140–41, 144; saintly portrayals of, 147, 150, 230, 233–34; vicepresidential bid, 191–92. *See also* Foundation, Eva Perón; Peronism
Perón, Juan Domingo: announcement of "Perón Wants to Know" letter writing event, 192–93; attacks on unjust commerce, 84, 94, 96–97; celebrations of consumer abundance, 162; conception of social rights, 127; exile and return, 248, 257; formulation of the vida digna, 1, 67–75; Labor Secretary, 63–65, 128; letter writers' views on, 2, 209; origins and early career, 62–63; overthrow, 246, 251; presidential election campaigns,

74–75, 191–92; relations with young supporters, 245–46; role during October 1945 protests, 73–74; role in the June Revolution, 62–74; style as speaker, 67–68; views on consumer waste and austerity, 169, 225–26, 232–33, 235–36; views on state planning, 65, 76–77

Peronism: authoritarian features, 126–27, 166, 196, 218–20, 233–35, 252–53; cabildo abierto, 191–92; conceptions of domestic life, 64, 69–70, 170–75, 182; consolidation and expansion of movement, 222, 233–35, 238–40; definition of unidad básica, 112; democratic features, 7, 191, 195–96, 219, 234; "democratization of wellbeing," 134, 137; figure of the descamisado, 163–64, 174, 209, 226; ideology, 234–35; leadership's conceptions of gender roles, 8–9, 119–21, 197; media control and censorship, 126–27, 233–34; movement versus regime, 9–10, 189, 197, 207, 220; as the "Organized Community," 126–31, 153, 196, 208, 214, 260, 283n21; patronage networks, 108, 121, 123, 143, 149, 252–53; political mobilization of women, 111–12, 169–73; popular complaints about officials, 2–3, 201–4; problem of false Peronists, 208–9, 211; problem of hegemony, 220, 223, 238, 256; problem of voice and loyalty, 207–14, 220; relationship with Argentine left, 72–73, 106, 160, 256; scholarship on, 3, 9–10; tactics of popular negotiation and supplication, 142–51, 238–39; transnational influences on, 63, 82–83; views of authorities on just marketplace, 85–86, 94–98, 107–18, 255–56; visions of technological progress, 14, 79, 136, 138–39, 193, 240–43. See also citizenship; civil society; vida digna

Peronist Party: doctrine, 127–31, 144, 234–35; letters from local party organizations, 195–96, 208, 210–13, 216; as mediating institution in consumer politics, 116, 127, 170–72, 226, 236; neoliberal turn of, 258; Partido Peronista Femenino, 111–12, 127, 170–71, 195, 226; predecessors, 74; role in contemporary Argentina, 251–52, 260. See also elections

Peru, 5, 176, 249

Pinedo, Federico, 57–58, 66

Plan Económico (1952): design of austerity measures, 223–25, 249; impact on spending power, 228–31, 236; and Peronist citizenship, 231; popular support of, 227–28; propaganda about, 225–26; and road to recovery, 231, 241

planning: business and military conceptions of, 58–62, 105; and commercial regulation, 99, 107, 118; high modernist varieties, 22, 83, 190–94, 218–20, 255, 257; and household

management, 172, 184; and letter writing, 188–220; Peronist conceptions of state's role in, 65–67, 75–82, 94, 162; popular appropriations of rhetoric, 193–98, 219–20, 228; relationship to populist politics, 94, 144, 186, 249–50; under post-1955 military dictatorships, 248, 257; and welfare state, 126, 238. See also Five-Year Plan, First; Five-Year Plan, second; Ministry of Technical Affairs; Plan Económico

populism: and consumer society, 170, 186, 243, 255; in contemporary Latin America, 258–59, 263n18; critics of, 252, 256, 263n18; and economic morality, 86, 94, 116, 201; and economic obstacles, 222–23; definitions, 5, 261n6, 273n49; in midcentury Latin America, 5–6, 8, 83, 254, 273n49; Peronist conceptions of "the people," 70–71, 156, 190, 212; "populist constitutionalism," 128, 151; role of regional brokers, 202; and state planning, 192, 203, 218; trivializing depictions of, 5, 259

Prebisch, Raúl, 248

La Prensa (newspaper), 25, 106, 127, 279n62

print media: commentary on consumer spending, 88, 93, 95, 100, 105, 157, 228; coverage of antispeculation, 112–14, 201, 236; coverage of social politics, 37, 41, 57; as mechanism to encourage thrift, 171–72, 227, 236; as part of commercial culture, 18, 32, 50, 90; Peronist control of print media, 126–27, 164, 180, 230; Peronist magazines, 150, 180–84, 187–88, 215, 226; union newspapers, 42, 44, 48–49, 108, 154, 233; variety of publications in midcentury Argentina, 25, 28; women's magazines, 33, 95, 165, 182, 227, 247

productivity: economic, 37, 247–48, 250; National Congress on Productivity and Social Welfare, 233; and Plan Económico, 224–25, 250; relationship between labor and consumption, 20, 110, 118, 210

propaganda: on consumer conditions, 114–15, 162–63, 173; and creation of Peronist subculture, 126–27, 130, 234–35, 253; criticism of Peronist uses of, 106, 159–60, 247; depiction of average worker's day, 187; following Eva Perón's death, 230–31, 239; on letter writing, 150, 215–16, 239; pamphlets, 130, 134, 137, 173, 242, 281n6; on social assistance, 119–21, 130–31, 134–36, 139–40; on social rights, 128–29; Subsecretariat of Information, 96, 129–30, 134–36; on thrift, 154, 167, 169, 226–27, 232–33

public works: requests regarding, 194–97. See also Ministry of Public Works

El Pueblo (newspaper), 93, 106

Quilmes, Buenos Aires (suburb), 109, 176

race: anti-Semitism, 70, 97; cabecita negra stereotype, 9, 158, 164, 166, 181; creoles, 9,
37–38, 70, 233, 266n40; immigrants, 47, 97,
233; indigenous people, 38, 158, 209; and
merchant stereotypes, 97, 114; and Peronist
citizenship, 9, 70–72
Radical Party, 45, 47, 55, 61; performance in 1951
elections, 191–92; reactions to constitutional
reform, 128; relations with Peronist movement, 64, 74, 106, 202
radio: broadcasts of Perón and Evita speeches, 1,
94–95, 206–17, 225, 235; and midcentury
commercial culture, 25, 28, 46, 90–91;
mechanism for disseminating Peronist propaganda, 67, 120, 131, 169, 173, 230; Peronist
control of broadcasting system, 126–27, 129,
180; radio receivers as consumer goods, 26,
30–32, 36, 49, 90, 138
La razón de mi vida (book), 140–41, 144
redistribution, income: in contemporary Argentina, 252, 258–60; Peronist model of, 13, 53,
66, 75–83, 91, 254; and Peronist national
development, 221–23, 248; and social assistance, 137; state efforts to slow the pace
of, 230–31, 235–36, 249–50; and the threat of
postwar inflation, 85, 95, 108, 167–68; views
of 1930s social reformers on, 47, 50, 56
religion. *See* Catholicism
Renzi, Atilio, 124, 148
retail stores, 18, 26, 113, 164; almacén (corner store),
29, 44, 164, 177–79, 203, 227; butcher, 88, 99,
101, 204, 228, 235; clothing, 88–90; letters
from owners of, 102, 104, 204–5; Peronist
forms of, 177–80; restaurants, 22–23, 46,
88, 99–100; sales statistics, 87, 92–93, 104,
276n21; self-service shopping and supermarket, 29, 114, 227. *See also* antispeculation
campaigns; commerce; cooperatives, department stores; Foundation, Eva Perón
Revista de Economía Argentina (journal), 37, 167,
266n33
Revolución Libertadora, 130, 246–49, 251
Rico Tipo (magazine), 157–58
rights. *See* citizenship
Rivas, Nelly, 245–46
Romero, Manuel, 46–47
Rosalinda (magazine), 33
Rosario, Santa Fe (city), 23, 26, 29; letters from
residents of, 79, 115, 199, 211, 213

Salta province, 96, 198
San Juan province, 71
Santa Fe province, 27–29, 56, 96, 236; letters from
residents of, 144–45, 47, 150, 217
Santiago del Estero province, 44, 163, 174
Santos Discepolo, Enrique, 173
saving, 89, 172–73; Caja Nacional de Ahorro
Postal, 89, 172–73, 276n1. *See also* thrift

Secretaría de Trabajo y Previsión (Labor Secretariat): division for women workers, 70; and
the formation of the Peronist movement,
64–65, 67–75; relations with business,
72–73. *See also* Departamento Nacional de
Trabajo
Schorske, Carl, 254–53
Scott, James C., 219
Secretariat of Industry and Commerce, 61–62, 64,
95–96, 98, 104. *See also* Ministry of Industry
and Commerce
Señalando rumbos (film, 1949), 119–21, 127,
135–36
SIAM Di Tella, 31, 59–60, 105, 241, 246
Socialist Party, Argentine, 43, 54; critiques of
consumer conditions, 44, 47–48, 57, 106;
relations with Peronist movement, 72, 74,
106, 159–60; target of Peronist repression,
127, 235
Sociedad Rural, 56, 58, 72
social assistance programs: and 1930s reform
movements, 54–57; business owner views
on, 58–60, 204–5; in contrast to charity, 122,
131, 137, 141; as counterbalance to consumer
austerity, 238–39; definition of, 121–22; Eva
Perón Foundation as provider of, 122–25,
140–42, 144–51; finances, 125–26; letter
writer views on, 142–51, 199, 205; and
Peronist mass consumption, 1, 13–14,
125–26, 132, 151; Peronist organization of,
122–26; propaganda about, 119–21, 129–31,
134–36, 19–41; and public health, 75–76, 123,
136, 179, 226–28; and social rights of citizens, 127–29; state provision of, 66, 75, 78,
81, 122–23; as technologically modern, 136,
284n47; and tourism, 1, 123–24, 126, 131–34;
union-run, 64–65, 122–23, 126, 133–37,
281n11. *See also* housing; welfare state
social justice, vii; as element of Peronist leadership's rhetoric, 68–69; historicizing, 8; letter writer invocations of, 149, 201, 214; and
mass consumption, 79–80, 110, 115, 118, 169,
254; in the midcentury moment, 152–53,
254; Peronist conceptions of, 3–4, 15, 76,
118, 178–79, 239–40, 253. *See also* citizenship; standard of living; vida digna
social politics: and 1930s reform movements, 19–
21, 34–42, 50–51, 253; comparisons between
Argentina and the world, 36–37, 54, 59–60,
152; and obstacles faced by advocates,
40–41; Peronist approach to, 53, 75–80, 87,
122; and postwar planning, 55–67, 81. *See
also* social assistance programs
social scientists: and assessments of Peronist-era
consumption, 88, 167; influence on early
Peronist movement, 63–69, 81; and postwar
planning, 53–54, 55–60; role in 1930s reform
movements, 20–21, 34–42, 54–55; surveys

of purchasing power, 29–31. *See also* social politics; standard of living

Soffici, Mario, 28, 134–36

South Korea, 257

Soviet Union, 13, 59, 132, 219, 229n74, 278n50, 291n3

Spain, 26, 31, 39, 161, 267n43

speculator. *See* antispeculation campaigns; morality

standard of living: and antispeculation campaigns, 84–85, 110; as centerpiece of Peronist citizenship, 3, 7–9, 13–14, 53, 250, 255; and constitutional rights, 129; and consumer purchasing power, 89, 106, 180, 185, 187, 255; definitions of, 35–37, 54; as English concept, 69, 82; elevation by Peronist state, 75–81, 83, 232, 243; as growing part of political lexicon, 42, 50, 53–54, 220; impact of austerity measures on, 223–33, 243; as keyword of midcentury politics worldwide, 12–15, 35–37, 59, 69, 82–83; and labor productivity, 233; and legacies of Peronism, 257, 259; letter writer conceptions of, 121, 151, 197–200, 207–10; and nutritional studies, 13, 38, 40, 63, 88, 128; and Perón's wartime formulation of the vida digna, 63–65, 67–72; and postwar planning debates, 55–60, 62, 67; regional differences in, 37–38; and social assistance, 122, 127, 135–36, 151, 156; and surveys of working-class budgets, 37–42. *See also* consumption, mass; social assistance programs; vida digna

Stalinism, 4, 253, 261n4. *See also* Soviet Union

state: bureaucratic competition, 124–25; corruption, 56, 101–2, 202, 208, 258; growth in bureaucracy, 271n30, 285n65; nationalizations, 91–92; Peronization of bureaucracy, 148, 234, 238; as route for social mobility, 143–44; technocratic impulses, 55, 61, 71, 79, 95, 144, 190–92; wartime intervention, 56, 60–67. *See also* planning

Subsecretariat of Information, 96, 129–30, 134–36. *See also* propaganda

Taiwan, 257

taste: and alleged tackiness of Peronist sympathizers, 157–59; and Argentina's democratic social tendencies, 26; and design of social assistance, 132–42; and midcentury mass politics, 290n74; and norms of cultured comportment, 159, 181–84; and Peronist emulation of "bourgeois" lifestyle, 120, 137–42, 152, 181–84; and Peronist retailing, 176; and working-class consumers in the 1930s, 48–50

thrift: and consumer "little economies," 32; as female responsibility, 23–34, 167, 169–73, 180, 185, 227; and Plan Económico, 226–30;

and Peronist consumer education, 154–56, 166–75; and politics of late Peronist period, 232–33, 250; popular reactions to thriftiness campaigns, 173–75, 210, 212, 229–30; and populist redistribution, 222–23, 263n18

Thompson, E. P., 42

Trabajador de la Carne (newspaper), 154–55

tourism. *See* social assistance programs

Tucumán province, 108, 110, 202, 233, 272n34

Unión Cívica Radical (UCR). *See* Radical Party

Unión Industrial Argentina (UIA): relations with Peronist regime, 72–74, 78, 205; role in postwar planning, 58–62, 66, 81

Union of Secondary Students, 245–46

unions, labor: consumer cooperatives, 47, 176–78, 216; early alliance with Perón, 64–66, 68–74, 79–81; Federación de Trabajadores de Luz y Fuerza, 235; La Fraternidad, 42, 48–49; letter writing, 148, 195–96, 208, 218; meatpackers, 154–55; metalworkers, 237; and rural workers, 2, 65, 72; social programs, 64–65, 122–23, 126, 133–37, 281n11; strikes and negotiations under Perón, 80–81, 109–10, 168, 229–30, 233–37; sugar harvesters, 110, 202, 233; support for antispeculation campaigns, 108–10; Unión Ferroviaria, 47–49, 64, 123; unionization statistics, 43, 80, 268n53; views on mass consumption in the 1930s, 47–50; and women workers, 70, 171. *See also* Confederación General del Trabajo

United States of America: business presence in Argentina, 30, 103, 242; as Cold War patron in East Asia, 257; commercial regulation in, 85–86, 117; and comparisons with Argentine consumer society, 10–11, 22–23, 30–33, 37, 117, 152; as a "consumers' republic," 254, 257; diplomatic relations with Peronist government, 79–80, 242, 274n62; food consumption in, 88; influence of film and television on Argentina, 28, 134, 142, 152, 157; New Deal, 59–60; retail chains in Latin America, 185; State Department reports, 296n17; travelers' opinions about Argentina, 22–23, 32, 160–61; working-class living standards in, 30–32, 37

upper class, 88, 122, 133, 155–56; Peronist attitudes concerning elite lifestyles, 71, 120, 135–37, 152, 162, 181–84; and Peronist criticism of greed, 86, 94, 103, 109, 116, 141, 208; as unpatriotic oligarchy, 1, 14, 86, 141, 183, 213

urbanization, 12, 16, 23, 27–28, 200; Peronist-era suburbanization, 79, 89 90, 152, 187, 194–97, 200

Uruguay, 54

La Vanguardia (newspaper), 127, 290n70

Vargas, Getúlio, 5, 290n74

vehicles, motor: automobile as marker of consumer modernity, 24, 30–31, 37; import permits, 243; Peronist commentary on, 69, 135, 233; Peronist production of cars and motorcycles, 14, 242–43

Venado Tuerto, Santa Fe (town), 28, 51

Venezuela, 83, 259

vida digna: in contemporary Argentina, 257–60; and employment, 143, 200; as interpretive tool, 3, 8–9; labor leader views regarding, 162–64, 167, 169, 224–25; letter writer allusions to, 189, 199, 203–4, 209–10; and mass consumption, 13–14, 87–92, 136, 151, 222, 253–56; obstacles to realizing, 84–86, 93–96, 117, 188–89, 197–206; Perón's wartime formulation of, 53, 68–75, 81, 83; as political problem in midcentury world, 16–17; and propaganda about Peronist policies, 127–39, 134, 162–64, 185, 187; and symbolism of chalet californiano, 119–20, 129, 133, 135. *See also* citizenship; Peronism; propaganda; social assistance programs; social justice; standard of living

wages: in 1930s Argentina in comparative context, 30–31; and ethics of commercial exchange, 43, 48; evolution over Peronist rule, 162, 231; family subsidy, 41, 50, 56, 60, 167; and the financing of social assistance, 124–26, 134; impact of austerity measures on, 228–31, 235–37; and Labor Department surveys, 40–41; and Peronist income redistribution, 64, 71, 74–76; popular complaints about low wages, 2, 109–10, 174, 198–200, 209; and worker share of GDP, 75, 249; and working women, 171. *See also* cost of living; redistribution, income; unions, labor

war on speculation. *See* antispeculation campaigns

welfare state, 14, 75, 83, 119–22, 152–53. *See also* planning; social assistance programs

women: advertising representations of, 33, 90, 171; as agents of household thrift, 23–34, 167, 169–73, 180, 185, 227; Eva Perón Foundation's norms of femininity, 137–42, 178; fashion and the female body, 159, 183; and labor unions, 70, 171; and Partido Peronista Femenino, 111–12, 127, 170–71, 195, 226; and Peronist citizenship, 8–9; Peronist political organization of 111–12, 169–73; as voters, 7, 128, 191–92; in workforce, 33, 171. *See also* family; Foundation, Eva Perón, gender; Perón, Eva Duarte de

working class: and critiques of prodigal spending, 93–94, 154–66; and fears of social unrest, 52–53, 56, 59, 68; household budgets, 30–31, 39–41, 63, 198; and increase in consumer purchasing power, 74–81, 86–92, 164–65, 178–80; as object of inquiry by 1930s reformers, 19–21, 34–42, 87; as object of political concern during war, 53, 63–64, 68–71, 76; and partial integration in 1930s consumer society, 25–26, 29–34, 49–50; and Perón's definition of the vida digna, 68–71; and Peronist citizenship, 7–8, 13–14, 68–71, 209–11, 254–55; and Peronist ideals of family life, 8, 119–21, 170–72, 187; and Peronist norms of respectability, 119–21, 131–36, 161–64, 177–84; productivity, 110, 210, 224–25, 233, 247–48, 250; stereotypes about, 57–58, 163–64, 182–83, 187; statistical estimate of size, 265n25; supposed emulation of middle-class consumers, 25–26, 49–50, 265n16; as target of social assistance, 55, 56, 132–36. See also family; gender; standard of living; unions, labor

World War, Second: and Argentine views on reconstruction, 79, 84, 160; impact on formation of Peronism, 52–53, 79–80; 82–84, 253–54; political and economic effects on Argentina, 52–53, 56–57, 84; victory gardens, 226

Yrigoyen, Hipólito, 20, 55